That Broader Definition of Liberty

That Broader Definition of Liberty

The Theory and Practice of the New Deal

Brian Stipelman

LEXINGTON BOOKS
Lanham • Boulder • New York • Toronto • Plymouth, UK

Published by Lexington Books
A wholly owned subsidiary of The Rowman & Littlefield Publishing Group, Inc.
4501 Forbes Boulevard, Suite 200, Lanham, Maryland 20706
www.rowman.com

10 Thornbury Road, Plymouth PL6 7PP, United Kingdom

British Library Cataloguing in Publication Information Available

Library of Congress Cataloging-in-Publication Data
Stipelman, Brian.
  That broader definition of liberty : the theory and practice of the New Deal / Brian
Stipelman.
      p. cm.
  Includes bibliographical references and index.
  ISBN 978-0-7391-7454-8 (cloth : alk. paper)—ISBN 978-0-7391-7455-5 (electronic)
  1. New Deal, 1933-1939. 2. Public welfare—United States. 3. United States—Social
policy. 4. United States—Social conditions. 5. United States—Politics and government.
I. Title.
  E806.S816 2012
  973.917—dc23   2012027954

Printed in the United States of America

To Wilson Carey McWilliams and Elayna Eve Stipelman. For the world he fought for and the one she deserves

Contents

Acknowledgments

In the spring of 2003, my second year of graduate school, I took an independent study with Dan Tichenor, where I first learned about Thurman Arnold. Arnold was fascinating, and seemed a worthy subject for a dissertation. Two years later I was ready to begin, and asked Carey McWilliams if he could recommend a good book on New Deal thought, so Arnold could have some context. McWilliams, who knew just about every book ever written, told me none existed, and that I should write it myself. *A Better Kind of Liberty* is the result.

This is my first book, so there is a long list of people that need to be acknowledged. I will try to be brief, and ask you to forgive my lack of synonyms for the word thanks. Sometimes it is just the right word for the job. Paul Franco, Larry Simon, and Jean Yarborough must be thanked for instilling in me a love of philosophy and political theory. Jean especially deserves credit for seeing potential in an obnoxious undergraduate who could not write and thought he knew everything. It was she, more than anyone, who started me down the road that has culminated here, and for that I owe her a tremendous debt. It is my sincerest hope that even if she disagrees with the politics of this book (which she almost certainly will) she can at least take some small measure of pride in helping me transition from an obnoxious C- reaction paper on *The Apology* to what you are about to read.

Gordon Schochet and Dennis Bathroy were a constant source of wisdom and encouragement during my time at Rutgers, and I am grateful for it. Gordon, I am sorry that I never followed through on that John Stuart Mill project, but at least he makes an appearance here. Steven Bronner in particular played a pivotal role shaping me into a theorist. His influence should be clear to anyone who knows him and his work.

I was fortunate enough to surround myself with a particularly talented cohort of young political scientists, each of whom has read and influenced at least part of this work. So thank you Brian Graf, Alexandra Hoerl, Geoffrey Kurtz, Marilyn LaFay, Saladin Ambar, Aaron Keck, Amy Linch, Nichole Shippen and James Mastrangelo.

I owe an even greater debt to Wilson Carey McWilliams for inspiring this book and inspiring me. Every iteration of this project finds me more drawn to the questions and the concerns he dedicated his life to, and I wish he could have lived to see it. I hope that whatever is of value in this project is worth adding to his legacy. Dan Tichenor took over as a dissertation advisor after McWilliams' untimely death, and was about as wonderful a mentor as I could have asked for, in terms of both his personal support and vast knowledge. This is a far stronger book for his involvement.

I would also like to thank Jane Junn, Donald Beahm, Ryan Mueller, Sam Nordberg, Chuck Carlise, Jared Stipelman, and Michael Thompson for each reading and commenting on some (or all) of the manuscript at various stages of completion, as well as the many people who offered feedback during innumerable conference presentations. A special thanks to Dan Tichenor, Dennis Bathroy, Stephen Bronner, and Jim Morone (whose chapter on the New Deal in *Hellfire Nation* convinced me that this project was doable) for shepherding me through the dissertation process.

I am grateful to my colleagues Donald Beahm and Carlos Cunha for providing a nurturing and supportive professional environment that allowed me to complete this.

Thank you to Melissa Wilks, Alison Northridge, Stephanie Brooks, Jennifer Rushing-Schurr, and the people at Lexington for all your help guiding this to print.

What value there is in this work owes much to their influence. The problems are mine alone.

None of this would have been possible without the love and support I have been able to lean on outside of my professional life. Thank you to my friends in The Risen and at Red Mosquito, for keeping me sane and teaching me the value of community, virtual and real. This would have been written a lot quicker without you, but I would have enjoyed myself a lot less. Thank you Pearl Jam, R.E.M., Dan Bern, Mark Lanegan, and Tom Waits for the musical accompaniment. Thank you to Susan Eddy for actually reading and editing parts of this manuscript. How many mothers-in-law would do that? Thank you to Peter Eddy for always reminding me why this book is necessary. Thank you to Michele and Charlie, my mother and father, for always believing in me, especially since I did not always believe in myself. And you were right, doing that honors project my senior year of college was a good idea.

And of course there aren't words for what I owe to my wife, Hilary, who has stood by me, kept me grounded, and given me love and support for more years than she can remember. And last but not least, thanks to my daughter Elayna, for turning me into an adult. I love you both.

Thank you for the gifts you have given me. Thank you for the debts I cannot repay.

A Note on Sources

Frequently-cited works are footnoted with the following abbreviations.

Chat　　　　　Franklin Roosevelt. *FDR's Fireside Chats*. eds. Russell Buhite and David Levy. New York: Penguin Books, 1993.

Constitution　　Henry Wallace. *Whose Constitution?: An Inquiry into the General Welfare*. New York: Reynal & Hitchcock, 1936

Courage　　　　Eleanor Roosevelt. *Courage in a Dangerous World: The Political Writings of Eleanor Roosevelt*. ed. Allida Black. New York: Columbia University Press, 1999.

Democracy　　Henry Wallace. *Democracy Reborn*. ed. Russell Lord. (New York: Da Capo Press, 1973).

Folklore　　　　Thurman Arnold. *The Folklore of Capitalism*, Washington, D.C.: Beard Books, 2000 (reprinting 1937).

Frontiers　　　Henry Wallace. *New Frontiers*. New York: Reynal & Hitchcock, 1934.

Leave Behind　Eleanor Roosevelt. *What I Hope to Leave Behind: The Essential Essays of Eleanor Roosevelt*. ed. Allida Black. New York: Brooklyn, 1995.

Moral Basis　　Eleanor Roosevelt. *The Moral Basis of Democracy*. New York: Howell, Soskin & Co, 1940.

Speeches   Franklin Roosevelt. *Great Speeches.* ed. John Grafton. New York: Dover Publications, 1999.

Statesmanship   Henry Wallace. *Statesmanship and Religion.* New York: Round Table Press, Inc., 1934.

Symbols   Thurman Arnold. *Symbols of Government.* New Haven: Yale University Press, 1935.

Voltaire   Thurman Arnold. *Voltaire and the Cowboy: The Letters of Thurman Arnold.* ed. Gene Gressley. Boulder: Colorado Associated University Press, 1977.

Part I: Introduction

Chapter 1
The Political Theory of the New Deal

We were against revolution. Therefore, we waged war against those conditions which make revolutions—against the inequalities and resentments which breed them.

—Franklin Roosevelt[1]

We cannot remove sorrow and disappointment from the lives of human beings, but we can give them an opportunity to free themselves from mass restrictions made by men.

—Eleanor Roosevelt[2]

In brief, the New Deal places human rights above property rights and aims to modify special privilege for the few to the extent that such modification will aid in providing economic security for the many.

—Henry Wallace[3]

The greatest destroyer of ideals is he who believes in them so strongly that he cannot fit them to practical needs.

—Thurman Arnold[4]

Our political ideals, the inchoate political theory possessed by American citizens, set the moral boundaries and concrete expectations of our collective public lives. They tell us what we owe to each other, what we owe to our larger political community, and what that community in turn owes us. These ideals are a collection of expectations and obligations, told in the form of a story peopled with heroes and villains, the worthy and the unworthy. The struggle for the hearts and minds of democratic citizens is a battle of competing moral narratives, and the limits of what is politically possible are determined in large measure by which narratives we choose to adopt, and how well we adapt them to the stage we act them out upon. This work seeks in part to analyze the story of the New Deal, and how its strengths and limitations were shaped by that adaptation.

Time magazine's November 24, 2008, cover featured the headline "THE NEW NEW DEAL"—with president elect Barack Obama's head superimposed over Franklin Roosevelt's body.[5] The doctored photo speaks to the enduring legacy of the New Deal story. When we have lost our faith in the masters of the markets, if not the markets themselves, and when we realize in moments of crisis and desolation that individual liberty without security means little more than the freedom to starve, we still look to the New Deal for inspiration. The electrifying promise of the Obama campaign, against the backdrop of our most severe economic crisis since the Great Depression, made it easy to see the election of 2008 from the standpoint of 1932. It remains to be seen if history will remember George W. Bush as a second Herbert Hoover, but anxious Americans looked to Obama, as they once looked to FDR, to restore their faith in American economic institutions, American democracy, and the American dream. We wanted, *Time* told us, to once again act out the story of the New Deal.

FDR's administration was the most consequential of the twentieth century, and the ambition of its vision is still striking. The New Deal sought to save capitalism and democracy by democratizing the former and expanding the scope of the later, arguing that these steps would foster a more robust and vital, less cramped and circumscribed, individualism. While it understood the nature and the limits of citizenship in a modern democracy, the New Deal sought to overcome the narrow consumerist impulses that we Americans so often confuse with "freedom"—one might recall President Bush's squandering of our post-9/11 moment of national unity by informing Americans that their greatest patriotic duty was to shop.[6] And even though the world is a dangerous place, the New Deal showed Americans that we can live free of fear as long as we have faith in our democracy—which is to say faith in ourselves. *Time*'s November 24 cover story concludes, rightly, that the success of Obama's "new liberal order" will depend on his ability to appropriate the character of the New Deal, to play FDR to Bush's Hoover, to restore the faith that we have lost. If he proves successful, "he will establish a Democratic majority that dominates U.S. politics for a generation."[7]

That was, and continues to be, one way to tell the story of our recent political history—that the time is ripe for a 'new New Deal' and that the potential exists for a major progressive political realignment. But it is not the only narrative in play. For others, the political misfortunes that characterized the last years of the Bush administration, or even a negative overall assessment of his presidency, does not equal a condemnation of conservative ideology. Newt Gingrich, for one, has argued that Republican defeats in 2006 and 2008 reflect a popular rejection of Bush's performance, not his principles. In other words, the problem was not conservatism, but Bush's unwillingness to be conservative *enough*, a conclusion embraced by the Republican base that received at least superficial public validation in the 2010 midterm elections. As such, the political right can still speak of figures like Ronald Reagan with awe and reverence, even as they distance themselves from Bush. The failure of the practice does not require them to reject the vision. Their fundamental narrative holds, and has made the Republicans a bold and aggressive opposition party.

Conversely, progressives—or at least the Democratic Party—have long seemed to be a weak and ineffectual party, unable to institutionalize their platforms despite broad public support for many of their preferred policies. Part of the problem may reflect the general failure of Democrats, outside of Obama's 2008 campaign, to articulate a vision—to tell the American people the story they need to hear. As a result, the Left has been forced to confront Reagan-style conservatism on the terms set by the Right, which denies a positive role for government in people's lives and transforms a principled defense of property rights into a practical defense of oligarchy. But the failure of conservative institutions and policies, and the crisis that has followed in its wake, now give progressives an opportunity (closing fast, perhaps) to regain control of political discourse in the United States—to redefine the limits of what is possible, just as the Great Depression revitalized a progressive orientation brutalized by the 'return to normalcy' that followed World War I. The Left has its policy prescriptions and a broadly sympathetic president. It knows what it wants to do. What it needs now is a narrative; a compelling and coherent story capable of providing the energy and unity that will legitimize its program and rally Americans behind it. Its politics, in other words, need a vision. Barack Obama's call for "change" was inspiring, but lacks substance without a connection to a larger, clearly articulated narrative. Without that story Obama can produce policy, but not vision, and vision, easy to lose sight of in frantic moments of crisis and the slow grind of politics, is essential to any long-term challenge to America's institutionalized conservatism.

In short, Americans are a schizophrenic people, at all times tempted by the angel and the devil hovering just over their shoulders, whispering in their ears, pulling us towards either a liberal orientation that utilizes public strength to guarantee private freedom, or a conservative worldview that sees that strength as a fundamental threat to the very values it claims to protect. No single election, regardless of its outcome, seems capable of fully purging either perspective, and history has disproven every claim to the contrary. Ours is a divided soul, and the ideological struggles that inform our politics are about which half of that soul is dominant—for a time.

Political theorists orient themselves to the past. They use the great works, great minds, and great conflicts of history to help illuminate the present and prepare for the future. This legacy is part of our inheritance as a people, and its insights enable us to avoid reinventing the wheel every time we need to push something up a hill. This work looks to the theory of the New Deal, arguing that in it contemporary progressives can find their wheel, their story—a vision of a new future made possible in the retelling of an old story. The present-day context may be different from 1932, but the philosophy of the New Deal neverthe-less offers all of us a way to recapture the radical possibilities of what is best in America. The New Deal remains, as it has always been, a potent symbol, one which speaks the language of the American experience and understands the lim-its of reform in a land of people suspicious of the government they depend on, who identify as consumers more than citizens and cling to pre-industrial concep-tions of individual autonomy and agency. The New Deal's political theory is not perfect, by any means; but its principal defects are reflections of larger problems intrinsic to American character, modernity, and capitalism as a whole. Until there is widespread support for a second American revolution, we, as a nation, need to look instead towards discovering ways to simultaneously accept and transcend our cultural, institutional, and political limitations. We must treat cor-porate capitalism and consumer culture the same way the Founders treated inter-est—as a force to be channeled and directed, rather than resisted. As a theory of means and ends, practice and principles, the New Deal is both an excellent place to begin and—particularly given its historical importance and the esteem in which we still hold FDR—a scandalously untapped resource. Our political fu-ture will be determined in the ongoing fight over its interpretation and appropr-iation.

This book has several aims, which I will expand upon after a brief introduc-tion. The first is to explore the normative content of the New Deal, its theory of ends. The New Deal is a largely unexamined era of American political thought, inexcusable given the monumental historical importance of the period. Compar-ative scholarly neglect of the New Deal's political theory has resulted in the perpetuation of misperceptions regarding its theoretical significance, and its underutilization as an ideological framework. One does not have to stretch too far to see the New Deal as a third American founding, a moment where we rede-fine the fundamental relationship between citizen and state no less fundamental-ly than the Revolutionary and Civil Wars. In short, the legacy of the New Deal is the adoption of a new social contract, and so understanding the nature of that contract should be a concern of any citizen who wants to understand their de-mocracy, regardless of their personal political orientation.

Second, this book explores the New Deal as a theory of political practice, examining the relationship between its means and ends. In fact, the emphasis placed on how to institutionalize ends is perhaps the New Deal's most interest-ing and unique contribution to American political thought. One of the reasons the New Deal has not been taken seriously as a body of theory is the tendency within political theory to abstract the normative component of theory out of its historical, institutional, and political context. It is not surprising, therefore, that much of the best work on the New Deal has been written by historians and scho-lars of American political development, as they are often more comfortable with the tangled relationship between ideas and institutions. This work argues that political theory cannot responsibly ignore the question of how to achieve articu-lated ends, even if it is at the expense of theoretical purity. Politics is reactive and uncertain, and political theory has to embrace complexity, contingency, and imperfection, as the New Deal does. Like the New Deal and New Dealers, political theorists and practitioners must learn to adapt their ends to available means while working to transcend them.

This work focuses in particular on the importance of storytelling as one of the most important bridges between theory and practice. This is not to say that a public commitment to a different set of ideals is capable of overrunning the well-fortified ideological and institutional defenses of the status quo, but this public commitment is certainly a necessary precondition for the creation of any sort of alternative.[8] Nevertheless, no ideological story is told in a vacuum. It must be shaped to the contours of its stage, and in order to understand why the New Deal was such a dizzying mixture of hope and disappointment we need to understand its institutional context, and how that context affected how it acted and how it dreamed.

Thomas Jefferson hoped that every American generation would attempt an act of refounding, and in the spirit of a 'living constitution,' rewrite its social contract to align with the wants, needs, and circumstances that defined the lives of its current citizens. At the same time, in a country founded on progressive principles moments of renewal might sometimes take on the form of a recovery, and as Morton Frisch argues, the New Deal's was a conservative progressivism because our traditions are "sufficiently open to the progressive solution of the current problems without radical change."[9] Following Frisch, I argue that the New Deal offers the most promising theoretical frame capable of reminding a conservative electorate of the importance of the radical impulses at the heart of what they are trying to conserve, and progressives (and all Americans) would do well to appropriate it.

What Political Theory?

A second-class intellect but a first-class temperament.
—Oliver Wendell Holmes[10]

The New Deal has largely been written out of the conventional story of American liberalism, at least at the theoretical level. When it is considered at all it is typically accounted as either political opportunism or a warmed over progressivism.[11] Peter Coleman argued that "a dominant characteristic of the New Deal was the absence of a coherent, integrated philosophy and program. Pragmatism, compromise, ad hoc invention, moderation, and political opportunism seem more aptly descriptive."[12] James Young's treatment is fairly typical. In an otherwise superlative *Reconsidering American Liberalism*, Young spends thirty pages unpacking progressivism and ten pages on the New Deal, much of which focuses on the differences between the two periods. His assessment was that the "New Deal produced virtually nothing in the way of serious political thought" and goes on to argue that "there was no single, coherent intellectual position that could be passed on to later generations of reform leadership."[13] Young's assessment is buttressed by historians like James McGregor Burns, and Alberto Romanasco, the latter of whom concluded:

> Ideologically Roosevelt and the New Deal were a no-man's land. Roosevelt's leadership and the New Deal had nothing to do with logic or consistency. Instead Roosevelt used his position of power to carry out what was essentially an exercise in political electivism; he drew freely from a wide and contradictory variety of ideological programs both home-grown and imported, and more often than not he used them simultaneously.[14]

Even prominent New Dealers like Raymond Moley and Francis Perkins[15] denied the existence of any overarching logic to the New Deal, although Rexford Tugwell insisted that "a bright thread of intention ran through [its] confusions and contradictions"[16]

If there was no clear understanding of what the New Deal was, few people seemed to mind all that much. Perhaps the New Deal was a victim of its success. As long as New Deal liberalism was dominant in practice its supporters felt little need to codify or defend it. Its truths were, in important ways, self-evident. By the time a defense was needed the American Left had largely left the New Deal's intellectual framework behind, adopting a more adversarial and in certain ways narrower frame that privileges particular narratives of interest and oppression. But even if people were looking for a theory of the New Deal, a few common misperceptions would have made it difficult to find. To start, the New Deal's political calculations and alleged opportunism were themselves facets of a theory of practice, the end result of political actors attempting to institutionalize a welfare state in a conservative context. Samuel Lubell understood this when he reflected back on the period. "As a reporter in Washington I had shared the general belief that the New Deal was hastily improvised and animated by no coherent philosophy. When one translated its benefits down to what they meant to the families I was interviewing in 1940, the whole Roosevelt program took on a new consistency."[17] The New Deal was an instance, perhaps the most compelling instance in American history since its founding, of democratic theory in practice, where our leaders were theorists (or became theorists because they were leaders). Perhaps even more than the founding generation, New Dealers were forced to theorize a new state while simultaneously governing the old one. Their ideological commitments were mediated through pre-existing political institutions and a conservative electorate, each resistant to change. New Dealers were forced to alleviate the hardships of the Depression, hold the nation together, and win elections while simultaneously rewriting our social contract. Theory and practice are irrevocably intertwined under these circumstances, ends shaped by the limitations imposed by available means.[18]

The second misperception is the fact that thinking about New Deal theory frequently, and erroneously, starts and stops with Franklin Delano Roosevelt (FDR). While FDR will undoubtedly be the central focus of any discussion of the New Deal, he is not the sum total of the New Deal. It is only by looking at FDR in conversation with other important New Deal thinkers that a clearer picture of the philosophy emerges.

There have been past efforts to articulate the philosophy of the New Deal, of which Morton Frisch's *Franklin D. Roosevelt* is perhaps the best example. Recently there has been a greater support for the proposition that the New Deal has a coherent theory behind it. In the field of American Political Development, for instance, scholars like Robert Eden, Sidney Milkis, Jerome Mileur, James Morone, and David Plotke,[19] have all argued to some degree for the existence of a New Deal political theory. Philip Abbot's *The Exemplary Presidency* is a compelling look at the way Roosevelt absorbed the political thought and public personas of previous presidential exemplars to make his defense of a welfare state palatable for an American audience. Historian Anthony Badger provides a clear and compelling overview of the way constraints limited the policy choices available to New Dealers, and Alan Lawson's New Deal history explores the tension between the American traditions of individualism and commonwealth.[20] Cass Sunstein's *The Second Bill of Rights* is one of the most recent and arguably the best attempt by a political theorist to articulate the normative content of the New Deal. This book takes their work as a starting point, and aims to provide a fuller synthesis of the theory and the practice of the New Deal, arguing that one cannot be understood without reference to the other.

Finally, the New Deal was more than Franklin Roosevelt, and this work focuses in particular on crucial figures like Eleanor Roosevelt, Henry Wallace, and Thurman Arnold who illuminated critical aspects of the New Deal (its republicanism, its theory of political agency, and the tensions between its democratic theory and political practice) that have been given insufficient attention in scholarship centered around FDR. It is the author's hope that through this expanded focus a richer conception of our still developing sense of the New Deal's political theory will ultimately emerge.

A Brief Overview of New Deal Theory

The deeper purpose of democratic government is to assist as many of its citizens as possible, especially those who need it most, to improve their conditions of life, to retain all personal liberty which does not adversely affect their neighbors, and to pursue the happiness which comes with security and an opportunity for recreation and culture.

—Franklin Roosevelt[21]

The political theory of the New Deal grapples with the question of necessity in a liberal democratic society—the relationship between both necessity and expectations (often codified as rights), and necessity and practice. As Robert Eden put it, "Events on the scale of the Depression remind us that a republican people, even one blessed with the greatest resources, is subject to accident and force, and can guide its affairs by reflection and choice only within very narrow limits."[22] The New Deal challenged facile understandings of liberty and freedom by embracing (and whenever possible transforming) the relationship between means, ends, and constraints. As such, when the New Deal explored the relationship between economic power and political governance its emphasis was on the distribution of power within a capitalist system—the effect of power on social conditions rather than the way that power constituted itself.[23]

The key to the New Deal's assault on laissez faire capitalism is its argument that unregulated economic power in private hands represents a type of arbitrary power that democratic citizens have both a right and duty to limit. As New Dealer Thurman Arnold argues:

> It is the private seizure of industrial power that builds the kind of irresponsible organizations which can wreck a democracy. That power is subject to no election every four years. It is acquired in secret. Its operations are veiled in the mystery of meetings of boards of directors, dominated by single individuals and with interlocking lines of interest and control. It recognizes no public responsibility. It must not be allowed to get a foothold.[24]

But beyond recognizing the threat that unaccountable corporate power poses to democracy, the New Deal also identifies economic power as a form of governance, and that in the face of business's abdication of its responsibilities as a governing institution our political government has an obligation, born of necessity, decency, and the promise of democracy, to protect the rights of all citizens.

Here the New Deal demands that we revisit our traditional interpretation of the Declaration of Independence's constitutive commitments, arguing that our society has the capacity to elevate the pursuit of happiness to a status equal to that of liberty, and that society (acting through either its private or public governing structures) is obliged to give us the basic tools we need to take advantage of these rights. In short, security (defined economically, physically, and psychically) is the precondition of the meaningful possession of our rights, and that we should expect our governing structures (private and/or public) to guarantee that security. As FDR argued, "the time has come in our civilization when a great many of these chances should be eliminated from our lives."[25] Liberty is ultimately privileged over equality, even if the security caveat raises minimal standards of equality. Happiness is not guaranteed, but our success or failure to find it should reflect as much as possible our own agency, rather than structural forces we cannot control.

In order to give this view legitimacy, the New Deal claimed it necessary to view our expectations from the standpoint of an interdependent community— that our individual rights could only be protected and enjoyed in a larger social context. The New Deal rejected the category of class, finding it both divisive and alien to American sensibilities. It sought instead to utilize our identities as consumers, recognizing that what we longed for in the darkness of the Depression was the restoration of that identity. However, the New Deal understood both that consumption had become synonymous with the exercise of freedom, and that our focus on consumption can privilege the most anti-social and anti-political aspects of our individualism.[26] Therefore, it sought to mitigate the worst excesses of consumption in the same way that the welfare state sought to take the sting out of markets. It saw consumption and security as the place where meaningful citizenship and self-development began, rather than ends in themselves. They became a prerequisite of freedom, rather than its actualization.

This was the goal, at any rate. The New Deal, following Machiavelli (even if it could not publicly claim him as a patron), was always cognizant of the limits of reform. It possessed a pragmatic sensibility about ideology, staying faithful to its broad ends while remaining undogmatic about its particular means. It focused on the institutional contexts that interfered with reform, looking for ways to circumvent them without jeopardizing the possibility of future progress. In particular, New Deal theory highlighted the limitations imposed by the electorate and the difficulties of reform in a liberal democracy whose constitution was, in the words of Chief Justice Charles Evans Hughes, "the greatest instrument ever designed to prevent things from being done."[27] The New Deal had a complicated relationship with democracy, holding it up as an ideal and working to elevate public discourse,[28] while simultaneously understanding the limits of that discourse and the need to frame its ambitions within the confines of those limits. The complicated relationship between democracy, administration, and social justice was mediated through a philosophic liberalism that, while prepared to blur the line between education and manipulation, would not force people to be free.

The opportunity to change the way we think about our social contract was made possible by the physical and psychic dislocations of the Depression. By 1933 US Steel, the nation's first billion-dollar corporation, had cut its full time workforce down from 224,980 to zero.[29] Twenty-five percent of Americans were unemployed on the eve of Roosevelt's election, national income had fallen to half of its pre-depression level, and thousands of banks had closed with hundreds of millions in deposits lost.[30] America's system of private charities and local relief were, exhausted and it was not uncommon to see people collapsing from hunger in the middle of the streets, or prowling in the garbage dumps for spoiled meat to fill an empty belly. One mother was absolved of the murder of her child, whom she killed to spare the pain of starvation.[31] The bitter irony was that while over twenty percent of the students in the New York City school system suffered from malnutrition,[32] wheat sold for the same price it fetched in the reign of Elizabeth the 1st 300 years earlier.[33] In Iowa a bushel cost less than a pack of gum. Not surprisingly, six counties in Iowa were under martial law,[34] and President Hoover had chained shut the gates of the White House and turned the armed forces against its own veterans.

As Anne O'Hare McCormick, a writer for the *NY Times* magazine observed: "If Mr. Roosevelt goes on collecting mandates, one after another, until their sum is startling, it is because all the other powers—industry, commerce, finance, labor, farmer and householder, state and city—virtually abdicate in his favor. America today literally asks for orders."[35] But while the nation asked for orders, there were still clear limits to what it would follow, and for how long. Perhaps remembering Woodrow Wilson's warning about the fleeting nature of progressive movements, Roosevelt feared (presciently) that the return of prosperity would be accompanied by a resurgence of the 'ruthless self-interests' that caused the Depression in the first place. As the middle class returned to normalcy, the New Deal reminded us, sometimes in vain, that we have obligations to that one-third of the nation that remained "ill-housed, ill-clad, ill-nourished."[36] However, the fact that the people at the bottom were worthy of attention was something remarkable. Here is the president of the United States declaring for a truly universal conception of substantive citizenship, marking his determination "...to make every American citizen the subject of his country's interest and concern...The test of our progress is not whether we add more to the abundance of those who have much; it is whether we provide enough for those who have too little."[37] Although some movements outside the New Deal offered more egalitarian programs and policies, in the end the ambitions of these movements far exceeded those of the American people. The New Deal's temperament, echoing the sentiments of a momentarily (and comparatively) radicalized electorate, reflected a liberal populism rather than socialism. Happiness still had to be earned; failure remained a type of justice as long as it was deserved. Americans resented the disconnect between work and reward, not inequality.

The response of one worker to National Recovery Administration (NRA) wage regulations cut right to the heart of this sentiment.

> You can guess that the money is handy. With the $41.80 coming to me we can do a lot. But there is something more than the money. There is knowing that the working man don't stand alone against the bosses and their smart lawyers and all their tricks. There is a government now that cares whether things is fair for us. I tell you that is more than money. It gives you a good feeling instead of all the time burning up because nothing is fair.[38]

Workers wanted to know that there were people in power ensuring that the game was fair—not simply by preventing legal barriers to opportunity, but by minimizing as much as possible the impact of luck and chance, what John Stuart Mill called "the accident of birth." That, the New Deal declared, is the new obligation of our social contract, ensuring that economic, as well as political barriers to success were neutralized so that the possibility of happiness was finally in our own hands.

The New Deal was an aptly chosen phrase. The New Deal offered the 'forgotten man'[39] of America a new deal, but it never offered to change the game, nor were Americans tired of playing it. By the end of World War II *Fortune* magazine could confidently declare that the average American does not "want a new America. He wants the old one—only more of it."[40] The Great Depression did not lead to a full rejection of traditional American values like 'minimal' government or the pursuit of happiness facilitated by choice in the marketplace. The New Deal instead took steps to protect those values from the predatory and destructive tendencies of capitalism. Roosevelt argued that "[l]iberalism becomes the protection for the far-sighted conservative...I am that kind of conservative because I am that kind of liberal"[41] and Francis Perkins, his Secretary of Labor and long-time member of his inner circle, declared Roosevelt to be just "a little left of center." That is accurate, but lest we overstate the point, it is worth emphasizing just how far from the center political discourse and institutions had shifted. A return to the center, if the center is seen as a firm commitment to the expansive humanism enshrined in the Declaration of Independence and Preamble of the Constitution at the heart of the New Deal, is in itself a radical move.

For all its promise, the New Deal remains a problematic theory. Of particular concern is the ultimate refusal of the New Deal to seriously engage the dynamics of capitalism that threatened to undermine so much of what the New Deal tried to accomplish. However, it is important to draw distinctions between the failures of New Deal theory to address these questions and the failures of the Roosevelt administration to institutionalize a response. In the end the administration may not go far enough or the theory may perhaps be too timid, but this begs an important question: was it possible, in practice, to go further and be more aggressive? Are the limitations of New Deal theory in fact limitations inherent in the liberal, capitalist, democratic framework that we have adopted and show no signs of abandoning—and if so where does that leave us? We will return to this discussion in the conclusion.

Political Theory

There is a tendency among students of political theory to seek more formal and abstract presentations and to implicitly accept a sharp distinction between the worlds of intellect and of action.

—Philip Abbot[42]

One of the arguments running through this work is that political theory has to be political. A normative vision of the good life that makes no reference to political contexts and institutional realities is more concerned with moralizing than with politics. Political theory has to account for the constraints that necessity imposes on both theory and practice. The Roosevelt administration had to confront the contradictions and failures of industrial corporate capitalism in the midst of the country's greatest depression, in the looming shadow of fascist aggression, and largely lacking the necessary national administrative capacity to do so. FDR

understood what was at stake.[43] "Shortly after Roosevelt took office, a friend
told him that if he succeeded in the task he had set for himself, he would go
down in history as the greatest American president; but if he failed, he would be
condemned as the worst. Roosevelt replied quietly, "If I fail, I shall be the
last."[44] To complicate this further, the electorate was not sufficiently organized
to provide the mass base for the more radical moments of the New Deal. Nor is
it clear that this base existed. FDR's mandate always was to save capitalism, not
replace it. As Barry Karl argues, the radicalism of the period prior to the New
Deal was defensive, an expression of self-protection more than revolutionary
intent. Likewise, Americans in the 1930s, even in the heart of the Depression,
blamed their government more than they blamed capitalism. "Americans did not
want a new constitution; they wanted the one they had to work. Roosevelt assured them that it would, and he provided the politics that proved him right."[45]
The public endorsed Roosevelt as a reformer, not a revolutionary.

Clearly there is an important role for political theory as moral critique, as
meaningful public policy requires clear ends and evaluative standards, both of
which have normative components. But policy exists in a political context,
where it competes against other interests, other needs (the urgency of relief or
the rise of fascism), institutional restraints (southern racial hierarchies), and the
reality of uncertainty. Any transformative theory needs to account for both how
that transformation is supposed to occur and the pressures the agents of that
transformation operate under. It is also worth remembering there is nothing inevitable about reform. The response to the Depression in Europe was very different than the response in the United States, and as David Plotke argues
throughout *Building a Democratic Political Order*, political decisions actively
drove the reform agenda. "The new political order was not a necessary response
to economic breakdown or changing socioeconomic relations. Many other domestic courses were proposed, and the diverse international response to the Depression, show that economic collapse did not necessitate any single political
direction."[46] The welfare state institutions developed by the Roosevelt Administration were just one of several possible alternatives, coming into existence due
to the political skill of New Deal partisans. To be successful, New Dealers had
to learn how to communicate with an electorate, how to organize the interests
that supported its vision, how to navigate congress, party, and bureaucracy. This
product will always be imperfect, but as Jerome Mileur notes:

> that [FDR's] achievement entailed compromises—half a loaf where the true be-
> lievers wanted the whole loaf—attests not to a weakness of leadership but in-
> stead, especially in the context of his consistent and revolutionary purpose, to
> the importance of political leadership in a constitutional system designed pre-
> cisely for such leadership.[47]

This political focus helps to explain the comparative moderation of the New
Deal, especially measured against some of its more ambitious rhetoric and the

expansive dreams of fellow travelers. While the New Dealers saw themselves as educators (and, when necessary, manipulators) they were also liberal democrats, unwilling to push the nation much farther than it was prepared to travel. As Roosevelt argued "[p]ublic psychology and, for that matter, individual psychology, cannot, because of human weakness, be attuned for long periods to a constant repetition of the highest note on the scale"[48] There were limits to how much the New Deal could appeal to principle without falling back on interest, and questions of interest are almost always simultaneously questions of power that demand negotiation and compromise. There was also the matter of a conservative electorate anxious for a return to its old prosperity and familiar relationships. Roosevelt shared Woodrow Wilson's conviction that progressives in the United States had only a brief window every generation to bring about substantive reform.[49] The New Deal would by necessity be limited in what it could accomplish in the short term. This is why such a great emphasis was placed on the immediate institutionalization of reforms, however imperfect. They would alleviate the distress of the depression and, once in existence, would be open to the possibility of future expansion and improvement.[50]

Roosevelt's tongue-in-cheek comments about how his job would be easier if he were a dictator were no less true for being facetious. Any reforms in a democracy require the broad electoral consent of the voters, at least if the programs wish to maintain any legitimacy and the administration wishes to stay in power (and reform is impossible without power). Therefore, as Sidney Milkis argues, Roosevelt "was sensitive to the uneasy fit between energetic central government and the Constitution. It was imperative, therefore, that the New Deal be informed by a public philosophy in which the new concept of state power would be carefully interwoven with earlier conceptions of American government."[51] The more radical the reform the more important it was to make that reform seem familiar, so that Americans would not push against their gradual socialization towards the new values and priorities of the New Deal.

This should not be confused with Burkean style conservatism. There was an awareness of and respect for the power that the past holds over the minds of the electorate, but tradition was something to be constructed and interpreted, rather than something received in a fixed and finished form. The sense of mastery that informed the New Deal, the conviction that social institutions were not beyond human control, let it approach tradition as a way to facilitate, as well as constrain, agency. Here the New Deal was aided by both the broad elasticity and radical promise of America's founding ideals of liberty, equality, and the pursuit of happiness. What the New Deal hoped to conserve was, by its very nature, fundamentally progressive. Therefore, while James MacGregor Burns, Paul Conkin, Howard Zinn,[52] and others have highlighted the conservatism of the New Deal, they often downplay the radical possibilities inherent in New Deal 'conservatism.' In this regard the reactionary opposition had a clearer idea of what the New Deal was trying to accomplish, and the hysteria of that opposition speaks to the power of the broadside challenge the New Deal posed to conservative American values. President Hoover prophesized that if Roosevelt was elected "grass will grow in the streets of a hundred cities, a thousand towns; the weeds will overrun the fields of millions of farms."[53] General Smedley Butler testified before the House of Representatives that "during the summer of 1934 a group of Wall Street brokers had urged him to lead a fascist march on Washington and overthrow the government in order to protect business interests."[54] What is particularly remarkable here is that these brokers were organizing a coup not during the overheated populist rhetoric of the 1936 campaign, but during the First New Deal, when high commodity prices and business confidence were seen as keys to economic recovery, and industrial interests were writing the National Recovery administration's (NRA) regulatory codes themselves. The equally hostile *Chicago Tribune* tried a more democratic approach to overthrowing Roosevelt. In the weeks leading up to the 1936 election, the switchboard operators at the *Tribune*'s offices were instructed to remind callers "that there are only X days to save your country" (from Roosevelt).[55] While he had strong support among rank and file journalists and workers, he always faced tremendous opposition from the nation's editors and business elite, to the point that many refused even to say his name. Roosevelt became simply 'that man in the White House.' This visceral hatred was not simply a consequence of unfavorable policy. Instead it reflected fears that the New Deal was challenging the basic premise of what had become the American story.

A Better Type of Story

Every individual…constructs for himself a succession of little dramas in which he is the principal character. Those who are unable to construct a worth-while character for themselves in any particular situation lose morale; they become discouraged, ineffective, confused.

—Thurman Arnold[56]

The New Deal walked a fine line between education and manipulation in its relationship with the voting public. The rational voter was the ideal, one the New Deal worked to nurture, but at the same time it understood that the electorate is irrational and emotive before it is rational and reflective. Our political thinking is informed by what Thurman Arnold calls our folklore—the stories, ceremonies, and symbols we use to legitimate both the world around us, our place in it, and our aspirations for it. And any effective political program needs to not only be able to offer policy prescriptions, but tell a compelling story that speaks to the categories and experiences of the electorate and frame them in a way that makes existential sense.

The New Deal understood this, and this is a lesson contemporary political actors would do well to heed. Modern progressives are understandably eager to trump what they see as conservatism's record of failure. But a record of failure is not sufficient. Short of a total collapse, facts can only destroy the dominant story if we have a compelling alternative waiting to replace it. Otherwise, as Arnold argues, we can find some kind of ceremonial way to rationalize the disconnect between our principles and reality, even if that ceremony is no more than apathetic resignation. The bleak historical record of contemporary conservatism may mark a moment of institutional failure, but the failure of the old order does not automatically birth the new. We are perfectly capable of limping along, if not indefinitely, then to a point of truly catastrophic failure, where there is no telling what awaits us when the smoke clears.

The Nation commemorated the seventy-fifth anniversary of the New Deal with a series of articles highlighting what contemporary progressives should appropriate from the New Deal. What was missing was a systematic discussion of how the various aspects of the New Deal cohered together—the nature of its comprehensive vision and how this legitimated the various programs and innovations *The Nation* celebrates. The absence of that discussion is particularly troubling because Richard Parker, in the lead article, acknowledges the importance of articulating a vision.

> Crucial among the gifts of a true democratic leader, as FDR clearly was, is the ability to share not so much policies but stories, parables that incorporate moral and ethical vision, narratives of who we are and where we came from, and why we are together and where we can go, and what we can achieve if we work together.[57]

But what Parker, and the rest of the authors participating in *The Nation's* New Deal forum seem to miss is that the recitation of facts, figures, and policies is not the same thing as telling a story. We require universal narratives that convey stories in a language that generates the emotional attachments capable of conferring legitimacy and stability. This involves more than framing particular issues a certain way. Tactical use of language is part of storytelling, but is not its entirety. The language itself proves effective only when it serves as a bridge to a larger symbolic context. The New Deal provides us with a story, one that offers an expansive vision of the United States as an inclusive community balancing collective obligation with individual right, accepting the limits of what is possible while working to expand those limits. It accomplishes this by utilizing symbols and categories that speak to the way Americans understand their experiences, grounding it in their folklore, and connecting the promise of the past with the reality of the present and potential of the future.

Methodology

For the purposes of this work I am drawing a distinction between the New Deal and the Roosevelt administration. The New Deal represents a comprehensive vision of the American welfare state, grounded in a new understanding of rights. In its most progressive moments the Roosevelt administration sought to articulate this vision to the voting public and institutionalize it within the federal government. But Roosevelt was not always a New Dealer himself (sometimes for political reasons, sometimes out of conviction, or lack thereof),[58] nor did New Dealers ever fully control his administration. Likewise, no single New Dealer encompasses the vision as a whole. The theory is greater than the sum of its parts. So when the phrase New Deal is used in the context of this project it will be referring to the theory of welfare state liberalism this project synthesizes. The presidential administration in power from 1933 to 1945 I will refer to as the Roosevelt administration. They are not the same thing.

I also assume that there is a basic unity cutting across the New Deal during this entire period. Scholars since Basil Rauch, who wrote the first significant history of the New Deal,[59] have commonly made reference to two New Deals: the first occupying the period of the Hundred Days and the AAA/NRA experiments (recovery), the second accounting for progressive social legislation like the wages and hours bill, social security, and the Wagner Act (reform). Those who wish to argue that there is no thematic coherence to the New Deal frequently point to the seemingly contradictory policies of these two eras, although this criticism often conflates means and ends, overlooking the vision that unified disparate approaches to policy.

Milkis argues, persuasively, that after the 1936 election we can identify a third New Deal focused on the tasks of executive reorganization and institutionalizing the accomplishments of the first two New Deals. For Milkis, the reorganization framework inspired by the Brownlow report, FDR's court packing plan, and his failed attempt at party realignment via his 1938 "purge" were all efforts to empower the executive branch with the political strength it needed to manage what the New Deal now assumed to be legitimate and permanent functions of the government.[60] The goal was to provide the state with the administrative capacity necessary to address the perpetual crisis of modern capitalism, even when that crisis was not formally recognized. This formulation of three New Deals is a useful analytic tool for subdividing the various phases of New Deal reform, even though it leaves out an aborted "fourth" New Deal that would have advanced commitments to the Second Bill of Rights (although this can be seen as a return to the principles of the second New Deal if one looks to subdivide the New Deal conceptually rather than chronologically). Nevertheless, cutting across all these phases of legislation and policy initiatives is a common set of concerns—they were all animated by a coherent vision present throughout each of these New Deals.

As I argued earlier, one of the reasons that many scholars have had a hard time finding a systematic New Deal theory is the understandable emphasis placed on the person of FDR, rather than casting a broader net that encompasses the minds he surrounded himself with—who influenced him, shared his political and theoretical goals, and often articulated them in a more systematic fashion. This study crafts its synthesis chiefly (but not exclusively) by examining the thought of four New Dealers: Franklin Roosevelt, Eleanor Roosevelt, Henry

Wallace, and Thurman Arnold, figures chosen for several reasons. First, they all occupied places of great significance within the Roosevelt administration. Although only FDR and Wallace (in 1940) were ever actually elected, they were all accountable to the electorate in ways that the great public intellectuals of the period (figures like Stuart Chase, John Dewey, Felix Frankfurter, Max Lerner, Sidney Hook, Walter Lippmann, and company) were not. New Dealers had to practice political theory in the trenches, where ideological purity and even clarity is forced to surrender to necessity. As such they offer us insight into what practical political theory looks like. The study of the political thought of accountable political actors—those who theorize on the battlefield—is an underdeveloped area of enormous potential wealth. This is especially the case in the United States where, as Henry Commager argues, "[t]hroughout most of the history of the Republic, the major political philosophers had been statesmen, not savants or academicians."[61]

All four of these theorists were able and prolific communicators, and understood that the clear and simple transmission of otherwise complicated principles are an essential element of democratic statesmanship. FDR was a brilliant speaker, whose fireside chats aimed to demystify the process of government; marking an attempt to bridge the distance between citizen and ruler, to make the modern administrative state less alienating at worst, more democratic at best. Eleanor Roosevelt was one of the most popular political columnists of the age, while Wallace was a prolific writer and lecturer, as well as the standard-bearer of New Deal liberalism during the later years of the Roosevelt administration. Arnold himself was a best-selling author, a frequent contributor to the leading intellectual journals of the period, and "a key spokesman for the evolving New Deal."[62] All of them saw themselves not just as politicians and administrators, but also as educators and propagandists. They were all political actors actively and self-consciously engaged in an attempt to sell a foundational political vision to the American people in a way perhaps not seen since Madison and Hamilton penned the Federalist Papers.[63] It is true that, with the possible exception of Arnold, none of their works will be held up as first-rate works of conventional academic political theory, but to dismiss them on those grounds is to misunderstand their significance and purpose, their democratic and political character.

The Great Depression, and the institutionalizing of the welfare state as a response, required changing how Americans had long understood their relationship to the government, and to each other. The work of the thinkers examined here needs to be seen first and foremost as an attempt to make the unfamiliar familiar, their style a response to the alienation of their time. It was a reaction to the fact that we are, in ER's words, "separated too widely from each other and are unable to understand the daily problems of people in more limited circumstances."[64] They made themselves open and accessible to others, showed them a larger world, and communicated in clear, unaffected language how the well-being of one was related to the well-being of all. It is political theory aimed at the mass, not the elite, a distinction of great import in a democratic nation.

These figures were chosen for other reasons besides their twin roles as popularizers and members of the administration. Each of them offers a critical piece of the overall New Deal theory, filling in the gaps and articulating the assumptions that underpin Roosevelt's speeches and public declarations. Without considering these four thinkers as a group we are left only with shadows and outlines of a larger theory. But just as this is a study of the New Deal, rather than the Roosevelt administration, this is not a systematic look at each of these theorists. This is a work of synthesis, aiming to construct a philosophy of the New Deal from its component parts. There are tensions within the individual thought of each that this study will largely ignore, unless it speaks to problems within the larger synthesis as a whole. Still, it is a secondary hope of this project that it draws attention to these figures as political theorists in their own right. With the very slight exception of Franklin Roosevelt and Thurman Arnold, the most self-consciously "academic" of the four,[65] the closest we have to systematic presentations of their individual thought is usually found in their biographies. There have been thematic studies done on aspects of the Roosevelt administration[66] but they are divorced from the totality of New Deal political theory.

As previously mentioned, all four are figures of particular political importance. Franklin Roosevelt's relevance is self-evident. He was the body and soul of the New Deal, and his less progressive moments paralyzed New Dealers who had no idea how to proceed without him. Henry Commager sees in FDR the embodiment of generations of progressive political theory.

> It would be difficult to find a more representative figure or one who combined more harmoniously all those attitudes and principles which distinguished twentieth century political thought. He had the emotionalism of Bryan without his intellectual flabbiness, the magnetism of Theodore Roosevelt without his economic immaturity or his fatal tendency to compromise on essentials, the pragmatic hardheadedness of LaFollette without his inflexibly or harshness, the idealism of Wilson without his doctrinaire intellectualism. With a rationalized philosophy of government he combined an instinct for practical politics: more fully than any president since Jefferson he saw government as both an art and a science.[67]

That is high praise, and it is possible that FDR the man is not deserving of it. After all, his most important speech, the Commonwealth Club Address, was largely written by advisor Adolph Berle, and while FDR was closely involved in the drafting of his important public statements, he employed numerous talented people as speechwriters throughout his administration. But this project considers FDR as a public figure—the symbol that delivered the words and embodied the message is what is relevant for our purposes.

While FDR will be the central figure of any study of the New Deal, Eleanor Roosevelt (ER) is almost as important. Despite the incredible controversy she could engender, she frequently topped lists of the most admired women in the world, and her approval ratings were sometimes higher than her husband's.[68]

She was held in such high regard that one political cartoon featured a child mistaking the Statue of Liberty for her while another, on the occasion of her death, featured a group of awed cherub's breathlessly awaiting her entrance into heaven. She was FDR's conscience, and his eyes and ears on the ground. ER developed what was essentially a shadow administration within the White House,[69] and was one of the chief advocates within the New Deal for blacks, women, the young, and other dispossessed people whose lack of political power and organization otherwise silenced their voices. Her *My Day* newspaper column was one of the most popular in the country. In 1940, *Life* magazine summarized her previous eight years. She had traveled more than 280,000 miles (and been to every state but South Dakota), written one million words, donated over half a million dollars (almost all the money she made from writing and speaking), shaken more than half a million hands, and given hundreds of lectures.[70] In doing she became the voice of the New Deal's vision and the shape of its future.[71] As Barry Karl reminds us, "it was Eleanor Roosevelt's positions on social and moral issues that post-New Deal young liberals—Hubert Humphrey, Eugene McCarthy, George McGovern, even Adlai Stevenson—remembered as the legacy of the New Deal."[72]

Henry Wallace was, next to Franklin and arguably Eleanor Roosevelt, the great standard-bearer of New Deal liberalism, and FDR's hand-picked successor.[73] He was "the most articulate and reflective of the New Dealers," in the opinion of Louis Hartz,[74] and its most prominent prophet. He was also, with the possible exception of the Roosevelts, the most popular American statesman in the world. By any measure he was a figure of impressive intellect and energy, who authored the first econometric study in the United States, invented strains of hybrid corn, edited the *New Republic*, and formed a third party to challenge the rising Cold War consensus that claimed figures like Eleanor Roosevelt.[75] In between this he wrote and traveled extensively,[76] served two terms as secretary of agriculture, one term as vice president, and as secretary of commerce was Roosevelt's choice to oversee both the world's reconstruction and the internal transition back to a peacetime economy that would attempt to institute an economic bill of rights and guarantee full employment.[77]

Thurman Arnold was a former mayor, member of the Wyoming state legislature,[78] lawyer, judge, dean of the West Virginia law school, member of the Yale Law school faculty and major figure in the legal realism movement. James Young considered Arnold to be "the one striking exception to my statement that the movement produced little theory,"[79] and Wilson Carey McWilliams described Arnold as "the most articulate of the New Dealers who accepted the reinterpreted doctrine of the liberal tradition"[80] In *Age of Reform* Richard Hofstadter remarked, "Thurman Arnold wrote works of great brilliance and wit and considerable permanent significance...the most advanced of the New Deal camp."[81] Arnold performed legal work for the AAA in the early and mid-thirties, but he was brought into the inner ranks of the New Deal based on the strength of his two most important works, *The Symbols of Government* and *The Folklore of Capitalism*, written in 1935 and 1937 respectively. *The Folklore of*

Capitalism brought him national attention, and was particularly well received amongst the high-profile New Dealers in the Roosevelt administration. They were determined to find Arnold a permanent place within the administration, and in 1938 he became the assistant attorney general in charge of the Department of Justice's Anti-Trust Division. This was a surprising appointment, since *The Folklore of Capitalism* contained a biting analysis of the Sherman Anti-trust Act where he argued that it was a piece of symbolic legislation designed to address public angst over the existence of trusts rather than actually control them.[82] Once in power Arnold reinvigorated and revolutionized the division, winning a large number of anti-trust prosecutions, introducing innovative and effective new tactics that addressed systematic abuses, and greatly expanding its administrative staff. Under Arnold's leadership the Antitrust Division became an agency both capable of meaningful action and inclined to take it.[83] The advent of World War II sapped the Roosevelt administration's desire to battle large concentrations of economic power, and Arnold, growing increasingly frustrated, left the division in 1943.[84] Nevertheless, his time there, and his updating of traditional anti-trust policy for modern economic conditions represent, as Alan Brinkley has argued, the last significant challenge to the power of capital offered by the Roosevelt administration.

While the four figures highlighted here are essential, they by no means exhaust the pool of New Deal theorists. The New Deal drew many great minds into its orbit, almost all of whom wrote about their experiences in some capacity. Certainly there is great value behind further exploration of figures like Robert Jackson, Jerome Frank, Ben Cohen, David Lilienthal, Frances Perkins, Harry Hopkins, Harold Ickes, allies outside of the executive branch like Felix Frankfurter, Charles Murphy, and Robert Wagner, to say nothing of the many fellow travelers (Stuart Chase) and sympathetic critics (Max Lerner) not part of the government.

Perhaps the most controversial exclusion is the lack of focus on members of FDR's original advisors—his 'brains' trust. This decision was made for two reasons. First, Adolph Berle and Raymond Moley, while undeniably an influential part of the first New Deal, do not necessarily reflect the final evolution of its thought, and tie the New Deal too closely to its earliest initiatives. Berle left the administration early, and Moley eventually found himself in opposition to it. Tugwell lasted longer and wrote prolifically, but he was, in important ways, an outlier to the administration, a political liability eventually forced out, whose positions were frequently out of synch with even other New Dealers. He was gone shortly after the start of Roosevelt's second term, whereas Wallace and Eleanor Roosevelt were major figures from day one right through FDR's death. While Arnold was a minor actor until his appointment as head of Roosevelt's anti-trust division, he also headed the last major New Deal initiative, and one of its most significant. His inclusion is also necessitated by the fact that his principle works of theory, *Symbols of Government* and *The Folklore of Capitalism*, represent the two most systematic and sophisticated articulations of the theory of practice that informed the New Deal.

My second reason reflects the political orientation of this project. FDR, ER, and Wallace were political actors in a way that the brain trusters, more conventionally academic, never were, and it is the thought of these political actors that best reflects the fusion of theory and practice, vision and salesmanship, at the heart of the New Deal. Having said that, there is certainly great value in the closer study of these and other New Dealers not included here. Any act of synthesis is forced to make difficult choices about where to focus, and future discussion of excluded thinkers can only further enrich and enliven the theory as a whole.

It is worth clarifying the use of certain terms, especially *progressive, liberal*, and *democracy*. All three words are used in multiple ways throughout the project, and while the context should make the particular definition clear, the reader should still be forewarned. *Progressive* is used to refer to both a general left-leaning political orientation as well as the Progressive movement and the values it broadly held.[85] Similarly *liberal* will refer to the politics that follow out of the theory of the New Deal (and is used less inclusively than *progressive*), but it also refers to the classical form of liberalism (usually identified with the laissez faire descriptor) and the broader theory of philosophic liberalism, with its emphasis on constraints against arbitrary power and epistemological skepticism. Finally *democracy* refers both to the institutional arrangements (voting for representatives, etc.) as well as the moral ideal of democracy, with its emphasis on self-direction and moral equality.

Overview

> How are we constructing the edifice of recovery—the temple which, when completed, will no longer be a temple of money changers or of beggars, but rather a temple dedicated to and maintained for a greater social justice, a greater welfare for America—the habitation of a sound economic life.
>
> —Franklin Roosevelt[86]

This work is divided into four parts. Chapter 2 continues to lay introductory groundwork by offering a brief look at the Populist and Progressive movements that constitute previous responses to the excesses of laissez faire capitalism. Chapters 3 and 4 look at the New Deal's theory of ends, its argument for why reform is necessary and what a reconstructed society should look like. It defines the New Deal's vision, the substance of its story. Chapters 5 and 6 look at the New Deal's theory of practice—how should reformers confront a conservative electorate and account for institutions resistant to change? How should it tell its story? Given that the primary purpose of this study is to craft this synthesis and articulate a complete theory of the New Deal, we will withhold critical evaluation until the end, so as to not interrupt the presentation of the theory itself. We therefore conclude with chapter 7, which marks our initial attempt to assess the strengths and limitations of New Deal theory.

Chapter 2 looks at the theoretical antecedents of the New Deal. The chapter begins with an overview of the philosophic defense of laissez faire capitalism that dominated public discourse during the Gilded Age, 1920s, and the modern era running from Reagan until the present, although the focus is primarily on its incarnation as Social Darwinism. This theory becomes a deeply internalized piece of modern American folklore, and any progressive attempt to minimize the power and reach of capitalism will be forced to confront it.

The Populist and Progressive movements represent the first great American responses to the power and scope of that conservative ideal, and each in their own way influence the direction the New Deal will take. We will look briefly at the populist political style and its attempt to reassert the political and social agency that was lost in the process of economic modernization. The progressive era was more directly influential on the New Deal, and here we introduce some of the basic concepts that the New Deal would appropriate into its own theory. Of particular importance, however, is the way the progressives rejected politics in the name of civic purity. While the New Deal would internalize many progressive values and attempt to institutionalize others, it is the New Deal's embrace of the political that marks the most significant point of departure from progressivism.

The third chapter looks at the guiding assumptions that serve as preconditions of the New Deal's theory of ends, and the New Deal's progressive inheritance will be on display. We will examine the New Deal's argument that private economic power is a type of governance and therefore should be subject to the same limitations we place upon our political government to protect ourselves from arbitrary power. The purpose is to legitimize the right of the state to intervene in the case of (or to prevent) market failure—not just for the good of capital, but for the good of the citizen who rightly expects his government, be it economic or political, to ensure that he is furnished with the security he needs to exercise his rights.

The chapter concludes with a look at the other basic preconditions of New Deal theory. It asserts the right of the state to intervene, outside of wartime, in what was previously held to be a sacrosanct economic sphere. The assumption is that all citizens are entitled to a certain basic standard of living (this will be explored more in chapter 4) and that when private governance (the economy) cannot furnish it society (acting through the state) has both the right and obligation to ensure those standards are met. Animating this belief is a progressive faith in mastery, that human beings are capable of manipulating their social order to openly challenge the presence of necessity in our lives. Of course, the New Deal argues, one of the things that make Americans fortunate is that they had conquered the problem of scarcity. The Depression reflects a failure of our ability to distribute our abundance, rather than any fundamental lack or want. A cooperative state is possible because we have (ironically thanks to laissez faire capitalism) left the Hobbesian state of nature behind us. The task before us is one of gradual socialization, moving us away from an economy of scarcity towards one of abundance. The New Deal recognized that this would take time, and that self-interest might always remain a powerful frame capable of undermining progressive policies. As such, an effort was made to highlight our essential interdependence. Our former frontier individualism is largely a myth in a modern economy, and our own broad economic health was bound to our ability to accept responsibility for the material conditions of our fellow citizens.

Chapter 4 looks at the substance of the New Deal's positive political theory. There are two main arguments—that the pursuit of happiness should be accorded a status equal to liberty and that certain substantive preconditions must be met before either right can be enjoyed. Here we find the justification for the New Deal's security state—security incorporating not just our basic rights to food, shelter, and safety, but new rights to work, comprehensive education, and leisure. Following the emphasis on interdependence above—as well as reflecting a larger commitment that the leadership of a democracy should represent its entire people, even those who do not support it—the New Deal sought to find a basis on which it could construct a national community. It ultimately rejected the category of class, settling instead on consumer.

However, the New Deal did appreciate the dangers of positing the consumer as the central agent in its theory, choosing consumers as much for a lack of viable alternatives as for its own merits. The hope of the New Deal was that the narrow individualism and private orientation associated with consumption could be directed towards public ends—that the act of consumption could provide the preconditions for more meaningful (although ultimately voluntary) forms of freedom. Here the emphasis was on citizenship and Millian self-development, both of which move us away from narrow and baser private interests towards something public and higher. And when that failed there was always the Tocquevillian emphasis on religion, as a way to soften the excesses of consumption.[87]

This new understanding of happiness and security was to be institutionalized in a new social contract—implicitly at first, although as it became possible to think past World War II the New Deal started taking bolder, more public action to make these rights explicit—culminating in the declaration of a Second Bill of Rights. Steps were also taken to make space within this contract for groups that had historically been excluded from mainstream American society—the young, women, blacks, and those so mired in poverty that they had essentially been forgotten. Although there were limits to what the New Deal could do for them in practice—due to both a lack of political organization and, in many cases, powerful and organized hostility against them—their conditions were publicly addressed, their rights asserted, the New Deal going so far as to concede that until these groups were incorporated into American society the society itself had little right to expect their loyalty and obedience, a claim whose radicalism is difficult to overstate.

Chapter 5 examines the New Deal's theory of political agency. It discusses the nature of the New Deal's political pragmatism, situating it more in the tradition of Machiavelli than Dewey, concerning itself far more with limits on practice, the necessity of compromise, the perfectibility of politics and the nature of power than with larger epistemological and ontological questions of truth and experience. The chapter's primary focus is on Thurman Arnold's theory of symbolic politics, which examines the way our political culture provides both opportunities for and constraints upon reform.

Arnold's central argument is that ideas and institutions mutually constitute themselves. Ideas are of small consequence outside of the institutions that embody them, but these institutions themselves cannot function without ideas to give them morale, energy, and legitimacy. He looks into how these ideas are formed, the irrational manner in which we hold them, the ceremonial fashion in which we address the tension between our practice and our ideals, and the ways in which political actors are forced to engage these symbolic frames if they wish to connect with the electorate. His argument, which all the New Dealers profiled here accept, is that in times of institutional collapse, reformers need to learn how to manipulate the symbols of that failed order, which maintain an emotional relevance long after they cease to correspond with reality. New institutions require legitimacy, and reformers are forced to co-opt older, established symbols while new ones develop. The job of the theorist becomes, for Arnold, providing reformers with the conceptual tools they need to convince the electorate to do what they want, a fundamentally manipulative approach that stands in tension with the more rigorous conception of citizenship that the New Deal embraces as the ideal. The second half of the chapter looks at the way the New Deal sought to both undermine and appropriate the symbols of the old order, focusing on our symbols of business, welfare, the state, religion, the frontier, and the Constitution.

Chapter 6 looks at the other institutional limitations on New Deal reform, separate from, but still informed by, our conservative folklore. It briefly explores the nature of the conservative coalition that stymied the New Deal, the relationship between FDR's court plan and labor's sit-down strikes, as well as the weak federal state and the lack of preexisting infrastructure. The second half of the chapter looks at what Milkis calls the third New Deal, the attempts to institutionally strengthen the executive branch, as well as the complicated relationship between president and party. It highlights the New Deal's emphasis on organization as a way to enforce liberal accountability and involve groups in the democratic process (along with the state's obligation to help the unorganized organize themselves, of which labor is the most prominent example). Finally, it provides an overall look at the limits to reform imposed by a liberal democracy (the limits imposed by capitalism are discussed in chapter 7).

Chapter 7 concludes the argument. After a brief summation of the New Deal theory and its strengths, it explores several of the tensions that should be addressed if the theory is to be appropriated for reimagining contemporary progressive political discourse. These include the limits of interest group liberalism, the tension between an administrative state and Jeffersonian localism, the problems attendant upon trying to craft a common good on the back of a consumer identity, the possible incompatibility between the democratic ideal and manipulative practice, and above all else the ultimate inability of the Roosevelt administration to confront the presence of capital in the system.

New Deal theory is imperfect, but its weaknesses highlight in important ways its very strength as a theory. The assumption underpinning both the New Deal and this work is that, for now at least, capitalism is here to stay—that there is no mass movement capable of peacefully overthrowing it, and our political focus needs to be on figuring out ways to humanize and democratize it. While it articulates an aspirational understanding of citizenship it is fully aware of the limits of what we are capable of as citizens. It insists on the sanctity of our political traditions and institutions, and makes its peace with their flaws even as it struggles to overcome them. As a result the process of reform will be proximate and imperfect, but the political theory of the New Deal is aware of what is at stake, understands the nature of political agency in a modern democracy (American democracy in particular), and offers us a theory and practice capable of reconstructing a nation that so often fails to live up to its own ennobling ideals.

Notes

1. FDR from a 1936 campaign speech. Quoted in Bruce Miroff, *Icons of Democracy* (Lawrence: University Press of Kansas, 2000), 258.

2. ER, *The Moral Basis of Democracy* in *Courage*, 57.

3. Wallace, *Frontiers*, 252.

4. Arnold, *Folklore*, 393.

5. Franklin Delano Roosevelt will be abbreviated as FDR throughout much of this work.

6. "Continued participation and confidence in the American economy," in his words. George Bush, "Address to Joint Session of Congress" September 20, 2001. http://archives.cnn.com/2001/US/09/20/gen.bush.transcript/Bush

7. Peter Beinart, "The New Liberal Order" *Time Magazine,* November 20, 2008.

8. As Kim Phillips-Fein argues, the political right certainly understood that the corporate counterrevolution against the New Deal would be fought on an ideological as well as an institutional level, and that much of that revolution's phenomenal success can be traced back to its emphasis on creating an alternative ideological story to counter the New Deal worldview. Kim Phillips-Fein, *Invisible Hands: The Businessmen's Crusade Against the New Deal,* (New York: Norton, 2009).

9. Morton Frisch, *Franklin D. Roosevelt: The Contribution of the New Deal to American Political Thought,* (Boston: Twayne Publishers, 1975), 58.

10. Apocryphal quote attributed to Oliver Wendell Holmes regarding FDR. Jean Edward Smith, *FDR.* (New York: Random House, 2007), 311.

11. Even though progressive historians themselves cannot come to any real consensus over what progressivism actually stood for.

12. Peter Coleman, "The World of Interventionism," in *The New Deal and Its Legacy: Critique and Reappraisal,* ed. Robert Eden, (New York: Greenwood Press, 1989), 50.

13. James Young, *Reconsidering American Liberalism: The Troubled Odyssey of the Liberal Idea*, (Boulder: Westview Press, 1996), 169. I agree with Young insofar as the lack of a clearly articulated New Deal theory means that the American Left has no theory about the origins of their welfare state.

14. Albert Romansco, *The Politics of Recovery*, (New York: Oxford University Press, 1983), 5.

15. Frisch, *Franklin Roosevelt,* 24. Frisch argues that New Dealers may have been too immersed in the thick of the period's politics to get a handle on what was taking shape.

16. Tugwell quoted in Adam Cohen, *Nothing to Fear: FDR's Inner Circle and the Hundred Days That Created Modern America*, (New York: The Penguin Press, 2009), 285.

17. Samuel Lubell, "The Roosevelt Coalition," in *The New Deal: Analysis and Interpretation,* ed. Alonzo Hamby. (New York: Longman Inc., 1981), 162.

18. One could even argue, as Robert Eden does, that the perception itself was shaped by political considerations—namely that FDR was reluctant to carefully define what the New Deal was before he had found a way to institutionalize it, a strategy that makes sense given how ideologically divided the Democratic Party was. Robert Eden, "On The Origins of the Regime of Pragmatic Liberalism: John Dewey, Adolf A. Berle, and FDR's Commonwealth Club Address of 1932." *Studies in American Political Development* 7, (Spring 1993), 111-112.

19. See Hubert Humphries, *The Political Philosophy of the New Deal,* (Baton Rouge: Louisiana State University Press, 1970); Frisch, *Franklin Roosevelt*; Barry Karl, *The Uneasy State: The United States from 1915-1945* (Chicago: The University of Chicago Press, 1983); Philip Abbot, *The Exemplary Presidency*, (Amherst: University of Massachusetts Press, 1990); Sidney Milkis and Jerome Mileur. "Introduction: The New Deal, Then and Now" in *The New Deal and the Triumph of Liberalism,* eds. Sidney Milkis and Jerome Mileur, (Amherst: University of Massachusetts Press, 2002); James Morone, *Hellfire Nation*, (New Haven: Yale University Press, 2003); David Plotke, *Building a Democratic Political Order: Reshaping American Liberalism in the 1930s and 1940,* (New York: Cambridge University Press, 1996). Cass Sunstein, *The Second Bill of Rights*, (New York: Basic Books, 2004).

20. Anthony Badger, *The New Deal: The Depression Years 1933-1940,* (Chicago, Ivan R. Dee, 1989), Alan Lawson, *A Commonwealth of Hope: The New Deal Response to Crisis,* (Baltimore: The Johns Hopkins University Press, 2006).

21. FDR, "State of the Union Address," January 6, 1937.

22. Eden, *Origins*, 104.

23. The New Deal was not prepared, theoretically or politically—although a good deal of that theoretical commitment was informed by its assessment of political possibilities—to fully engage capitalism at a structural level. This will pose some serious problems for the theory as a whole, which will be discussed in the concluding chapter.

24. Thurman Arnold, *The Bottlenecks of Business*, (New York: Reynal & Hitchcock, 1940), 110-111.

25. FDR quoted in Sunstein, *Second,* 91.

26. It does not have to, of course. As Lawrence Glickman makes clear in *Buying Power: A History of Consumer Activism in America* the idea of the consumer as an ethical agent capable of turning the private sphere into a public one has a long, albeit occasionally forgotten, history in the United States. The New Deal hoped to strengthen the bonds between citizen and consumer, although this was never a political or organizational priority. Lawrence Glickman, *Buying Power: A History of Consumer Activism in America*, (Chicago: The University of Chicago Press, 2009).

27. Hughes quoted in Morton Keller, *America's Three Regimes: A New Political History*, (Oxford: Oxford University Press, 2007), 37.

28. It is hard to imagine President Bush (or Clinton or Obama, for that matter) telling Americans to roll their maps out onto the floor so he could explain the geography of the war on terror to us, the way FDR did to explain the problems of supplying our troops in the Pacific during WWII.

29. Irving Bernstein, *A Caring Society: The New Deal, the Worker, and the Great Depression*, (Boston: Houghton Mifflin Company, 1985), 18-19.

30. Sunstein, *Second*, 36-37.

31. Badger, *New Deal*, 12.

32. Cohen, *Nothing to Fear,* 16.

33. Smith, *FDR*, 289.

34. Smith, *FDR*, 327.

35. Ann O'Hare McCormick, "Vast Tides That Stir the Capital," *New York Times Magazine*, May 7, 1933, in *The New Deal and the American People,* ed. Frank Freidel, (Englewood Cliffs: Prentice-Hall, Inc., 1964), 5.

36. FDR, "Second Inaugural Address," January 20th, 1937, in *Speeches*, 61.

37. FDR, *Speeches*. 61.

38. Quoted in M.D. Vincent and Beulah Amidon, "NRA: A Trial Balance," *Survey Graphic,* July 1935, in Freidel, 40-41.

39. A phrase of Social Darwinist William Graham Sumner's, appropriated by the New Deal in a wonderful moment of irony appreciated by theorists, if no one else.

40. Quoted in John Jeffries, *Wartime America: The World War II Home Front* (Chicago: Ivan R Dee, 1996), 189.

41. Quoted in Young, *Liberalism*, 171.

42. Abbot, *Exemplary*, 8.

43. It was this lack of administrative capacity that Badger consistently argues helps explains many of the limitations in the farm, industrial, and welfare programs of the New Deal.

44. John Wettergreen, "The Regulatory Policy of the New Deal," in Robert Eden, ed. *The New Deal and Its Legacy: Critique and Reappraisal*, (New York: Greenwood Press, 1989), 200.

45. Karl, *Uneasy*, 98 and 153.

46. Plotke, *Building*, 85.

47. Jerome Mileur, "The 'Boss': Franklin Roosevelt, the Democratic Party, and the Reconstitution of American Politics," in Milkis and Mileur, *New Deal*, 87.

48. FDR quoted in Sidney Milkis, "New Deal Party Politics, Administrative Reform, and the Transformation of the American Constitution," in Eden, 314.

49. Wilson, following Jefferson, estimated this to be every twenty years.

50. Although, as Badger notes, that opportunity rarely came.

51. Sidney Milkis, "Franklin D. Roosevelt, the Economic Constitutional Order, and the New Politics of Presidential Leadership," in Milkis and Mileur, *New Deal*, 35.

52. James MacGregor Burns, *Roosevelt: The Lion and the Fox*, (New York: Harcourt Brace & World, 1956); Paul Conkin. *The New Deal*, (Arlington Heights: AHM Publishing, 1975); Howard Zinn, ed., *New Deal Thought*, (Indianapolis: Hackett, 2003).

53. Hoover quoted in Cohen, *Nothing to Fear*, 34.

54. Basil Rauch, *The History of the New Deal 1933-1938*, (New York: Creative Age Press, 1944), 137. Apparently these would-be fascists were not aware that General Butler voted for Roosevelt.

55. Editor's introduction, *Speeches*, 57.

56. Arnold, *Symbols*, iii.

57. Richard Parker, "Why the New Deal Matters," in *The Nation*, April 7, 2008. http://www.thenation.com/doc/20080407/parker/4

58. He was realistic about the money Congress would appropriate for New Deal programs, was sincerely troubled by the presence of deficits, and largely open to various, even contradictory, approaches to increasing consumer spending, for instance.

59. Rauch, *History*.

60. Milkis, "Economic," 41.

61. Henry Steele Commager, *The American Mind*, (New Haven: Yale University Press, 1950), 346.

62. Lawson, *Hope*, 192.

63. And, like the Federalists, the key to selling this radical reconceptualization of government was to hide its radical character.

64. ER, *Moral Basis*, 63.

65. No doubt due to Arnold's former career as a law professor, although Arnold was famous for his decidedly sardonic, unconventional writing style. If he was an academic, he was an unconventional one. Regardless, even here the amount of secondary work done on Arnold is quite small.

66. See, for instance, Theodore Rosenof's *Economics in the Long Run*, (Chapel Hill: The University of North Carolina Press, 1997), and, more recently, Sunstein, *Second*.

67. Henry Steele Commager, *Mind*, 354.

68. In fact, Louis Howe, FDR's chief political advisor until his death in 1936, was convinced he could get ER elected as president if she wanted to run. She declined to test his theory.

69. As Blanche Wiesen Cook, one of ER's most recent biographers, describes:

> Throughout the White House years, ER was to spend between sixteen and twenty hours a day running actually a parallel administration concerned with every aspect of national betterment. Domestically, nothing was beyond her range of interest, and she monitored every department through a friend or agreeable contact. FDR never credited ER with a job well done or publicly acknowledged her political influence. But little of significance was achieved without her input, and her vision shaped the best of his presidency.

Blanche Wiesen Cook, *Eleanor Roosevelt: Volume II 1933-1938*, (New York: Viking, 1999), 30.

70. David Emblidge, ed., *My Day: The Best of Eleanor Roosevelt's Acclaimed Newspaper Column 1936-1962* (Da Capo Press: 2001), 44.

71. Following FDR's death she would become the elder stateswoman of the Democratic Party and oversee the drafting of United Nations Declaration of Human Rights.

72. Karl, *Uneasy*, 175.

73. FDR refused to run in 1940 if Wallace was not approved as his running mate. Exhausted by 1944, FDR did not put up a fight to preserve Wallace's position on the ticket, given his deep unpopularity with the party leadership (due in large part to his combative liberalism). Even so, Wallace almost received the nomination based on his grassroots support that could not quite overcome the organized opposition and machinations of the Democratic Party machine.

74. Louis Hartz, *The Liberal Tradition in America* (San Diego: Harcourt Brace, 1955), 271.

75. Although, perhaps attesting to ER's greater political acumen, Wallace's third party bid cost him the good will of both the Democratic Party and mainstream progressives in general.

76. In 1934 alone Wallace traveled 40,000 miles, made appearances in every state, wrote twenty articles, published two books, and one significant pamphlet. John Culver and John Hyde, *American Dreamer: A Life of Henry A Wallace*, (New York: W.W. Norton & Company, 2000), 151.

77. A conservative Congress, recognizing the threat that Wallace posed, immediately stripped the office of secretary of commerce of much of its power.

78. In 1920 he was the only Democrat elected in the entire state of Wyoming during a banner year nationwide for the Republicans. An anecdote from his autobiography perfectly captures the irreverence of his personality.

> On the fateful day the legislature assembled to elect a speaker there were a number of flowery speeches made for the leading candidate. After they were over and the question was about to be put to a vote, I rose and said, "Mr. Speaker, the Democratic party caucused last night, and when the name of Thurman Arnold was mentioned, it threw its hat up in the air and cheered for fifteen minutes. I therefore wish to put his name in nomination for speaker of this House. " I then sat down, but I got up immediately and seconded the nomination. I said, "I have known Thurman Arnold for most of my life, and I would trust him as far as I would myself. "
> Everybody laughed except the Speaker pro tem. My nomination was not on his carefully prepared agenda, and he did not know what to do. People were waving at him from all directions. So I rose a third time, and said, "Mr. Speaker, some irresponsible Democrat has put my name in nomination and I wish to withdraw it. " After that, the train got on the track again.

Thurman Arnold, *Fair Fights and Foul*, (New York: Harcourt, Brace & World, Inc, 1965), 33.

79. Young, *Liberalism*, 174.

80. Wilson Carey McWilliams, *The Idea of Fraternity in America*, (Berkeley: University of California Press, 1973), 551.

81. Richard Hofstadter, *The Age of Reform*, (New York: Vintage Books, 1955), 317.

82. Control was actually impossible, Arnold would argue, since we had no economic institutions capable of replacing trusts. The Sherman Act was designed to blind us from the truth that ideologically distasteful trusts were, at the time, structurally necessary.

83. For an excellent overview of Arnold's DOJ tenure see Alan Brinkley, *The End of Reform*, (New York: Vintage Books, 1996), 105-122.

84. He served briefly as a judge, but he felt he lacked the reverence necessary to perform in that role. He resigned after several years to open a private practice in Washington. His prestigious firm produced a future Supreme Court Justice (Abe Fortas), blocked several attempts by the Postmaster General to censor magazines he deemed ob-

scene, and played an instrumental role in defending victims of Senator McCarthy's witch-hunts.

85. Of course figuring out what Progressives believe is itself something of a cottage industry. See Eldon Eisenach's *The Lost Promise of Progressivism* (Lawrence: The University Press of Kansas, 1994) and Robert Wiebe's *The Search for Order,* (New York: Hill and Wang, 1967) for two of the better books on this.

86. FDR, "Assessing the New Deal," October 22, 1933, Fireside Chat, in *Chat*, 39.

87. The ceding of religious language to the Right has given it a potent monopoly over one of our most potent symbols (see, for instance the perverse formulation of what constitutes 'values' voting in contemporary political discourse). The New Deal reminds us that within religion we have a powerful set of categories capable of inspiring progressive reform. Christianity has been enlisted into the causes of prohibition, nativism, censorship, and bigotry, but it was also the backbone of the abolitionist movement, the reformism of the social gospel movement, and the inclusivity of Martin Luther King.

Chapter 2
The Evolution of Reform: Populist and Progressive Forebears

It was not only that Americans had to adjust themselves to changes in economy and society more abrupt and pervasive than ever before. It was rather that for the first time in their national experience they were confronted with a challenge to their philosophical assumptions.

—Henry Steele Commager[1]

The New Deal was not America's first attempt to address the physical and existential challenges modern capitalism poses to both the individualism and agency that Americans have long regarded as their birthright. The Populist and Progressive eras each confronted the violence unreconstructed laissez faire capitalism inflicted on those who fell behind in the competitive struggle for survival and advancement: poor wages, terrible working conditions, and a suffocating loss of agency that called into question the reality of the "American Dream." The New Deal would build upon their theoretical innovations, granting previously radical ideas and political approaches the mainstream legitimacy and stability necessary to institutionalize a dramatic and enduring change to our social contract.[2] As Thurman Arnold argues, real structural innovation requires not only a failure of the existing order, but a coherent ideology (or folklore) capable of legitimating new aspirations and institutions. In that sense, the New Deal was perhaps as dependent on the intellectual framework produced by these earlier movements as it was on the crisis of the Great Depression.

33

There is much excellent scholarship (albeit less consensus) on the Populist and Progressive movements,[3] and a detailed analysis of these periods is beyond the scope of this work. Instead, this chapter focuses on the aspects of Social Darwinism, populism, and progressivism relevant to the subsequent development of New Deal thought, in particular the nature of their challenge to the ideological and institutional power of large-scale capitalism.

The New Economic Order

Man became economic man, democracy was identified with capitalism, liberty with property and the use of it, equality with opportunity for gain, and progress with economic change and the accumulation of capital.

—John Blum[4]

That the post Civil War rise of a modern, industrialized America came at a tremendous human cost is clear, even if one accepts (as FDR did) that it was, on balance, worth the price. The crop-lien system response to a limited monetary supply, with its ruinous credit rates, destroyed the vaunted independence of the farmer, chaining him to an exploitative system of finance that left him little more than a slave while mockingly insisting that he was free. The farmers' increasing productivity simply pushed him deeper into debt by driving down farm prices, perverting the values of hard work and delayed gratification that were such vital components of American character, robbing him of any sense of agency. As Lawrence Goodwyn chronicles in *The Populist Moment*, "[a]s thousands, then millions descended into the world of landless tenantry, the annual output expanded, but both the soil and those who worked it gradually became exhausted as a result of the desperate cycle of crop lien, furnish, cotton harvest, failure to pay out, and new crop lien."[5] The farmer was well and truly trapped, and his struggle to free himself only further tightened his chains. He was faced with a collective action problem classical American ideology simply could not conceptualize, let alone address. The small American farmer was simply irrelevant next to the systemic power of national and global markets, finance capital, trusts, and forerunners of modern agribusiness, but our Jeffersonian folklore continued to celebrate the farmer's now largely illusory agency, closing off the possibility of a collective response to his marginalization.

Life was no better in the city, with unemployment soaring as high as 16 percent during the frequent periods of depression, and many of those who had regular employment found themselves barely scraping by, brushing up against a $500 poverty line that 40 percent of industrial workers lived below. Only about 15 percent of American workers enjoyed what was considered a decent standard of living, earning between $800 to $1100 a year.[6] Beyond their limited wages, these Americans were often forced to live and work in conditions ranging from substandard to inhuman, with hundreds of thousands dying on the job and millions more injured by the "mechanized violence inherent in the industrial work place."[7] By 1890 the richest 1 percent of Americans made more in wages than the bottom 50 percent and owned more property than the bottom 99 percent.[8] The country was seemingly ripe for class revolution, and third-party presidential candidate James Baird Weaver[9] described the impending conflict in language that made Thomas Paine a model of understated restraint.

> The American people have entered upon the mightiest civic struggle known to their history...We must expect to be confronted by a vast and splendidly equipped army of extortionists, usurers ad oppressors marshaled from every nation under heaven. Every instrumentality known to man,—the state with its civic authority, learning with its lighted torch, armies with their commissions to take life, instruments of commerce essential to commercial intercourse, and the very soil upon which we live, move, and have our being—all these things and more are being perverted and used to enslave and impoverish the people. The Golden Rule is rejected by the heads of all the great departments of trade, and the law of Cain, which repudiates the obligations that we are mutually under to one another, is fostered and made the rule of action throughout the world. Corporate feudality has taken the place of chattel slavery and vaunts its power in every state.[10]

Weaver describes an America (indeed, an entire world) that had been completely co-opted by those who utterly reject any sense of mutual obligation, reciprocity, or even human dignity. His use of the language of slavery would have had particular resonance to a people whose Civil War wounds were still raw, and Weaver's words would strike a chord with the millions of citizens who were convinced that their birthright, the promise of America, had been stolen from them.

Despite the apocalyptic visions (twenty years later, still confronting the same systemic threats to the American Dream, President Theodore Roosevelt would declare "We stand at Armageddon and we battle for the Lord"), fiery rhetoric, and organizational talents of the Populists, the revolution never came. The question is why. One major factor was a lack of institutional vehicles for reform. The mainstream political parties were simply unequipped to take on this system, even if they were willing. Party politics served primarily as a source of identity and entertainment. It was sport and gossip rolled into one, and lacking the hierarchical national organization of the kind that would be necessary to impose order on a parochial system. The national parties did not control nominations, dictate campaigns, or write platforms. The president was rarely more than a factional leader. The city machines, who justified their existence by providing basic welfare services, were perhaps capable of providing some sort of local order, but were unable to act with sufficient scope and national authority to tame what was truly a national economic system. Even on those rare occasions when the federal government chose to act—Grover Cleveland's belief that "[t]hough the people support the government; the government should not support the people" was the norm—it lacked the administrative capacity to enforce its decisions. "National policy was an illusion..." Robert Wiebe argues. "With neither the will nor the apparatus for continuous supervision, administrators in Washington declared the law at the outset and perhaps checked a few of its results at some later date."[11] In fact, the only figures really capable of acting on a national level were industrial leaders, but their national field of action reflected their own narrow interests.

That this lack of national capacity to address the costs of capitalism was largely tolerated reflected the legitimacy of that system in the eyes of most Americans. In part this was because the reality of the violence present in everyday life was hidden and obscured.[12] The sheer scope and distance of finance capitalism enabled businessmen to be cavalier about the ways they decimated far-off communities. Workers could be ignored, poverty cordoned off in slums, and no one had to bear witness to the human costs of this new system. But there was also a powerfully argued, clearly articulated justification for this new order, advanced by theorists like Herbert Spencer, William Graham Sumner and John Fiske. These men embraced our acquisitive instincts as both a moral virtue and evolutionary adaptation, and provided an enduring pseudo-scientific justification for an otherwise morally questionable position: that greed was not only beneficial to the individual, but also advanced the common good.

There was an elegant simplicity to the theory of laissez faire. All men applied themselves to the acquisition of wealth, according to their natural ability. The best ones would find innovative ways to exploit our common inheritance and advance society through the accumulation of wealth. So far this is straight out of a standard reading of Locke, although Locke would likely dispute the claim of Russell Conwell that "to make money honestly is to preach the gospel."[13] Unlike Locke, however, for these men society retained the sense of violence and conflict that categorized the state of nature, since theirs was a world categorized not by abundance, but scarcity. We lacked the resources to meet the needs of all, and so over time the unfit would necessarily, and for the good of society, be eliminated. As society became more and more complex those not prepared for it had to be left behind. After all, it was Spencer, and not Darwin, who coined the term "survival of the fittest," and it was self-evident that the nation would be better off by allowing the fit and unfit to respectively reward and remove themselves. In this, we see the time-honored American concern with purity[14] playing itself out with economic/class, rather than its more traditional racial overtones (although few doubted that the Anglo-Saxon race would ultimately produce those most fit to survive). It was a dark vision of a humanity struggling against a state of nature that owed more to Hobbes than Locke.

The brilliance of the argument came from equating this process with the laws of nature and evolution, both of which are material theories of progress from which few more obligations may properly be drawn. This theory's scientific veneer allowed its adherents to render irrelevant any pangs of conscience that came with the human costs of "progress." It made no more sense to lodge a moral protest against gravity as it did this new economic order. As Andrew Carnegie argued in *The Gospel of Wealth*, "whether this change [modern capitalism] be for good or ill, it is upon us, beyond our power to alter, and therefore to be accepted and made the best of. It is a waste of time to criticize the inevitable."[15]

But the defenders of this "Social Darwinism" also understood the power of the happy ending. The teleological idea of 'progress' worked, as any teleology does, to justify the absence of obligations and constraints, assuaging the guilt felt by those still bound by traditional moral concerns—in the end it would all be worth it, if we remain patient just a little while longer. Spencer disciples like John Fiske further softened Spencer's position by equating industrialization with God's plan for a more just world. Others, like William Graham Sumner, gave the philosophy a middle-class veneer, focusing as he did on the 'forgotten man' whose hard work drives our social evolution. As Henry Commager argues, this was a heady philosophy.

> Progress was no longer a mere conclusion of logic but a necessity of nature. Scientific determinism lost its terrors when it was seen to be benevolent, shaping Nature and Man for ends that could justly be called divine...Morality itself was furnished, for the first time, with a scientific foundation. Reason and intuition had wrestled vainly with the problem of evil in a universe logically or ideally good, evolution made the problem irrelevant, for evil, which was now seen to be but a maladjustment to nature, was destined inevitably to disappear in that larger harmony which was good.[16]

Out of the Hobbesian darkness comes utopia, with an inexorable and inevitable force that greatly appealed to the sentiments of a nation long convinced of its central place in a divinely ordered history. That this philosophy legitimated the status quo in such a glorious way made it especially appealing to elites and those who wished to curry favor with or aspire to be them.

With evolution doing the heavy lifting, government simply had to maintain order so that progress could naturally unfold. However, order clearly privileged the great men and great interests who were the engine of that progress. Although not the star of history, the restrained role of the state was nevertheless remarkably important because the future was, in spite of the weight of science, history, and destiny, remarkably fragile. As Young (quoting Wiebe) points out, "[i]f any slight departure from the straight and narrow of non-interference could derail the whole, presumably inevitable, train of progress, then, 'by imputing such power to a few errant men, the theorists mocked the grandeur or their own fundamental laws."[17] Union agitation, worker and consumer protections, indeed any attempt to humanize the system could cause the whole thing to collapse, and as a result the great electoral contests of this period understood themselves as titanic struggles for the soul of civilization. For the Social Darwinists, we could only bring about the future by surrendering our sense of free will and agency to the workings of the market and the unfolding of history and evolution. Freedom became synonymous with the lives we created for ourselves within the market, and at no point was there a sense that citizens, operating through democratic institutions, could direct the process and determine its outcome.

In practice the state ignored the glaring disconnect between the gospel of competition and the reality of pools, trusts, holding companies, and cooperation that mocked the very competition supposedly driving evolution. The dominance of the laissez faire ideology carried over into the nation's fundamental law, granting it an unquestioning legitimacy usually enjoyed only by scripture.[18] Sumner argued that our only self-evident right is the right of competition and the Supreme Court, under the leadership of Justice Stephen Field, agreed. The Fourteenth Amendment and the Declaration of Independence were read as strict defenses of private property, trumping all other rights and concerns. Property became a way to legitimize the idea of mastery in a democratic society and constitutional innovations like substantive due process protected this new, increasingly oligarchic but widely supported, understanding of property. Corporations were granted legal personhood and their stockholders given limited liability, making it even easier to dehumanize workers and obscure the social costs of this system. Any freedom other than the freedom of contract was deemed both paternalistic and unconstitutional. Attempts to regulate wages and hours took away the 'liberty' of people to work and buy how they choose. The very idea of freedom as democratic political agency functionally ceased to exist, replaced by a more narrow view of freedom as submission to the needs of the market and (eventually) consumer choice. Although an exasperated Justice Holmes commented in his 1905 *Lochner* dissent that "The Fourteenth Amendment does not enact Mr. Herbert Spencer's Social Statics," the Supreme Court clearly disagreed.

It was a powerful theory, made more so by its roots in various aspects of American folklore. As Wiebe notes:

> The theory, for all of its harsh qualities, drew upon a rich tradition of village values. Equal opportunity for each man; a test of individual merit; wealth as a reward for virtue; credit for hard work, frugality, and dedication; a premium upon efficiency; a government that minded its own business; a belief in society's progressive improvement; these and many more read like a catalogue of mid-nineteenth century values.[19]

The Spencerian vision survived, in various forms through the Gilded Age, the "Roaring Twenties" and up into our present era precisely because it managed to link itself to these classical American values, This is the folklore that every left-leaning movement oriented towards economic justice is forced to confront, although true to its name Social Darwinism proved to be a highly adaptable theory, with figures like Herbert Hoover and Ronald Reagan softening its harsh edges. While the New Deal launched what was arguably the most far reaching and totalizing assault on this worldview within mainstream American politics, it did so by building off of the populist and progressive attempts to break the "steel chain"[20] of laissez faire.

Populism

I believe that both parties are afraid of Wall Street. They are not afraid of the people.

—L.L. Polk[21]

Although populism built off of the same tensions that had been fueling third party protest throughout the post Civil War era, the historical movement formally known as populism began with the Farmer's Alliance (which became the National Alliance in 1889 and later the Populist Party).[22] Populism's high-water mark was its highly successful insurgent campaign in 1892 (which produced the famous Omaha Platform) and the 1896 William Jennings Bryan fusion campaign with the Democratic Party. Bryan's defeat at the hands of McKinley left a movement, already in the midst of an identity crisis that inevitably accompanies the move from insurgency to mainstream, dispirited and functionally broken.

The populist style, heavily influenced by Jacksonian democracy, tends to reduce politics to a binary clash of "the people" versus "the interests." Of course who makes up the people and what constitutes an interest is an open, political question. Some populists like Thomas Watson made significant attempts to broaden the movement's appeals to immigrants and blacks, but for the most part populism as a political movement accepted traditional racial and ethnic understandings of who constituted an American. Likewise, while certain interests were familiar populist villains (railroads and Wall Street) Bryan's "Cross of Gold' speech" and the larger debate about free silver and monetary policy can be read in a very different light when one realizes that the silver interests of the mountain west were strong supporters of the Bryan candidacy.

However one defines the people and the interests it was clear that this was not simply a conflict of interests or a war between classes, but a larger moral struggle, a Manichean battle between Good (the people) and Evil (the interests), the kind of language FDR would adopt in his 1936 reelection campaign.[23] The side of the people represents all that is best within America and its traditions, while the interests represent a co-option at best, a perversion at worst, of those basic ideals. Populism is frequently suspicious of constitutional and liberal checks on power because those checks are seen as tools of special interests, the weapons they use to subvert the will of the people—not a crazy position in light of a long string of counter-majoritarian Supreme Court decisions, of which *Lochner v. New York* is only the most famous.[24] Tocqueville describes an early populism in *Democracy in America*, but Jacksonian democracy was ultimately optimistic and forward looking. It had the force of progress and history on its side. Populism is the angry side of Jacksonian democracy, the darker lamentations of a people who have seen their birthright stolen from them, their once free institutions hopelessly corrupted. The preamble to the Omaha Platform surveys the political landscape and its report is exceedingly grim.

We meet in the midst of a nation brought to the verge of moral, political, and material ruin. Corruption dominates the ballot-box, the Legislatures, the Congress, and touches even the ermine of the bench. The people are demoralized; most of the States have been compelled to isolate the voters at the polling places to prevent universal intimidation and bribery. The newspapers are largely subsidized or muzzled, public opinion silenced, business prostrated, homes covered with mortgages, labor impoverished, and the land concentrating in the hands of capitalists. The urban workmen are denied the right to organize for self-protection, imported pauperized labor beats down their wages, a hireling standing army, unrecognized by our laws, is established to shoot them down, and they are rapidly degenerating into European conditions. The fruits of the toil of millions are boldly stolen to build up colossal fortunes for a few, unprecedented in the history of mankind; and the possessors of those, in turn, despise the republic and endanger liberty. From the same prolific womb of governmental injustice we breed the two great classes—tramps and millionaires.[25]

"Corruption" infests politics, the press, the market, with the machinations of the interests undermining the very possibility of freedom. There is a conspiratorial element to this type of thinking to be sure, but the power elite does not cease to exist just because it is offensive to democratic sensibilities.

The economic component of populism is largely defined by the same producerist ideology that dominated Jacksonian democracy.[26] In strict Lockean terms, wealth belongs to the people who literally produce it. As the Omaha Platform puts it, "Wealth belongs to him who creates it, and every dollar taken from industry without an equivalent is robbery. 'If any will not work, neither shall he eat.' The interests of rural and civic labor are the same; their enemies are identical." The distant financers of Wall-Street who control the money supply, the Railroad executives who establish ruinous rates, right down to the shop-keeper who profits from the crop lien system, none of these men are entitled to the profits they earned from the rent of other people's hard labor. The wild success of Henry George's *Progress and Poverty*, which sought to solve almost every economic issue in America with a confiscatory tax on rent, speaks to the far reaching power of this ideal. Populism rejected the symbolic efforts of laissez faire to rebrand the great American individual as financier and businessman. While Carrol Wright assured our industrial leaders that "the rich and powerful manufacturer... is an instrument of God for the upbuilding of the race,"[27] the populists refused to bend a knee.

To protect the interests of producers, populists advocated for public control over industries like the railroads and the expansion of the monetary supply, precisely because these were seen as essential to the preservation of genuinely free markets that would promise rewards commensurate with work. The populists did not seek an entitlement state. They were not interested in welfare. Rather they saw the need for public regulation in order to ensure that reward is derived from effort and innovation, rather than power.[28] With the populists we find an expression of the idea that would come to dominate both progressivism and the New Deal—that safeguarding substantive individual freedom requires using public political power to break up or regulate private economic power. The populists did not really seek to replace capitalism, despite some promising experiments with cooperative organizations. Instead they challenged its scale and looked to correct a system that subsumed all rights and all questions of moral obligation under the "right to contract." What made the populists comparatively anachronistic compared to many of the progressives who would follow them was the fact that the small-scale producerism they championed was dying, an echo of the age of Jackson that history had left behind.

The importance of populism is not found simply in its critique of the emerging industrial order. Instead populism represented the first organized attempt to restore a sense of political agency to people in a system that was systematically stripping it from them. As Lawrence Goodwyn argues, the signature achievement of populism was its ability to awaken within a dispirited people "individual self respect and collective self confidence," which enabled them to respond to alienation and deprivation in an assertive, rather than passive fashion. For Goodwyn, the significance of populism is found less in the Omaha platform (once it became a national party it rapidly began to lose its identity) and more in its ability to create and sustain a movement culture. It was the totalizing character of this movement culture that enabled the populists to reject the folklore of laissez faire capitalism and mount a challenge to the existing order.

The importance of this movement culture cannot be overstated. It enabled the disaffected to immerse themselves in alternative social institutions that generated the solidarity and morale necessary for overcoming the apathy that can so easily paralyze the dispossessed. It was the creation of institutions like cooperatives, journals, and especially the lecture circuit that fostered a movement culture capable of empowering the dispossessed and, through collective membership, granting autonomy to individuals utterly overwhelmed by larger structures beyond their control.[29] As Goodwyn claims:

> In its deepest meaning, Populism was much more than the tactical contributions of Kansasans or Texans. It was, first and most centrally, a movement that imparted a sense of self-worth to individuals and provided them with the instruments of self-education about the world they lived in. The movement taught them to believe that they could perform specific political acts of self-determination.[30]

The lived experience of Populism reinforced a wavering faith in the power of democracy, and that as long as the United States remained a democracy its citizens "had a right to do whatever they had the ethical courage and self-respect to try to do."[31] This was not the rise of class consciousness—instead it was a rise of self-respect, with the individual's own sense of agency coming from his membership in this larger community. This realization, that only through collective strength can there be individual agency in this new industrial order, would be the most important insight progressives and New Dealers would appropriate from this populist heritage.

Progressivism

> Progressives celebrated the moral possibility inherent in the growth of human power over nature, that by transcending old limits, human beings might closely approach the ideal.
>
> —Wilson Carey McWilliams[32]

James Young argues that "liberals today might be said to be living still on the intellectual capital of progressivism," and no student of American political thought can dispute the importance of this era. In fact, most, if not all, of the New Deal's theory of ends can find its origins in progressive thought, although as Alonzo Hamby argues, it reflects "an evolutionary development"[33] more than simple continuity. But beyond recognizing its importance, it is difficult to encapsulate precisely what progressivism was. Robert Wiebe identified progressivism as a "search for order," while Michael McGreer, struck by the Victorian sensibilities animating the movement, categorized the era by its "anti-individualism." McGreer and Young differentiate the populist and progressive movements, while Commager views populism straight through to the New Deal as part of the same broad ideological trajectory. Most scholars highlight both Teddy Roosevelt and Woodrow Wilson as progressives, and frequently dissect the period through the competing frameworks of New Nationalism and New Freedom, but Eldon Eisenach, associating progressivism with nationalism, writes New Freedom out of his story.

Nevertheless, almost every overview of progressivism highlights two central features—the need for a public response to the private power of capital, and a faith in mastery—that human beings can understand and control the economic and political structures that govern their world. Both of these were bound up in the progressive understanding of democracy. As Wilson Carey McWilliams puts it, "Beyond mere order, Progressives were engaged in a quest for democracy on the grand scale, informed by the belief that the human spirit or conscience, guided by social science, could eventually create a vast and brotherly republic of public-spirited citizens."[34] The progressive vision of the better society was ultimately apolitical in the sense that the progressives hoped to eliminate the need for politics, replacing it with the concept of scientific expertise devoid of ideology and interest, and it is here that the New Deal most sharply diverges from the progressive era. While sharing much of the substantive vision of the progressive era, the New Deal tempered its aspirational notions of expertise with a healthy respect for the permanency of the political.

Robert Wiebe's classification of the progressive era as a search for order is perhaps the best place to begin. The progressives did seek to restore order and control to a world where older values of community were under siege in the name of a ruthless individualism achievable in practice only by a few, but Wiebe's formulation downplays that the laissez faire worldview possessed its own order and teleology. It might be more accurate to think of the progressive era as a search for universal agency. The goal was to preserve individuality by recognizing its social origins and to reawaken within Americans that powerful, driving sense of optimism which believes that we are capable of mastering any environment; social, economic, and political as well as physical.

Progressives utilized the populist 'people versus interests' framework. As Hamby argues, "[a]bove all, progressives saw themselves as fighters for democracy ('the people) locked in combat with 'the interests' (primarily concentrated corporate and financial power),"[35] and progressive like Charles Beard turn interest into an essential category of political analysis, urging political scientists to no longer "cling to a delusion that we have to deal only with an abstract man divorced from all economic interests and group sentiments."[36] The appeal of muckraking journalism was not found simply in its exposure of horrifying conditions (what student ever forgets reading Upton Sinclair's *The Jungle*?) and enervating corruption, but because these facts were seen as open sores on a once pure (and potentially purifiable) body politic. However, the progressives were bedeviled by how to quantify "the people." Eisenach argues that progressives identified 'Americaness' with the nation's new core (New York, Chicago and its other great and rising cities), but this of course has little to say to the rural Americans that populism spoke to. And, like the populists, the progressive era found itself divided over questions of racial and ethnic exclusivity, and some progressives championed eugenics, immigration restriction and a prohibition movement grounded in ethnic fear mongering with the same energy they fought for public regulation and greater democracy.[37]

The progressive emphasis on community also reflected a discomfort with what was seen as individualism run riot. While some progressives attributed the flaws within American society to structural problems related to capitalism, others pointed "to an atomistic individualism—the perversion of America's rights based culture that scorns the most limited standards of public life."[38] McGreer grounds this concern in middle-class Victorianism, arguing that:

> [T]he rich had perverted individualism itself. The Victorians balanced individual freedom with self control, hard work, and domesticity. The rich has seemingly cast aside those balance weights. In the hands of the upper ten, individualism became an excuse for complete autonomy, legitimization of indulgence and inequality, and a rationalization of the troubling national status quo.[39]

As such there was an attempt to reawaken a republican orientation within the American people—to turn our attention away from private pursuits and towards public concerns. However, this notion of public involvement did not necessarily sit easily with the progressive emphasis on the dispassionate expert, and the progressive concern with democracy (be it women's suffrage or the direct election of senators) was meant to empower people to choose administrators capable of overcoming self-interest and parochialism as much as it was to make them active participants in self-rule. Democracy may be, as Dewey argued "the idea of community life itself,"[40] but it was not at all clear what kind of participation within that community was desirable, or, if one were to ask chastened progressive Walter Lippmann, whether meaningful participation was even possible.

But the progressives are most celebrated for their more successful (compared to the populists) attempts to deal with the excesses of modern corporate capitalism, and the progressives set out to dissolve or control concentrations of wealth and power that could compete with the collective public power of the state. To combat the strength of capital, progressives attempted to centralize government and minimize the distance between the people and their institutions, to close the gaps through which capital can bypass democracy. Animating this effort was a deeply held conviction that economic laws were human constructs and therefore capable of control by dispassionate specialists acting in the name and interests of the people. This belief led to a rather substantive policy wish list meant to challenge the old economic and political order. As Eisenach observes,

> All of them heaped scorn on the idea that the fundamental principle of economic life and of the relationship of government to economics should be competitive markets and laissez faire. While they differed at the margins, almost all agreed on the need for legally recognized trade unions and arbitration of labor disputes; unemployment and worker compensation and safe employment bureaus; municipal ownership of utilities; national ownership or regulation of transport and communications; national incorporation laws and corporate regulation; the use of tariffs as a tool of national economic planning; the national compilation of industrial, agricultural, and financial statistics; state and federal regulation of hours and wages; public inspection of factories, mines, and tenements; federal and state progressive inheritance taxes; state and federal controls on the use of natural resources; public land use policy, and compulsory public education and free technical training.[41]

Through this ambitious agenda progressives sought to bring public order to a system governed by private, unaccountable power, and in the process restore to Americans a proper balance between individual and community, limiting the power and scope of "interests" in the name of a larger national unity simultaneously democratic and subject to apolitical administrative expertise.

Of course there were stark differences in the progressive community over the best way to achieve this, crystallizing around two camps, the Herbert Croly-inspired "New Nationalism" championed by Teddy Roosevelt and the Louis Brandeis-influenced "New Freedom" of Woodrow Wilson. The New Deal would incorporate elements of each into its own vision.

New Nationalism accepted the emphasis on size and mass that developed alongside corporate capitalism. It embraced the potential for efficiency and production, and focused on regulating trusts and combinations. Teddy Roosevelt distinguished between good and bad trusts precisely because trusts were a necessary economic unit in modern times. "Combinations in industry are the result of an imperative economic law which cannot be repealed by political legislation."[42] Accepting the basic rights of capital and rejecting the producerism of the populists, New Nationalism sought to humanize the inevitable trends towards size, efficiency, and rationalization. As Herbert Croly would argue, the promise of American life was no longer a preexisting condition Americans were born into. Modern technology and industry was capable of spreading its ever-increasing benefits to an ever-expanding number of people, but only if it was properly steered by the state, rather than the private economic interests that seemed to govern the Gilded Age. Democracy required that "the national public interest [be] affirmed by positive and aggressive action,"[43] and it was clear that this meant state action.

Woodrow Wilson's New Freedom, like Roosevelt's New Nationalism, accepted the need for an activist government, but disagreed sharply (in theory, if not in practice) with Roosevelt's acceptance of the new corporate order, reflecting a mixture of the populist's producerism and Brandeis' aesthetic aversion to size. Where New Nationalism hoped to use, in Croly's famous formulation, Hamiltonian means (a powerful national government) to secure Jeffersonian ends (greater freedom and opportunity for the average individual), the New Freedom remained far more suspicious of the idea that large concentrations of economic power could ever be co-opted or controlled in the name of democracy. "There is no salvation for men in the pitiful condescensions of industrial masters. Guardians have no place in a land of freemen. Prosperity guaranteed by trustees has no prospect of endurance. Monopoly means the atrophy of enterprise."[44] Wilson's New Freedom argued that large-scale economic units were fundamentally anti-competitive and that the state should use its power to offset this tendency towards concentration.

Nevertheless, both visions assumed a united people rising above narrow interests. Where they differed was on how to conceptualize that public. Roosevelt's stream of progressivism highlighted a truly national community while Wilson's focused more on the integrity of individual communities threatened by malevolent interests. Either way, James Morone argues, the Progressives "rested their vision on an imaginary republican people, rising above politics to proclaim an unequivocal public interest in a single voice."[45] This collective vision resonated precisely because individualism was losing its power as an explanatory ideal. It was growing increasingly difficult to separate the individual from his larger social context as more people crowded into increasingly smaller spaces and found themselves governed by distant impersonal forces. JP Morgan could claim that his success was due to "character" but the Progressives were no longer buying it.[46]

But if we are to have a united people, what forces actually serve to unite it? What could give this new society cohesion? Some progressives privileged exclusion, grounded in the pseudo biology of race science. Others argued for a great process of assimilation, the famous melting pot. Some progressives fixated on a publicly spirited nationalism, more administrative than democratic but animated by a republican spirit. Other progressives like Walter Weyl and Walter Lippmann embraced a new universal identity that could be grounded in the act of consumption—a view perhaps unique to a people particularly blessed with material abundance, and one the New Deal would go on to appropriate. Regardless, all progressives nevertheless took Dewey seriously when he argued that "To define democracy simply as the rule of the many, as sovereignty chopped up into mince meat, is to define it as abrogation of society, as society dissolved, annihilated."[47]

It was this desire for unity that led in part to the anti-political orientation of the progressives. For many progressives politics was synonymous with a localism that was parochial at best, hopelessly corrupt at worst. This position made a fair amount of sense at the time, as the progressives were reacting to very real and now (thanks to muckraking journalism) much publicized political corruption, the self-conscious pursuit of spoils and very little competition at the national level.[48] It was the open cynicism of the politicians themselves, progressives believed, that helped legitimate the laissez faire suspicion of public action. Whom could you possibly trust to administer a public program? This ran deeper than the simple mugwumpish aesthetic opposition to corruption that would mark Franklin Roosevelt's early political priorities. Progressives envisioned a strenuous, active and informed citizenry and had little patience for both the pageantry and limited scope of electoral politics. As progressive Samuel Batten would argue, "A good partisan cannot be a good citizen."[49] As Jerome Mileur observed, their preference for administration caused them to be hostile to the very

> activity of politics itself—the endless bargaining, trading, and dealing. Politics did not charm the idealists, the reformers, the men of education, morals and conviction. They saw no larger purpose in it, no higher good served by it, only a squalid enterprise, demeaning to intelligence, riddled with corruption, and culminating at best in the cheerful compromise of principle.[50]

As such, the progressives hoped to purify the nation of its politics, to drive out the devils infesting its political machines and redeem the city on a hill. They could never accept, as FDR eventually would, Tammany sachem George Plunkitt's distinction between "honest and dishonest graft."

A politics cleansed of corruption (by empowering the people to take on the interests) would clear space for the rise of the technocratic elite that citizens would have the good sense to elect. Government might not be by the people and of the people, but it would certainly be for it. This, as Morone points out, is the basic progressive contradiction—"government would be simultaneously returned to the people and placed beyond them, in the hands of the experts."

The New Deal would challenge this apolitical orientation. As Wiebe argues;

> most progressives "paid to human beings the highest compliment of believing that, once they knew the truth, they would want to act upon it." Yet they were an impatient, sometimes arrogant lot who abided very few human failings. The delusive assumption that all good citizens share their goals—or would as soon as these were explained—led them to trample sensibilities with little regard for the resentment that was accumulating about them.[51]

Where the progressives saw a general will most Americans, who had not internalized the progressive call to national unity, saw simply the will of all, the aggregation of individual preferences lacking the moral sanction that fed "the progressive passion for remaking other Americans."[52]

Not surprisingly, the more politically minded progressive figures like Presidents Roosevelt and Wilson attempted to address the lack of attention paid to the grind of politics. Wilson tried to use political parties as a buffer between the people and the state—a way to bridge the gap between public and private. Roosevelt, on the other hand, sought to establish the presidency as the pre-eminent symbol of national leadership—to embody the general will within himself. But, ultimately, the progressives rejected the founders' emphasis on institutions and artifice as a substitute for virtue. Instead they embraced the idea of disinterested virtue and supplanted institutions with expertise, in the process losing sight of Madison's warning that we would not be governed by angels, or that, as Morone notes "[f]or every public-spirited reformer, there were scores of industry spokesmen."[53] As McWilliams argues, "progressives were inclined to reject or downplay original sin in favor of the kind of sins that are mitigable or eradicable through education and law."[54] We have here the promise of the city on a hill without the puritanical modesty that limited its more wild ambitions. As we shall see, the New Deal accepted the reality of sin and therefore understood the necessity of politics.

New Deal Antecedents

For almost a century the modern American reformer has been the gadfly and the conscience, to a large extent the heart and the mind, of the only nation in man's history which has dared to live by the credo that any individual's rendezvous with his destiny is a rendezvous with a better tomorrow.

—Eric Goldman[55]

Although it would be a mistake to overly conflate these three great periods of reform, the New Deal took much from the populists and progressives, granting some of their ideas a mainstream legitimacy (abetted, no doubt, by a deep institutional collapse) and institutional permanence that the earlier movements could not quite achieve. As such, it is useful to see the New Deal as a descendent of these earlier periods, integrating their insights into its overall vision.

The emotional power of 'we the people' fueled all three reform movements. Populists and New Freedom progressives would use this idea of 'the people' to attack the existence of monopoly and concentrated power. New Nationalist progressives made their peace with a new order, and tried to reconceptualize freedom for an age of mass, where autonomy would be determined by how much you made, the conditions under which you made it, and what happened when you could not make enough, rather than the traditional distinction between producers and rentiers. The New Deal would find itself much more influenced by this strand of progressivism, echoing the sentiments of Teddy Roosevelt, who argued in his 1912 "Confession of Faith" that "it was abnormal for any industry to throw back upon the community the human wreckage due to its wear and tear." The New Deal would make the notion that charity is a public obligation rather than a private ideal the centerpiece of its welfare state, without ever fully abandoning the distinction between a deserving and undeserving poor.

Each movement confronted the difficulties inherent in facing the implications of capitalism in a country so devoted to its folklore. Commager makes the tension clear:

> There was the ethical problem which arose from the attempt to apply the individualistic moral code of the eighteenth and early nineteenth centuries—a moral code in which good and evil were significant terms, and responsibility personal—to the complex, impersonal practices of a twentieth-century economic order. There was the parallel difficult of accommodating a government based on the eighteenth-century principle that government is a necessary evil to the felt necessities of a welfare state. There was the problem of salvaging the individual in an economy dominated by vast, impersonal, and largely incomprehensible forces and of justifying individual effort in a deterministic philosophy which offered less play for free will than had any previous system of thought to which Americans had subscribed.[56]

Both the progressive and populist movements were adept at articulating their own responses to the economic and social crisis at hand. Neither ever truly appreciated the legitimating power of our old folklore and the institutional barriers to reform. The New Deal had the great advantage of drawing on these previous traditions, and so an established vocabulary was available to it. But the New Deal also recognized, in a way the other movements never did, how the presence of a theoretical vocabulary is not sufficient—that the vocabulary is a weapon in an ongoing and never-ceasing political battle for the soul of a nation, and that in a democracy politics will always be primary.

Populism, progressivism, and The New Deal each represented a major threat to the established order of their time, and threatened to expose the oligarchic sense of entitlement that underpinned categorical defenses of property. Wiebe's description of the reaction to turn-of-the-century reformers could just as easily be applied to the Liberty League's frothing denunciations of the New Deal or the panicked siege mentality of the business community during the conservative resurgence of the late twentieth century:

> In the baldest sense, they came to fear that in a democratic society the people might rule. Individualism, except as a mode of implicit contempt for the scattered sheep below, almost always referred to the rights of an elite to retain what they held and to acquire more; cohesion meant an imposed order, one that would necessitate a sharp-edged enforcement. Rather than anticipating the good that would eventually arise from crisis, they wanted to quash all disorder now, to forestall catastrophe by fitting society in a safe, sturdy mold. "Law" and

"property." The fundamental terms in their rhetoric, connoted a whole complex of social, economic and political privileges.[57]

The reaction to reform was elemental in its ferocity, its roots too deep to ever fully excise. And this marks the most important difference between progressivism and the New Deal. There was a teleology that underpins much progressivism, a belief, utilizing a framework similar to the Darwinism of their opponents, that we would eventually evolve to a point where we could not only master our environment, but truly master ourselves. Progressives might be impatient with the scope of reform, but they never doubted its inevitability, and this is why the catastrophe of World War I and its thudding aftermath was such an existential disaster for the movement.[58] Progressives were simply not prepared for that kind of a broadside challenge to their narrative. They did not know how to confront the failure of their teleology.

The New Deal, perhaps with the benefit of history and hindsight, had made its peace with imperfection and the flaws in human nature. The New Deal would appropriate the progressive desire for self-mastery and substantive citizenship as an ideal but was far more comfortable with the presence of leisure and pleasure in human life than their progressive forebears.[59] It is telling that one of the great triumphs of progressive social engineering, prohibition, was undone almost immediately by the New Deal. But more importantly, the New Deal never had the progressive desire to cleanse politics. It understood the power of interest, and the enduring strength and depths of old order. It offered a fundamentally more modest, and therefore more liberal, approach to reform. Even when the crisis of capitalism brought about by the Depression opened up possibilities like never before, the New Deal understood that this was a fleeting moment and any victories would be imperfect. There was no teleological safeguard for reforms, only the battles won with the help of questionable allies and the tactical logic of compromise in service to a strategic vision. The New Deal, in the end, fused the critique of capitalism and social vision of the populists and progressives with a political sensibility that leads to the type of political theory practiced by the framers and Lincoln—the mixture of theory and practice that characterizes any foundational period. We turn now to that theory.

Notes

1. Henry Steele Commager, *The American Mind*, (New Haven: Yale University Press, 1950), 43.

2. Stability, but not permanence. The New Deal accepted the contested and contingent (which is to say, political) nature of our folklore.

3. Personal favorites include Eric Goldman's *Rendezvous with Destiny* (Chicago: Knopf, 1952), Henry Steele Commager's *The American Mind*, Eldon Eisenach's *The Lost Promise of Progressivism*, Lawrence Goodwyn's *The Populist Moment* (Oxford: Oxford

University Press, 1978), and Robert Wiebe's *The Search for Order*, but this list is hardly exhaustive.

4. John Blum, quoted in Young, *Liberalism*, 128.

5. Goodwyn, *Populist*, 25.

6. Alan Trachtenburg, *The Incorporation of America*. (Hill and Wang: New York, 1982), 90.

7. Trachtenburg, *Incorporation*, 91.

8. Eric Foner, *The Story of American Freedom*, (New York: Norton, 1998), 117.

9. Weaver ran as the candidate of the Greenback party in 1880 and the Populist party in 1892.

10. James Baird Weaver, *A Call to Action* in Issac Kramnick and Theodore Lowi's *American Political Thought*, (New York: Norton, 2009), 795.

11. Wiebe, *Order*, 32.

12. Wiebe, *Order*, 9

13. Russell Conwell, "Acres of Diamonds," in Kramnick and Lowi, *Thought*, 738.

14. See Jim Morone's *Hellfire Nation* for a fantastic history of this impulse.

15. Carnegie, in Kramnick and Lowi, 731.

16. Commager, *Mind*, 87.

17. Young, *Liberalism*, 133.

18. Which, Arnold would argue, this functionally was. See chapter five.

19. Wiebe, *Order*, 136.

20. To use Eric Goldman's wonderful phrase.

21. L.L. Polk, President of the National Farmer's Alliance, quoted in Goodwyn, *Populist*, 134.

22. Populism refers to both the primarily agrarian political response to laissez faire capitalism that predated progressivism, and a particular political style which, although predating the populist movement, eventually took on its name. Both are consequential, as populism influenced the progressive theorists who in turn influenced the New Deal, and the New Deal would on occasion make use of the populist style.

23. The fact that he referred to that campaign as a "crusade" is telling in this regard.

24. The 1905 *Lochner* decision saw the Supreme Court overturning a New York state law imposing a maximum number of hours bakers could work per week. The court ruled that this undermined the liberty of contract that was implicit in the 14th amendment, and was therefore unconstitutional.

25. http://historymatters.gmu.edu/d/5361/

26. Kim Phillips Fein, in *Invisible Hands*, chronicles the particularly effective inversion of traditional populism, practiced by modern-day conservatism, which unites capital and labor (the producing classes) in a new class war against intellectuals, the media, bureaucrats, and other members of the new rentier class who seek to parasitically exploit the fruits of the former's labor. Phillips-Fein, *Invisible*, 218.

27. Quoted in Trachtenberg, *Incorporation*, 43.

28. Interestingly enough, Sumner shared the concerns of the populists regarding the way the political influence of plutocrats could undermine the evolutionary benefits of laissez faire capitalism.

29. Lecturers did not simply give speeches—they functioned as organizers and created a vibrant political culture that gave isolated victims of modern capitalism a sense of solidarity and collective purpose. The lines to hear Alliance lecturers would stretch for miles.

30. Goodwyn, *Populist*, 135

31. Goodwyn, *Populist*, 136
32. Wilson Carey McWilliams, "Standing at Armageddon: Morality and Religion in Progressive Thought," in eds. Sidney Milkis and Jerome Mileur's *Progressivism and the New Democracy* (Amherst: University of Massachusetts Press, 1999), 108.
33. Alonzo Hamby, "Progressivism: A Century of Change and Rebirth" in Milkis and Mileur, *Progressivism*, 57.
34. McWilliams, "Armageddon," 104.
35. Hamby quoted in Sidney Milkis' "Introduction: Progressivism Then and Now," in Milkis and Mileur, *Progressivism*, 4.
36. Beard, *The Economic Basis of Politics*, in Kramnick and Lowi, 1022.
37. See Eileen McDonough's essay "Race, Class, and Gender in the Progressive Era: Restructuring State and Society," where she argues that on many social questions the progressives were in fact regressive. Found in Milkis and Mileur, *Progressivism*.
38. Milkis, in "Introduction," 4.
39. Michael McGreer, *A Fierce Discontent: The Rise and Fall of the Progressive Movement in America 1870-1920*, (New York: Free Press, 2003), 56.
40. Dewey, *The Public and Its Problems*, in Kramnick and Lowi, 1038.
41. Eldon Eisenach, *Progressivism*, 142.
42. Roosevelt, quoted in Young, *Liberalism*.
43. Croly, *The Promise of American Life*, in Kramnick and Lowi, 1073.
44. Woodrow Wilson, *The New Freedom*, in Kramnick and Lowi, 1113.
45. James Morone, *The Democratic Wish*, (New Haven: Yale University Press, 1990), 113.
46. Weibe, *Order*, 134
47. Dewey, quoted in Eisenach, *Progressivism*, 188.
48. Morone, *Wish*, 100.
49. Quoted in Eisenach, *Progressivism*, 113.
50. Jerome Mileur, "The Legacy of Reform: Progressive Government, Regressive Politics," in Milkis and Mileur, *Progressivism*, 271.
51. Wiebe, *Order*, 212. The quote within the quote is attributed to progressive Florence Kelly
52. McGreer, *Discontent*, 127.
53. Morone, *Wish*, 119.
54. McWilliams, "Armageddon," 110.
55. Goldman, *Destiny*, 461.
56. Commager, *Mind*, 49-50.
57. Wiebe, *Order*, 78.
58. Wiebe, *Order*, 145.
59. McGeer, *Discontent*, 71.

Part II: Ends

Chapter 3
"Necessary First Lessons":
The Preconditions of the Welfare State

Government to [Jefferson] was a means to an end, not an end in itself; it might be either a refuge and a help or a threat and a danger, depending on the circumstances.

—Franklin Roosevelt[1]

The New Deal justified both its new social contract and the institutional innovations behind it as the natural next step in America's political development, working to minimize the impression that it represented a stark break from our received (and for many divinely sanctioned) political practices and commitments. It did not contest the substance of the American Dream, arguing instead that we had to rethink the preconditions necessary for achieving that dream. This chapter begins with the New Deal's assertion that our government should be dynamic and responsive to changing conditions, a 'living and growing thing,' rather than an increasingly static and anachronistic collection of institutions existing outside of time and place. It then moves into the New Deal's critique of reified laissez faire liberalism, focusing in particular on the argument that economic power is as potentially arbitrary and coercive as political power, and therefore subject to democratic accountability. It concludes with a look at the preconditions that make a more active state necessary, justifiable, and viable: affirming a faith in social mastery, replacing an economics of scarcity with an economics of abundance, and challenging the fiction of atomistic individualism with the reality of interdependence.

Political Maturation

The day of the great promoter or the financial Titan, to whom we granted anything if only he would build, or develop, is over. Our task now is not discovery
or exploitation of natural resources, or necessarily producing more goods. It is
the sober, less dramatic business of administering resources and plants already
in hand... of distributing wealth and products more equitably, of adapting existing economic organizations to the service of the people. The day of enlightened
administration has come.

—Franklin Roosevelt.[2]

The New Deal understood itself as the next phase in the development of American liberalism—embracing its fusion between democracy, rights, and capitalism,
but moving beyond the older, static, and pre-industrial formulations that previously informed America's liberal identity. Henry Wallace alternately likened
the New Deal's theory to a reformation of older thinking, or a doctrine designed
to help the nation transition from adolescence to maturity.[3] Both analogies are
apt. Like a reformation, the New Deal was simultaneously conservative and radical, familiar and threatening. It sanctified original principles while criticizing
their contemporary perversions, offering a restoration through reform. And like
growing up, it involved coming to grips with the wrenching loss of childhood
innocence and youthful irresponsibility, recognizing that it is not freedom, but
the inevitable reality of interdependence and obligation that mark the onset of
adulthood. The New Deal identified our existential sensitivity to change as the
single greatest obstacle to change in the United States, and great pains were tak-
en to ease the sense of mental disconnect and dislocation.

Although FDR did not always use the same analogies as Wallace, they
shared the insight that the New Deal could only safeguard old ends (the protection of liberty and the pursuit of happiness) with new means. Likewise, both
understood the importance of minimizing the psychic shock that follows new
ways of thinking. FDR took care, therefore, to ground the New Deal in the liberal tradition familiar to Americans, arguing in *Individualism, Romantic and Realistic*, more commonly known as the Commonwealth Club Address, that the
New Deal represents the next logical step in the historical process towards a
more idealized liberal democracy, a more perfect (but never perfected) union.[4]

The New Deal, following the logic of the founders, understood that while
government could be a source of tyranny, in the proper democratic context its
power could also be emancipatory. This is in fact, as Eden argues, the core message of the Commonwealth Club Address, "that liberty is the consequence of a
distinctive kind of tyranny, a liberating tyranny. The root of liberalism is realism
about the origins of modern liberty in tyrannical initiatives. An affirmation of
princely, entrepreneurial execution is the foundation of liberalism."[5] It would be
utopian to imagine a world without power, and liberalism accepts that the world
remains saturated in it. So it is not power in general that New Deal liberalism

confronts, but rather the arbitrary, undemocratic power that served a privileged few against the greater good of the community. Since its origins in Europe's religious wars, philosophic liberalism's primary concern has been the protection and expansion of individual freedom, achieved by minimizing the impact of arbitrary power in people's lives. This can be done through two complementary methods: democratically, by granting citizens a say in the rules that govern them, and institutionally, through due process and the impartial rule of law. Liberal thought was originally political in its origins, an immediate response to a disruptive and frequently violent context, and New Deal theory is in large measure an attempt to move an abstracted, reified understanding of government back towards its contextual roots, and in the process confront arbitrary power with democratic power.

In Roosevelt's account, national governments grew out of a desire for a central power to protect weak individuals from the machinations of feudal barons.[6] This desire for security justified centralized power; and while it undermined liberty for some (the barons), the vast majority of the people had no meaningful liberty to lose, and a great deal of security to gain.[7] As Roosevelt notes, the founders of the modern state took their cues from Hobbes, rather than Locke.

> [T]he creators of national government were perforce ruthless men. They were often cruel in their methods, but they did strive steadily towards something that society needed and very much wanted, a strong central state, able to keep the peace, to stamp out civil war, to put the unruly nobleman in his place, and to permit the bulk of individuals to live safely.[8]

These men were ruthless because history demanded it of them—because in the early stages of creation, when leaders must pacify a violent world and craft order out of chaos, ruthlessness is a necessity. In the interests of security, and the possibilities it creates, society is willing to suffer concentrated power and its attendant excess. Necessity requires it. Sacrifices must be made to create the preconditions for the exercise of freedom. Freedom may be a natural right but its actualization may, perhaps paradoxically, require giving grants of enormous power to people not shy about using it.

But history unfolds without ever arriving. The development of modern political theory is in large measure the attempt to reintroduce the idea of freedom as a dynamic process back into a system that tends to freeze freedom and its opposition at a particular moment in history. Americans still cling to the spirit of Thomas Paine's ringing declaration in *Common Sense* that "government even in its best state is but a necessary evil; in its worst state an intolerable one," missing that the government Paine refers to is not our constitutional republic, but the English monarchy. The American people have trapped their understanding of freedom and the constraints that act against it in a Revolutionary era that, while symbolically resonant (symbols the New Deal would have to appropriate) had little to say about the actual context in which they live their lives.

Therefore, highlighting the fluid nature of development (of ideas and institutions) is one of the primary goals of the Commonwealth Club Address. FDR
argues that while the threat to individual liberty has always been arbitrary power, the source of that power changes as material and institutional conditions
change. The first major modern shift moved from the power of unaccountable
warring barons to the power of the unaccountable monarch. The very success of
the state builders was the source of their own demise: the peace and security
provided by the monarch created the space in which individual liberty could take
root, and the powers granted to the monarch became onerous, no longer necessary to guarantee security and counter-productive to the well-being of individual
citizens.[9] FDR walks us through the gradual introduction of checks on arbitrary
power that followed; constitutional limitations, expanding democratic participation, and the increasing power of the moral ideal that "a ruler bore a responsibility for the welfare of his subjects," and that their welfare, as defined by the
subjects themselves, was the ultimate source of moral right and political legitimacy.[10]

Opposing the monarch were the capitalist, merchant, and middle classes,
whose rising strength and influence were derived from money and trade, not
land and tradition. Modern liberalism was born from this struggle. This tradition,
therefore, was originally concerned with limiting the power of absolute political
authority through increasingly democratic institutions, constitutional checks, and
using economic power to counterbalance political power—all in the name of
individual emancipation. Although some of its more libertarian offshoots would
attempt to deny the existence of power outside of political government, the
mainstream Hobbesian/Lockean tradition that would inform the American
founding accepted the permanent presence of power, and sought instead to regulate, control, and disperse it.[11]

Because it was these democratizing and liberalizing currents that produced
the American Revolution, suspicion of (if not outright opposition to) centralized
political authority formed the core of our political philosophy. Economic independence became the primary external check on the power of an already anemic
state. As long as the people needed or wanted little from it, the central government could be kept weak and unthreatening.[12] Over time, however, we forgot
both why we were suspicious of government and why we prized economic freedom. Initially, these served as a means to liberty, but both gradually came to
define it. The American people adopted the paradoxical view that theirs was a
free government, yet any action taken by that government, especially in the economic realm, was a form of tyranny. We became a self-governing people who
rejected the possibility of self-government. A practical philosophy based on political and historical experience became a form of rigid and unsophisticated
dogmatism.

For the first half of our history, the paradox could be ignored insofar as national government was not really necessary. A rural country with vast untapped
stretches of land could afford to equate liberty with minimal government and
unregulated economies because those who were left behind could always 'go

west.'[13] In this best of all possible worlds, "when a depression came a new section of land was opened in the west; and even our temporary misfortune served our manifest destiny."[14] Soon, however, the industrial revolution would offer seductive visions of a newly mastered world, which would change our attitudes towards government and economics, and legitimize a certain type of interference, one that promised the freedoms of adulthood without recognizing the corresponding responsibilities.

As Roosevelt observed, the machine age dangled the possibility of ever-rising standards of living in front of our eyes, and the powers of the government were put into the service of the great industrial barons of the day. There was often a spectacular human cost, but such is the price of progress. The honor they received reflected the results, "irrespective of the means they used."[15]

> So manifest were the advantages of the machine age, however, that the United States fearlessly, cheerfully, and, I think, rightly, accepted the bitter with the sweet. It was thought that no price was too high to pay for the advantages which we could draw from a finished industrial system.[16]

As long as our "financial Titans" were producing results, the republic could absorb their excesses, and the open frontier was there to absorb those left behind.[17] To oppose this was to oppose our manifest destiny, and to therefore stand outside of history and place yourself in opposition to God's plan for his new chosen people.

Roosevelt consciously moves to tie the New Deal to this old folklore. As with the state builders of old, the people of the nation were prepared to tolerate concentrations of power in the name of the material progress promised by a modern economy. And just as the philosophy of divine right sought to legitimate the power of the monarch, our new lords sought legitimacy in political theory. However, no divine right needed to be imposed on the American people from the top down. The sheer abundance of land and opportunity, as well as a liberal mindset predisposed to celebrate economic strength and convinced that power was meritocratically distributed, created a set of circumstances in which the great mass of people exalted their new masters of their own volition, in large measure because they believed that they too would someday be masters. And while the self-made millionaire myth was precisely that,[18]

> Because the society was so open and the continent so underdeveloped the scramble for wealth and shares of power did not unduly disrupt American life: instead it became the very essence of American life. The development of the country was so manifestly a positive-sum game that the growth of one persons' wealth and power did not necessarily mean the shrinkage of another's.[19]

This is the core of the "American Dream," where the presence of opportunity meant that hard work (and perhaps a little luck) was all that was needed for a life of self-sufficient mastery. But rather than guaranteeing that dream, an active government (outside of granting public funds for private investment) was perceived as its primary threat. As Commager notes,

> [Americans] tolerated with mere ceremonial protest the looting of the public domain or the evasion of taxes or the corruption of the legislatures, so long as these things brought visible profits, and resented government interference with private enterprise far more than private interference with government enterprise.[20]

Reactions to the worst excesses of industrial power could remain largely ceremonial because for the first century or so of American history there was a reasonable correlation between myth and reality. Prior to the end of the nineteenth century no source of industrial power was large enough to impact the lives of great masses of people. The largest factories did not employ more than a few hundred workers, and even the largest concerns were usually capitalized at less than a million dollars.[21]

With the end of the nineteenth century, however, came a reassessment of industry's promise. The Census Bureau declared the frontier closed, and with it, the opportunity of last resort.[22] This was accompanied by the rise of the trust, the holding company, and phenomenal concentrations of economic power, further constricting the possibilities of those without great wealth. As FDR reminds us, "the turn of the tide came with the turn of the century. We were reaching our last frontier; there was no more free land and our industrial combinations had become great uncontrolled and irresponsible units of power within the state."[23] By 1890 railroads employed over a hundred thousand workers, corporations became multinationals, and capitalization was in the hundreds of millions of dollars. By 1901 US Steel gave the United States its first billion-dollar corporation. This was, without a doubt, the centralization of power that the founders feared and Tocqueville had prophesied. Opposition to it, even the great Populist movement, rose only in fits and starts, waxing in times of depression and waning once general prosperity was resorted, rarely reaching beyond America's alienated underclasses or intellectuals.

As George Eads argues, echoing Arnold (and Commager), in times of prosperity material wealth and psychological well-being meant that only superficial observance need be given to the older liberal values of competition and independence, the values the Populists were so anxious to restore. "So long as the competitive ideal was embodied in statues and industrial and political leaders paid lip service to it, there was a general willingness to leave it at that."[24] Hence—as Arnold realized—even significant regulations like the Sherman Anti-Trust Act were largely symbolic measures, designed to affirm our fealty to principles of competition and independence without sacrificing the large concentrations of economic power required for modern development.

By the time of the Great Depression, however, there was a general atmosphere of crisis, and a pervading lack of confidence that the system would reset itself as it had in the past. Ceremony and symbolism alone would no longer be sufficient. As the Commonwealth Club Address illustrates, the New Deal's response to this crisis rejected the language and imagery of Marxism—cold, alien, and offensive to American sensibilities that have always rejected class analysis even when talking about class issues. Instead it harkened back to the familiar concepts of liberal theory. Just as Tocqueville predicted,[25] liberty in America was threatened by a new set of American 'feudal barons' that undermined our economic freedom as surely as the European barons of old took away our political freedom. In 1816 Jefferson wrote of his hope that "we shall crush in its birth the aristocracy of our monied corporations which dare already to challenge our government to a trial of strength, and bid defiance to the laws of our country."[26] As Roosevelt toured the country one hundred and sixteen years later, he warned that, "we are steering a steady course toward economic oligarchy, if we are not there already."[27]

The problem, as Arnold argues in *The Folklore of Capitalism*, is that even when material circumstances change, and old institutional arrangements no longer prove viable, "the words still remain and make men think that the institutions are still with them. They talk of the new organizations which have come to take the place of the old in terms of these old words."[28] Classical liberalism is in many ways a pre-industrial philosophy, designed for a pre-corporate world. The concepts it celebrates—the rule of law, our equality before it, and an economic system based on freely negotiated contracts between equals—would become fictions in the new corporate industrial economy. The classical liberals themselves would have conceded this. Patron saint Adam Smith, for one, warned that corporate organization would lead to a dangerous lack of accountability.[29] This was further exacerbated by the Supreme Court's insistence that corporations had all the legal rights of citizens, alongside far fewer constraints on their behavior due to legal advantages like limited liability laws. After the industrial revolution and the rise of industrial (later finance) capitalism, new forms of liberalism were necessary to deal with the impact of arbitrary economic power in people's lives (particularly corporate power).[30] But in spite of this, American political thinking failed to recognize changing conditions, so strong was our faith in our rugged individualism and endless opportunity. Those who heeded the prophecies of Tocqueville, the American Cassandra who warned that industrialization would be the door through which "aristocracy and the permanent inequality of social conditions" would "infiltrate the world once again,"[31] were the voice of the minority in American political life. They spoke of limits in a land without them, and threatened to undermine the American individualism believed to be the source of its collective greatness. It would take the shock of a long depression and an utter abdication of responsibility on behalf of the private economy to create the space necessary for a new liberalism, and the New Deal seized that opportunity. Roosevelt's Commonwealth Club Address argues that America in 1932 had reached a moment in its economic development analogous to that revolutionary moment in its political history, where the forces of democracy rose up to take control of the state, however imperfectly, for the betterment of its citizens. The industrial plant had been built, the country unified through railroad and radio, telegraph and telephone. The sacrifices had been made, necessity had been overcome, and it was time for the United States to shift from an economy of scarcity to the progressive vision of an economy of abundance.[32] The time had come, in short, to begin the process of economic democratization.[33] America had to reform itself. Its people and its institutions needed to grow up and realize that the Great Depression represented the systematic failure of pre-modern individualism and capitalism.

Like Roosevelt, Wallace understood that getting the American people to accept this was in large measure a matter of symbolic education, of pointing out the ways in which, thanks to economic developments, old categories are no longer easily mapped onto a modern world, even if they have maintained their emotional resonance. For the Framers, "property" referred to tangible assets like land, not abstractions like intellectual property, brand loyalty,[34] or even capital. "Industry" meant industriousness, "manufactured goods" were largely produced by hand, and "commerce" referred to the local act of buying and selling.

> A man who owns a house or a barn or a piece of land can do what he likes with that property. A man with ten shares of stock in a billion dollar corporation has no more influence in deciding what the corporation will do than the most ragged vagrant in a breadline. It was on this old kind of "property," when a man had both control and ownership, that our whole theory of private enterprise, now sadly shaken, was built. The modern corporation, with its vast anonymous powers, has cracked this theory from stem to stern.[35]

Perhaps the biggest change of all was in our understanding of the word *liberty* itself: Wallace argues, "in the last half of the nineteenth century, liberty began to be thought of... as meaning the free initiative of capital to expand as it pleased and the free right of employers to drive such bargains as they could."[36] The Fourteenth Amendment—clearly intended to protect the individual rights of freed slaves—was transformed into a shield safeguarding the great consolidation of industrial power that defined the twentieth century, absolving that power of any sense of responsibility for the welfare of the society it came to dominate.

The New Deal believed that our limited state had once been capable of managing the decentralized economic forces of the past (or, perhaps more accurately, that those forces could manage themselves), but concluded that those days are over. Economic power, highly centralized, can easily overpower political attempts to balance it. New institutions were necessary to meet these new challenges, but they could not be born until the people accepted their legitimacy. The American people would not abandon their old order until they ceased to believe in it. Getting there would require a new understanding of what liberty and property had come to mean in practice. And this, by extension, would require the nation to realize that the problems facing a democracy in times of industrial centralization are very different from the problems facing a democracy of agrarian freeholders. But this realization was slow and painful.

In *Whose Constitution?* Wallace likened this to the process of growing up. The great symbols of frontier individualism were the symbols of youth and immaturity, where one could dismiss larger questions of responsibility, obligation, and interdependence, and think only of himself.

> The country hankered for its youthful irresponsibility, which it thought of as "normalcy." But "normalcy" such as the country wanted was a dream and a delusion. The nation had yielded up its innocence, and would have to pay the price in one way or another. It was an adult nation, whether it wanted to be or not.[37]

If we were so inclined, we could blame the depression on the refusal of the United States to "grow up." Our inability to recognize that advances in technology and centralization create problems alongside possibilities, together with our failure and refusal to acknowledge changed circumstances and changed obligations, is a reflection of our fundamental immaturity. This analogy also offers a new way to interpret the traditional charge that the welfare state is paternalistic. If the goal of the welfare state were to infantilize the nation, this would be a damning accusation. If, on the other hand, the goal is to help facilitate the transition into adulthood, then this is the kind of paternalism that manifests itself by providing a child with an advanced education or money to buy a house or start a business. It is a grant in aid designed to foster independence, not permanent dependency. Certainly this is how the New Deal understood it.

The stark consequences of clinging to our youthful understandings of individualism and liberty were all too clear. As Wallace observes,

> Rugged individualism for farmers in 1932 meant 6-cent cotton, 10-cent corn, 2-dollar hogs and 30-cent wheat. For small businessmen it meant a losing fight against the chain stores and the corporations which, with their built up reserves, could survive the depression. For the 15 million unemployed heads of families and unemployed young people it meant the liberty of taking the road to look for non-existent jobs, the liberty of holding out the hat for private or local charity, the liberty to move in with relatives to have a roof over their heads or to go back to the old homestead and add to mother's troubles on the farm.[38]

We have the tools to address these problems, Wallace argues. "[T]he Constitution envisioned a true nation, to be controlled by the people, and with powers to deal nationally with national problems."[39] It was the intention of the Founders, Wallace claims, for each generation to identify its own problems and develop the tools for addressing them.[40] Following Jefferson, each generation should rewrite and renew their social contract. Doing this effectively would require making it clear to the American people that eighteenth century categories could not be applied to a twentieth century world. Above all else this meant demonstrating that concentrations of economic power pose as serious a threat to the exercise of individual freedom as the concentrations of political power we so zealously guard against. If this could be shown, it would be possible to justify a welfare state capable of enforcing a new social contract that made good on the great promises of the Declaration of Independence and Constitution: "the pursuit of happiness" and securing "the blessings of liberty to ourselves and our posterity."

Economic Governance

The greatest threat to liberty in the United States lies in the very excess of that kind of liberty which puts great economic power in a few private hands. Economic liberty is never won and fixed forever; its benefits continually tend to gravitate toward the stronger or shrewder elements of society, leaving other elements with little or no liberty.

—Henry Wallace[41]

The central concern of liberalism is the restraint of arbitrary power, limiting the reach of authority grounded in coercion rather than consent. Traditionally this meant the coercive power of the government, and in the United States this view was so hegemonic, the idea of government so reified in its political formulation, that it completely obscured the ways in which private economic power, especially in its corporate form, has actually become a form of government, unaccountable to the public in any meaningful way. This insight is at the heart of New Deal theory, and as such convincing the public of its validity was central to its educational efforts. The New Deal asks us to think of government expansively, to regard it as any force that constrains, through the use of power, our ability to live our lives as we see fit. A free people, according to liberal categories, will insist that they have some protection against the abuse of that power. A free people, according to democratic categories, will have some role in determining how those protections are structured. The key to institutionalizing these protections is to awaken the recognition within citizens that their freedom is threatened by arbitrary economic power, and that they have a legitimate right to limit that power.

This is why it was so vitally important to make Americans aware of the expansive power and influence that corporations have. As Wallace argues in *Whose Constitution?*,

The power to start and stop a plant at will is relatively harmless in the hands of the small businessman, but to give this same right to our huge impersonal corporations which employ millions of people is quite another matter. The time has certainly come to set up some social safeguards; there is enough dynamite in the exercise of this power to wreck our whole economic structure, including the corporations themselves.[42]

When an organization possesses the power to devastate communities with cuts in wages or jobs, or when the officers sitting on a board of directors can highjack the economic or environmental well-being of entire regions, they cease to be private citizens. When their actions place the security of thousands at risk, they have "forgone their privilege as 'persons' and taken on some of the responsibilities of public institutions."[43] They essentially become a type of government, against which the individual has no meaningful protection. Wallace warns that [c]apitalism was built upon the principle of open and fair competition between free and evenly matched men, but this has become a farce in the face of monopolies. "No individual can hold his own against a billion-dollar corporation."[44] As such these economic constructs require a degree of regulation and democratic control that had not been previously necessary.[45]

This is at the heart of Tocqueville's fear of an industrial aristocracy prophesized one hundred years prior. Aristocracies in ages past were required to shoulder social responsibilities in exchange for their power and position. They, in theory, had to recognize fundamental obligations to their communities, acknowledging that with their power came responsibilities. The industrial aristocracy of modernity recognizes no such responsibility, nor have we been conditioned as a people to demand that they do. As Tocqueville observes,

> The industrialist only asks the worker for his labor and the latter only expects his wages...they are not linked in any permanent way, either by habit or duty...The landed aristocracy of past centuries was obliged by law, or believed itself obliged by custom, to help its servants and to relieve their distress. However, this present industrial aristocracy, having impoverished and brutalized the men it exploits, leaves public charity to feed them in times of crisis.[46]

Those who wield economic power have convinced themselves that their business is private, devoid of public responsibility or obligation beyond any incidental benefits that derive from the pursuit of their self-interest. What's more, this new aristocracy recognizes no obligations but still demands privilege, lobbying for favorable laws and public supports.

Roosevelt makes clear what is at stake in his 1936 acceptance speech. He reprises themes from the Commonwealth Club Address, especially the history of American and liberal thought as a struggle for freedom against "some restraining power."[47] But this time he has ratcheted up the language. Now that the immediate scare of the Depression is over, and that the New Deal is both empowered by the labor movement and less interested in conciliating a business community that has turned against it,[48] Roosevelt can more clearly define the new threat to our freedom, in language far more combative than the sympathetic critique of capitalism offered in the Commonwealth Club Address. References to a growing, almost involuntary tendency of corporate power to resemble feudal baronies are replaced by the self-conscious machinations of "economic royalists," agents, rather than passive actors.

> For out of this modern civilization economic royalists carved new dynasties. New Kingdoms were built upon concentration of control over material things. Through new uses of corporations, banks and securities, new machinery of in-

dustry and agriculture, of labor and capital—all undreamed of by the fathers—
the whole structure of modern life was impressed into his royal service.[49]

The royalists quickly seized control of the political process to consolidate and
legitimate their power.

> [T]hese new economic dynasties, thirsting for power, reached out for control
> over movement itself. They created a new despotism and wrapped it in the
> robes of legal sanction. In its service new mercenaries sought to regiment the
> people, their labor, their property. And as a result, the average man once more
> confronts the problem that faced the Minute Man of seventy-six.
>   The hours men and women worked, the wages they received, the condi-
> tions of their labor—these had passed beyond the control of the people, and
> were imposed by this new industrial dictatorship. [50]

Tyranny is tyranny, and though the context changes the struggle against it remains timeless. Economic freedom once created the space for political freedom
by weakening political and tyrants, today our democratic political freedom must
be used to limit the arbitrary power of economic tyrants.

> For too many of us the political equality we once had won was meaningless in
> the face of economic inequality. A small group had concentrated into their own
> hands an almost complete control over other people's property, other people's
> money, other people's labor—other people's lives. For too many of us life was
> no longer free; liberty no longer real; men could no longer follow the pursuit of
> happiness.[51]

Economic freedom and political freedom are inextricably linked. No longer can
we bracket the two and keep them separate. "If the average citizen is guaranteed
equal opportunity in the polling place, he must have equal opportunity in the
market place."[52]

The New Deal argues that what ultimately matters is the expansion of human freedom, of creating larger spaces in which we can pursue our happiness.
This process cuts across both economic and political life. Liberty requires more
than the opportunity to vote for a candidate. "Liberty requires opportunity to
make a living—a living which gives man not only enough to live by, but something to live for."[53] In times past, laissez-faire economic policies were a way to
guarantee political freedom. Now, the New Deal argues, we must use our hard-
won political liberty to guarantee our economic liberty. Some degree of agency
and mastery over our economic conditions is a necessary pre-requisite to the
meaningful exercise of freedom as surely as any political right. In fact, the separation between politics and economics is artificial, arbitrary, and dangerous. As
Roosevelt warned Congress in 1938, "[t]he liberty of a democracy is not safe if
the people tolerate the growth of private power to a point where it becomes
stronger than their democratic state itself."[54] The Great Depression made very
clear that the tyranny of the plant closure could devastate the life and liberty of a

community as surely as rebellion and invasion. Starvation wages, or no wages at all, are as powerful a limit on individual freedom as the most arbitrary of laws.[55] Without a responsive, powerful, democratic state there are few mechanisms through which citizens can redress their economic grievances other than violence.

The preservation and expansion of substantive opportunity will therefore require a "re-appraisal of values," Roosevelt argues. Just as the monarch's privileges were no longer necessary once the feudal barons had been put down, the "financial Titan" no longer need be granted the same leeway he once enjoyed. In fact, to continue to do so would only serve to stifle the cause of liberty and the possibility of individual self-development. The world has been conquered, the industrial plant built. What is needed now is the administration of that plant for the good of the people as a whole, although the people are still understood to be a collectivity of individuals, their good being whatever maximizes their chance to pursue their own ends without harming others in the process.[56]

Capitalism itself should be preserved, of course—economic liberty is needed to balance the power of the state. The New Deal, especially in the aftermath of the NRA experiment, privileged two compatible approaches to balancing that power—both of which recognized that in a liberal democracy capital could pose a greater threat to liberty than the state. Each method kept the government out of the day-to-day management of the economy but utilized state power to ensure that economic power did not harm the public. The first method looked to the preservation of competition, using the power of the state to break up what Arnold called "bottlenecks," restraints on competition and concentrations of economic power derived from control over markets rather than superior innovation and service. The second approach privileged regulation,[57] to ensure that concentrated corporate power serves the community as a whole instead of a narrow band of stockholders. Those with economic power must be subjected to the same types of democratic regulation that compel those with political power, however imperfectly, to work in favor of the interests of the people. They must be compelled, in short, to recognize themselves as a type of government possessing obligations to their citizens.

Without regulation to enforce those obligations, our liberty and the democracy that protects it cannot long survive. Roosevelt reminds us:

> Because we cherished our system of private property and free enterprise and were determined to preserve it as the foundation of our traditional American system, we recalled the warning of Thomas Jefferson that 'widespread poverty and concentrated wealth cannot long endure side by side in a democracy...And so our job was to preserve the American ideal of economic as well as political democracy, against the abuse of concentration of economic power that had been insidiously growing up amongst us in the last fifty years, particularly during the twelve years of preceding Administrations. Free economic enterprise was being weeded out at an alarming pace.[58]

The New Deal recognizes that a broad distribution of private property and competitive markets are constantly threatened by arbitrary economic power. This requires safeguards guaranteed by the state.

However, Americans had become conditioned to see the primary threat to their prosperity as excessive government power, unreflectively ripping the maxims of Paine, Jefferson, and Thoreau from one context and transplanting them to another.[59] Citizens needed to understand that the threat was no longer governmental power. As Adolph Berle, a member of FDR's Brain Trust, argued,

> When nearly seventy per cent of American industry is concentrated in the hands of six hundred corporations; when not more than four or five thousand directors dominate this same block; when more than half of the population of the industrial east live or starve, depending on what this group does; when their lives, while they are working, are dominated by this group; when more than half the savings of the country are dominated by this same group; and when the flow of capital within the system is largely directed by not more than twenty great banks and banking houses—the individual man or woman has, in cold statistics, less than no chance at all.[60]

Left to his own devices, the average individual has no chance to defend himself against great concentrations of economic power. Thus, for the New Deal, the old individualism championed by Hoover and the Liberty League was a fiction, its promise a lie.

As the Commonwealth Club Address reminds us, with the industrial infrastructure of the country finally built, extremes of wealth and power are no longer justifiable in terms of efficiency, and offer little benefit to the average investor or independent businessman, let alone a wage laborer or small farmer. Like public political power, concentrations of private economic power should exist at the sufferance of society, and only as long as they provide a meaningful social benefit. This, the New Deal argues, is the true nature of Lockean liberalism, not the laissez faire perversion that had long dominated American thinking. Regulation and taxation guaranteeing that corporations serve a public purpose is completely legitimate. Without regulation, private enterprise becomes "a kind of private government and is a power unto itself—a regimentation of other people's money and other people's lives,"[61] and these circumstances are unacceptable no matter where the power is lodged. And so Roosevelt would argue "I am against private socialism of concentrated private power as thoroughly as I am against governmental socialism. The one is as equally dangerous as the other; and destruction of private socialism is utterly essential to avoid governmental socialism."[62]

As Abbot points out in *The Exemplary Presidency*, what the New Deal has done is essentially to identify, following Marx, that a ruling class with separate interests has come to dominate the economic (and with it the social) destinies of the American people, and their interests are separate from those of the great mass of citizens. However, "[u]nlike the Marxists, FDR had identified, not a proletariat, but a mass of tiny capitalists whose dreams of 'living in their own homes' each 'with a two car garage' were shattered by an irresponsible ruling class."[63] Our salvation was to come at the hands of the democratic dictatorship of an expanding bourgeoisie. The question remained whether or not the ruling economic elites could be made to recognize their status as a ruling class and shoulder the responsibilities that followed. Capitalists must acquire an ethic of stewardship if they wish to limit the necessity of public regulation and control. As Wallace argues, they must come to realize they "have extraordinary powers over the social structure, and they have not learned to exercise these powers in the social interest."[64] Due to our folklore, classes of people profiting enormously at the expense of others "think they are just enjoying their liberty."[65] It is not until they come to understand the power that they wield, and the destructive ways in which they wield it, that they can grasp why the New Deal is necessary.

The hostility of businessmen towards the New Deal reflected their difficulty in accepting this new position. W.M. Kiplinger, a Washington journalist, offers a summary of their opposition that grounds it not in a hopeless antagonism, but from a skewed perspective. Their views were narrow, but:

> They are 'narrow,' in the sense that they are focused on their particular interests, and that they think of their business as the end rather than the means of getting things done for the community or the nation....they are apt to think that anything which interferes with their operations, their 'freedom,' their 'liberty' is wrong.[66]

This truncated vision prevents them from seeing their proper role in a free-market society. In actuality "[b]usinessmen are our principal class of public servants, although it would shock them to be told so. The fact is that they in the aggregate control the destinies of most of us to a far greater extent than do government officials."[67] Some New Dealers in favor of greater government control were often loath to recognize this fact. Businessmen certainly were. But in a market economy they will remain our primary provider of essential services, and the question becomes whether or not they can be reoriented towards recognizing this obligation. The extent to which they can is the extent to which the need for regulation and coercion is minimized.[68]

Certainly prior to the New Deal the business community, Tocqueville's industrial aristocracy, had failed miserably on this score, abetted by its refusal to recognize its privileged position in society. As Bertrand de Jouvenel, no cheerleader of the welfare state, concedes:

> If an aristocracy is false to its duty when it takes to shuffling out of responsibilities and risks, and making its sole aim the security of its possessions and position, then no other aristocracy ever made greater haste to leave its post than the capitalist.[69]

There are numerous reasons why this was the case. In part there was the tendency on the part of laissez faire capitalists to selectively read Adam Smith or John Locke, overlooking the sections where Smith declares that private property is inviolable only when it is used "without injury to his neighbor" or Locke's argument that our claim to private property is justified by improving and expanding the common inheritance of humanity. The social element of private property has always been there, but questions of obligations and limitations were narrowly interpreted out of existence. This is in part the great legacy of Herbert Spencer and William Graham Sumner's appropriations of Darwin, as we find within their work the true intellectual origins of modern laissez faire capitalism. Here the accumulation of individual wealth and power does humanity a service not by giving, but by taking. Ripping the threads of the small and weak from our social tapestry is not only a prerogative born of power, but a moral duty that will leave behind a work of art far more beautiful for the culling.

For those desiring a softer interpretation there remains the uncritical assumption of laissez faire capitalism that the creation of wealth is the sole public responsibility of economic man. Its distribution will somehow take care of itself without direction or regulation. Attempts to interfere in this system in a positive capacity can only destroy its ability to function. In either case, greed and self-interest are elevated to a public good, one that utterly denies the need for those with economic power to recognize their positive responsibilities. The question becomes whether or not this failure reflects systemic contradictions, as Marxism argues, or whether it can be overcome through education or, failing that, mitigated through regulation.

The New Deal assumes good will is possible on behalf of all actors involved, public and private, political and economic. The New Deal's economic program rejected the assumption that orientations towards individual interests are irreparably opposed to the common good.[70] The problems here are not inherent to the logic of capitalism—instead the New Deal believed it was possible to craft a more publicly oriented ethic onto capitalism. The intention was to supplant the current fusion of capitalism and the radical rugged individualism born of the frontier and tortured readings of Darwin, a fusion made troubling by its immaturity, its denial of the central fact of our interdependence. As Wallace reminds us, the Depression made clear that "[t]he hard but necessary first lesson we all must learn is that we cannot prosper separately."[71] Private, isolated self-sufficiency is no longer a viable option, nor is it what corporations practice. Their scope is (inter)national—transcending local boundaries. As Wallace notes

> I agree with the corporations that the government should leave all possible initiative with private citizens and local communities—provided corporations do likewise. But insofar as corporations have transcended localities and have reached out for governmental power, it seems essential for a democracy to develop a mechanism for handling them fairly and in the public trust.[72]

Confronting the reality and reach of corporate power, and controlling it democratically, is one of the critical psychological and institutional steps necessary to ensure a transition to an economy of abundance.

An important step here is attacking the wall of separation that laissez faire liberal theory imagines exists between the economic and political realm, one reinforced by the academic separation of economics and politics into independent disciplines. Until their connection is reasserted, it will be difficult to make the case that economic authority is governing authority. Throughout his speeches, FDR takes pains to dispel for Americans who had not yet read their Charles Beard the myth that America has traditionally tolerated no government interference in its economy.[73] Business has always welcomed, and in many cases demanded, government aid in the form of subsidies and tariffs, even military aid when confronting worker's movements. Wallace notes that the great banks have long assumed that "they and the government were essentially one in the matter of monetary and financial policies."[74] It would not be long, after all, before Charles Wilson, head of GM, would declare that "what is good for General Motors is what's good for America."

The New Deal worried that the decentralized, unregulated nature of the American economy allows some sectors of the economy to avoid shouldering their fair share of burdens, and principally rewards those who can see private opportunity but remain blind to public obligation. The problem becomes devising a way to ensure that the public derives a greater benefit from the private generation of wealth. Can we modify its structure to increase "its capacity to provide our people with work at adequate wages, to build purchasing power as well as profits, to promote consumption as well as production?"[75] "Can cooperation and social invention replace the competitive seizure of opportunities for wealth"[76] as the new mechanism of progress? A failure to do so dooms us to a continuous cycle of boom and depression until the long-term consequences of short-term exploitation finally catch up with us.

The Myth of Private Property

> The reason why old myths create such a problem in times when old institutions are not functioning effectively is that they induce men to act in direct contradiction to observed facts.
>
> —Thurman Arnold[77]

The New Deal argues that private economic units are forms of governance, responsible for meeting the needs of those they rule, and subject to the control of political government if they fail in those responsibilities. Thurman Arnold explores the nature of our stubborn resistance to this idea, making this case most strongly in *The Folklore of Capitalism*. It is because, Arnold argues, we conceptualize corporations as rugged individuals, not institutions that govern our lives. It is not the government who controls our food supply, gasoline, power, heat, water, health, and credit, yet we continuously resist the need to assert democratic oversight over these industries. In part this was due to our faith in self-regulating markets capable of policing themselves. Umpires and rules are needed for isolated instances of individual malfeasance, but no regulation is needed to ensure that everyone enjoys the benefits of capitalism.[78] That was part of the folklore's appeal, the assumption that anything that generated wealth would flow back down to the population at large. Interfering in this automatic and natural process was bad public policy.

Any empirical defense of the status quo, however, is limited insofar as it can be empirically disproven. Economists can demonstrate whether or not wealth is more equitably distributed under different regulatory regimes and levels of taxation, and the results seem to clearly demonstrate that there is no necessary natural correlation between the generation and distribution of wealth.[79] Fortunately, business was further protected from regulation due to the profoundly held moral conviction that these entities were the private property of their owners and therefore beyond the scope of public concern, playing off the traditional liberal divide between public and private spheres of action. As Arnold argues:

> There was something peculiarly medieval in the faiths which sustained the business government in America. In the first place, men...actually believed that it was not government at all. The American Telephone and Telegraph Company and the United States Steel Corporation were "individuals" who "owned" their industries. Such intangible things as morale, a trained personnel, institutional habits, public acceptance and good will, indeed all the elements which distinguished a going concern, were thought of as private property, owned by an intangible individual, just as it was once thought that the King of France "owned" the State.[80]

The idea of corporate personhood is nonsensical, Arnold argues, since the elements that make up a corporation—morale, habits, personnel, good will, etc., are all constituted by collectivities, not individuals.[81] Nor are these corporate entities entitled to lay private claim to the fruits of these massive organizations in any classical sense. The corporate governors at General Motors have not mixed their labor with the factory floor to justify their claims of ownership by the classical liberal standards established by Locke. Yet, Arnold argues, our folklore lacked the symbols and language necessary to conceptualize industrial organizations in any other fashion, nor was it willing to surrender the belief that capitalism always served the cause of freedom.

In Arnold's analysis, the only ceremonial mechanism available to bridge the gap between our ideals and the feudal nature of large-scale organizations was to have the courts discover that a proper reading of the Constitution granted these organizations the status of individuals, with the attendant rights, privileges, and protections. No matter how many people a concern employed, no matter how much the health, livelihood, and well being of employees, consumers, and entire regions might be at the mercy of this private organization, any attempt at regulation was a priori illegitimate, as these were private organizations (and legally individual entities), not governments subject to public control. Large organizations "owned" their industries, and it was the duty of the government to protect their private property from tyrannical usurpation by "the people," who could only constitute themselves through an inefficient government whose actions make things less productive in the long run.[82] To claim otherwise would be to call our entire governing folklore into question.

Perhaps the most striking example of the double standard in the American thinking about business and political government is evident looking at our symbols of taxation. One of the great psychological factors limiting what government can accomplish is the conviction that government spending invariably costs the public money and whatever businesses do will eventually make money, or at least not cost the public. Public governments squander our wealth; private entrepreneurs invest in the future. Governments are coercive and take our property without mandate.[83] Taxation is a form of punishment at best, theft at worst. Corporations are individuals who spend their money, and spending money in a free market is a celebration of freedom.[84] These distinctions, Arnold argues, are nonsensical.

> [W]hen the government wasted, it was wasting the taxpayer's money. When a railroad, or a public utility, wasted, it was wasting its own money—which, of course, every free individual has a right to do unless you are willing to change your "system of government" and adopt "Socialism." Of course, the great industrial organizations collected the money which they spent from the same public from which the government collected. However, in the case of a public utility, or textile concern, or a building corporation, the collection was voluntary, since men could do without clothes, light, or houses. Indeed, they *should* go without them, if they had no money to pay for them because if they didn't they would become dependent on the government. When the government collected, the collection was an involuntary tax, which in the long run fell upon the poor, because of the great principle that it is unjust to tax the rich any more than you happen to be taxing them at the time, and that the rich will refuse to hire the poor if taxed unjustly.[85]

If we so choose, our folklore tells us, we can refuse to pay for food, water, electricity, car payments, and the like. These are choices, and the symbols of taxation are reinforced by our belief that the inability to afford necessities reflects a personal failure. Class is a moral, rather than an economic category, and dependency and redistribution are its sins. But we are forced to pay our taxes. Public spending is coercive. Private spending is optional, and a celebration of freedom—the freedom to find entertainment, medical care, clothing, shelter, and food, or the freedom to starve. Again, Arnold observes:

> Rent, light, heat, transportation to and from work, were regarded as services purchased voluntarily. Police protection, libraries, parks, were paid for involuntarily by taxes. Therefore, the real danger to the income of the small man was supposed to be taxes and not prices, because he had a choice in the matter of purchases. Therefore it was public waste of funds that had to be watched. Private wastes of funds would take care of itself, since the profit motive prevented businessmen from wasting. Government had no profit motive and therefore was bound to waste more because of the extravagant theories habitually entreated by those who do not work for profit. And then, anyway, private funds, when

wasted, only affect the individual who wastes them (and corporations were individuals), whereas the waste of public funds affects posterity, since they will
have to be repaid by the taxpayers of the future.[86]

It might in fact be cheaper if the government took over certain essential services
supplied by private organizations (or vice versa, but we readily concede the alleged virtues of privatization). They might even deliver these services more effectively to more people. This is an empirical question, but one the folklore of
capitalism will not let us answer. It tells us the profit motive is the only non-
tyrannical mechanism of social development and accountability. To even test
this theory creates dependency on government, which, according to our folklore,
would lead to an expansion of political tyranny, to say nothing of the ruinous
effects this would have on the characters of the American people.

While the alternative is dependency on private economic power, this does
not have the same negative symbolic value as public government spending,
since our folklore refuses to identify private economic organizations as governing bodies. Spending money on essential services provided by a private business
or corporation is a choice, not a tax. If prices are too high we can do without. If
advertisers manipulate us into paying for products we do not need, it is our fault
for being suckered in. However, we have no choice but to pay our taxes.[87] Arnold continues:

> By means of this folklore a curious set of mental habits grew up. People grew
> to distrust service rendered them by that type of organization called the State,
> because they felt they would be "taxed" to pay for it. They preferred the servic-
> es of great industrial organizations because they did not consider their contribu-
> tions to such corporations as taxation. Men in America were so conditioned that
> they felt differently about taxes and about prices. The former was an involunta-
> ry taking; the latter a voluntary giving. Prices were something a person could
> pay or not pay as he chose. Thus all government activity became associated
> with a very unpleasant symbol, that of forced contributions. Business activity
> was correlated with the pleasant symbols of a free man going into the market
> place and buying what he chose. So it was that men opposed government ef-
> forts to furnish them with light, power, housing, credit, and looked with suspi-
> cion at government efforts to solve national problems. Everything that the gov-
> ernment did meant higher taxes, involuntarily paid.[88]

As Arnold points out, in reality it makes no difference to the individual if his
money goes to private corporations or to the government. In fact, money that is
paid to the government is potentially subject to greater oversight and democratic
accountability. But our folklore has convinced us that the law of supply and demand, the profit motive, and the other mystical forces that together form the
invisible hand of the market make active regulation unnecessary at best, tyrannical at worst.[89]

As a result, not only are we incapable of recognizing that industrial power is
a form of government, we are blind to the possibilities of public investment. We

are unable to assign value without some kind of financial metric to evaluate its success. Building parks and houses, putting the idle to work, subsidizing museums, and providing health care and education are all seen as expenditures that burden the future, not investments for its benefit.

> We cannot build schools and hospitals, preserve our water supply, improve recreational areas, or train doctors, because such programs are not self-liquidating in money terms. A trained doctor, for example, is not an asset, because his benefit to society cannot be expressed in monetary terms. Hence his training at public expense is an economic sin and burden on the taxpayers and leads hellbent to inflation.[90]

In the eyes of the New Deal, failing to invest in public infrastructure and social services costs us real wealth. In the eyes of traditional economic thinking, we are better off having done nothing.

As long as we remain bound to a folklore which convinces us that public action is tyrannical and private action is the only legitimate source of freedom, we will fail in our efforts to provide for our people to the best of our productive capabilities. As Arnold argues:

> The problem facing the American economy is a psychological one...Man is a slave to his vocabulary. Adjustment to the industrial revolution of the twentieth century will be accomplished only when we invent new words to describe the problems that face us. Today we need a set of words that will convey the idea that the wealth of the union consists of its capacity to produce goods, the programs for the public welfare that cannot be translated into monetary terms are nevertheless assets of incalculable value.[91]

Without new ways to think about value, especially public value, we leave the ability to invest in ourselves in the hands of private individuals under no obligation to think of themselves as public actors with public responsibilities. Moving past this will require a broader conception of the legitimate role of the state in the lives of citizens.

Rethinking the State

> What is the State? It is the duly constituted representative of an organized society of human beings, created by them for their mutual protection and well being. "The State" or "The Government" is but the machinery through which such mutual aid and protection are achieved.
>
> —Franklin Roosevelt[92]

The New Deal has a neutral, at times almost mechanistic, view of the state. It is not romanticized as the embodiment of the nation, nor is it demonized as an implacable enemy of individual liberty. It is a tool of organized society, which can be configured to enhance both the protection *and* well-being of its citizens, assuming those citizens are sufficiently organized to utilize it. It is a servant of whoever engages it, nothing more. Society, on the other hand, has a moral obligation (and, potentially a legal one, depending on how our social contract is institutionalized) to provide for its members. Meeting these obligations through our private economic government is fine, arguably even preferable. The New Deal is, after all, a liberal philosophy, always wary of centralized power. But the needs of citizens must be met; and the state offers us the capacity to meet this obligation when private industry is unwilling or unable to do so.[93] This, Secretary of Labor Francis Perkins argued, was Roosevelt's most important idea:

> The idea that government had a positive responsibility for the general welfare. Not that government itself must do everything, but that everything practicable must be done. Whether government does it, or private enterprise, is an operating decision dependent on many factors—but government must insure that something is done.[94]

Under normal circumstances, private enterprise can be entrusted with meeting the needs of the general welfare. But when it fails to do so, the government must step in to make sure basic needs are met.

Early in his second inaugural address, Roosevelt argues that through government we find "the instrument of our united purpose to solve for the individual the ever-rising problems of a complex civilization."[95] His choice of the word *instrument* is instructive. The government exists as a tool of democratic society, a servant of our will rather than a source of oppression. It enables us to master the world, working in tandem with private initiative and picking up the slack when private initiative fails. Other nations must grapple with the problem of necessity, but in America the primary obstacle to mastery is our own fear, hesitation, and timidity—our unwillingness (bordering at times on a superstitious and reactionary stubbornness) to use the public tools at our disposal. There is also a reminder that our civilization is complex and interdependent, easily capable of overwhelming isolated citizens. It is increasingly difficult for individuals to confront modernity on their own. We need to act collectively to solve the problems that impede the individual, because these impediments are beyond the ability of the individual to master.

The democratic machinery of government is meant to aid us. Rather than being a necessary (and necessarily hostile) force existing outside of and in opposition to society, it was a tool that society could use to advance its own collective interests, a power to be harnessed, not simply feared or resented.[96] Positive state intervention can help to create space in which individuals can empower themselves—by providing security and by making capital accountable to community and consumer—and the state's excess can be policed, its direction determined, through democratic institutions, in a way that a system of economic consolidation (masquerading as free markets) and exploitation (the profit motive) cannot match.

If employment at a living wage is a right (as the New Deal claimed), and if we wish to avoid excessive government involvement in our lives, then those who control the "great industrial and financial combinations which dominate so large a part of our industrial life"[97] have an obligation to make sure that those fundamental rights are met. In Roosevelt's eyes, corporations were a public trust, and while private industry was entitled to profit, that profit had to be balanced out against the services they provided to the community. This in itself is nothing new. Rather, it is a return to an earlier understanding of incorporation, which occurred at the sufferance of the community and for its benefit.[98] The failure of private corporations (or business in general) to protect our economic rights requires the government to safeguard those rights through regulation or intervention—as surely we would expect it to guarantee our rights to speech, assembly, or due process.

As Wallace argues, "The days when corporations and capitalists could do pretty much what they pleased are over. From now on, more and more they will enjoy only that liberty which they have purchased by continuously and consciously exercising self-restraint on behalf of the general welfare."[99] A capitalism that accounts for (or is forced to account for) the general welfare is far superior to unrestrained competition looking only to personal advantage, accountable to no one. Through a *continuous* assertion of political will, the public interest can force corporations to "accept the doctrine that capital and management have received from government a grant of power which entitles them to make profits on condition that certain rules of the game are observed with respect to production, prices, wages, and savings."[100] Through the government we have the possibility of democratic control and accountability, and there is one, and only one, standard the people can use to justify regulation, a "concern for social justice and social charity—in other words, the greatest good for the greatest numbers."[101]

Roosevelt refers back to Lincoln. "I believe with Abraham Lincoln, that "[t]he legitimate object of Government is to do for a community of people whatever they need to have done but cannot do at all or cannot do so well for themselves in their separate and individual capacities."[102] The moral obligation of the state to intervene, however, is not sufficient in itself, even with the moral authority granted by quoting Lincoln. There are several remaining assumptions that underpin not only the right of intervention, but the confidence necessary to justify exercising that right. They are the possibility of mastery, of asserting agency and direction over institutional processes; the existence of sufficient abundance to challenge an economic framework oriented towards scarcity; and finally the fundamental interdependence (economic and social) of Americans—that even if the individual remains our primary conceptual category, we must recognize that these individuals function in an interdependent context, rather than remaining isolated and atomistic.

Mastery

There is no unsolvable problem if we face it wisely and courageously.
—Franklin Roosevelt[103]

The laissez faire tradition is noteworthy for its fundamental denial of human agency regarding social questions. It saw people as prisoners of natural (market and evolutionary) forces whose complexity we cannot grasp and whose power we cannot master. The boundaries they impose upon us cannot be challenged. Attempting to do so is the worst kind of hubris, inviting disaster not only to the individual, but the entire nation. There is something peculiarly un-American about this kind of paralysis and submission, alien to the temperament of a people who challenged a monarchy and conquered a continent, but Americans resolved that discomfort in three ways. First, some argued that in the long term these laws would provide for the well-being of all Americans (though this was always more a question of faith than demonstrable process). The Social Darwinist corollary to laissez faire individualism, second, assured us that if we could not look forward to a rising tide lifting all boats, we could at least take comfort in the fact that the least seaworthy vessels would sink so we need not worry about them again. And finally, of course, there was always a healthy Malthusian pessimism, which argued that poverty was an inevitable part of the human condition and that fear of privation was therefore the principle motive force behind labor. Ultimately all three of these positions had one thing in common—they absolved their adherents from any obligation to confront problems of economic and social injustice by denying the possibility of effective intervention. If anything, inaction was more humane because of our capacity for negative agency. We could not make things better, but we could certainly make them worse.

This pessimism is surprising given our natural inclination towards mastery—to look upon necessity as a challenge rather than a prison. A restless people would be inclined towards the possibilities of agency, rather than the passivity of limits. As Ann Norton observes,

> The passion to surpass the God of Nature in the making of a world manifests itself in every aspect of life of Americans: in where they live and what they eat, in what they wear and where they play... there is no pleasure that cannot be enhanced, no pain that cannot be lessened, no effort that cannot be eased, no want that cannot be supplied, no need so small that it need not be answered, no provision so complete it cannot be improved.[104]

It is telling that two of the fastest growing cities in the United States, Phoenix and Las Vegas, are found in deserts that have no business supporting metropolitan populations. Their growth is the continuation of our manifest destiny—to overcome the challenges nature places before us in the name of American greatness. Given this passion for mastery it is a testament to the folklore of capitalism that a civilization capable of building a transcontinental railroad shrank at the thought of regulating markets and confronting privation.

Any progressive political theory has to challenge this basic pessimism. It has to assume that positive change, however incremental, piecemeal, and imperfect it may be, is possible and desirable. As Isaiah Berlin has noted Roosevelt, and through Roosevelt the larger New Deal, embraced that possibility (not its inevitability) with arms wide open.

> Roosevelt stands out principally by his astonishing appetite for life and by his apparently complete freedom from fear of the future; as a man who welcomes the future eagerly as such, and conveyed the feeling that whatever the times might bring, all would be grist to his mill, nothing would be too formidable or crushing to be subdued and used and moulded into the building of which he, Roosevelt, and his allies and devoted subordinates would throw themselves with unheard-of energy and gusto.[105]

When people speak of FDR's ability to restore confidence and optimism to a demoralized nation this is what they are referring to. The New Deal restored Americans' faith in their agency. It assured Americans that they did not have to hope that social problems would fix themselves independent of human intervention. With hard work, determination, and pragmatic flexibility human beings (and especially Americans, given the material abundance at their fingertips) have the power to master necessity.

Explicit in the writings of all the New Dealers profiled here is the belief that the limits on action are primarily psychological, an insight that can be traced back to progressives like Lester Ward. Given the fact that America has conquered scarcity (more on this below), the only things preventing a more just distribution of its abundance were our own self-imposed limits. "The chief difficulty is with human hearts and human wills," Wallace tells us, and one of the aims of the New Deal's public writings was to inspire confidence in the possibilities of mastery.[106] FDR recognizes this when he argues that we must respond to the Depression as we would a war. He is not calling for martial law, or even martial virtues. Instead, he refers to the way in which war focuses our attention, concentrates our energies, and can override selfishness (in some) in the name of a larger public endeavor. War is the moment that historically has been easiest for us to overcome our fear of public mastery, and the New Deal did not hesitate to appropriate that symbolic language in order to overcome the psychic limitations of the American people.[107]

When we are not bound by necessity the limits of our mastery are a question of desire and will. Americans wanted to tame an entire continent and set about doing it, the terrible human cost legitimated by the ideology of manifest destiny. The task of conquering want, of providing security and opportunity, is more difficult because the 'laws' of capitalism tell us it is impossible. One goal of the public writings of New Dealers was to help us recognize that there are no

static or transcendent economic laws. Just as we discovered that the power of
kings was actually sanctioned by subjects instead of God, "[w]e must lay hold of
the fact that economic laws are not made by nature. They are made by human
beings."[108] Laws created by humans can be made to serve them.[109]

In fact, New Deal theory largely rejects the language of laws entirely. There
is something too ironclad and mechanistic about thinking of human institutions
as governed by laws. As Charles Kessler reminds us, governments and social
institutions owe their origins to Darwin, not Newton—they are responsive to
their environment, change as conditions change, and are capable of artful manipulation.[110] The nature of that manipulation will be discussed in chapters 5 and
6, but the key move here is recognizing that they are capable of direction. This is
an assumption that the progressive must assert and defend at every opportunity,
even if he shies away from a conception of administrative elitism in favor of a
more democratic distribution of authority. Without it the conservative can take
refuge in the insolvability of social problems, retreating from the moral implications of their position by highlighting the impossibility of the task and, in the
process, turn hard-headed reformers in tune with the realities of power into star-
ry-eyed dreamers who do not understand how the world really works. The New
Deal accepted this challenge head-on and gave the American people faith that
capitalism could be preserved, and even improved, if we are willing to subject it
to human direction. This was, as Arnold called it "the social philosophy of tomorrow"—our increasing willingness to demystify the world so that we can
assert control over it.[111]

Abundance

We live by ancient standards of withdrawal and denial in a world bursting with
potential abundance. The fears, coupled with the narrowness and hatred of our
forefathers, are embodied in our political and educational institutions and bred
in our bones. It will only be a little at a time that we can work ourselves free.
—Henry Wallace[112]

Of equal importance was the New Deal's broadside challenge to scarcity economics, a particularly bold move given that it took place during America's worst
depression. FDR makes clear in his First Inaugural Address that the Depression
is a problem of our own making.

Only a foolish optimist can deny the dark realities of the moment. Yet our distress comes from no failure of substance. We are stricken by no plague of lo-
custs. Compared with the perils which our forefathers conquered because they
believed and were not afraid, we have still much to be thankful for. Nature still
offers her bounty and human efforts have multiplied it. Plenty is at our doors-
tep, but a generous use of it languishes in the very sight of the supply.[113]

In short, the New Deal was governed by a conviction that we had conquered necessity; that the basic material goods needed to provide every American with a decent life (security enough to exercise liberty and pursue happiness) exist.[114] Our problem is that we are socialized into an economics of scarcity—which assumes that people will only work when threatened with privation and that competition, not cooperation, is the only viable path to progress. The New Deal aimed at a reorientation towards what Wallace and Rexford Tugwell called an economy of abundance, in which it is possible to both address our wants and satisfy our needs.[115]

Although Americans were socialized into an economy of scarcity that focuses on production and the attendant values of thrift, restraint, and self-denial, the rising emphasis on consumption and consumerism meant that we were also ready to accept the implications of prosperity. In fact, as Hofstadter notes, the assumption of abundance was with us from the beginning, implicit in the image of the frontier and manifested in the lack of class consciousness within American workers, who believed as an article of faith that there was enough to go around and whose anger came from a feeling that they were being denied their chance to partake of prosperity.[116]

Eleanor Roosevelt took this argument further, arguing that the assumption of scarcity is our primary stumbling block in fostering a cosmopolitan perspective privileging social justice. The immediate problems are fear and ignorance, creating intolerance and apathy and caused by privation. Fear is a ruling passion: its presence undermines self-governance and makes the trust and affection essential to democratic citizenship almost impossible to cultivate. "The worst thing that has come to us from the depression is fear; fear of an uncertain future, fear of not being able to meet our problems, fear of not being equipped to cope with life as we live it today."[117] Trust and affection are only possible in the absence of fear. Where there is fear we find intolerance, and where there is intolerance there cannot be democracy. ER was quick to associate intolerance with scarcity, be it a scarcity of material goods, understanding, or attachment. In principle, she argues, there were few disagreements that were fundamentally irreconcilable provided we could avoid the problem of scarcity. Democracy requires abundance. "We must maintain a standard of living which makes it possible for the people really to want justice for all, rather than to harbor a secret hope for privileges because they cannot hope for justice."[118] The welfare state is therefore essential for the preservation of democracy.

> [D]emocracy requires a standard of citizenship which no other form of government finds necessary. To be a citizen in a democracy a human being must be given a healthy start. He must have adequate food for physical growth and proper surroundings for mental and spiritual development.[119]

The measure of a state's ultimate effectiveness, and validity, is its ability to provide those preconditions of citizenship (physical security, education, and time—all of which are threatened by the assumption of scarcity) for all its citizens, even members of the underclass that American society had long rendered invisible.

While Eleanor Roosevelt cuts to the heart of why the assumption of abundance is important, it is in the work of Henry Wallace that we find one of the New Deal's most sophisticated discussions of the subject. He saw the failure of capitalism as a failure not of production, but as a system of distribution that had not kept up with advances in our productive capacity. Wallace classified the old order as an economics of scarcity, one that privileged ruthless competition and assumed that the needs of all citizens could not be adequately met. This in turn legitimated inequality and privation. It denigrated ideas of trust and cooperation as both naive and counter-productive. Wallace concedes that scarcity economics had its uses: it liberated the grasping, selfish energy that created the truly staggering amount of industrial potential the welfare state hoped to tap. But its moment in history has come to an end. For the first time in human history we have the capacity to end want, to create a world categorized first and foremost by abundance. The question for Wallace is whether or not we can embrace these new possibilities.

Wallace finds the American people at a crossroads, between adolescence and maturity, between an exhausted land and a promising frontier, between an economy of scarcity and an economy of abundance. At this crossroads we have to make a choice, one Wallace invests with a millennial weight. If we remain bound to the economics of scarcity and competition, if we refuse to embrace the potential for abundance that a capitalism harnessed to the public interest offers us, we are doomed to repeat the cycle of depression/recovery/depression that has plagued capitalism throughout its history.

Until the development of a modern industrial economy, escape from economic scarcity was never an option, since we lacked the ability to conquer necessity. We never had the physical capacity to produce the goods necessary to supply all people with a decent standard of living, but by the 1920s (in Wallace's estimation) this was no longer the case. Want was now artificial, a failure of our social, political, and economic systems to keep pace with the potential of modernity. In his first inaugural FDR blames that failure on our economic governors.

> Primarily this is because the rulers of the exchange of mankind's goods have failed, through their own stubbornness and their own incompetence, have admitted their failure, and abdicated. Practices of the unscrupulous money changers stand indicted in the court of public opinion, rejected by the hearts and minds of men. True they have tried, but their efforts have been cast in the pattern of an outworn tradition.[120]

Wallace, while not denying FDR's basic accusation, offers us a more psychologically nuanced explanation. The problem is less incompetence and stubbornness (although this is still present) and more a failure of our folklore. The Great Depression reflects the inability of the United States to come to grips with its own potential, the Depression caused by "our failure to learn to live with abundance," our inability to "create a social machine that will help us distribute, fairly, the fruits of our labor."[121] We find ourselves trapped, instead, in a mindset that privileges competition over cooperation. "We could not trust ourselves with joy and beauty because they ran counter to our competitive search for wealth and power."[122] We need no longer live in those times, Wallace argued, but we have yet to realize this.

An economy of abundance privileges social justice. It challenges a profit motive that claims that men can only be motivated by greed or the threat of privation, and that the idea of justice is utopian because we lack the resources to achieve it. In the heart of the Depression we suffered not from scarcity, but from a collapse of markets and purchasing power. Needs could be met, and goods could be produced, but they could not be distributed under our economic system. The great task ahead of the reformer is to provide not only social institutions that will focus on maximizing distribution, but to give citizens a framework through which this new system can be legitimated. The questions we have to ask ourselves, Wallace reminds us, is whether we can awaken our souls "to the need for social justice, and have we souls rich enough to endure abundance?"[123]

Wallace's use of the word "endure" is worth noting. Prosperity requires a reshuffling of our philosophy and ideology, as well as our reading of history. These moments of critical reflection and growth are never easy, as maturation is never easy, and he understands the need to approach these questions while exercising a sensitivity towards the past. The United States, like a child coming of age, is eager to embrace the benefits of adulthood but reluctant to assume the obligations. These new obligations cannot be forced onto a people if we expect them to be internalized, the ultimate expression of legitimacy. Instead, the New Deal argues, we must move slowly and carefully, fusing a new tradition onto the old one, gradually sublimating it. This requires progressive leaders to carry out a truly massive effort aimed at political and social reeducation, one that also demonstrates sensitivity for the needs and prejudices of the student. As Tocqueville observed, Americans have always been hostile to "alien" and "foreign" ideas.[124] The majority of citizens will accept only what is comfortable and familiar to them. The New Deal understood this, and also knew that it would be impossible to replace a rugged individual with a cooperative individual without grounding this transformation in familiar traditions and symbols.[125]

Wallace, who in this vein made copious use of America's Christian heritage, compares the experience of the United States to Job. We are being tested, and if we pass we will be rewarded with a life more abundant than ever before, provided we reject the advice of our false friends and recognize scarcity economics as "the dead hand of the past trying to make a profit by blocking the progress of business."[126] This dead hand speaks for a worldview that denies the possibility of cooperation and rejects pride and love as potential (and powerful) forms of motivation, privileging greed and suffering.

One aspect of modern scarcity economics is the belief that men will work only when they are hungry and that they will stop work when they have enough money to keep their bellies full for three or four days. This cynical attitude of exploitation of the many for the benefit of the few has no place in modern civilization. The moment the many are taught to read and write, to build better homes, to eat better food, to see an occasional movie, to listen to the radio, desire is created and markets are enlarged. People want more and are willing to work to get what they want. This increased longing of the people for *light and abundance* is going on at an increased tempo all over the world.[127]

Wallace does not doubt that the viciousness of scarcity economics enabled it to conquer, and we have been gifted with the industrial plant it built, even if we are disingenuous about confronting the costs of our inheritance. But to continue legitimating that worldview represents a form of moral bankruptcy. "It is only in an economy of scarcity that the few can sit on the top and scorn the misery of those below."[128] Instead, the New Deal argues, we need to create an ideological climate that rejects the moral poverty of scarcity economics and acknowledges that at the intersection of interest and cooperation we find widespread prosperity.

For essentially their entire history Americans have privileged economic needs over all others. But that time has ended. "The economic and business machine should be subjected more and more to the religious, the artistic and the deeper scientific needs of man," Wallace argues.[129] It is here, not in the realm of economics and business, that we will find the logic and inspiration needed to begin the next stage of history. Those old laws are not irrelevant, but they no longer are entitled to a pride of place within our folklore.

I am not denying either evolution or the law of supply and demand. But I am denying the right of a philosophy based on such laws to guide humanity toward the infinite richness which is resident on the one hand in human nature itself and on the other hand in the capacity of science to exploit the material world for our benefit.[130]

In fact, the more complete our mastery of the world becomes, "the more certain the destruction" unless we manage to change.[131] Our control over the world has, for Wallace and the New Deal, emancipated us from many of its limits, and unless we adjust our social values to account for that, we risk losing control of history and drifting from one catastrophe to the next, an insight at the core of modern environmental politics.

The problem America faces is a lack of vision. We are unable to transition from an economics of scarcity towards one of abundance. Our productive possibilities are greater than we can imagine, but only if we can approach these issues with good sense, good will, and good management. This requires a national conversation about what we want to do with the economic machinery of the United States, as well as the assumption that we are entitled as a nation to discuss the use to which it is put. The beneficiaries, the New Deal claims, need to be the people who work for a living, as on top of any moral question of dessert, they are the ones who will provide the spending that will drive a peacetime economy. This requires at least paying a decent wage but there is more. "[L]abor wants more than a job, wants more than decent wages; it wants to be appreciated, to feel that it is contributing toward making this world a better place in which to live."[132] Wallace highlights the latent cooperative instinct that he hopes to bring to the fore. There is more than wages and hours at stake here, even though the New Deal never pushed this far after the collapse of the NRA. Workers want a voice in how industry is run. They want to make creative decisions. They want to be a partner in the creation of their future.[133] Wallace, never one to shy from prophecy, embodies both the New Deal's faith in mastery and the possibilities of a more abundant future when he argues that:

> Sooner or later, the question, "What is there in it for me?" will have to be translated into, "What is there in it for all of us?" I know how hard it is to change human nature but human nature does respond to changed conditions and it becomes plainer all the time that modern capitalistic society faces the choice between a widely, generously shared prosperity or none at all.
> The millennium is not yet here, although the makings of it are clearly in our hands.[134]

Interdependence

> As contrasted with this basic interdependence, the competitive aspect of our society is to a large extent superficial. As competitors we may forget the extent to which we are all literally dependent on the labors of thousands of other people.
> —Henry Wallace[135]

The question "what is there in it for all of us" cuts right to the heart of the final grounding assumption of New Deal theory. While there was always a focus on matters of interest, the New Deal recognized that any permanent legitimacy the welfare state hoped to enjoy would have to appeal to a greater unity amongst the American people. Without that sense of unity a people habituated towards competition would inevitably look upon the welfare state as a form of theft—taking the hard earned resources of A and transferring them to B, who did not earn them and therefore has no claim to them. While Wallace in particular hoped for the eventual transformation of human nature, something more immediate would have to do during the interim. Here the emphasis was placed on our fundamental interdependence, which built off of our individual self-interest while tying our fate towards the fate of our larger community. As Miroff notes, "[f]or Franklin Roosevelt, [and the other New Deal publicists] interest and morality were never set in opposition to one another. Instead, his discourse integrated pluralistic interests into a larger structure of interdependence that was moral as well as economic."[136] In short, we had to recognize the ways in which our individual well-being was dependent in turn on the well-being of those who shared our social context. New Dealers privileged different aspects of that context, some focusing more on ethical relationships while others highlighted material interests, but each approach understood the importance of recognizing the ways in which our well-being was entwined with that of our fellow citizens.

We have left the world of the independent farmer, the small shopkeeper, and the frontier behind, New Dealers argued. Neither states nor citizens can exempt themselves from the affairs of one another, solving local problems as they see fit. Our world is complex and interdependent. It refuses to recognize artificial boundaries. Our political understanding of economic life must keep pace. State lines are no longer demarcations of economic importance, and states do not have the tools necessary to meet modern problems. Nor, in a modern economy, can we isolate ourselves from the well-being of others without consequences. As one New Deal publicist argued:

> Unemployment is like a contagion also because it spreads. When a big factory is shut down, its whole neighborhood and city suffers. The livelihood of all who have been selling their goods and services to those wage earners is affected—storekeepers, landlords, doctors, barbers, owners of movie houses, and, in turn, the workers whom they employ and those who produce the goods they sell. When large numbers of people in one part of the country are without earnings, families on farms and in cities hundreds of miles away may find their living less secure...[137]

While the farmer still served as the archetype for American rugged individualism, agriculture had long ceased to be a local concern, and Wallace notes that "[w]ere agriculture truly a local matter in 1936, as the Supreme Court says it is, half of the people of the United States would quickly starve."[138] As long we allowed ourselves to be captured by the letter, rather than the spirit, of 1787, the nation could no longer meet the obligations laid out in the Preamble. In fact, Wallace argued, that there "is as much need today for a Declaration of Interdependence as there was for a Declaration of Independence in 1776."

The preservation of a healthy (as opposed to pathological) individualism requires both the recognition of interdependence and acknowledging that certain forms of predation must be restrained. We have long accepted that reasonable limitations on private actions are not tyrannical. The New Deal asked us to accept that the same is true of our property rights. Our right to use our property (especially economic property) needs to be measured against the competing rights claims of others. These conflicts are to be resolved by referring them to the standard of maximizing individual freedom for the greatest number possible. In the end, minimum wage laws may take away the freedom of the employer to pay what he wishes, but the sacrifice is justified by the increased opportunities that higher wages afford the worker (which will trickle up to aid the employer in terms of increased consumption).[139]

For Eleanor Roosevelt, realizing our interdependence is a question of cosmopolitan education, of expanding our horizons of interest and concern beyond a narrow parochialism, which, as historian Alan Lawson notes, was one of the principle goals of the WPA's mural project.[140] ER hoped that the crisis would succeed where Dewey's exhortations in *The Public and Its Problems* failed. The Depression taught Americans (at least temporarily) the reality of interdependence; that "one part of the country or group of countrymen cannot prosper while the others go downhill, and that one country cannot go on gaily while the rest of the world is suffering."[141] If we can recognize our interconnectivity we can begin to understand why it is essential to provide the basic necessities of life to everyone, so that they can become citizens worthy of governing us. We are all forced to live in the world we collectively build together, and the standards we demand for ourselves must be made universal.

Wallace approached the question of interdependence from a more material basis. In an argument reminiscent of Tocqueville's "self-interest rightly understood," our interdependence justifies investment in the welfare state because we all benefit from the maximization of our individual potential, although Wallace's focus was often directed towards more material concerns than ER's focus on citizenship and self-development. Wallace, who never missed a chance to quantify something, argued in 1944 that "[t]he greatest economic sin is waste of human labor. In the decade of the thirties waste of human labor deprives this country of 200 billion dollars of goods we might have had, or more than the war has cost us to date."[142] Improvements in health, housing, education, farming, and rural electrification results in Americans who are more productive, better situated to consume the products of our economy, and more willing to shoulder the burdens and obligations of democracy.[143] A truly healthy national market requires a thriving population across the entire country, regardless of race, class, or economic sector. Roosevelt devoted his first fireside chat in sixteen months (two months before the 1936 election) to this very idea, as he attempted to unite farmers and laborers together in mutual bonds of interest and citizenship. Without recognizing our interdependence it will be impossible for us to generate and sustain the political and moral will needed to usher in our economy of abundance.

Roosevelt concludes his First Inaugural Address merging principle and interest, with a sense of urgency reflective of that moment.

We now realize as we have never realized before our interdependence on each other; that we can not merely take but we must give as well; that if we are to go forward, we must move as a trained and loyal army willing to sacrifice for the good of a common discipline, because without such discipline no progress is made, no leadership becomes effective. We are, I know, ready and willing to submit our lives and property to such discipline because it makes possible a leadership which aims at a larger goal. This I propose to offer, pledging that the larger purposes will bind upon us all as a sacred obligation with a unity of duty hitherto evoked only in time of armed strife.[144]

The larger purpose is the creation of a society in which interdependence need not depend on interest for its grounding, one that ultimately privileges cooperation more than competition. A tall order, to be sure, but one that New Dealers believed we were closer to than we might imagine. Our interdependence, based on increasing specialization and a highly developed division of labor, attest to the cooperative core of American society. The task of the reformer becomes figuring out ways to remove the competitive veneer. This may only be possible through a long-term change in the expectations, trust, and obligations we are willing to invest in each other, a process of reeducation that could take generations.[145] The New Deal will not be complete until we achieve what Henry Wallace called the "quarter turn of the human heart."

Conclusion

We shall strive for perfection. We shall not achieve it immediately—but we still shall strive. We may make mistakes—but they must never be mistakes which result from faintness of heart or abandonment of moral principle.
—Franklin Roosevelt[146]

Before the New Deal could redefine the nature of the American social contract it had to first demonstrate the failure of the old order. This meant more than simply arguing that FDR was not Hoover. Such an electoral strategy might have helped secure a Democratic victory in 1932, but it could not guarantee that with the return of prosperity voters would not return to their old habits and old allegiances. Constructing a new institutional order and investing the order with new principles (or at least new priorities) would require a comprehensive new vision of the relationship between citizen and state, individual and community, agent and environment. It necessitated a new story, a new governing folklore. This chapter looked at the assumptions that would inform that new story.

1. The New Deal, while clearly a movement for change, was conservative insofar as it sought to restore the United States to its founding values, undoing what had become a perversion of our founding ideals. So for all its comparative radicalism it clearly tried to situate itself within the tradition not only of American reform, but as part of the long and never-ending attempt to 'form a more perfect union.' Its radicalism became a type of restoration, its "new structure a part of and a fulfillment of the old."[147]

2. It argued that Americans possessed a stagnant, reified conception of the nature of government that blinded them to the coercive presence of economic power in their lives. Recognition of that power was an essential first step in justifying a larger, more energetic national state capable of   addressing the recurring crises of capitalism and protecting the vic-

tims of an economic system that dehumanizes those who participate in it as subjects, rather than masters.

3. The state became the primary vehicle through which society could not only meet its obligations to its members and address the shortcomings of capitalism, but also do so in a way that fostered democratic accountability.

4. The New Deal had confidence in the state's ability to meet these challenges due to a faith in humanity's ability to master its social conditions. It was animated by a conviction that social arrangements were contingent, products of choice and capable of control and direction.

5. Mastery was possible in large measure because the United States had conquered necessity. It possessed the industrial capacity necessary to provide all of its citizens with a reasonable standard of living. However, we were accustomed to an economy that presupposed scarcity rather than abundance, and the nation needed to be resocialized towards the implications of abundance.

6. This process of socialization would take time, which meant more immediate short-term appeals to interest would be required. In that vein, the New Deal highlighted the fundamentally interdependent nature of modern society, arguing that individuals had to think of themselves as situated in a social context where their prosperity and well-being was connected to that of their fellow citizens.

The New Deal, believing in the power of citizens to master their politics and themselves, aimed to establish a public philosophy and political institutions that could facilitate Wallace's 'quarter turn' as much as circumstances would allow. It left us with a new vision of the state ready to go to great lengths to support a new, expansive social contract. "We were ready to abandon that definition of Liberty under which for many years a free people were being gradually regimented into the service of the privileged few." It was time to institutionalize "that broader definition of Liberty under which we are moving forward to greater freedom, to greater security for the average man than he has ever known before in the history of America."[148] The nature of that new liberty is the subject of the next chapter.

Notes

1. FDR, "Commonwealth Club Address," 23 Sept. 1932, *Speeches*, 20
2. FDR. "Commonwealth," 24-25.
3. Wallace, *Statesmanship* and *Constitution*.
4. The Commonwealth Club Address was largely drafted by Adolph Berle, with input and editing from Roosevelt. However, for simplicity's sake, I am attributing it to Roosevelt, as the speech was written for him to deliver and take credit for.

5. Eden, *Origins*, 147.

6. The Commonwealth Club Address' account of how the nature of power shifted over time and in response to changing material circumstances is broadly accurate, and surprisingly sophisticated for a campaign address. Of course the whole process is given an inevitability and consensus that would be pleasing for the non-adversarial approach to American history that is part of our national culture. Roosevelt's claim that we 'cheerfully' accepted the costs of the machine age overlooks decades of bitter and violent protest, and the causal ease with which Roosevelt describes our opportunities to start over reflects the power of the Horatio Alger myth. It is not entirely clear if Roosevelt is oversimplifying this story because he does not want to challenge the received assumptions of our American mythology, because he himself believes them, or if this version of the story helps set up the substantive argument he goes on to make about the need for more energetic government. I suspect it is all three.

7. This argument will be made in greater detail in a later chapter, but political liberalism is not only about the possession of rights claims, but discovering ways for the state and society to adjudicate what happens when those claims rub up against each other. In those cases some form of utilitarian calculus is almost always used.

8. FDR, "Commonwealth," 19.

9. A lesson FDR would learn in his second term as returning prosperity once again made the American people cautious and channeled their fear towards conservative, rather than progressive ends.

10. FDR, "Commonwealth," 19. While the Declaration of Independence declares the existence of natural, transcendent, and inalienable rights, it is also clear from the document that it is up to all people to define those rights for themselves and judge when they have been violated.

11. Every since Louis Hartz wrote *The Liberal Tradition in America*, just about every major work of American political thought has been compelled to respond to the Hartz thesis. And while works like Carey McWilliams' *The Idea of Fraternity in America*, and Rogers Smith's *Civic Ideals* (New Haven: Yale University Press, 1997) highlight the presence of non-liberal (or at least non-Lockean) traditions within American political thought, it is hard to escape his conclusion that Lockean liberalism has been the dominant, if not exclusive, theoretical framework Americans use for thinking about their state and society. Of course one of the implicit arguments of this project is that that liberalism is a far more elastic theory than Hartz gives it credit for, an argument made explicitly by James Young in *Reconsidering American Liberalism*.

12. The opposition was not to power per se, just federal power (due in large measure to the regional diversity of economic interests and the potential threat that centralized policy posed to those interests. We see this playing itself out during the Roosevelt administration in regards to Southern opposition to wages and hours policies that undermined its comparative economic advantage afforded by cheap labor). State laws were frequently more invasive and far-reaching than federal laws could possibly aspire to be. Why we were so suspicious of one form of power, and tolerant of another, is an interesting question. Certainly state power was seen as more legitimate, as it was theoretically more democratic—although many states were slow in enfranchising all their citizens, and poll taxes kept millions of blacks and poor whites from the polls well into the New Deal. Arnold argued that the hostility to federal government was a form of ceremony—a way for Americans to celebrate their independence from government without actually undermining the practical need and desire for government. They celebrated their principles at the federal level and practiced their opposite at the state and local levels.

13. Unregulated economies in theory. Of course in practice, the business apostles of laissez-faire capitalism (as opposed to its philosophic apostles) used their considerable political clout to get favorable tariffs, free land, etc.

14. FDR, "Commonwealth," 21.

15. FDR, "Commonwealth," 21.

16. FDR, "Commonwealth," 22.

17. Whether or not this option existed in practice was in important ways irrelevant. This type of thinking was supposed to provide moral and existential legitimacy for the status quo, not represent an accurate reflection of the world.

18. For instance, Howard Zinn observes that 90 percent of textile, railroad, and steel executives came from middle- or upper-class families. Howard Zinn, *A People's History of the United State*, (New York: The New Press, 1997), 188.

19. Thomas K. McGraw, "Business and Government: The Origins of the Adversary Relationship," in *Business and Government in America Since 1870: The New Deal and Corporate Power*, Robert Himmelberg. ed. (New York: Garland Publishing, Inc., 1994), 187-188.

20. Commager, *Mind*, 13.

21. McGraw, "Business," 190.

22. To say nothing of the lost dynamism and innovation that derived from the need for continual foundings which accompanied western expansion. See Frederick Jackson Turner, *The Significance of the Frontier in American History*, 7, July 1893. http://xroads.virginia.edu/~Hyper/TURNER/

23. FDR, "Commonwealth," 22.

24. George Eads, "Airliner Competitive Conduct in a Less Regulated Environment: Implications for Antitrust," in Himmelberg, 72.

25. See "How an Aristocracy May Emerge From Industry" in Alexis de Tocqueville's *Democracy in America,* trans. Gerald E. Bevan, (London: Penguin Books, 2003), 645-648.

26. Jefferson quoted in Thomas Nace's *Gangs of America*, (San Francisco: Berrett-Koehler Publishers, Inc. 2005).

27. FDR, "Commonwealth," 24.

28. Arnold, *Folklore*, 121.

29. "The directors of [corporations]...being the managers rather of other peoples' money than their own, it cannot well be expected that they should watch over It with the same anxious vigilance with which the partners in a private guild frequently watch over their own... Negligence and profusion, therefore, must always prevail, more or less, in the management of the affairs of such a company." Smith quoted in Nace, *Gangs*, 40.

30. The socialist tradition, on the other hand, also sought to replace capitalism with more public or collective forms of ownership. The more radical edges of the New Deal, particularly its planned communities, flirted with these ideas, but only the Tennessee Valley Authority achieved mainstream prominence, and even there efforts were made to incorporate the TVA into the larger capitalist system.

31. Tocqueville, *Democracy*, 648.

32. Note, however, that not all liberal reforms shared this assumption. The NRA, for instance, was an attempt to preempt Senator Hugo Black's bill to create a thirty-hour work week, which was based on the fear that there was no longer room for growth and that we had reached what John Stuart Mill had called a stationary state in which our focus should shift from growth to the distribution of finite resources.

33. This is not necessarily the same thing as workplace democracy. The goal was to distribute the fruits of the economy more equitably, not to redistribute power (beyond the empowering of Unions, which was conceived of as a way to increase purchasing power, not to redefine the industrial order).

34. Wallace and Arnold use the term *good will*, but this is what they are referring to.

35. Wallace, *Frontiers*, 268

36. Wallace, *Frontiers*, 49.

37. Wallace, *Constitution*, 61.

38. Wallace, *Constitution*, 82.

39. Wallace, *Constitution*, 35.

40. Wallace cites, among other people, Hamilton from "Federalist 31." "A government ought to contain in itself every power requisite to the full accomplishment of the objects committed to its care, and to the complete execution of the trusts for which it is responsible, free from every other control but a regard to the public good and to the sense of the people." Wallace, *Constitution*, 205.

41. Wallace, *Constitution*, 102-103.

42. Wallace, Constitution, 160.

43. Wallace, *Constitution*, 162.

44. Wallace, *Constitution*, 163.

45. The form this regulation could take might vary. During the NRA/AAA stage the New Deal attempted to develop cooperative relationships between capital, labor, and consumers. The later stages of the New Deal, souring on the possibilities of cooperation, privileged forms of countervailing power.

46. Tocqueville, *Democracy*, 648.

47. FDR, "Acceptance Speech," 27 June 1936, *Speeches,* 48.

48. In part because new sources of political strength (unions and blacks especially) gave the New Deal the political cover to be more aggressive.

49. FDR, "Acceptance," 48-49.

50. FDR, "Acceptance," 49.

51. FDR, "Acceptance," 49.

52. FDR, "Acceptance," 50.

53. FDR, "Acceptance," 49

54. Quoted in Miroff, *Icons*, 260. As Miroff goes on to note, "This was perhaps the last time that a president raised in a serious manner the problem of corporate power in a democracy."

55. Unlike Jacksonian-era social critics like Orestes Brownson, the New Deal never seriously challenged the legitimacy of wage labor itself. There were numerous experiments, especially in smaller, planned, agrarian communities, to restore control over the means of production to the community itself, but this was never seriously addressed on a national scale beyond early hopes for greater cooperation between capital and labor. Throughout the New Deal the principle concern was to make sure that work paid, not to grant workers control over the work itself.

56. A formulation that comes directly from John Stuart Mill's *On Liberty,* (Indianapolis: Hackett Publishing Company, 1978), although he was rarely cited by important New Dealers as an influence. This formulation is offset, however, by a republican emphasis on the mutual obligations and civic duties that attend membership in any community that is much less prominent in Mill.

57. As Jean Edward Smith points out, FDR preferred to use the word *cooperation* over *regulation* when possible, both due to a natural conciliatory streak and as a rhetori-

cal move, as regulation has a more pronounced element of coercion. Having said that, when FDR talks of cooperation he usually means regulation. Smith, *FDR*, 84.

58. FDR, "Campaign Speech: Chicago," 14 Oct. 1936, *Speeches*, 53.

59. Both Paine and Jefferson were anti-monarchy, not anti-government. Even Paine's insistence that "government, even in its best state, is but a necessary evil" needs to be juxtaposed with the proto-welfare state he endorses at the end of *Rights of Man*.

60. Berle quoted in Jordan Schwarz's *Liberal: Adolf A Berle and the Vision of an American Era*. (New York: The Free Press, 1987), 77.

61. FDR, "Campaign," 14 Oct. 1936, *Speeches*, 54.

62. FDR quoted in Joseph Lash, *Dealers and Dreamers: A New Look at the New Deal*, (New York: Doubleday, 1988), 201.

63. Abbot, *Exemplary*, 55.

64. Wallace, *Frontiers*, 12-13.

65. Wallace, *Frontiers*, 128

66. W.M. Kiplinger, "Why Business Men Fear Washington," *Scribner's* (October 1934) in Freidel, 92.

67. Kiplinger, Business, 93.

68. Similarly, as Berle warned Roosevelt, the New Deal could not be too antagonistic towards business interests, as the nation's economic recovery would be dependent on the recovery of private enterprise. "We have not, in the absence of a large Government ownership program, any class or group to whom we may turn for economic leadership." The two side's relationship was no less symbiotic for the mutual antagonism. Berle quoted in H.W. Brand's *Traitor to His Class* (New York: Doubleday, 2008), 487.

69. Bertrand de Jouvenel, *On Power*, (Indianapolis: Liberty Fund, 1993), 386.

70. Both laissez faire capitalism and socialism reject this formulation to a degree. Laissez faire generally denies the existence of a common good, at least one that can be advanced through social policy. Socialism, on the other hand, emphasizes a cooperative, class orientation to a much greater degree than the New Deal.

71. Wallace, *Frontiers*, 29.

72. Wallace, *Frontiers*, 33-34.

73. And, as Roosevelt never tired of observing as relations between the two sides got increasingly hostile, the nation's banking and business interests were begging for the government to do something about the Depression when Roosevelt took office.

74. Wallace, *Frontiers*, 43.

75. Wallace, *Constitution*, 155.

76. Wallace, *Frontiers*, 274.

77. Arnold, *Folklore*, 136.

78. According to the folklore of capitalism, market failures are always the fault of individual organizations or people who refuse to play by the rules, never the result of systemic defects.

79. Witness the phenomenon of the "jobless recovery" from the 2007-2008 economic recession.

80. Arnold, *Folklore*, 110-111.

81. Arnold takes this argument further and points out that the notion of purely private property even in our own lives is increasingly suspect. I own a computer and car, but would be powerless to fix them if they broke. Ownership implies a degree of self-sufficiency that just does not exist anymore.

82. There was a great public outcry against the use of sit-down strikes in the mid 1930's because no distinction was drawn between the property of an individual and the

property of an organization. Opponents would make the argument that strikes, if not stopped, would eventually lead to strangers invading their living rooms and hold sit-down strikes there. The strike would destroy the organization and then destroy the family. Arnold, *Folklore*, 52.

83. The fact that the appropriations are made by elected representatives is conveniently overlooked when this argument is made.

84. See Foner, *Freedom*, and David Hackett Fischer, *Liberty and Freedom*, (New York: Oxford University Press 2005).

85. Arnold, *Folklore*, 264.

86. Arnold, *Folklore*, 267-268.

87. Although our resentment about this fact has created an entire industry revolving around finding ways to cheat the government out of taking our hard-earned money. We would be horrified to find people were applying the same principles to not paying their bills.

88. Arnold, *Folklore*, 268-269.

89. Arnold walks us through the whole convenient process. If something is too expensive, that company will drop its price or go out of business—unless of course it has a monopoly. This is not a concern, since we have anti-trust laws to take care of that, and when they prove to be ineffective we can just blame that on the greedy politicians who are in bed with business and refuse to enforce the rules. Prices regulate themselves as long as everyone follows the proper economic principles. Plus business is run by the profit motive, which prevents waste. When the government spends our money, the laws of supply and demand are carelessly brushed aside by politicians interested only in their own personal advantage (which, unlike the profit motive of the businessman, will not increase the general good).

90. Arnold, *Fair Fights and Foul*, (New York: Harcourt, Brace & World, Inc, 1965),103-104.

91. Arnold, *Folklore*, 276-277

92. FDR, "Message to the New York State Legislature," 28 August 1931, *Speeches*, 10.

93. It is the use of state power to deal with economic matters that is significant here. As James Morone demonstrates in *Hellfire Nation*, the state had always been active in intensely personal matters. Religious blue laws had been with us from the beginning, and abolition was a moral crusade. The New Deal began at the tail end of the prohibition experiment (in fact, it ends it), which was a massive intrusion into private life, justified by both the social ills caused by alcohol and the impact it had on our character (especially the character of the poor and foreign). These intrusions were justified by appealing to moral and religious sensibilities, even when there was an economic component to them. Roosevelt understood the power of the crusading mentality that was constantly simmering below the surface of the American people, waiting to be tapped. By making economic concerns moral concerns, the New Deal was able to expand state power into previously forbidden areas.

94. Frances Perkins, *The Roosevelt I Knew*, (New York: Viking Press, 1946), 476.

95. FDR, "Second Inaugural Address," 20 Jan. 1937, *Speeches*, 58.

96. The emphasis here is on the democratic elemental control. New Deal theory was aware of the possibilities of the private capture of this machinery, although as we shall see in chapter 7, the Roosevelt administration did not take sufficient steps to defend against that possibility.

97. FDR, "Commonwealth," 25-26.

98. Nace, *Gangs*. 46-55. Nace focuses in particular on the threat of charter revocation, exercised with some regularity when the corporation in question was demonstrably failing to benefit the public. It was not until after the Civil War that this system was rapidly abandoned for "general incorporation," which effectively eliminated the democratic protections offered by the charter system.

99. Wallace, "Capitalism, Religion and Democracy," in *Democracy Reborn*, ed. Russell Lord, (New York: Da Capo Press, 1973), 141.

100. Wallace, "Technology, Corporations, and the General Welfare," *Democracy*, 124.

101. Wallace, *Frontiers*, 20.

102. FDR, "Government and Modern Capitalism," 30 Sept. 1934, *Chat*, 62. Of course who constitutes 'the people' is itself a contestable question, as it has always been. It should also be noticed that references like this are attempts to tactically exploit the love and prestige attached to certain figures in American history. Whether or not FDR actually shared Lincoln's views is irrelevant from this perspective. What matters is the good will the connection generates.

103. FDR, "First Inaugural Address," 4 March 1933, *Speeches*, 31.

104. Ann Norton, *Republic of Signs: Liberal Theory and American Pop Culture*, (Chicago: The University of Chicago Press, 1992), 21-22.

105. Berlin quoted in Sunstein, *Second*, 93. Sunstein goes on to note, rightly, that this makes FDR one of the most quintessentially American president, embracing, rather than running away from, the political implications of the American drive for mastery.

106. Wallace, *Statesmanship*, 94.

107. FDR peppered his speeches with martial references, urging Americans in his Inaugural Address to "move as a trained and loyal army willing to sacrifice for the good of a common discipline, and ensuring his supporters in his 1936 acceptance speech that he is "enlisted for the duration of the war." *Speeches*, 51. The appeal of that language remains with our modern tendency to declare 'war' on any large-scale social problem that requires massive social resources and public power (drugs, poverty, terrorism, etc.).

108. FDR, "Acceptance Speech," 2 July 1932, *Speeches*, 16.

109. Cass Sunstein explores this argument at length in *The Second Bill of Rights*.

110. Charles Kessler, "The Public Philosophy of the New Freedom and the New Deal," in Eden, 156.

111. Interestingly enough, Arnold points to the increased (by 1936 standards) tendency of the media to cover electoral politics like a game as a sign of progress. "Even at the height of the last campaign the bitterness was softened by the realization that a play was being staged. This is a new thing in our political thinking. It holds the promise of giving us greater control over our ceremonies and creeds, without losing any of their emotional drive. " Arnold, *Folklore*, 344. The problem, as we've seen in the intervening years, is that the focus on pure entertainment has not developed into a more scientific and diagnostic approach to policy formation.

112. Wallace quoted in Norman Markowitz, *The Rise and Fall of the People's Century* (NY: The Free Press, 1973), 1.

113. FDR, "1st Inaugural," 30.

114. Contra to the recent assertion of Amity Shales, who argues that the New Deal assumed a posture of permanent scarcity. Amity Shales, *The Forgotten Man*, (New York: Harper Collins, 2007). Shales is right when she argues that Roosevelt (and Hoover) doubted the ability of the American economy to repair itself, but Roosevelt's emphasis on

regulation, safety nets, and even occasional redistribution reflected a lack of faith in un-regulated markets to distribute abundance, rather than its capacity to create.

115. Here they build off the ideas of progressive economist Simon Patten, although his terms are economies of pleasure and pain.

116. Brinkley, *Reform*, 10.

117. ER quoted in Joseph Lash, *Life Was Meant to Be Lived: A Centenary Portrait of Eleanor Roosevelt*, (New York: W.W. Norton & Company, 1984). 61.

118. ER, *Moral Basis*, 78.

119. ER, "Insuring Democracy " *Collier's* (15 June 1940), *Courage*, 74.

120. FDR, "First Inaugural," 30.

121. FDR, "First Inaugural," 5.

122. Wallace, *Frontiers*, 275.

123. Wallace, *Statesmanship*, 8.

124. Perhaps this intellectual conservatism is a reaction to the dislocation caused by our quick embrace of new technologies, an attempt to compensate for a world continu-ously moving ahead of us.

125. This will be explored in much greater detail in chapter 5, and this notion is currently enjoying a renaissance under the notion of "framing." George Lakoff is argua-bly the most influential figure in this new movement. See *The Political Mind* (2008) and *Moral Politics* (1997).

126. Wallace, "America Can Get It," 9 Feb. 1944, *Democracy*, 31.

127. Wallace, "Get It," 32. Emphasis mine.

128. Wallace, "Get It," 34.

129. Wallace, *Statesmanship*, 127.

130. Wallace, *Statesmanship*, 130.

131. Wallace, *Statesmanship*, 130.

132. Wallace, "What America Wants," 4 Feb. 1944, *Democracy*, 18.

133. Although the New Deal never made this type of economic democratization one of its political priorities, desirable though it may be.

134. Wallace, "The Cotton Plow Up," 21 Aug. 1933, *Democracy*, 55.

135. Wallace, *Constitution*, 311.

136. Miroff, *Icons*, 246-247.

137. Mary Ross, "Why Social Security?" *Washington D.C's Social Security Board*, 1936, in Freidel, 78.

138. Wallace, *Constitution*, 93.

139. In *Supercapitalism*, Robert Reich argues that there are more effective tools for promoting the economic well-being of low-wage workers than minimum wage laws. The New Deal would be fine with this. What matters is the commitment. The particular ways in which those commitments are met should be subject to empirical evaluation.

140. "[T]he effort to link day-to-day life with myth and historical destiny lent the program some cultural significance while it conspicuously promoted its sponsors' ideal of a cooperative commonwealth that would link local mores with national purpose." Lawson, *Hope*, 137.

141. ER quoted in Joseph Lash, *Eleanor and Franklin*, (History Book Club, 2004), 382.

142. Wallace, "What American Can Have," 7 Feb. 1944, *Democracy*, 29.

143. Wallace, ever the statistician, notes, "The people of the United States would be at least thirty percent more efficient if they were in maximum good health. " Ibid., 25.

144. FDR. "First Inaugural," 32.

145. A project undertaken, with great success, by conservatives in the aftermath of the New Deal. Again, see Kim Phillips-Fein's *Invisible Hands.*

146. FDR, "Fourth Inaugural Address," 20 Jan. 1945, *Speeches*, 162.

147. FDR, "Answering the Critics," 28 June 1934. *Chat*, 51.

148. FDR, "Government and Modern Capitalism," 30 Sept. 1934, *Chat*, 62.

Chapter 4
"That Broader Definition of Liberty": The Social Contract of the New Deal

The Fourth of July commemorates our political freedom—a freedom which without economic freedom is meaningless indeed. Labor Day symbolizes our determination to achieve an economic freedom for the average man which will give his political freedom reality.

—Franklin Roosevelt[1]

Americans think of their rights in terms of the Declaration of Independence's holy trinity: life, liberty, and the pursuit of happiness. In practice, however, the rights to life and liberty had long trumped the pursuit of happiness, and all these rights were understood to be manifestations of a broader right to property. The New Deal offered a broadside challenge to this traditional view, elevating the importance of happiness and grounding all three rights within a robust right to both physical and psychic community. And while these rights were natural in the sense that they were universal, they were aspirational rather than extant, an ideal to achieve rather than a reality to protect.

Despite this change, and the expanded role the state would play in the protection and facilitation of these rights, the New Deal shared traditional liberal concerns with minimizing arbitrary power and maximizing the possibilities of individual liberty. As a liberal movement, it continued to privilege private means to achieve these ends, never fully relinquishing a suspicion of public power even as it sought to permanently consolidate it. Where it differed from the dominant laissez-faire form of liberalism was in its willingness to use the state as a democratic tool, to promote liberty and happiness by filling in the gaps left by the manifest failures of private (economic) government to protect and empower the citizens in its care. As Tennessee Valley Authority (TVA) director David Lilienthal put it, "[g]overnment is not exclusively an umpire...the technical services of the government have a job to do."[2]

Thus the New Deal expanded the sphere of legitimate state action, but it did not view the state as having interests separate from the political process. It was a set of neutral machinery designed to facilitate democratic ends, hopefully a set of ends animated by a sense of the common good, but recognizing the reality that this machinery would serve whoever could organize to capture it. While there was no conception of the state as an entity independent of its component parts,[3] there was a belief that a mass of citizens consists of more than an aggregation of individuals. Instead they constitute a society (of individuals) with certain basic common interests, and a just social contract is one that maximizes those interests. The New Deal's understanding of rights—or, better, the state's role in the enforcement of those rights— was utilitarian, but the content of those rights were self-defined. The common interest was the right of every American to liberty and happiness, liberty interpreted largely as the freedom to pursue a self-directed understanding of happiness. Choice and contentment form our base ends, and the state (and society) was to furnish the security and opportunity necessary to realize those ends.

While the New Deal would refuse to impose a particular understanding of happiness, it was not entirely neutral in terms of the ends it deemed worthy of pursuit. The self-development of the individual and the exercise of citizenship were the highest forms of happiness and liberty, and society should, when possible, orient its citizens in that direction. There is a tension here between the individualistic orientation of liberal thinking and the communitarian orientation of society, a tension that any welfare state liberalism has to address.[4] Alan Ryan captures the attempt at resolution:

> It is communitarian rather than aggressively individualist, but it is individualist rather than aggressively collectivist. It achieves this by asserting that individuals are products, or even facets, of the life of the community and then going on to insist that the community itself exists only in the life of associated individuals.[5]

We cannot escape the brute fact of our sociality, nor the benefits and obligations we derive from it. We are political animals, but at the same time a legitimate social order is one that fosters our individuality, invites our participation voluntarily, secures it out of interest and attachment and safeguards a right to dissent.

The New Deal conceptualized a national community that was, at least in theory, as inclusive as possible. Reacting against the divisive violence that characterized both the communist and fascist revolutions, the New Deal rejected frameworks that abandoned the possibility of consensus.[6] It ultimately privileged the category of consumer over race, class, or nation, and its interpretation of freedom and happiness centered, at least initially, on the act of consumption as a vehicle for achieving security and happiness (the former acting as a prerequisite for the later). It attempted to mitigate the private, materialistic, and enervating tendencies of happiness-in-consumption by, following Tocqueville and Mill, fusing it with three alternative perspectives: the development of individual potentiality, a religious worldview—grounded in but not limited to Christianity—privileging compassion and love, and a call to democratic citizenship.[7] Once Americans had achieved security and comfort, the logic went, we could begin to seek this more elevated and sublime understanding of happiness.

The social contract was rewritten with these ends in mind, with this understanding of freedom and happiness as intimately linked, each unachievable without the other. It becomes the obligation of society, acting through the state, to ensure that the basic preconditions of liberty and happiness were guaranteed—namely material and psychic security. Happiness was ultimately to be defined by an autonomous individual agent, and no social arrangement can (or should) guarantee its realization. Such a promise would require an end to autonomy and alienation, rendering it both totalitarian and utopian. Nevertheless, the state can help ensure that the greater balance of any failure to achieve happiness rests in the hands of the individual and the choices made, rather than the imposition of material conditions difficult to master. Happiness, the New Deal argued, should be dependent on agency, not chance or necessity, and our institutions should be structured with this end in mind.

This chapter will explore the logic and concepts animating the New Deal's social contract. It begins with a look at its universalism, manifested in the category of the consumer, as well as the attempt to mitigate the individualist excess of consumerism. Next it examines the way the New Deal sought to institutionalize material and psychic security, the preconditions of liberty and the pursuit of happiness, as an all-inclusive public right. It concludes with a look at how the New Deal attempted to make space for groups that had historically been written out our social contract.

A Government for All the People

[T]his machinery will not run for long without the motive power of some unifying force....The old efforts to attain unity failed to provide anything enduring, it seems to me, because they were based on greed and prejudice and fear and hatred, on the hope of banding together to resist, grab, or conquer.

—Henry Wallace[8]

The New Deal, while recognizing the partisan nature of democratic politics, believed the government had to serve the interests of all members of the community, not just the ones who voted for a particular administration. It attempted, following Jefferson in 1800,[9] to be partisan while simultaneously transcending partisanship—to recognize the essential importance of key constituencies and the need to secure political power, tempered by a desire to govern not only a party, or a constituency, but a nation.[10] As James Morone points out, "[a]t the heart of Roosevelt's moral talk lay his utopian picture of a shared community."[11] Therefore a critical part of the New Deal project was finding common ground from which it could reject our historical Manichean conflicts (between black and white, capital and labor, state and market) and articulate an inclusive vision of the public good. Roosevelt's Four Freedoms and Second Bill of Rights were each attempts to conceptualize that vision, but the New Deal also leaned heavily on the moral authority of the Declaration of Independence and Preamble to the Constitution, as well as our common religious heritage. The emphasis on the past situates the New Deal not as a radical point of departure, but as the current stage of a long historical process of human emancipation.

The New Deal would use the language of the general welfare to pursue a vision of individual autonomy. Unity was possible insofar as we realize that autonomy can best be achieved in the context of a cooperative community. Obligations can be imposed on recalcitrant citizens, but only as long as those obligations respect individual rights, broaden the ability of the great mass of citizens to live freely, and are subject to democratic controls.[12]

There are two assumptions implicit in this approach. The first is that the Great Depression settled, at least for the time, the question of whether or not the state has a role to play in this process.[13] In his 1936 acceptance speech, Roosevelt eloquently reflects on one of the great lessons of the Depression: "Better the occasional faults of a Government that lives in a spirit of charity than the consistent omissions of a Government frozen in the ice of its own indifference."[14] And, with the exception of the Liberty League and its descendents and fellow travelers,[15] for a generation the Republican Party broadly accepted the framework and accomplishments of the New Deal, arguing that their issue was with its expansion and administration rather than its aims.

The second major assumption made by the New Deal is that there is a general public interest the government can act on behalf of. While this common good was liberal and privileged the individual in its calculations, it assumed that this framework would have broad support and that the needs and grievances of dissenters could be adequately addressed within it. This framework had majoritarian and universal elements to it. It was majoritarian insofar as it assumed the American people would ratify this framework but accepted their right to reject it.[16] It was universal because the New Deal could not conceptualize any meaningful dissent from that order, outside of ignorance or greed (self-interest improperly understood). Intelligent, patriotic, moral, and farsighted public policy was capable of binding disparate groups together. The slogan of the NRA was, after all "We Do Our Part," and FDR reminded the nation that "while the shirking employer may undersell his competitor, the saving he thus makes is made at the expense of his country's welfare."[17] Clearly this is more than just simple pluralism. The common good is not what is left over when the bargaining is done.

The New Deal rejects the claims of Walter Lippmann in *The Phantom Public*, that there can be no coherent public with its own position and interests. "[T]he citizen," Lippmann argues "gives but a little of his time to public affairs, has but a casual interest in facts and but a poor appetite for theory."[18] The New Deal was far more optimistic about the possibilities of citizen interest and agency, and attempted to restore, on a massive scale, the older idea of commonwealth, an idea that finds its most theoretically sophisticated defense in fellow traveler Dewey's ideal of a great community.[19] This community could only be achieved imperfectly over time, especially in the face of industrial alienation and the socialization of scarcity, but given the actual absence of necessary scarcity, it became possible to envision a society defined by meaningful interactions between citizens, colored by real respect and compassion. It required, once again, the "merest quarter turn of the human heart" to recognize the possibilities of a shared world of abundance.[20]

The belief in a universal democratic commonwealth, the possibilities inherent in that 'quarter turn,' is the source of much left-leaning critique of the New Deal's frustrating incrementalism. Within New Deal theory there is a principled refusal to adopt a permanently adversarial posture, to deny recalcitrant citizens participation and representation in both the democratic process and its aftermath. FDR rejected the advice of Felix Frankfurter, in regards to the relationship between business and the state, to "recognize that here is war and act on that assumption."[21] Even at the moments of its greatest militancy the New Deal would qualify its broadside attacks on capital. FDR would argue, in defense of a minimum wage, that we should not:

> let any calamity-howling executive with an income of $1000 a day, who has been turning his employees over to the government relief rolls in order to preserve his company's undistributed reserves, tell you—using his stockholders' money to pay the postage for his personal opinions—tell you that a wage of $11 a week is going to have a disastrous effect on all American industry.[22]

However, the vehemence shown here, or in his frequent denunciations of economic royalists in the 1936 election, was almost always followed by the caveat that these figures were exceptions, that this "type of executive is a rarity with whom most business executives most heartily disagree."[23] The New Deal always (in rhetoric *and* in substance) held out hope that a better type of corporate citizen could reform the structural imperatives of capitalism, even if it was willing to insist on regulation while these citizens first reformed themselves (and to ensure good behavior). The New Deal believed that when all interests were granted equal representation and imbalances of power were neutralized, otherwise narrow partisans would be capable of making sacrifices for the good of the society as a whole. Some would do it willingly, others might require appeals to religious beliefs, patriotism, long-term interests, and even coercion through the law, but the hope was that all but the most unreconstructed would come around, and that legal coercion would be minimal. Because a common good was possible, Roosevelt hoped that the profit motive was capable of voluntary restraint by appeals to decency and self-control, and believed that "the responsible heads of finance and industry, instead of acting each for himself, must work together to achieve the common end. They must, where necessary, sacrifice this or that private advantage; and in reciprocal self-denial must seek a general advantage."[24] In fact, the primary enforcement mechanism for the NRA was the appeal to patriotism—with compliance came the opportunity to display the blue eagle in the window.

FDR's optimism and the way he radiated a sense of public spiritedness made this type of vision possible. In a land of plenty, people could afford to be generous. In a world of progress, cooperation would pay both short- and long-term dividends. People are decent enough to look past their grasping, acquisitive natures and sacrifice for the good of society.[25] Frances Perkins captures FDR's thinking.

> He would insist on moral and social responsibility for all the institutions of human life; for the school, for the family, for business and industry, for labor, for professional services, for money management, for government—yes, even for the Church. He would insist in his way of thinking that all of these institutions should accept and practice a moral responsibility for making the life of the individuals who make up the life of the common people 'more decent,' and in the common people he included the rich and poor alike.[26]

The justifications for almost all New Deal programs were to be found in these appeals to the national community. People were not asked to sacrifice for particular interests, but for the good of their friends and neighbors, whether those neighbors are found in the east or west, north or south, city or country, farm or factory. Of course, Roosevelt was politically astute enough to follow these pleas with the observation that increasing the purchasing power of your neighbors would increase their ability to consume your own goods (self-interest rightly understood), and enough of a political "realist" to recognize that appeals to principle and interest themselves might need to be supplemented by law, but nevertheless this principled belief in the possibilities of cooperation animated the New Deal, blunting the force of its coercive moments.

This commitment was anchored in The New Deal's belief that underneath our disparate self-interests was a public interest—a public good—that could be shared by all Americans. FDR believed that common ground could be found between competing interests,[27] and that the reality of interdependence[28] could create bonds of fellow feeling that united Americans across boundaries of class, race, ethnicity, religion, region, and gender.[29] It was the job of the president "to find among many discordant elements that unity of purpose that is best for the nation as a whole."[30] This is one reason why the New Deal sought to shift economic discourse away from the battle between capitalists and workers, labor and finance, and instead emphasize our commonalties as consumers. Inclusion was always preferable to irreconcilable hostility as the theoretical starting point.

Perhaps in defiance of history, and certainly in defiance of Marxism, the New Deal refused to abandon its belief that a concert of interests between business, labor, and consumer was possible.[31] Thus, while Roosevelt encouraged Perkins to represent labor interests early in his first term, telling her "I think the Secretary of Labor ought to be *for* labor,"[32] the interests of labor were only a participant in a larger conversation that privileged no one voice. Even at its most militant, the New Deal was quick to blame particular business (or labor) leaders for their short sightedness, rather than condemn capitalism or unions as a whole, and would it not accept the presence of irreconcilable ends. The tensions between rich and poor, capitalist and laborer, which color both the Marxist and populist analysis of political economy, are absent here.[33] Distinct interests certainly existed, but there was nothing permanently divisive about them. There was a ruling class, but their narrow interpretation of their interests reflected a false consciousness, and progressive businessmen like Albert Filene, who supported minimum wages and collective bargaining, demonstrated that emancipation from this false consciousness was possible.[34] The Marxist critique of capitalism argues that the interests of capital and labor are irrevocably opposed to one another. Its politics are necessarily adversarial. Consensus was false consciousness. The New Deal rejected this standpoint as "un-American," which is to say completely at odds with our self-understanding as an inclusive, united, middle-class society.

The New Deal rejected the category of class because its divisive overtones not only negated the ideal of universal (middle-class) community, but had proven to be ineffectual as a political framework.[35] As Dewey noted, "In spite of the disparaging tone in which 'bourgeois' is spoken, this is a bourgeois country; and an American appeal couched in the language which the American people understand must start from this fact."[36] The American worker did not reject bourgeois values, or the idea of wealth. What they hated was their exclusion from it, their inability to reap the rewards perceived as a birthright and hovering so tantalizingly close.[37] These values were so embedded in the American psychology that their rejection would have required an act of self-negation. Instead, the battle lines were between the selfish and the virtuous—those who would abuse their power versus those who use it to expand the access of others to the American Dream. The lines between the two groups are moral and fluid. There are no static class barriers and no hopeless antagonisms. The poor were not members of a class with permanently separate interests. Rather, they were people who needed aid to facilitate their rise to the middle class, where they could pursue their own particular vision of happiness

Finally, the reluctance to engage in more narrow class appeals can only be understood in the larger context of the times. For the New Deal, indeed most liberals of the time, the politics of class, conceived explicitly in those terms, were colored by the twin specters of communism and fascism. The fear, reinforced by events in Europe, was that discussions of class centered on irrevocable conflict would likely end in violence, any victory too costly to be worthy of the name. Beyond that, even the more militant liberals like Dewey believed that such a conflict would be far more likely to see the forces of fascism prevail.[38] The possibility of collapse, of the end of the American experiment, loomed large in an administration that felt a keen sympathy for John Winthrop's millennial expectations for the United States as a "city on a hill."

What then is the substance of the common good of the American community? While we will find disagreement on the question of means (although the effectiveness of any given means is an empirical question subject to empirical validation), the New Deal assumes that there are certain ends on which the vast majority of Americans can agree: We want our government to use its powers openly (to assure accountability) and aggressively to preserve equality of opportunity, free enterprise, and the largest possible sphere of self-initiative—to preserve, in short, our individual rights to life, liberty and the pursuit of happiness.[39] Whatever radical moments it may have had, the New Deal never abandoned these fundamentally liberal concerns. The government can best secure our liberty by preserving our freedom of thought and worship, providing access to opportunity, and ensuring the security of our persons and property (property understood in a more authentically Lockean sense than the way in which he is normally appropriated).[40]

It was in its broader understanding of personal security that the New Deal represented a departure from previous governing interpretations of liberalism, as it created public obligations to ensure the welfare of its citizens—through private economic government when possible, through political governance when necessary. While this represented a new governing philosophy, it was justified by appealing to the oldest of American ideals. As Wallace argues:

> We can sum this all up in one word and say that what America wants is the pursuit of happiness. Each individual before he dies wants to express all that is in him. He wants to *work hard*. He wants to play hard. He wants the pleasures of a good home with education for his children. He wants to travel and on occasion to rest and enjoy the finer things in life. The common man thinks he is entitled to the opportunity of earning these things. He wants all the physical resources of the nation transformed by human energy and human knowledge into the good things of life, the sum total of which spells peace and happiness.[41]

What Wallace describes here is a broad framework for happiness, with an emphasis on work, education, family, and leisure that makes the self-definition and achievement of happiness possible. Within this framework the individual's search for happiness becomes a public concern, and while the individual must ultimately determine for himself what happiness is, society has both an obligation and an interest (the two are always closely linked) to facilitate its pursuit.

Two questions remained for the New Deal to answer. How do we determine what constitutes the public—a task made especially difficult in a political system designed to foster competing private interests, and how could the government help secure our pursuit of happiness without paternalistically defining what happiness is? The New Deal, concerned about inclusion, answered the first question by utilizing the category of consumer. The question of happiness would be more difficult to answer, in part because the New Deal sought to facilitate happiness in both body and soul, and as Tocqueville warned one hundred years prior, the desire for comfort in America has grasping, totalizing tendencies that can overwhelm all other considerations.

The Consumer and the Common Good

The American citizen's first importance to his country is no longer that of a citizen but that of a consumer.

—Muncie newspaper editorial[42]

Originally the New Deal did not identify one particular interest with the common good, hoping to strike a balance between capitalist, worker, and consumer, but the failure of the NRA demonstrated that privileging one of these groups might be necessary. The seemingly implacable hostility of the business community towards the New Deal eliminated them as a possibility. The public's fragile acceptance of labor meant that they were not a viable option politically, and the New Deal never had much of a romantic attachment to unions to begin with.[43] As a result the New Deal settled on the category of consumer. It was certainly broad enough to include all people—not everyone works for a wage, nor does everyone own stock or a business, but we are all consumers. This approach appealed to the egalitarian instincts of the New Deal, as attempts to address the depression through increased consumption would more immediately impact a great mass of citizens than expanding industrial production. Finally, it made space for the acceptance of leisure as a basic right.

But what made this framework especially compelling is the way that consumption had *already* become a fundamental aspect of our American identity—both in terms of how we see ourselves and how we define freedom. David Hackett Fischer has traced our fascination with material abundance back to the early days of American history, where it became "an artifact of liberty and freedom."[44] Claude Fisher argues that "Americans today may be entranced by consumer glitter, but so were Americans centuries ago."[45] For Fisher all that has changed is the access the average American has to these goods (and the number of choices available). Our history has been shaped in part by the way we have "democratized luxury." And as Eric Foner notes in *The Story of American Freedom*, the rise of truly mass production, advertising, and chain and department stores finally offered this part of our identity sufficient soil to fully bloom. Even if many Americans could still not fully participate until the comparative egalitarian leveling that followed World War II, consumer consumption has for decades, if not centuries, established itself as a key cornerstone of the American Dream.[46] The Depression did not represent a rejection of the values of the 1920s, but reflected the despair of Americans who feared those values were now lost to them. Given how Americans have long equated happiness with material possessions, and freedom with the right to choose them, any public philosophy encouraging consumption seems a natural fit. The New Deal found the consumer, for better or worse, the most widespread and authentically American identity available, and recognized that any frontal assault on its primacy was politically impossible.

From the beginning this understanding of consumption as freedom was in tension with an earlier competing understanding of freedom as economic autonomy—the yeoman farmer or the independent shopkeeper were free because they were independent. But despite the protestations of Jacksonian populism, for the vast majority of Americans that autonomy disappeared alongside the rise of industrial capitalism. It would only be natural, Arnold would argue, that the ideal of freedom as consumption would grow in prominence as a form of ceremonial intervention—a way for Americans to still convince themselves they enjoyed the same old liberty.[47] As Fischer notes, freedom itself changed "from a spiritual idea to a material condition."[48] We may not be able to master the forces that govern our lives, but we can choose the products that fill them. As one advertising executive put it, "[e]very free-born American...has a right to name his own necessities."[49] Thus choice, with its intimations of privacy, abundance, reward, and fulfillment, was given a normative coloring, and came to trump older, more aristocratic understandings of liberty that privilege sacrifice, self-denial, and the exercise of citizenship in a public space. The New Deal aimed at bridging the gap between the two conceptions of liberty, believing in the possibility of their reconciliation, although the consumerist impulse would by necessity remain dominant for a time.[50] Older conceptions of freedom as a spiritual ideal could serve to temper, but not replace, its newer material orientation.

In the intervening years it is easy to read this history critically, informed as it is by the excesses of the modern consumer economy and damning indictments like Benjamin Barber's *Consumed*. Barber's position itself harkens back to the critique that many progressives leveled against the reconceptualization of freedom as consumption and leisure that accompanied the democratization of entertainment and the rise of the mass production of consumer goods.[51] Progressives resisted the tendency of entertainment to exalt individualism and redirect energy they hoped could be used for progressive purposes. Jane Addams lamented the lack of 'reforming energy' she found amongst the young, and blamed this on their new emphasis on personal gratification.[52] An orientation towards consumption socializes us to look inward instead of outward, and place private satisfaction over public need.

But this is not the whole story. Other progressives, like Walter Weyl, argued that the fact that consumers were "overwhelmingly superior in numbers to producers" made them a potentially influential agent of change. As Lawrence Glickman argues in his history of American consumer movements, "[O]nce mastered, Progressives believed, the logic of interdependence empowered consumers and served as an object lesson in how to redeem citizenship in a new era, one in which interdependence rather than autonomy was the watchword."[53] The New Deal, while somewhat sympathetic to the progressive critique of entertainment, consumption, and irresponsible leisure, nevertheless embraced the consumer as their central category, as did fellow travelers like John Dewey and Stuart Chase. And we should be careful not to downplay this connection between responsible consumption and responsible citizenship. As Lawrence Glickman observes, "The 1930s was perhaps the only decade in American history when commentators could speak of 'consumer society' as a potentially radical force,"[54] and the House Committee on Un-American Activities charged the consumer movement of the 1930s with allowing communist principles to enter into American society.[55] There were public components to this private act.

Despite the alleged potential for consumer-citizens to become communists, it made sense for the New Deal to embrace the category of consumer. Besides the fact that consumption could help stimulate the economy and deemphasized class struggle, access to radios, automobiles, electricity, and other labor-saving devices led to demonstrable improvements in the quality of people's lives.[56] An abundant society was a positive goal in itself.[57]

It was also politically necessary, as Americans defined themselves as consumers first, citizens second. As Philip Abbot argues, "Supporters as well as critics have assumed that the essence of America lies in its nature as a commercial society. To be an American is to be one who sells and buys. The measure of the health of our society, perhaps our only measure, is general prosperity."[58] Our ability to consume, and to choose what we consume (even if we do not fully understand the ways in which we are conditioned to make certain choices) is an act of freedom. And as Anne Norton argues, the more that we experience labor in terms of repression and impotence, the more we need to exercise freedom through consumption. Labor is experienced as dependence and subordination, while consumption is "the exercise of freedom and choice."[59] The New Deal would place great emphasis on the psychological importance of work, but work was fulfilling more as an act of citizenship and obligation than it was an act of self-creation.

Tocqueville speculates on the origins of our consumer instincts in *Democracy in America*. In part he sees an emphasis on consumption as a natural byproduct of a country without fixed class distinctions, where there are no hereditary barriers to wealth. The absence of formal limits to acquisition animates within people a restless craving for more, in part to stave off the fear of losing what they have.[60] Tocqueville's emphasis is on comfort, but he wrote at a time where another form of freedom, freedom experienced as autonomy, was far more widespread, and Tocqueville sees these differing conceptions of freedom competing for attention within the American personality. By the 1930s consumption represented more than the chance to be comfortable. Due in large measure to the accuracy of Tocqueville's warnings about the rise of industrial aristocracies, consumption had become our primary means of self-creation and self-determination, the way we experience freedom.[61] The opportunity to consume is a celebration of freedom independent of questions of need and necessity. It offers the chance to create an identity not afforded to us elsewhere. It is through the satisfying of excess wants, as Norton points out, that we experience power and a limited form of agency.[62] Freedom was to be found in the act of buying in a competitive marketplace, a celebration of an individual choice, freely made, that stood in stark contrast to the paternalistic (and sometimes tyrannical) control that the average American was subjected to at work.[63]

The New Deal's emphasis on consumption was possible due to the fact that real (as opposed to artificial) scarcity was not an issue for an industrial power like America. As Thurman Arnold wryly notes, "From an engineering point of view Mr. Hoover's guess about two chickens in every pot was entirely too conservative."[64] Equating consumption with democracy, freedom, and the health of American society obviously appealed to a people long governed by their desire for material comfort—and it offered a promised restoration of the American dream after the privation and hardship of the Great Depression. Any public philosophy intending to resonate with American voters must address this promise. We have long been a people willing to put up with sacrifice and denial only temporarily, and primarily in the service of a more abundant future.[65]

Using the well-being of consumers as a test for public policy also enabled the New Deal to weight benefits towards the middle and working classes—groups that enjoy fewer structural advantages in the American economy and therefore are more in need of government protection—who spent a much greater percentage of their income and who would benefit from plans designed to boost consumption.[66] The Fair Labor Standards Act, the Wagner Act, Social Security, the Works Progress Administration, National Youth Administration, Civilian Conservation Corps, and the Home Owners Loan Corporation and Farm Mortgage Assistance program all need to be understood in this light.[67] A focus on consumption also enabled FDR to argue that consumer-friendly legislation served to fight the Depression, creating a demand for goods that would stimulate the economy and put people back to work. As a neutral category, the consumer enabled Roosevelt to bypass traditional class conflicts and offered a comparatively easy way to test the public usefulness of both businesses and policy. Did it serve its clients efficiently and effectively? If the answer was no, government regulation was justified. This approach came to dominate New Deal policy, especially during its later anti-trust phase.[68]

Alan Brinkley has called this anti-monopoly crusade the most prominent public initiative of the late New Deal, and Thurman Arnold was both a powerful administrator and a tireless public advocate, defending it with a missionary zeal.[69] Roosevelt's new approach represented a repudiation of the NRA, and reflected a new attitude towards concentrated economic power, privileging an approach more in line with the traditional American love of consumption, embrace of competition, and suspicion of power. It saw itself more as a restoration, using state power to protect the competitive markets that consumers benefited from. It consisted:

> not in hiring experts to make broad general plans but in breaking up, one at a time, the restraints on production and distribution of goods...It does assume...that the future of industrial democracy does not lie in any more gov-

ernment control than is required to remedy specific evils. It believes that in the long run the most efficient production and distribution of goods will come from private initiative in a free market. It is based on the premise that most of our troubles have come because we have allowed private groups to protect themselves against the inconveniences of being force to compete with new enterprise.[70]

Arnold understood his role in the Anti-Trust Division as requiring him to challenge any and all restraints that artificially constrained markets and created bottlenecks in the process of distribution. This meant not only attacking 'bottlenecks' caused by corporations (like G.E.) and industries (oil) but professional groups like the American Medical Association; even unions on occasion. Economic organizations were to be judged solely on the effects those organizations had on consumers. Did they both enhance and distribute our material abundance? Did they allow us to take full advantage of our industrial capacity and maximize our ability to consume it?

Arnold and the New Deal chose to privilege consumers because they comprised, according to Arnold, the 85 percent of the population for whom the cheaper and more widespread distribution of goods (as well as increases in wages) would have a measurable impact on the quality of their life. No other group in the United States could make a comparable numerical claim, and it had strong appeal to the utilitarian philosophy (and electoral calculations) of the New Deal. A movement indifferent to size, privileging increased wages and lower prices, and designed to facilitate consumption, would not only affect the greatest number of people, but also serve as an engine to drive the nation's economic development and productive strength.

Of course there are dangers attendant in so strongly equating freedom with the act of material acquisition—of equating political consciousness with consumer consciousness.[71] As Abbot argues, "if the publicly shared ideal is private acquisition, then there is no public."[72] Private acquisition plays into the most publicly enervating understanding of freedom, precisely the danger Tocqueville identifies in *Democracy in America*.

There is, indeed, a most dangerous passage in the history of a democratic people. When the taste for physical gratifications among them has grown more rapidly than their education and their experience of free institutions, the time will come when men are carried away and lose all self-restraint at the sight of new possessions they are about to obtain...It is not necessary to do violence to such a people in order to strip them of the rights they enjoy; they themselves willingly loosen their hold.[73]

Tocqueville here speaks to the older conception of freedom that privileges autonomy and mastery, but there is also the assumption (also made by Progressive-era reformers as well as contemporary critics like Barber) that private comfort likely comes at the expense of public concern. Self-interest turns individuals from public citizens to private consumers and predisposes them to support any government program that provides them with personal benefits regardless of the overall costs and consequences of said program.[74] "Thus men are following two separate roads to servitude; the taste for their own well-being withholds them from taking a part in the government, and their love of that well-being forces them to closer and closer dependency on those who govern."[75] While Tocqueville's concern here is with a centralized administrative state, it is easy to translate this concern into a passive acceptance of corporate governance, acquiescing to its private arbitrary power provided our comfort does not suffer in the process.

In this regard Tocqueville shared Jefferson's fear that a country cannot be both wealthy and public-spirited. "What a cruel reflection," Jefferson laments, "that a rich country cannot long be a free one."[76] With wealth comes moral decline, and with abundance (as opposed to self-sufficiency) comes a narrow self-interest. Both Jefferson and Tocqueville share an abiding skepticism about whether or not a person who spends their time focused on their private interest will be able to enter the community to discuss the public good. The New Deal departs from Jefferson and Tocqueville on this score, arguing that, given the connection between freedom, happiness, and necessity, freedom is most likely safeguarded amidst prosperity. However, this departure is not made without reservations. In fact, the New Deal shared Tocqueville's prescriptions for reigning in the inevitable excess that comes with an emphasis on materialism— particularly the emphasis on citizenship and religion as ways to transcend our own private, self-regarding concerns.

However, this was not the only approach the New Deal adopted. While material comfort and well-being was embraced as an end, and a worthwhile one, it was not the highest of ends. The New Deal was sensitive to the critique of Woodrow Wilson's biographer who lamented, "Our government has ceased to be a duty, to be sacrificed for, and becomes a privilege somehow to be used for ministering to our needs and our greeds."[77] If we have no higher conception of citizenship than materialism—if, as President Bush argued, our principal obligation as citizens was to hug our children and go to the mall it becomes all too easy to think of the government solely as an ATM, and social welfare programs as mere special interests. Instead, the New Deal sought to reframe comfort as a means to more sophisticated forms of happiness: self-development and citizenship. And here the New Deal embraces what are arguably the most progressive aspects of the liberal tradition, taking its concerns for individuality and autonomy and attempting to channel them into something higher.

Self-Development and the Common Good

[Democracy] is a method of government conceived for the development of human beings as a whole.

—Eleanor Roosevelt[78]

New Deal theory was liberal, but while Locke's *Second Treatise* is rightly regarded as a foundational liberal text, it is not the culmination of the liberal tradition, nor the primary theoretical inspiration behind the New Deal. To blunt the consequences of our excessive individualism, the New Deal looked to liberals like John Stuart Mill, and while it did not specifically claim Mill as a patron theorist (nor did Mill primarily think in terms of rights), the New Deal's understanding of liberty and happiness is indebted to Mill.

For Mill, happiness is found in the liberty to develop our own unique individuality—discovering for ourselves where our talents and potentialities lay; by developing them we achieve and celebrate our humanity. As he says in *On Liberty*, "Human nature is not a machine to be built after a model, and set to do exactly the work prescribed for it, but a tree which requires to grow and develop itself on all sides, according to the tendency of the inward forces which make it a living thing."[79] To be a human being is to be someone who makes choices, who grows through self-definition and self-discovery. "The only freedom which deserves the name is that of pursuing our own good in our own way."[80] However, there is more at stake here than just autonomy, the freedom to make unfettered decisions. Instead autonomy is a precondition of a larger purpose, the development of our individual human potential. This process is private insofar as no one individual has the authority to define for another how he must live (subject to the caveat that they follow Mill's harm principle), but it is public insofar as societies and the individuals who comprise them are better served by creating a dynamic environment in which the best in others helps us maximize the possibilities within ourselves.

According to Mill, individuality is aspirational, not something possessed in full.[81] Almost any obstacle barring its development must be removed. "Whatever crushes individuality is despotism."[82] Much of Mill's argument is to be read in the context of free thought and expression, but he notes elsewhere that one cannot easily pursue self-development in the face of material hardship. As Mill argued, "first amongst existing social evils may be mentioned the evil of Poverty," whose presence stifles our individual and collective potential.[83] It is exceedingly difficult to plant a beautiful garden in poor soil.

The fate of the individual is of interest to society, as the overall quality of our aggregate individuality is a common inheritance and the source of a people's greatness. Any state in which the people live in some type of bondage (be it the psychic bondage of conformity or the physical bondage of privation) stunts its own potential.

> It is not by wearing down into uniformity all that is individual in themselves, but by cultivating it and calling it forth, within the limits imposed by the rights and interests of others, that human beings become a noble and beautiful object of contemplation and as the works partake the character of those who do them, by the same process human life also becomes rich, diversified, and animating, furnishing more abundant ailment to high thoughts and elevating feelings, and strengthening the tie which binds every individual to the race, by making the

race infinitely better worth belonging to. In proportion to the development of his individuality, each person becomes more valuable to himself, and is, therefore capable of being more valuable to others.[84]

This individual concern with self-development blends seamlessly for Mill with the idea of self-government. Without sufficient attention devoted to the process of self-development you will not be fit to govern yourself, let alone others. We see here too the emphasis on what Mill calls his harm principle. The criteria for determining the right of the collectivity to interfere in the life of the individual is grounded in the way the individual's actions affect the collective as a whole. Mill is reluctant to define what harm is (although he is clear that harm has to be other-regarding) and in fact the end of *On Liberty* is devoted to laying out the ambiguity of his harm principle, making it clear that these definitions are often arbitrary social constructs, politically constituted and subject to democratic guidance. But while the definition of harm may be in play, the progressive ends of self-development are not, and Mill argued that few human beings could devote time and energy to the development of their human faculties as long as society is confronted by the reality of scarcity.

The New Deal shared both Mill's conception of the good life and its relation to government—namely that institutions should maximize the self-development of their individual members. This is, as Mill put it, "utility in the largest sense, grounded on the permanent interests of man as a progressive being."[85] Laws, government, and all forms of social organization that impose obligations on their members are legitimated in reference to this end. Happiness, that fundamental right, is expanded to include not simply the possession of property, but also the possibility of self-development. Happiness becomes the opportunity to discover and develop the unique talents and abilities that create individual meaning. Material wealth and comfort, both in terms of labor-saving devices and as means to relax, to recharge both body and soul, made this deeper concern with self-development possible. Only now that we have conquered scarcity could we being to approach the possibilities of human development. Eleanor Roosevelt was the most articulate of the New Dealers on this issue:

> The attainment of life and liberty required most of our energy in the past, so the pursuit of happiness and the consideration of the lives of human beings remained in the background. Now is the time to recognize the possibilities which lie before us in taking up and developing of this part of our forefather's vision.[86]

The issue with previous defenses of American values that emphasized the protection of property divorced that protection from its larger context—the necessity of property as a material precondition of self-development, which is to say, happiness. Note that this notion of self-development is fundamentally liberal. Only the autonomous individual can decide what choices in life affect his happiness. This cannot be imposed on another human being. Society has the right and duty to prevent external interference in an individual's right to author the conditions of his life—but it cannot force us to choose wisely. Our obligation to one another, as citizens and as human beings, is to facilitate the ability of each to discover their own unique sources of happiness, not to coerce them into doing so (or to conform to our own). A free society will maximize the ability of all its members to achieve self-defined happiness, and in this way we grant a basic level of human dignity to the autonomous individuals who compose that society.

Thus while the New Deal is informed by a rich conception of the good life, part of that conception involves the recognition that people must ultimately decide for themselves how best to live. One can still be wrong—neither Wallace, nor the Roosevelts were moral relativists, and each would trace much of their thinking to the Social Gospel of the progressive era—but respect for autonomy means that we usually have to grant people the freedom to be wrong. Both Mill and the New Deal are opposed to paternalistic social forces that interfere with autonomy and pressure individuals into making choices requiring, as Mill puts it, "no other faculty than the ape-like one of imitation."[87] It is its resistance to paternalism that the New Deal argues makes liberal democracy the best (although not perfect) form of government for facilitating self-development. It is dynamic, responsive, and the only political arrangement that can realistically hope to maximize the greatest good for the greatest number while letting each member define that good for herself. That freedom, alongside a basic level of material and psychic security, is the essence of dignity.

It is also the source of our strength as a nation. The New Deal argued, following Mill, that by unleashing the individual potential of every citizen, we impart to society a restless dynamism that benefits all its members. Without this energy, society becomes static and enervated, and the possibilities of a deeper happiness are denied to us both as individuals and as a collectivity. In the past, our orientation towards scarcity prevented us from seeing past our more immediate (and legitimate) material interests, but these past limitations need no longer bind us. Now we must make sure that we have not "been so busy making a living that we have less time really to live."[88] Nurturing our potential requires both leisure time and the opportunity to do something of consequence with it.[89] This creates new needs and new obligations. "The arts are no longer a luxury but a necessity to the average human being," ER argued, "and they should be included in any department which includes health, social security, and education."[90] Guaranteeing a diversity of experiences is essential if we wish to develop the broad perspective necessary to understand our larger connections to one another.

> No city child should grow up without knowing the beauty of spring in the country or where milk comes from, how vegetables grow and what it is like to play in a field instead of on a city street. No country child who knows these things should be deprived, however, of museums, books, music and better teachers because it is easier to find them and to pay for them in big cities than it is in rural districts.[91]

A citizen in a country with both rural and urban populations should be entitled to the experiences of both; indeed, that experience is essential if we want them to identify with one another as members of a "great community." It is the only way that a robust, cosmopolitan democracy is possible.

Within this framework individualism was not to be abandoned, but the way in which our individuality is rooted in a complex interdependent society must be highlighted, so that happiness could come to mean more than consumption, that it was found in the creation of shared spaces that stimulate individual potential. FDR sought to remind Americans that:

> Happiness lies not in the mere possession of money; it lies in the joy of achievement, in the thrill of creative effort. The joy and moral stimulation of work no longer must be forgotten in the mad chase of evanescent profits. These dark days will be worth all they cost us if they teach us that our true destiny is not to be ministered unto but to minister to ourselves and our fellow men.[92]

This was the ideal. In reality, most Americans would continue to define themselves as consumers—but the hope was that consumption would both combat the very real poverty many Americans found themselves in and create the secure physical and mental spaces necessary to allow for at least the possibility of self-development. However, both of these orientations are still fundamentally private—even if they carry with them a public benefit, the benefit is derivative from the private advantage. The New Deal still required some way of reorienting people outside of themselves. It looked in two directions; one privileging America's Christian heritage (broadly understood, and inclusive to the point of encompassing non-Christian religions), the other placing an emphasis on democratic citizenship. Rather than oppose, these two streams of thought complement and clarify each other. Roosevelt famously described his political philosophy by stating "I am a Christian and a Democrat, that's all." While often dismissed as a vacuous dodge, Roosevelt is pointing to a deeper synthesis between the two. For the New Deal democracy is a religion, Christianity (properly understood) is fundamentally democratic, and attached to both are strenuous political and social obligations that take us outside ourselves and soften the worst excesses of the consumer-based individualism and the private nature of self-development. Without democracy Christianity cannot fulfill its larger goals of human emancipation. Without Christianity our democracy will remain chained to our baser interests and instincts.

Religion and the Common Good

[R]eligion which gives us a sense of obligation about living with a deeper interest in the welfare of our neighbors is essential to the success of Democracy.

—Eleanor Roosevelt[93]

The appeal to religion as a way to soften the excesses of self-regarding individualism will be familiar to readers of Tocqueville, who highlighted both the strength and superficiality of American religious devotion, where many "Americans follow their habits rather than their firm beliefs when they worship God."[94] This had not changed much in the intervening hundred years. As Commager observed in *The American Mind*, "It is scarcely an exaggeration to say that during the nineteenth century and well into the twentieth, religion prospered while theology went slowly bankrupt."[95] And there is a utilitarian coloring to the way that the New Deal discussed religious faith—highlighting the ways in which its principles supported its politics, and avoiding the nuance that would color the analysis of more sophisticated theologians like Reinhold Niebuhr.[96] However, the happy intersection of belief and expediency does not change the fact that the belief was deeply held by many principal New Dealers, and the strength of this belief elevated religious public discourse above pandering and electioneering.

Religion played two key roles for the New Deal. It served to ground both democratic obligation and the welfare state. As FDR stated, "We call what we have been doing 'human security' and 'social justice.' In the last analysis all of those terms can be described by one word; and that is 'Christianity.'"[97] The New Deal's Christianity is the Christianity of the Sermon on the Mount.[98] Here the New Deal was very much indebted to the Social Gospel movement and figures like Jane Addams and Walter Rauschenbush. Social justice trumps concerns about moral character, and there was an inclusivity about it that put it in opposition to Father Coughlin's Social Justice movement, which combined a reactionary populism with anti-Semitism, fascist sympathies, and the worst elements of American nativism. Its second role was to serve as a symbolic language used for communicating the New Deal's aims to the American public. We will discuss the second role in greater detail in chapter 5 in the context of Henry Wallace's *Statesmanship and Religion*. Here we focus primarily on the writings of Eleanor Roosevelt, which most clearly and consistently articulated the role of religion in American life, as well as the connection between religion and citizenship.

Religion was, in the words of Eleanor Roosevelt, a "belief and faith in the heart of man which makes him try to live his life according to the highest standard which he is able to visualize."[99] It is "the striving of the human soul to achieve spiritually the best that it is capable of and to care unselfishly, not only for personal good but for the good of all those who toil with them upon the earth."[100] Spirituality is defined by a feeling of independence and curiosity.[101] Education and religion go hand in hand. Reason and revelation need not oppose each other.[102]

While Wallace and the Roosevelts were firm believers in the institutional separation of church and state, neither could imagine a healthy democracy whose citizens were not in some way Christian, a belief shared with liberal patrons Locke and Smith. In the words of Wallace, the government is charged "to devise and develop the social machinery which will work out the implications of the social message of the old prophets and of the Sermon on the Mount; but it remains the opportunity of the Church to fill men's hearts and minds with the sprit and the meaning of those great visions."[103]

These words could be alarming in an era of politically well-heeled religious fundamentalism and religiously inspired terror, but the understanding the New Deal had of Christianity, and religion in general, was profoundly undogmatic and fully inclusive—references to Christianity reflected its centrality to the American experience, but Christianity was hardly the only legitimate public manifestation of the religious impulse. Any set of beliefs sympathetic to these commitments is acceptable. ER is quick to note that the religious spirit that grounds the sense of community, care, and cooperation essential for democracy are not the exclusive domain of the Christian faith. Any worldview that teaches "that we cannot live for ourselves alone and that as long as we are here on this earth we are all of us brothers, regardless of race, creed, or color"[104] is sufficient.

ER moves beyond the soft toleration that characterizes much of the liberal tradition. We are not obligated to accept difference simply because the material costs of denying it are too high, nor should difference be embraced because it is socially useful. Difference is in some respects made irrelevant in the face of our commonalities as human beings. Instead, ER argues, "what is needed is really not a self-conscious virtue which makes us treat our neighbors as we want to be treated, but an acceptance of the fact that all human beings have dignity and the potentiality of development into the same kind of people we are ourselves."[105] ER's standard may require the proactive highlighting of difference in order to make it familiar, to uncover the shared humanity underneath it. But in the end the ultimate goal is to negate difference as a category.

Her broad understanding of Christianity moves past even Locke's watered-down list of Christian essentials.[106] One need not even accept the divinity of Jesus; only recognize that he lived an exemplary moral life. Beyond that, "fundamental law is really changeable human provision for certain conditions. There is very little actual fundamental law. Really only 'love one another.'[107] The rest is all interpretation—even the Ten Commandments."[108] Any religion or philosophy that prioritized this teaching was acceptable. Any that does not is incompatible with the democratic ideals of the New Deal.

All our moral and political obligations find their ultimate grounding in this requirement to 'love thy neighbor.' Love, ER argues, becomes the substance of democracy.

> The principle...of the responsibility of the individual for the well-being of his neighbors which is akin to "Love thy neighbor as thyself" in the New Testament, seems always to have been a part of the development of the democratic ideal which has differentiated it from all other forms of government.[109]

For the more millennial thinkers like ER and Wallace, true democracy represents our best attempt at redemption on Earth, and in a democracy no one is beyond salvation. The ultimate fate of the individual and the collectivity are intimately (and perhaps problematically) linked. Given ER's robust understanding of democracy, it is clear that its practice will be demanding. It requires a "Christ-like" way of living.[110] However, "if we once establish this human standard as a measure of success the future of democracy is secure."[111] The emphasis on the human standard is important: because Christ was human, the rest of us could conceivably hope to duplicate his public example.

The health of a society is largely determined by its ability to put these religious teachings into public practice, to look past narrow private interests towards the larger concerns of the whole community. "Loving thy neighbor as thyself" becomes the starting point for the resolution of all conflicts of interest.

> What is the trouble between capital and labor, what is the trouble in many of our communities, but rather a universal forgetting that this teaching is one of our first obligations. When we center on our home, our own family, our own business, we are neglecting this fundamental obligation of every human being.[112]

"Loving thy neighbor as thyself" not only involves recognizing our shared humanity, but acting on it—applying to others the same standards of justice we would apply to ourselves. It creates a strenuous cosmopolitan responsibility, requiring that our narrow communities expand ever outward to embrace state, nation, and eventually the world.[113] There is no way forward politically or socially without the recognition of this fundamental obligation. Instead of Christian democracy we have at best competing interest groups and a politics of isolation, conflict and despair.

It was that sense of embattled isolation that the New Deal sought to combat, and the long-term health of its institutions would depend on fostering this sense of cosmopolitan community. ER observed that "[m]any people are feeling that life is too hard to cope with. That feeling would not exist if out of this depression we could revive again any actual understanding of what it means to be responsible for one's brother."[114] Nurturing this sense of attachment to one another is essential if we are to endure the sacrifices democracy requires of us. A common religious heritage (broadly understood as a commitment to religious principles of charity, dignity, and love) provides us with the framework we need to develop these attachments.

The New Deal claims that we are confronted with an economic and spiritual poverty that prevents us from rising above purely selfish interests and establishing the goodwill necessary to address them. New Dealers like ER and Wallace saw the Great Depression as a millennial moment, a time of fear, doubt, and uncertainty that offers the possibility of regenerating spiritual values lost in the "mad haste for more and more money and more and more luxury."[115] These values have a long and deeply ingrained tradition in the American heritage, and we must be reminded of that heritage. The New Deal believed, as an article of faith, that it is possible eventually to overcome the baser priorities that consistently lead to depression and war. The problem is not conquering necessity or fortune: instead we must master ourselves and our suspicions of each other and in doing so create the political will necessary to remake the world over. Only a state whose foundations are constructed on the love and trust we find in the New Deal's broad understanding of Christianity can grant permanence to the social innovations of the New Deal. Whether or not this kind of meaningful love is possible in the cosmopolitan sense that ER and Wallace refer to remains to be seen. Perhaps in the end it is an assumption that must be made for even incremental change to be possible. Regardless of the answer, there was a recognition that such an attempt at meaningful human sympathy, if not fraternity, was at the heart of the New Deal enterprise.

Citizenship and the Common Good

> The motivating force of the theory of a democratic way of life is still a belief that as individuals we live cooperatively, and to the best of our ability serve the community in which we live.
> —Eleanor Roosevelt[116]

The New Deal also attempted to offset the worst excesses of a consumer oriented individualism by appealing to citizenship and the ideals of democracy. It understood democracy in two ways: first, as a mechanistic set of procedures and institutions designed to facilitate some degree of self-government; second, as a moral idea, less a system of government than a calling—a lived experience, not a set of institutional arrangements. As callings go, there are none higher: living the life of a true democratic citizen requires you to give of yourself so that others can create themselves, an act of mutual self-generation. While we are obligated to provide others with the opportunity for self-development, they in turn are supposed to use the talents and abilities so nurtured to become active citizens, thereby creating a dynamic social environment that benefits all.[117] There is an appeal to interest, to be sure, but service and citizenship are their own rewards.

It is here that the New Deal moves beyond Mill's liberalism into the republican tradition, albeit a particularly democratic and egalitarian reading of that tradition. We see this especially in the writings of Eleanor Roosevelt, the New Dealer most engaged with questions of citizenship. Echoing Rousseau's maxim that "freedom is adherence to the laws we make for ourselves," ER writes: "[w]hen you come to understand self-discipline you begin to understand the limits of freedom. You grasp the fact that freedom is never absolute, that it must always be contained within the framework of other people's freedom."[118] In a democracy, we attain liberty when we recognize, submit to, and work to enhance the bonds of fellowship that bind us to one another.

Democratic freedom involves not only effort, but sacrifice, the kind that comes from making public what was once private.

> Our basic sacrifice is the privilege of thinking and working for ourselves alone...If we are able to have genuine Democracy we are going to think primarily of the rights and privileges and the good that may come to the people of a great nation...It means that we no longer hold the fruits of our labor as our own, but consider them in the light of a trusteeship...we will execute to the best of our ability every piece of work which we undertake and give our efforts to such things as seem to us to serve the purpose of the greatest number of people.[119]

She recognized that this is a lot to ask, and it is why the development of friendship and attachment is so vital to the success of the enterprise. Since the New Deal envisions an active society in which people are expected to sacrifice for the greater benefit of all, the question of political obligation is central. How do we justify the sacrifices we expect others to make? Political theory offers four possibilities: duty, interest, love, and fear. The later, while the choice of Machiavelli and Hobbes, is not democratic. Democracy involves citizens freely choosing the laws that will govern them, and choices made under the influence of fear are not freely made. While New Deal thought makes frequent appeals to duty, duty is not an end in itself. The nation must earn our obligation, the New Deal argues, even if our neighbors are entitled to it. If we can sufficiently demonstrate our interdependence then we can justify sacrifice as an exercise in "self-interest rightly understood," and this was undoubtedly an important, if not the most important part of the New Deal approach. But interest is rational and dull, incapable of stirring people to act for others when their short-term interests may suffer, or when the benefits of sacrifice are felt at a macro, rather than personal level.

That leaves love, coupled with the idea of dignity (as a way to limit the authoritarian, grasping excesses of love), to form the core of the New Deal's democratic liberalism. We sacrifice for what we love—indeed, only through love is it possible to generate the fellow feeling necessary to make the sacrifices demanded of a welfare state. Without this love, without a feeling of attachment towards fellow citizens, the welfare state (and redistributive justice) becomes a form of theft, the taking of my hard-earned resources to help someone else who has no claim over me.[120] Our fellow citizens cannot be adversaries in the marketplace, but must instead be friends and family whom we are willing to aid. Our obligations to the state, to each other, and to ourselves should be grounded in an expansive, generous conception of love, one that will have difficulty taking root in a society where perceived scarcity makes love too costly.

For both the Roosevelts and Wallace, this love finds its origins in God, and its most expansive incarnation can be found in the life of Christ. Tactically this is a smart way to proceed, as there are fewer symbols with more potency in American life.[121] This does not mean pandering to the basest elements of organized religion. But it does involve recognizing that in order for an ideal to take hold in the public consciousness it needs emotional relevance. Democratic politics requires salesmanship, and the progressive theorist is ultimately selling the idea of the welfare state. Doing so successfully means appealing to those symbols that have the most resonance with the buying public. This does not require the sacrifice of principles in the name of tactics: all traditions can be read differently and symbols can be reinterpreted in new and expansive ways. The symbols of Christianity can lead to a politics of condemnation or a politics of forgiveness, but these symbols are potent and the great progressive leaders of the 20th century (ER, FDR, Wallace, MLK) understood their power.

Democracy asks that we sublimate, at least partially, the elements of individualism that ask us only to act for ourselves, and instead learn to consider and care for others. This requires knowledge of the self and knowledge of our interdependence: democracy creates for us "a problem we cannot escape: we must know what we believe in, how we intend to live, and what we are doing for our neighbors."[122] However, our neighborhood extends far beyond its apparent boundaries. Given the fundamentally interconnected nature of society this creates an obligation:

> To the coal miners and share-croppers, the migratory workers, to the tenement-house dwellers and the farmers who cannot make a living. It opens endless vistas of work to acquire knowledge and, when we have acquired it in our own country, there is still the rest of the world to study before we know what our course of action should be.[123]

It is demanding, but that is the price of democratic citizenship. The rewards for these sacrifices come from the joy of membership in a community of consequence, as well as the self-satisfaction that comes from knowing that we are actively participating in the decisions that affect us, creating the boundaries that will define our opportunities for self-development. It offers a life of genuine, albeit strenuous, freedom.

New Dealers were savvy enough (or liberal enough) to understand that when principle could be linked to interest, when it could be shown that there are material benefits that come from making others more secure, it is easier to sacrifice, even to love. But the appeal to interest was always tactical, and the New Deal held out the hope that over time it would no longer be necessary, that we could develop a different way of understanding our place in, and obligation to, the rest of the world. We return, once again, to Wallace's "quarter turn of the human heart."

This is complicated by the fact that love and attachment are usually intimate, local feelings, and mitigating the excesses of capitalism requires a large, likely impersonal state. This larger state creates extra demands and poses new dangers. The New Deal is philosophically liberal, and the central concern of all liberals is with limiting the abuse of arbitrary power. The empowered state given life by the New Deal frightened classical liberals because of the undeniable potential for abuse. However, ER argues, we need fear the state only if we fail in our obligations as citizens to police it. "Each of us, ultimately, is responsible in large part for the welfare of his community, for the kind of government he has, for the world he lives in."[124] If we wish to live free of the arbitrary power of the state and market, our government must be as democratic as possible. This involves both increasing the ability of citizens to comprehend the work of an increasingly complicated bureaucracy and developing new avenues of communication between citizen and representative. As such, FDR's fireside chats were as much an effort at democratic education as manipulation. As Milkis observes, "The president was confident that if he did his job as teacher, the people would pass the lessons on to their representatives on Congress."[125] FDR made a remarkable effort to educate the public, in language that was non-technical without pandering, about the economics behind the banking crisis or the difficulty inherent in supplying troops in the Pacific theater of World War II. But this was still controlled, hierarchical communication.

Ideally, the New Deal insisted, communication is also instigated at the bottom and taken seriously at the top. This in part is ER's justification behind her "I want you to write me" campaign, where she received (and answered) over 300,000 pieces of mail in her first year as First Lady.[126] It is vitally important, ER insisted, that we regard the government as a friend to be cultivated, not an evil to tame. "The feeling of friendship, the feeling that in the house where government resides, there also resides friendship, is perhaps the best safeguard we have for democracy."[127] The development of this friendship, achieved through participation and education, will create newer, stronger, and necessary attachments to our communities (national and local).

To aid in the creation of these attachments, the New Deal sought to infuse our understanding of property with a sense of trusteeship, across both space and time. Our current inheritance is due to the sacrifices of generations past, and we must act as stewards for generations to come. The social contract binds us to the future as well as the present, and acting on behalf of the future means creating a more just and equitable present.

This commitment to justice is based on more than a theoretical obligation to the unborn future. The New Deal's democratic theory is sympathetic to the Lockean and Jeffersonian right of revolution. While never abandoning faith that the United States could meet the needs of all its citizens, the New Deal places the burden on the state to deliver on the promise of its social contract, not for its citizens to meekly accept what was given to them. People can be legitimately disaffected when society fails to address their grievances. Unless they are provided for, there is no reason for minorities or the *poor to be loyal, nor was* there any reason for the young to bleed on foreign shores. ER quotes with sympathy a WWI veteran who claims:

I am a veteran of the last war, my father, his father, and his father before him fought in wars and I think that I am a loyal and true American, yet I am not sure that I wouldn't rather have a full stomach and shelter under some other regime than to be hungry and homeless under the present one.[128]

This radicalism, as Barry Karl argues, was grounded in self-protection, rather than ideology, which made the New Deal sympathetic to the impulse.[129] Roosevelt echoes the sentiment of the veteran when he argued in his 1944 State of the Union Address that "[p]eople who are hungry, people who are out of a job are the stuff of which dictatorships are made."[130] The burden here is not on the veteran to sublimate his own interests to that of the state, but the obligation of society, acting through market and state, to ensure that we offered our citizen-consumers the material prosperity necessary for the possibility of self-development and meaningful citizenship. We could not fight World War II without first having a WPA or CCC (or later a GI Bill) to give soldiers a reason to defend their country. The attraction the dispossessed felt towards communism, socialism, or even fascism should be seen less as a threat to security and more as a mark of failure on the part of the nation.

> We need not fear any "isms" if our democracy is achieving the ends for which it was established... [and it can only function by] each individual knowing his own community and taking responsibility for his part as a citizen in a democracy....you must have a minimum of economic security in order to have a true democracy, and for people to love their government and their country. You cannot love anything which does not allow you to have anything which makes life worth living.[131]

This offers an important twist to traditional republicanism. Our loyalty to our society is not given. It asks much of the individual, but it in turn must justify the sacrifice it calls for. If the United States was worth saving, if in fact it could be saved at all, it would be absolutely essential to reengage the population laid low by the Depression, to give them some reason to feel attached to the larger national community. This, as Lincoln noted one hundred years prior, is a problem every generation of Americans must face.[132] It is in the name of this reengagement that the New Deal rewrote our social contract.

A New Social Contract

> Little by little it is being bore in upon us that it's not only life which we have a right to preserve, but there is something more precious which the need of material things may stamp out of the human soul. Therefore it behooves us so to order our civilization that all can live in the security of having the necessities of life, and that each individual according to his abilities and his vision may at the same time preserve his hope for future growth.
>   —Eleanor Roosevelt[133]

For all of its definitional ambiguity, the Declaration of Independence clearly made two promises to the American people—that they would have both the opportunity to govern themselves and craft, on their own terms, a life worth living. For most of the founders, the principle threat to these rights was found in the exercise of arbitrary political power. Certainly the Bill of Rights reflects that concern, given its emphasis on political, and its silence on economic, rights. This makes sense, given the founders' colonial experiences and the seemingly limitless economic possibilities furnished by an empty continent in an agrarian age. Historically, the social contract of the United States interpreted self-governance as the absence of political restraints (our functional definition of liberty), and happiness as the pursuit of wealth and property. There was little need for economic rights, as it was believed that the abundance of land, opportunity, and the mechanics of the market would ensure that opportunity was perpetual, success deserved, and immorality punished. Americans agreed with Thoreau and Sumner, two otherwise very different thinkers, that freedom and happiness were found where government was absent. Contexts change, however, and a reified understanding of rights informed solely by the founding experience cannot speak to the needs of Americans living in an age of industrial (later finance) capitalism. The Great Depression made this clear.

As a response to the Depression, and building off the progressive elements of the liberal tradition, the New Deal sought to reinterpret our understanding of rights and in the process redefine our social contract. New Dealers argued that the rights to life, liberty, and happiness had economic as well as political dimensions, and that unaccountable corporations and markets could tyrannize a people as effectively as any state. Liberty was understood increasingly as a protection FROM as much as protection FOR property, and happiness was redefined as the chance for self-development more than the protection of property (especially capital). Property was a means, not an end, to a more robust understanding of liberty and happiness that owed more to John Stuart Mill than the gospel of wealth.

Underpinning these changes was a new emphasis on security as a foundational right, without which neither liberty nor happiness are substantively possible. While Thomas Hobbes argued in *Leviathan* that security is the condition that makes liberty possible, liberal thought has a tendency to interpret the idea of security narrowly, as protection from physical violence. But in order to secure freedom and happiness, "that broader definition of liberty,"[134] as FDR put it, the state must provide individuals with security, not only from the threats of crime and invasion, but also from the vagaries of an indifferent market and the existential dread derived from economic uncertainty. Finally, this new conception of rights (and the state that guarantees them) needs to address how our individualistic understanding of rights perverts, as Eleanor Roosevelt said, "any actual understanding of what it means to be responsible for one's brother."[135] The preservation of individual rights requires a collective commitment, and if we can no longer rely on one another we must turn to the state.

The New Deal's theoretical importance in the American tradition is derived not only from its conceptualization (and perhaps more importantly, institutionalization) of security as a precondition of happiness, but by attributing to security both material and psychic components. It is not only the presence of scarcity, but apprehension about the future, that must be addressed. We cannot have security while we know fear. Without security we cannot sustain the driving optimism necessary to grow and expand as a people—both in terms of our material development and in our capacity to love one another as citizens, neighbors, fellow members of a great community prepared to protect and defend the rights of one another.

These are exceedingly ambitious goals, and in some of its more millennial moments it was not clear how far the New Deal hoped to push. Wallace, for instance, might begin a campaign speech by declaring, "We believe that in this New World we will build an even newer world, in which there shall be comfort and security, and freedom and dignity for all. We believe that we are destined to create on this newer soil a higher standard of human freedom and a wider distribution of wealth and happiness."[136] But these rhetorical flights were often supplemented by programmatic moments when the New Deal would attempt to use the collective power of society, acting through its government, to minimize to the uncertainty that came from being an individual in a market economy that no longer privileged individuals. This manifested itself in necessarily imperfect concrete proposals—social security, work relief, wages and hours legislation, and the like could never fully bring about the emancipation Wallace prophesized. But they still made a measurable difference in the quality of people's lives. The material benefits were obvious—individuals cannot pursue happiness when they are hungry or homeless—but the significance of the psychic benefits, the preservation of hope and the possibilities of Wallace's "New World," should not be overlooked.

At the most basic level, the New Deal argues that it is necessary to stop the physical and spiritual harm caused by the uncertainty of survival. It is simply unreasonable to expect people who have no idea how they are going to feed their children to be engaged and responsible citizens. But our obligations to each other do not stop at mere survival. As our society grows more sophisticated, so do our needs. Once we have conquered necessity we must look to our self-development and happiness. Critics of the New Deal, and of the welfare state in general, miss the ways in which the social contract is constantly evolving with changed material conditions, the way in which, as Hiram Canton put it, "all mature states are welfare states."[137] Nurturing our potential requires culture, recreation, leisure. Access to diverse experiences is essential if we wish to develop the broad perspective necessary to understand our larger connections to one another, to enhance the realm of experience that makes richer conceptions of social obligation possible.

This move was without question a radical one, as it calls for a revision of how Americans understood the rights that were their inheritance, even the idea of rights themselves. The old laissez-faire, Spencerian interpretation argued that while no one had a right to deny another's happiness,[138] most of us would be preoccupied trying to secure our rights to life and liberty from a hostile world. In this old order our rights were uncertain but precious prizes to struggle to maintain. The New Deal, on the other hand, saw rights as entitlements, expectations that citizens could and should demand that society help them meet. In fact, our allegiance to society is contingent on its ability to guarantee those rights. ER argues, in words remarkable for a First Lady, that:

> [a] civilization and an economic system which does not recognize its responsibility to answer this question of how work at a living wage can be furnished to every individual, should be held in as great contempt as we used to hold the individual who had the attitude that he could go through life effortlessly and expect the world to look after him.[139]

The older social contract was both unsustainable and undesirable. The United States could not survive (and did not deserve to) if it could not become more democratic, which meant living up to the great promises found in its founding documents: the Declaration of Independence and the Constitution. However, The actual body of the Constitution was just machinery, a set of blueprints. Its soul was found in the preamble, and when the New Deal talked about the Constitution, it referred to the promises made by *We The People*, not the mechanisms used for achieving them.[140]

Of special importance is the way that the preamble makes clear the intergenerational nature of our social contract. Even if Jefferson is right and "the earth belongs in usufruct to the living," even if every generation should be allowed to rewrite the rules that govern it, those new rules should never undermine the freedom and possibilities of those that will come in the future. The potential of the present is a product of our collective inheritance. Wallace argued that:

> For the first time in the history of the world, we have here in the United States the possibility of combining into a truly harmonious whole all the prerequisites to the good life. We have the natural resources, the accumulated capital, the democratic traditions, the educational institutions and the agencies for instantaneous communication of ideas...not a single nation is so universally blessed.[141]

Blessed we may be, but that blessing was the product of the dedication, work, toil, and sacrifice of generations past. As such, our obligation to "our Posterity" may even be greater than our obligations to each other, since our descendents have no voice in the creation of the conditions that will govern them. Therefore, it is a moral duty to the future as much as it is to the present to address the systematic inequalities that keep certain classes, ages, races, and regions in perpetual poverty. We must ensure that success is no longer so heavily contingent on the accident of our birth.

The New Deal argues that the spirit of this preamble's mission is eternal, enduring for the life of the nation.[142] The Union will forever be in need of perfecting, the general welfare in need of promotion, the blessings of liberty never permanently secured. Only the material context has changed. We must be reminded of the Preamble's spirit of unity, its commitment to social justice, and its insistence that being an American obligates us to the future as well as the present. This is the central truth of the Constitution, and "[u]nity in the name of the general welfare has all too long been delayed by those who have made the theory of States' rights a refuge for anti-social activity,"[143] enshrining the worst aspects of individualism in constitutional law.

In his essay "The Public Philosophy of the New Freedom and the New Deal,"[144] Charles Kessler highlights the significance of this move, as it brings a different sort of Darwinian interpretation to our founding documents—one emphasizing not the Darwinism of Spencer, but the progressive Darwinism that highlights the impermanence of our conception of rights. While the New Deal would not go so far as to say that natural rights do not exist, by leaving their interpretation subject to changing material conditions, natural rights become something more akin to a process rather than an end, rooted in impermanent moments in time. It requires us, in essence, to take Jefferson's natural rights doctrine and square it with the reality of social evolution. It also highlights the political moment in this whole process. Rights are not transcendent, but are instead products of society—which places the whole political process of framing, defining, and selling a political ideology at front and center. How the electorate chooses to interpret and prioritize our rights to life, liberty, and the pursuit of happiness, how they interpret the Preamble, and most importantly, how political elites act to guide and craft that interpretation, determines their ultimate meaning (for now).

Freedom and Security

> The first who came here to carry out the longings of their spirit, and the millions who followed, and the stock that sprang from them—all have moved forward constantly and consistently toward an ideal which in itself has gained stature and clarity with each generation.
>
> —Franklin Roosevelt[145]

The New Deal's liberalism is not the Hobbesian (or even Lockean) liberalism of fear. It self-consciously sets itself against uncertainty and scarcity, articulating a liberalism for times of potential and plenty; defiantly sticking to this message at even the darkest moments of the Depression. While accepting that people form governments for security, the New Deal understood that expectations change over time and we may come to look for more from government than the protection of life and property. We come to view a serious opportunity to pursue happiness as an entitlement. The opportunity for self-development becomes a basic human right. This creates a rich set of obligations for democratic governments. They must guarantee their citizens education, a home, a living wage, health care, and the opportunity to develop talents not strictly essential for survival, but vital for individual development. A life without recreation, without joy, is not a free life. As ER defines it:

Freedom from want means being sure that if you want to work, you can get a job and that that job will pay you sufficiently to give you and your family a decent standard of living. A decent standard of living means that your shelter shall be adequate for healthful living, that your food shall be adequate and of the kind which will keep your family and yourself in good physical condition; that you shall have medical care as needed, by some something which your government may agree on; and that there shall be a margin of income to provide the necessary clothing, educational, and recreational need.[146]

We have a right not only to food, but healthy food. We have a right not only to clothing and education but free time. Without these things we cannot say we are secure. We certainly cannot call ourselves free. Freedom requires a degree of material *and* mental security, a basic level of protection from the constraints imposed by necessity and fear.

While the New Deal's definition focuses on the individual's experience of freedom, New Deal theorists also concerned themselves explicitly with the relationship between individual freedom and the health of the larger community. The New Deal recognized from the beginning that no democratic restoration was possible without first addressing the sense of fear and powerlessness that had dampened the optimism that is the source of American strength. A healthy state is one whose people are capable of love, trust, solidarity, and hope, and the Depression demonstrated both the fragility of any society that refused to institutionalize the protection of its citizens and the limits of our reservoir of optimism and faith in democracy—which is to say faith in each other and faith in ourselves.

We had long been a people accustomed to movement, even after the census bureau formally declared the frontier closed. Even in times of hardship there was a sense of optimism invested in the possibilities of travel and relocation. If things are tough at home they are bound to be better elsewhere. "Go west, young man." But as Irving Bernstein notes in *A Caring Society*, the pervading sentiment behind migration in the 1930s was not hope but despair. "Folks migrated not so much because they expected life to be better elsewhere, but because they could no longer bear to stay at home."[147] The country fled from the very idea of commitment and community. Marriage and birth rates fell. As one man described it, "you lived in fear of responsibility for another person. You backed off when someone got close."[148] The strain on traditional families was pronounced. Men were loath to go home and confront the hungry faces that indicted their performance as a provider and as a man.[149]

In particular there was concern for a 'stranded generation.' Reporter Lorena Hickok, agent of Harry Hopkins and confidant of Eleanor Roosevelt, took to the road to chronicle for the WPA the circumstances of the unemployed. She worried most about "Men between 40 and 55, with families growing up—children in grade school, children in high school. Children growing up in families whose father isn't ever going to get his job back. Children growing up 'on relief'..."[150] Here we see one generation embittered and despairing, another growing up without the propulsive optimism that fuels a non-adversarial democracy. An orientation towards scarcity encourages you to grasp what you can before others take it in your stead. An orientation towards scarcity in a time of scarcity (whether artificial or real) will quickly turn a people into the kinds of scavengers that undermine a democratic state. As one victim of the depression described the times:

> You were a predator. You had to be. The coyote is crafty. He can be fantastical-ly courageous and a coward at the same time...I grew up where they were hated, 'cause they'd kill sheep...They're mean. But how else does a coyote stay live? He's not as powerful as a wolf. He has a small body. He's in such bad condition, a dog can run him down. He's not like a fox. A coyote is nature's victims as well as man's. We were coyote's in the thirties, the jobless.[151]

This was the situation confronting the New Deal—the destruction of the habits and mores of a free people—a nation "dying by inches."[152] And it was the obli-gation of the society, acting through its government, to address the sense of des-pair and fear, and replace it with the security and hope that make liberty, happi-ness, and democracy both meaningful and possible.

The New Deal understood all too well what was at stake. As Roosevelt ex-plained in a fireside chat, "Democracy has disappeared in several nations not because the people of those nations disliked democracy, but because they had grown tired of seeing their children hungry while they sit helpless in the face of government confusion and government weakness."[153] The precondition of free-dom is security. This can be traced back to the proto-liberalism of Thomas Hobbes, but Hobbes' arguments about physical security largely ignored eco-nomic security. Roosevelt's central claim was that 'freedom' is freedom in name only when people are uncertain about their future. We cannot have mea-ningful freedom without conquering both the reality of necessity and our fear of it. Therefore, the state needs:

> to try to increase the security and happiness of a larger number of people in all occupations of life and in all parts of the country; to give them more of the good things of life, to give them a greater distribution not only of wealth in the narrow terms, but of wealth in the wider terms; to give them places to go in the summertime—recreation; to give them assurances that they are not going to starve in their old age; to give honest business a chance to go ahead and make a reasonable profit, and to give everyone a chance to earn a living.[154]

Society, acting through the machinery of the state, must provide the security (social insurance, wage and hours laws, educational assistance, leisure time, recreational outlets) necessary to make the pursuit of happiness genuinely possi-ble for an ever-expanding number of Americans.

Given his liberal faith in progress, it is not surprising that five lines into his first inaugural address, FDR emphasized that "the only thing we have to fear is fear itself—nameless, unreasoning, unjustified terror which paralyzes needed efforts to convert retreat into advance."[155] In a land of abundance, as opposed to scarcity, human agency is limited primarily by its own self-doubt. In many ways, the crisis facing Americans during the Depression was an existential one. We had lost faith in our economic system, we had lost faith in the American dream, and, because these were always such critical aspects of our identity, we had lost faith in ourselves. Progress would be indefinitely stalled without a restoration of that faith. There is much that conspires against the expansion of liberty, but the principal threats are the fear and ignorance that follow in the wake of the loss of faith, the despair wrought by privation.

The most famous articulation of the New Deal's conception of a just society is arguably found in Roosevelt's "Four Freedoms"—which, FDR is careful to point out, are not simply an American entitlement, but "four essential human freedoms" that must be protected "everywhere in the world." The first two, freedom of speech and freedom to worship, are classical liberal values that need no further discussion here.[156] The third, freedom from want, is something new, a right for every nation to enjoy "a healthy peacetime life for its inhabitants."[157] This goes beyond freedom of opportunity. Instead, it implies that freedom means knowing not only that our necessities are met, but also that we can all share in the abundance that is the promise of American Life. Norman Rockwell's famous "Freedom From Want" painting shows a happy, middle-class family sitting down to enjoy a large meal in comfort together. "Freedom From Want" captured the imagination of the American people and articulated the vision of the New Deal—a society in which every family could enjoy a meal like this, whose health was measured by the number of people with the means and leisure to sit around the table and share that moment. Abundance was not simply the presence of material goods, but the possibility of experiencing them with friends and neighbors. One is left with the impression, viewing the painting, that the company is the most important component of the meal.

It is significant that absent from this formulation is "Freedom of Commerce" or "Freedom of Enterprise." Instead of being a foundational freedom in itself, the benefits of commerce and capitalism are bound up in its ability to address want. Business lost its privileged place at the top of our social hierarchy. We are a long way from Calvin Coolidge's declaration that business "is one of the greatest contributing forces to the moral and spiritual advancement of the race."[158] Freedom from want is represented strictly through its social dimension, through the advantages it gives to the consumer, or the family rather than the businessman, and it is this move, this existential challenge to the pride of place business had enjoyed in American life, more than any other cause, that accounts for the virulent hostility of the business community towards the New Deal

The fourth and final freedom is freedom from fear. A mother lovingly adjusts the blankets covering her two sleeping children, while their father gazes upon their bed with affection. All is well, but the newspaper in father's hand indicates that somewhere bombs are dropping, and this gives the scene a touching fragility. Rockwell's visual interpretation was obviously colored by the war. However, one could just as easily imagine the father looking down on his children wondering where the money will come to feed and clothe them, to keep them healthy and to keep the roof over their head. In either case the threat is a psychic one. Fear limits freedom because it limits our sense of possibility. When we know fear, when we lack security, we are unable to take advantage of our human capacities to dream, to better ourselves, and to seek our own visions of happiness—in short, to be truly free. This was a dangerous, transformative notion in a society whose official position on risk was more in line with Irene du Pont, who argued that "Men are by nature speculators, and Nature enforces the necessity of speculation on all of us."[159]

We have a right, the New Deal claims, to "a reasonable measure of security." Without security for our family and ourselves, we can never cast aside the anxieties standing in the way of happiness. The New Deal's liberalism never guarantees happiness, but society has a moral obligation to provide the security so that every individual can make a real attempt to achieve it. Without the guarantee of certain basic material needs (the right to have a job, the right to food and shelter, and later, the right to health care and, if so desired, an advanced education—first established with the GI Bill) the "pursuit of happiness" is hollow. The protection of our rights calls for more than an umpire or a broker state. It requires constructive aid to those most in need of help and a commitment from society, acting through the state, to foster the right of all citizens to pursue their own path to happiness, free from fear. It demands in short, a new set of economic rights to supplement our established political rights.

The New Rights of the New Deal

We have accepted, so to speak, a second Bill of Rights under which a new basis of security and prosperity can be established for all—regardless of station, race, or creed.

—Franklin Roosevelt[160]

Although it would use a utilitarian standpoint to address competing rights claims, especially in regards to property, the New Deal framed economic and social reforms as a question of rights, obligations the individual could impose on his larger community. What are needed are a set of economic rights to parallel our political rights, to recognize that the emancipatory role once played by unregulated economic power has ended, just as the absolute monarch eventually outlived its own usefulness. And, paralleling the development of political freedom, the first requirement of economic freedom is economic security. In *Leviathan*, Hobbes argued that all political rights are dependent first on physical security, which the sovereign is expected to provide. When we fear for our lives, we cannot be free. Likewise, we cannot actively pursue happiness if we live in constant fear of economic uncertainty.

The Liberty League, the premiere coalition of Roosevelt haters, tried to frame things differently. In their eyes, they were the great defenders of liberty (in particular, property rights), protecting our "right to work, earn, save and acquire property" from the tyranny of Roosevelt.[161] However, their classical understanding of liberalism was, temporarily, in decline. Property rights and the protection of profits were no longer sacrosanct. Liberty now meant something very different, as Roosevelt made clear responding to the criticisms of the League.

> There is no mention made here in these two things [property and profits] about the concern of the community, in other words, the government, to try and make it possible for people who are willing to work, to find work to do. For people who want to keep themselves from starvation, keep a roof over their heads, lead decent lives, have proper educational standards, those are the concerns of Government…another thing which isn't mentioned is the protection of life and liberty of the individual against the elements in the community which seek to enrich or advance themselves at the expense of their fellow citizens. They have just as much right to protection by government as anybody else.[162]

This was a direct challenge to the older, laissez-faire understanding of liberalism, with its reactionary fear of any positive government involvement in economic life beyond facilitating private investment. The New Deal attempted to change our understanding of rights—to move beyond formal political rights and recognize that we can be tyrannized in the economic realm as surely as in the political, that we can have our rights violated by what we lack as surely as by what is deliberately taken away. The right to work becomes as important as the right to vote. Economic democracy serves as the precondition for political democracy, and political democracy is the only way to guarantee economic democracy. The two realms are intimately connected. 'Natural rights' include the right to food, shelter, and safety from economic predation. In the end, moreover, freedom was no longer something naturally conferred upon us, but something that needed to be guaranteed through collective social force, checked by democratic and constitutional procedures. Society in turn was morally obligated to guarantee those rights for an ever-expanding number of its citizens.[163]

Some of FDR's strongest statements on new rights came long after the active phase of the New Deal had ended, when "Dr. Win the War" would come to, at least temporarily, eclipse "Dr. New Deal." In his 'Four Freedoms' State of the Union address of 1941, he reminded an American audience the New Deal stood for "basic things that must never be lost sight of in the turmoil and unbelievable complexity of our modern world."[164]

Equal opportunity for youth and for others.
Jobs for those who can work.
Security for those who need it.
The ending of special privileges for the few.
The preservation of civil liberties for all.
The enjoyment of the fruits of scientific progress in a wider and constantly rising standard of living.[165]

With the end of the war finally in sight, and reconstruction on his mind, Roosevelt sought to return the New Deal to a position of prominence within his administration, his 1944 State of the Union address the trumpet blast signaling its return.[166] Here we find concrete recognition that while freedom may be an inalienable right, without protection it means nothing. FDR's remarkable Second Bill of Rights is nothing short of a redefinition of the American social contract.[167] These rights include:

> The right to a useful and remunerative job in the industries or shops or farms or mines of the Nation;
> The right to earn enough to provide adequate food and clothing and recreation;
> The right of every farmer to raise and sell his products at a return which will give him and his family a decent living;
> The right of every businessman, large and small, to trade in an atmosphere of freedom from unfair competition and domination by monopolies at home or abroad;
> The right of every family to a decent home;
> The right to adequate medical care and the opportunity to achieve and enjoy good health;
> The right to adequate protection from the economic fears of old age, sickness, accident, and unemployment;
> The right to a good education.[168]

The scope of the list is staggering: rights to employment, a living wage, food, clothing, recreation and leisure time, health care, housing, education.[169] As Roosevelt points out "[a]ll of these rights spell security. And after this war is won we must be prepared to move forward, in the implementation of these rights, to new goals of human happiness and well-being."[170] With his Second Bill of Rights, the right to economic security becomes as essential to democracy as the rights to conscience and due process. Democracy, especially liberal democracy, functions only when it is able to provide for the material needs of its citizens. If it fails to do so, it breeds either the passivity of the subject rather than the fire of the citizen, or—possibly worse—the anger and fear that fuels revolution.

The right to property, the proverbial elephant in the room, remains, but the New Deal redefines it in terms of security. When the rights of the speculator or financier come up against the need of people to have security against old age, sickness, and unemployment, the right of security trumps the freedom to speculate and the right to hoard, for without that security, substantive expansions of liberty become impossible.

> It is important, of course, that every man and woman in the country be able to find work, that every factory run, that business as a whole earn profits. But government in a democratic nation does not exist solely, or ever primarily, for that purpose... It is not enough that the wheels turn. They must carry us in the direction of a greater satisfaction in the life for the average man. The deeper

purpose of democratic government is to *assist* as many of its citizens as possible—especially those who need it most—to improve their conditions of life, to retain all personal liberty which does not adversely affect their neighbors, and to pursue the happiness which comes with security and an opportunity for recreation and culture.[171]

Roosevelt's use of the word 'assist' here is instructive. The New Deal never abandoned the liberal belief that private choices, when meaningfully available, are usually less coercive and more preferable than public ones. But when needs cannot be met through private channels, society has a moral obligation to give people what they need to make their pursuit of happiness possible. That is the "deeper purpose of democratic government."[172]

For a few reasons, perhaps most importantly the political costs inherent in the process, the New Deal did not seek to formally enshrine these rights in the Constitution. Its focus, as Cass Sunstein argues, was on the creation of constitutive commitments, a fundamental change of basic expectations that would inform subsequent politics despite a lack of constitutional grounding.[173] Nevertheless, many of these rights were at least partially instituted through New Deal programs—Social Security provided a guarantee of minimum assistance, minimum wages attempted to ensure that workers could make a living, and the GI Bill greatly expanded the opportunity for Americans to go to college.[174] Housing programs existed to assist families in acquiring a decent home. And while health care was killed in part due to the opposition of the AMA, future generations would be offered partial guarantees through Medicare and Medicaid.[175]

The Right to Work

We must and do assume that the bulk of mankind who are able to work are willing to work, and that they will strive for something more than a doghouse subsistence on a dole.
—From *Security Work, and Relief Policies*[176]

It is worth spending at least a little time examining two of the central components of the Second Bill of Rights in greater detail—the right to work and the right to an education (bound up with the right to leisure). A 1935 poll indicated that, amongst respondents classified as poor, 90 percent felt the government should guarantee work to those who want it.[177] The New Deal embraced this view, seeing the work not as an act of charity, but as a right of citizenship. The language used in the Second Bill of Rights is instructive—"The right to a useful and remunerative job in the industries or shops or farms or mines of the Nation." This formulation is significant not simply for its standard emphasis on the utility of work, but for its claim that opportunities for work are not merely the possession of private individuals, but the collective property of the nation. As such, the nation, acting through its democratic machinery, could take steps to ensure that all people had employment. This employment was essential to both the mental and physical health of the nation. Roosevelt argues that the right to work matters for its 'moral and spiritual values' as much as for the wage it provides. Workers agreed. As Anthony Badger notes, "employment gave workers many of the values they cherished, status vis-à-vis their fellows, economic security, and a reputation as a good provider. The goal of the unemployed was to restore those values. A job would give them control of their own fate and restore their reputation for providing economic security for their families."[178] Work, even wage work, inculcates a sense of responsibly, obligation, and agency, if not autonomy. It enables us to contribute something positive to the community, to give back to the society from which we receive both tangible and intangible benefits. Without work, FDR argues, we feel that we lack value, that we are a drain on society.[179] "To dole our relief...is to administer a narcotic, a subtle destroyer of the human spirit...Work must be found for able-bodied but destitute workers."[180] Work provides us with the self-esteem necessary to begin to think past ourselves and look towards our larger community. As Susan Faludi argues in *Stiffed,* this is at the core of the American understanding of masculinity, as we have long been a culture that honored its builders, valuing those able to create "something tangible that was essential to a larger mission."[181] The New Deal understood the symbolic power that the idea of work (and through work contribution and sacrifice) had for Americans, especially males.[182] Without a job we quickly lose the vitality and sense of worth that make society dynamic and (potentially) progressive.

In this view Roosevelt was far from alone. ER was at the forefront of the fight to offer jobs to the unemployed, rather than the dole. Even on relief, people need work that makes them feel useful and, when possible, nurtures specific talents. Those fortunate enough to have meaningful work should have that work protected. People with sophisticated skills needed sophisticated employment. And for people who lacked basic skills it was vitally important that the government include some aspect of vocational training alongside relief.[183] Even the existence of a simple job was often enough to restore a sense of self-worth to a dispirited person. Frances Perkins tells a story of a near deaf, elderly lawyer, trained at Harvard but unable to find work during the depression. He was given a job with the Works Progress Administration acting as a caretaker at a small seaside park. He took great pride in his work and tearfully asked Perkins to pass along his thanks to Roosevelt for "an honorable occupation that made him feel useful and not like a bum and derelict."[184] His relief job kept him off the dole, granting him dignity and a chance to serve his community. The history of the New Deal is replete with similar stories.

While the New Deal rejected the idea that poverty was normally a result of character flaws, it worried that receiving public assistance could have an enervating effect on the sense of worth and initiative of the recipient. Hence the emphasis placed on work relief, and the fact that relief jobs paid better than the dole (and less than private industry).[185] Work relief was superior because it allowed the recipient to do something active and constructive with his time—to both give back to his community and give back to himself. The Federal Art, Writing, and Theater projects reflect the New Deal's commitment here. Out-of-work artists and performers had their own unique sets of skills, and needed to eat as much as anyone else. The result was both a flourishing and a democratization of art, moving it out of the museum and into the Post Office.[186] However, reflecting its liberal commitments and cognizant of the ideological sensitivities of the citizens it served, the New Deal believed federal employment should always be designed to avoid interfering with functioning private industry. The government should act as an employer of last resort, but private employment was better, because even beneficial government programs, as an option of last resort, could not help but be at least slightly paternalistic and a potential source of arbitrary power.[187] This was the logic behind the use of 'security wages' in government relief work. Wages had to be high enough so that families could be supported, but lower than the wages of private employment.

As the economy responded to war mobilization these programs were gradually discontinued by a hostile Congress, and have never returned. There was an attempt to institute a comprehensive plan for "full employment" after the war, centered around the National Resources Planning Board and its report *Security, Work, and Relief Policies*. As Alan Brinkley notes, "To many liberals, the document became something close to a programmatic bible; to conservatives, it was evidence of the generously statist designs of the NRPD and the New Deal as a whole."[188] However, the conservative view won the day, as "the NRPB fell victim to the frenzied efforts by conservatives in Congress—Democrats and Republicans both—to use the war to dismantle as much of the New Deal as possible."[189]

The closest thing we have today to a universal right to work is the unemployment insurance component of Social Security, and even these benefits can be subject to political gamesmanship.[190] The promise of a right to work remains largely unfulfilled. But while the New Deal ultimately failed to supplant the structural dominance of capital in American society, it nevertheless succeeded at least instituting a degree of "cradle to grave" security.[191] If it could not guarantee a right to work, it could at least protect workers "against some of the costs of the accident of not having any job at all."[192] However, the Serviceman Readjustment Act (which the American Legion coined the G.I. Bill of Rights) offered a tantalizing glimpse into what could have been. The G.I. Bill of Rights, "one of the most expansive social programs in American history," offered unemployment and pension benefits, educational assistance, job placement assistance, health care, and low cost loans—in short, it represented most of what the New Deal had hoped to offer all Americans after the war.[193] But it failed to expand the way Social Security did. This reflected both the strength of the old folklore. The G.I. Bill "reinforced invidious distinctions between 'deserving' and undeserving citizens and sustained the popular belief that public generosity should be reserved for those with a special claim to public attention."[194] It was the sacrifice of the soldier, rather than their status as citizens, which justified the benefits.

This in turn made it difficult to argue that the bill should serve as a model for a more generous welfare state, despite the tremendous success of its programs.

The Right to Education

> Learning to be a good citizen is learning to live to the maximum of one's abilities and opportunities, and every subject should be taught every child with this in view.
>
> —Eleanor Roosevelt[195]

As the failure to expand the GI Bill made clear, there would be limits to what the New Deal could institutionalize as long as Americans clung to parochial identities, an inflated sense of their own independence, and a view of the world colored by our old folklore. To that end, there was arguably no new right more important than the right to an education, broadly understood—a right that helped preserve and strengthen the constitutive commitments that constituted the New Deal's social contract.

There is an obvious material value to education—the connection between education and remunerative work has been long established, and programs like the National Youth Administration provided useful job training to students in need. But this was not the only focus of the New Deal's emphasis on our right to education, nor was it necessarily the most important. Instead, the New Deal privileged its social aspects—that through education we foster citizenship, self-development, and awareness of our interconnective unity that grounds a truly democratic society. As ER argued, "the true purpose of education is to produce citizens."[196] In her biography of ER, Ruby Black notes "her conviction that people can, if they are informed, really solve their problems,"[197] a conviction shared by most prominent New Deal theorists. Injustice is as much a function of ignorance as it is interest or intent, a lack of understanding that can be fixed through exposure to new ideas and experiences. Certainly this was indicative of FDR's personal biography. As Jean Smith points out, it was "[f]rom the poor people of Merriweather County, [that] Franklin learned what it meant to be without electricity and running water; for children to be without shoes and adequate clothing; for a simple grade school education to be beyond the reach of many who lived in the hardscrapple backwoods."[198] As such, the New Deal defines education in the broadest possible terms. Anything that enables us to draw connections between ourselves and the people around us is educational, and the lessons learned from interaction with and exposure to difference is among the most valuable of these experiences. Our education as citizens is a lifelong process, and the just (democratic) society will provide ample opportunities for that education, and the leisure to take advantage of them.[199]

The primary knowledge needed to be a good citizen is an understanding of our social interconnectivity, awareness of the reality of other people's sufferings, and the way that this suffering diminishes us morally and materially. Without this knowledge:

we will be unable to move forward except as we have moved in the past with recourse to force, and constant, suspicious watchfulness on the part of individuals and groups towards each other. The preservation of our civilization seems to demand a permanent change of attitude and therefore every effort should be bent towards bringing about this change in human nature through education.[200]

The very survival of the United States will therefore require a reprioritizing of values on the part of its members towards an understanding of an individual's social origins, a politics predicated on abundance rather than fear, and recognition of the new obligations these relationships entail.

It is through the process of education that we come to know ourselves— who we are and the kind of a world we want to build. It is through the opportunities and exposure that an education provides that we can come to understand, love and care for a larger community that was once strange, unfamiliar, even hostile. Participation in that community is essential, as it is how we come to develop our shared humanity, acknowledge injustice, and generate the commitment to oppose it through the defense of the New Deal's economic rights

The Forgotten

> [R]egardless of station, race, or creed.
> —Franklin Roosevelt.[201]

The ambitions of the New Deal were potentially staggering, especially when one accounts for the scope of inclusion. In his 1944 State of the Union Address FDR argues:

> We cannot be content, no matter how high that general standard of living may be, if some fraction of our people—whether it be one-third or one-fifth or one-tenth—is ill-fed, ill-clothed, ill-housed, and insecure[202]

The limits to what the New Deal was able to institutionalize are very real, and glaringly inadequate in certain areas. We will examine in subsequent chapters the sources of these inadequacies, but the existence of political limitations does not change the fact that, as a set of principles, the New Deal aimed to be expansive. Its social contract was written to include the excluded, to make space within its programs and certainly within its theory, for women, minorities, the dispossessed, and the young. The standard through which our social contract is to be measured and judged is its ability to secure its promised rights for all citizens, and the failures of the Roosevelt administration's policy can be critiqued from within the framework of New Deal theory, provided one accepts its assumption of liberal universalism—that within this framework it is possible for groups currently alienated from the 'American Dream' to both air grievances and be integrated in meaningful and satisfying ways.

In part for political reasons, in part as a question of commitment, and certainly as a matter of temperament, ER was at the forefront of the New Deal on these issues.[203] She sought to draw attention to those the Depression ripped from the social fabric of America and those who had been abandoned long before the 1929 crash. In defiance of prevailing American folklore, she sought to remind "many unthinking people that the unemployed are not a strange race. They are like we would be if we had not had a fortunate chance at life."[204] ER believed this dismissive attitude towards the marginalized is ultimately a product of ignorance, and she worked diligently to publicize the plight of the forgotten. Whenever possible she sought to expose people to the desperate living conditions of the truly poor.[205] She traveled thousands of miles drawing attention to the deep, feudal poverty some Americans were mired in.[206] A companion on one of these trips offered her "any money you want" to help address the issue provided he never had to go back and confront those conditions again.[207] A particularly striking story, told often by ER, involved a little boy's pet bunny.

> It was evident it was a most cherished pet. The little girl was thin and scrawny, and had a gleam in her eyes as she looked at her brother. Turning to me she said: "he thinks we are not going to eat it, but we are," and at that the small boy fled down the road clutching the rabbit closer than ever.[208]

Stories about parents who could only give their children raw carrots to chew on during Christmas and families who could not send their children to school because they could not afford clothes became the subject of press conferences, magazine articles, newspaper columns, and public addresses. ER worked tirelessly to expose the conditions some American citizens were forced to endure, to put a human face on poverty and turn an abstract problem into a personal tragedy. It was, as was so often the case, a question of education. This kind of hideous poverty can exist only insofar as it is kept hidden, or if we utilize folklore that allows us to distance ourselves from these circumstances.

Part of the New Deal's concern was a basic moral outrage which led ER to declare "we simply cannot sit back and say 'all people cannot live decent lives.'"[209] Beyond that basic commitment, dealing with America's stranded is essential for the sake of democracy. Democracy requires trust, and that trust is undermined by the fear born of poverty.[210] ER reminds us that "[y]ou can develop an interest in the community as a whole when you take away the dread of desperate want, the terror, insecurity, that these people had before...only when you have a little security do you have time to think of your neighbor.[211] It is only possible to care about a community when the fear caused by want and privation is eliminated. It is exceedingly difficult to create attachments while they are present.[212]

Although New Deal caseworkers and researchers generated statistical ammunition for some causes, and shined a light on what was previously hidden, at the most basic level, addressing poverty did not require reports or studies—people had a right to have a minimum amount of security in exchange for their labor.[213] Anyone who worked had a right to "receive in return for their labor, at least a minimum of security and happiness in life. They must have enough to eat, warmth, adequate clothing, decent shelter and an opportunity for education."[214] Any civilization that does not grant this basic right to its citizens should be regarded with contempt, and any failure to rectify this situation is inviting revolution.[215] ER warns "no civilization can possibly survive which does not furnish every individual who wishes to work a job at wages on which he can live decently."[216] Although perhaps a touch melodramatic, the New Deal did see itself as an attempt, if not to save American civilization from extinction, certainly to salvage its conscience and decency.

In the eyes of the New Deal, while this kind of desperate poverty was without a doubt a testament to the failures of our society to distribute its abundance, there is a sense in which these people had already been permanently lost. Alleviating their condition represents a moral imperative, but it lacked the political urgency that animated the concern for those found in the ranks of the newly dispossessed, those not yet so destroyed by poverty to have lost the capacity to demand the restoration of what was taken.

Youth posed a different sort of problem. During the years 1933 to 1940 there were between three and four and a half million Americans under the age of twenty-one unemployed, let alone the millions more who found themselves underemployed.[217] Here was an entire cohort quickly losing faith in their democracy, and ER confessed to "moments of real terror when I think we may be losing this generation. We have got to bring these young people into the active life of the community and make them feel that they are necessary."[218] When the fear caused by the Great Depression caused most Americans to retreat into themselves and their own needs, she became one of the primary advocates for an entire generation of American youth.

The problems facing the young (from the standpoint of the New Deal's democratic theory) were twofold. Their basic physical needs must be addressed, but they also had to be integrated back into the public life of their communities. They needed purpose as much as they needed relief, and they needed it soon. Young people had to be convinced that their problems could be solved democratically. Otherwise their feeling of powerlessness and alienation caused by the Depression might remain with them the rest of their lives, and those not resigned to a lack of agency might look outside our traditions for redress. Perhaps revolution was not quite in the air, but it was on the horizon.

Such was the logic behind service-oriented programs like the CCC and NYA.[219] The CCC, FDR noted, "can eliminate the threat that enforced idleness brings to spiritual and moral stability,"[220] and Jean Smith claims it "literally gave 3 million young men a new lease on life."[221] The NYA, in turn, gave "less privileged youth...at least a measure of participation in the economic, social, and educational life of an era which frequently seems to have no place for them."[222] The New Deal believed in the educational value of a year (or two) of public service—it would satisfy, as ER claimed, "certain things for which youth craves—the chance for self sacrifice for an ideal."[223] Engaging in public service employment and non-profit work would provide them with the practical exposure to new places and people necessary for a democratic worldview. "They should learn the meaning of citizenship in a democracy and should feel that they are obtaining some valuable experience in citizenship, and contributing to the well being of the nation during the period of service."[224] The process would hopefully develop both a feeling of commitment to the idea of democracy and attachment to the people in it.

However, there were limits to what the state could ask of its young, especially military service, without first giving them a more meaningful stake in society. As war became increasingly likely as the world fell apart in the 1930's, the problem of youthful disaffection became even more prominent. As ER argued,

> When we have given them nothing to live for, why should we expect them to be happy when we suddenly ask them to be willing to die?...We have not made democracy work so they can find their place in it. Why should they feel a responsibility for defending it until we prove it is worth defending?[225]

Adults, ER argued, bore responsibility for the disaffection of the young. They created the world that allowed the Depression, and were in violation of their half of the intergenerational social contract. Certainly they had no right to be "self-righteous and dogmatic" given how little they learned from World War I.[226] Youth were a group that demanded engagement. It was essential that the generations maintain "a free intellectual interchange of ideas between themselves."[227] Since both groups inhabit the world at the same time, both are entitled to some say in its construction and administration. She worried that her own generation was abdicating their half of that responsibility.

> We have made the world such as it is today, and we had better face the fact that at least youth has a right to ask from us an honest acceptance of our responsibility, a study of their problems, cooperation with them in their efforts to find a solution, and patience in trying to understand their point of view and stating our own.[228]

Instead of facing their obligations to the young, her generation instead fixated on the anger of the youth movement, feeding the anti-communist sentiment of the time.[229] Again there were real limits to what could be done for the young in practice, but what is of importance here is both the theoretical commitment, and the way the New Deal used the frames of stewardship (we have obligations to those who will be inheriting the world we are creating) and citizenship to conceptualize the problem. A democracy needs to ensure that all of its citizens have both a stake in society, and the tools they need to engage it. There is recognition that the bonds which unite us are tenuous, and that taking them for granted invites the real possibility of democratic failure, an entire generation either disengaged from or openly hostile to their society and its governing contract.

ER in particular also addressed the role of women in the framework of our social contract. Consistent with the New Deal's emphasis on inclusion and universality, as well as its tendency to reduce social issues to economic issues, we find little emphasis on the particularities of the experience of women, of any unique needs they might have. Her primary concern was to clear away their barriers for self-development, which meant emphasizing the right of women to be independent. This, in turn, given the economic emphasis of the New Deal, meant the right to work. "There are three fundamentals for human happiness," ER claims, "work which will produce at least a minimum of material security, love, and faith. These things must be made possible for all human beings, men and women."[230] While the Great Depression did not necessarily eliminate love and faith from the lives of Americans, it certainly created serious barriers for women who wished (or had) to work. Wages plummeted even more steeply for women than they did for men, and they were already making half as much. What's more, the one solution to the Depression that seemed to unite the country was that married women should be denied jobs so men could work. George Gallup reported that he never saw people "so solidly united in opposition as on any subject imaginable, including sin and hay fever."[231] Many even blamed the presence of women in the workforce for the Depression itself. Magazine editor Norman Cousins argued that the cure to the Depression was to "simply fire the women, who shouldn't be working anyway, and hire the men. Presto! No unemployment. No relief rolls. No depression,"[232] a scheme admirable for its elegant simplicity, if nothing else. The Economy Act of 1932 mandated that when a married couple was employed by the Federal Government the wife should be fired first whenever the workforce had to be reduced. As late as 1939, over half the state legislatures debated similar bills, although only Louisiana's passed. Married female teachers were often forced to quit.[233]

Given the pride of place work has in the pantheon of American virtues, it is not surprising that many women felt they needed to be able to work in order to feel like productive citizens.

> The fact that in our particular civilization the contribution of a human being is often gauged by the money which he can earn is probably one of the reasons why both men and women who do not have to earn a living still want to prove that what they do is worthy of receiving the reward by which success is ordinarily judged.[234]

But more was at stake than status or public judgment. Work was a psychic necessity. It represented freedom and provided security.

> Every human being has to earn his living or life has no savor. You may be fortunate to have the dollars you need for existence, but to earn a living means a great deal more than that. To earn a living a human being

must have a sense that he is making a creative contribution to the world around him.[235]

For some women (especially those in ER's circles) the problem was less a question of survival and more a matter of existential meaning. For many women, ER argued, raising a family provides them with all the self-satisfaction they need, but every woman is different, and some will find that their personal needs steer them towards paid work.[236]

Privileging the undifferentiated liberal universalism that informed so much of the New Deal, ER's goal was to make sure that all people had the opportunity to decide for themselves who they were and how they planned to contribute to their society. It was the place of the individuals involved, and not social norms, to determine what was necessary for a happy and fulfilling life. Women are no different. She posed the following questions to her *My Day* readers. "Who is to say when a man earns enough to support his family? Who is to say whether a woman needs to work outside her home for the good of her own soul?"[237] Central to the New Deal's thinking on equality was the belief that people had to answer these questions themselves. Society, at any level, could not impose the answer, but it was obligated to furnish those who wanted to work with the opportunity to do so.

Arguably there were no groups more permanently alienated from the previous social contract than blacks. The New Deal's awareness and appreciation of the problem of racism was slow to develop. It posed a particularly thorny problem for the New Deal, as any attempt to address it threatened to wreck the entire New Deal political coalition, and with it the chance to institutionalize a welfare state. Still, questions of racial justice were raised, and ER was one of the most prominent civil rights advocate in the New Deal, and as Harvard Sitkoff wrote, "no individual did more to alter the relationship between the New Deal and the cause of Civil Rights and ER's 'we go ahead together'...became a rallying cry." Nevertheless, there was definitely a degree of racism she was prepared to tolerate as a practical matter, as she thought there was no way to change hearts and minds other than the slow process of socialization. The New Deal drew distinctions between social equality and political/legal equality. The former could and must be cured through education and exposure, but this would take a long time.[238] The government had a formal obligation to impose the later as rapidly as possible.

The moral hypocrisy of a caste system in a democracy was particularly offensive to the New Deal, as was the notion that we should derive our principal identity from race rather than more universal categories like consumers, or, ideally, citizens. The problem of racism was the denial of democratic citizenship. As long as there is segregation, and as long as the benefits of community life and citizenship are denied to blacks, there can be no democracy.

We can have no group beaten down, underprivileged without reaction on the rest....We must learn to work together, all of us regardless of race, creed, or color. We must wipe out the feeling of intolerance wherever we find it, of belief that any one group can go ahead alone.[239]

The belief that racial prejudice diminished both whites and blacks can be traced back to Jefferson's *Notes on the State of Virginia*.[240] Both sides have not only a moral obligation but also a tangible interest in addressing the problem of racial intolerance in order to preserve democratic citizenship.

> The menace today to a democracy is unthinking action, action which comes from people who are illiterate, who are unable to understand what is happening in the world at large, what is happening in their own country, and who therefore act without really having any knowledge of the meaning of their actions, and that is the thing that we, whatever our race is, should be guarding against today.[241]

Racism is not compatible with an engaged and informed citizenry, or with a cosmopolitan sensibility. But the New Deal recognized that this democratic appeal alone was not sufficient.

To whites ER 'preached' that discrimination is inhumane, immoral, and undemocratic, and at a material level weakened the foundations of the nation. Not only did it stunt the moral growth of the racist, but also stifled the economic development of the region. On both counts, the burden was on whites to change, even if it caused serious upheaval in the southern power structure.[242] The intergenerational social compact means that whites have to accept responsibility for slavery's legacy, even if it was difficult for a generation not directly responsible to bear that burden. Although whites "are suffering from a difficult situation and it is always hard on the individuals who reap the results of generations of wrong doing..."

> ...We brought them here as slaves and we have never given them equal chances of reeducation, even after we emancipated them. They must be given the opportunity to become the kind of people that they should, and I often marvel that they are as good as they are in view of the treatment they have received.[243]

Regardless of the cost or disruption, the education of blacks was a moral and political necessity. Similarly important were attempts to increase the contact the races had with each other, since whites (and blacks) feared what they did not understand. Here she spoke from experience, and her personal example was likely her single greatest contribution to the cause of civil rights.[244] She allowed herself to be photographed with blacks and invited black school girls to picnic at the White House, infuriating southern Democrats by entertaining a "bunch of 'nigger whores' at the White House."[245] She resigned from the Daughters of the American Revolution when they barred the black singer Marion Anderson from performing in Constitution Hall,[246] and protested segregated seating by moving her chair to the aisle between black and white sections, despite a young Bull Connor's threats to arrest her for violating local segregation laws.[247]

At the same time she, like Booker T. Washington, called upon blacks to accept responsibility for improving themselves and their condition as much as possible within the existent social framework. Acceptance would come later. For now blacks had to focus their fight primarily on education and economics (the building blocks of citizenship), and here the New Deal offered more genuine opportunities than ever before, even if those opportunities were still far from equal. Black leaders largely shared this accommodationist stance. Desegregation was less a priority than black participation in New Deal aid programs.[248] Walter White, head of the NAACP, agreed with FDR's assessment that relief was more important than desegregation.[249] Leaders rarely mounted a direct challenge to the doctrine of separate but equal, but this grudging acceptance does not mean the importance of psychic recognition went unnoticed. As Christopher Lash noted, "This was what the Negro wanted—that he be seen and recognized as an individual and accepted in the fullness of a humanity that he shared with whites—and this is what the First Lady understood."[250] Friendship and support were given with "courage and enthusiasm and, what is far more important, without…the insufferable patronizing manner which so many persons in like position would manifest."[251] It was her hope that this example might encourage others to do the same.

The New Deal had faith that attitudes would change, but recognized that change would happen slowly. Blacks had a long road ahead of them, as any and all legitimate change had to happen through democratic channels dominated by a resistant, if not openly hostile, citizenry who chose to exercise their autonomy in reactionary ways. The realities of power (as opposed to justice) in the United States were such that the burden of proof was on blacks to justify their inclusion. They had to be better than their white counterparts, to rise above white intransigence. The New Deal recognized the injustice of necessity, but argued that ideals must bend to political reality in the interest of stability.

As Mary Stuckley argues, this strategy of deferral represented a typical response of the New Deal to deeply entrenched issues of identity (as opposed to economics). The New Deal would legitimate the grievances of minority parties, and then preach patience in the face of intransigent opposition.[252] A delicate, perhaps unworkable, balance was struck between privileging the stability of the system (which meant the continued marginalization of minority groups) while condemning that same marginalization. Bridging that gap will take time, and in the interim justice will have to yield.

> It seems trite to say to the Negro, you must have patience, when he has had patience so long; you must not expect miracles overnight, when he can look back to the years of slavery and say—how many nights! He has waited for justice. Nevertheless, it is what we must continue to say in the interests of our government as a whole and of the Negro people; but that does not mean we must sit idle and do nothing. We must keep moving forward steadily, removing restric-

tions which have no sense, and fighting prejudice. If we are wise we will do this where it is easiest to do it first, and watch it spread gradually to places where the old prejudices are slow to disappear.[253]

With its faith in progress, decency, and education, the New Deal believed time, patience, and diligence would eventually solve the seemingly intractable problem of racial exclusion from the social contract—institutionally and socially. Today this sounds like a dodge, and the Civil Rights Movement demonstrated that a more confrontational approach could prove effective. But we should not underestimate the New Deal's challenge to the race relations of the time. As Plotke observes, "The severely discriminatory character of the racial order meant that when new federal programs were not explicitly racist they put elements of that order in question."[254] Certainly there was enough of a challenge for the overwhelming majority of the black community to support the New Deal (DuBois voted for FDR four times),[255] and many whites turned away from the New Deal for precisely those same reasons.

The New Deal was unwilling to sanction a formal challenge to the fundamental order of society that bypassed existing political channels. Its commitment to American democracy prevented it. There was no problem that could not be solved within the boundaries of the system. This belief went far beyond racial issues. The New Deal did not worry about communist elements within youth organizations, but would never have tolerated behavior that fundamentally threatened the legitimacy of the Constitution. Despite the sexism present in the Democratic Party, ER never supported a third party for women. She was a strong supporter of unions, but felt a strike by public employees was illegitimate. Whenever a conflict of interest existed both sides were expected to submit, in good faith, to the rules and procedures of the system. Democracy is entitled to our loyalty precisely because it contained evolutionary and self-correcting ways to address grievances. The New Deal, its supporters would argue, is worthy of loyalty as long as it continued to work to expand the breadth and depth of our social contract.

Conclusion

We hold this truth to be self-evident—that the test of a representative government is its ability to promote the safety and happiness of the people.
—1936 Democratic Party Platform[256]

In the end, the New Deal's social contract, and the theory behind it, provides us with a much more robust understanding of traditional American values. Our understanding of security is expanded to include not simply protection from external threat and coercion, but protection from the violence that can be inflicted by the market and the existential fear that comes with insecurity. It is significant not only that our thinking about security is broadened, but that even in times of depression it is well within our ability to provide meaningful security for every member of society. We no longer need chain ourselves to those older understandings of liberty and fear that are derived from the assumption of scarcity.

As a result we are now able to focus our attention, as a people, to that third, oft-neglected part of the Declaration of Independence's trinity of rights—the right to pursue happiness. At bottom the New Deal interprets happiness as the ability to participate in a consumer society, but it is important not to reduce the New Deal to this. It was well aware of the way in which a consumerist orientation narrows our horizons, and it was always meant to serve not as an end, but as a beginning. Once comfortable and secure we could emphasize self-development and citizenship, the two feeding off each other in a cycle aimed at elevating Americans above their more narrow concerns and enabling them to recognize their interdependence, develop new attachments, and in the process better themselves.

This is the basis of the New Deal's social contract. It is a contract between Americans and their society—not the government per se. Ideally these goals should be provided privately, but when private means fail the burden is transferred to the public. If the contract is not honored, then the public has no moral standing from which to make any claims on its citizens, nor should it expect their loyalty.

Similarly, the contract is fundamentally expansive and in important ways unlimited. Each generation must determine for itself (although in conversation with the past and future) the prerequisites for the exercise of their rights, as well as the steps the government must take to protect those rights. Likewise, the logic behind the New Deal is universal, which means it must continue to spread until it covers the entirety of American society (or, if the internationalist strain within its thought is followed to its conclusion, the entire world). There is, in this respect, no stopping point—no moment in which the New Deal can be said to have reached its end. Its implications are far more radical, its ambitions far more profound, than the imperfect institutionalization begun during the Roosevelt administration and gradually expanded upon since.

There are several critical tensions running through the New Deal's social contract—most of which the theory is aware of and attempts to address. Are the kinds of attachments necessary to build a mass state on the foundation of love, respect, and dignity (as opposed to interest or fanaticism) possible in a society as large and differentiated as the United States? The New Deal demands more than just interest group liberalism. Can we have it? While the New Deal hopes to harness the consumerist impulse and steer it towards something more sophisticated and publicly spirited, it is not clear whether or not this move can be successful. History seems to say no, as today we are a nation of consumers first, and citizens a distant second at best. Is this a lost cause? Can we do better? We will address these issues in greater detail in the final chapter.

Another tension may not yet be readily apparent. The New Deal places a premium on having an involved and informed citizenry as the only truly reliable check on an expanding central government. The act of citizenship is also a noble and worthwhile enterprise in its own right. Such is the democratic theory of the New Deal. However, if a theory of ends wishes to be more than critique it must be attached to a theory of practice, and the New Deal's theory of practice may ultimately undermine the democratic theory that is so vital to the theory as a whole. Do the ends of the New Deal pay too high a price for its chosen means? It is to this theory of practice, the *political* component of political theory, that we now turn our attention.

Notes

1. FDR, "An Appeal to Farmers and Laborers," 6 Sept. 1936, *Chat*, 82.
2. David Lilienthal, *TVA: Democracy on the March*, (New York: Harper and Row, 1943), 120.
3. The Progressive movement (with the standard caveat that there were many types of Progressives and any blanket statement cannot cover all of them. See Rodgers, "In Search of Progressivism" *Reviews in American History*, Vol. 10, No. 4, Dec. 1982) was considerably more Hegelian than the New Deal in this regard. Many Progressives argued that the state was a 'moral agent' (Foner, *Freedom*, 152), while the New Deal's understanding of the state was far more mechanistic.
4. The advanced liberal tradition, beginning with Mill, adapts, whenever possible, a position of reconciliation, embracing the tensions between opposites as both likely contain insights into the character of human sociality and organization that should be embraced and incorporated into the social order. As Mill explains in *On Liberty*, "Unless opinions favorable to democracy and to aristocracy, to property and to equality, to cooperation and to competition, to luxury and to abstinence, to sociality and individuality, to liberty and discipline, and all the other standing antagonisms of practical life, are expressed with equal freedom and enforced and defended with equal talent and energy, there is no chance of both elements obtaining their due." Mill, *Liberty*, 45.
5. Alan Ryan, *John Dewey and the High Tide of American Liberalism*, (New York: W.W. Norton & Company, 1995), 109. Note that Ryan is describing Dewey, but Dewey and the New Deal face the same dilemma, and attempt to reconcile it in largely the same way.
6. As Rogers Smith and others have clearly demonstrated one can easily read American history as a history of exclusion and ascriptive prejudice, but these moments could always be (and were) challenged by referring back to the radical inclusivity promised in the Declaration of Independence. Smith, *Civic*.
7. However, these intellectual debts were never fully acknowledged.
8. Wallace, "On the Move," 11 March 1935, *Democracy*, 94.
9. "We are all Republicans; we are all Federalists" Jefferson remarked in his first inaugural address as he sought to position the Democratic-Republicans as the only party actually capable of representing the entire nation. Of course any party can claim to represent 'the people,' and most make that claim. The test is seeing who supports the party, how it treats the opposition, how inclusive or expansive its policies are.
10. At the same time, however, FDR was trying to bring about an ideological realignment and turn the Democratic Party away from an umbrella party towards one that

was primarily liberal. This need not be seen as a contradiction. The New Deal, while a liberal party, aimed at liberal inclusiveness and offered (it believed) a set of categories that offered the most room for common ground amongst American citizens. Nor do ideological parties undermine the conviction that even if a party represent a particular ideological position, it still has a duty to represent, as best it can, the legitimate (in reference to what the social contract entitles them to) interests of the opposition. See Sidney Milkis, *The President and the Parties*, (USA: Oxford University Press, 1993).

11. Morone, *Hellfire,* 354.

12. With the important caveat, as Chief Justice Hughes pointed out, that the phrase 'freedom of contract' did not appear in the Constitution and as such could not trump attempts to use "the protection of the law against the evils which menace the health, safety, morals, and welfare of the people." Rights meant more than property rights, freedom more than the freedom of capital to purchase labor. Quoted in Foner, *Freedom*, 205.

13. There was always a sense of urgency surrounding the New Deal because many New Dealers suspected that nothing was settled in the long term. While the hope was that the New Deal represented the beginning of a society structured on the assumptions of abundance, interdependence, and mutual obligation, there was also the realization that the New Deal was an opportunity afforded by the crisis of the Great Depression, and that there was a need to institutionalize as much as possible before the crisis ended and the conservative instincts of the American woke from their slumber. The language of the moral crusade, of sacrifice and the common good, is exhausting. While the presence of crisis and institutional collapse makes progressive innovation possible, what the people long for is the return of equilibrium, or, if you like, normalcy. Once the crisis ends the fear that led to reform quickly turns conservative, seeking to consolidate the small gains made. But that is often enough. As long as a policy gets institutionalized it becomes possible to expand its reach, as its presence becomes part of the heritage we wish to conserve.

14. FDR. "Acceptance,"50.

15. Formed in 1934 by disaffected (Al Smith) and conservative (John Davis—the 1924 nominee for president) Democrats and industrialists (the DuPont family, Prescott Bush), the Liberty League was devoted to defending the Constitution and supporting property rights by opposing Roosevelt. It spent upwards of $1.5 in lobbying and marketing, but it peddled a message that Americans were not ready to embrace again just yet.

16. As we shall see in chapter 5, this was one of the justifications behind Roosevelt's 'purge' of conservative democrats. Ideological parties make it easier for the nation to ratify or reject a particular framework.

17. FDR, "The First Hundred Days and the NRA," 24 July 1934, *Chat*, 35.

18. Walter Lippmann, *The Phantom Public*, (New Brunswick: Transaction Publishers, 1999), 14-15.

19. Even if, as we shall continue to see, agency was understood more in terms of ratifying or rejecting the performance of political elites. Political freedom is found in the act of accountability rather than administration.

20. Although Wallace was aware of how wrenching that quarter turn might be.

21. Frankfurter quoted in Nelson Lloyd Dawson, *Louis D. Brandeis, Felix Frankfurter, and the New Deal*, (Hamden: Archon Book, 1980), 103.

22. FDR, "Purging the Democratic Party," 24 June 1938, *Chat*, 127.

23. FDR, "Purging," 127.

24. FDR, "Commonwealth," 26.

25. Frequently the good of society meant the protection either of the most vulnerable (farmers, unions, industry in certain cases), those most capable of expanding production, or the most broadly based component of it (the consumer).

26. Perkins, *Roosevelt*, 333.

27. A common strategy used by Roosevelt when his advisors disagreed was to "Put them in a room together, and tell them no lunch until they agree!" Quoted in Burns, *Lion*, 183.

28. A theme he constantly hammered home whenever he campaigned. Local issues were always put into a larger national context. The plight of the small farmer who was not paid enough for his crops would be connected to the conditions of industrial workers who could not afford to buy them.

29. Race and gender were not top priorities for the New Deal. Compared to the progress made in later movements, the New Deal did very little, but to judge the New Deal too harshly on this score ignores both the political realities that confronted the New Deal and its universal language. Women and minority groups lacked the organizational power to defeat the forces of reaction marshaled against them, and had FDR expended political capital to fight for them, it would have destroyed the New Deal coalition that made other progressive change possible. Instead, Roosevelt gave women and minorities unprecedented access to positions of power and influence within his administration, and framed policy and programs in an inclusive way that made their future expansion possible. The New Deal was not the Civil Rights movement, but the Civil Rights movement may not have been possible without the groundwork laid by the New Deal. See Kevin J. McMahon, *Reconsidering Roosevelt on Race*, (Chicago: The University of Chicago Press, 2004); and Howard Sitkoff, *A New Deal for Blacks*, (New York: Oxford University Press, 1981).

30. Quoted in Burns, *Lion*,182.

31. Frances Perkins has noted that Roosevelt was never able to get inside the mind of the capitalist. "Roosevelt never understood the point of view of the business community, nor could he make out why it didn't like him. He did not hold that everything should be judged by whether or not it makes money, and this made the business people incomprehensible to him." Perkins, 155. Similarly, Perkins also argues that FDR never really understood the sense of adversarial solidarity that animated the labor movement, the way in which unions formed "unbreakable bonds which gave them power and status to deal with their employers on equal terms." Perkins quoted in Miroff, *Icons*, 262.

32. Perkins, *Roosevelt*, 215.

33. While the populist appeals to the difference between deserving and undeserving wealth, between the common man and the privileged few, colored the rhetoric on occasion (especially in the 1936 campaign), it did not creep into policy, or even the theory, beyond trying to address clear imbalances in the status quo distribution of power and wealth in society.

34. Fischer, *Liberty*, 475-477.

35. Not that this blunted the ferocious protestations of Al Smith and the Liberty League who argued that chief amongst the New Deal's crimes against America was "the arraignment of class against class. It has been freely predicted that if we were ever to have civil strife again in this country it would come from the appeal to passion and prejudices that comes from demagogues that would incite one class of our people against another. Quoted in David Pietrusza's "New Deal Nemesis," http://www.davidpietrusza.com/Liberty-League.html. For further discussion see Sey-

mour Martin Lipset and Gary Mark, *It Didn't Happen Here: Why Socialism Failed in the United States*, (New York: W.W. Norton & Company, 2000)

36. Dewey, quoted in Ryan, *Dewey*, 290.

37. McWilliams, *Fraternity*, 542. McWilliams goes on to note "This alone helps account for the consistent tendency of the unions to sacrifice every other good to the attainment of economic gain, a pattern made more compelling by the desperate need of members." McWilliams is broadly correct here. Frequently unions placed their right to unionize above questions of wages and hours, but once unionization was successful the primary focus was on the economic concerns of its members. The experience of the New Deal's resettlement programs is also instructive. Model cooperative communities were established to help the poor and displaced build new subsistence lives for themselves. The communities were popular amongst those participating in them, but never as a permanent arrangement. Instead they were seen as a way for the dispossessed to stabilize and reintegrate themselves into American society—a way to save up so they could someday own property themselves. These communities also earned the hostility of elements of the left, who saw them as planning for permanent poverty, or, in more conspiratorial moments, as an attempt to build "a sheltered peasant group as a rural reactionary bloc to withstand the revolutionary demands of the organized industrial workers." Louis Hacker quoted in Abbot, *Exemplary*, 90.

38. Ryan, *Dewey*, 302.

39. The devil is in the definitions, but what matters here is that there is a shared vocabulary that can be referenced and appealed to. There are no new ends that need be accepted. The goals themselves are legitimate—the battle is over their interpretation.

40. The right to profit from our labor, alongside the belief that this profit is legitimate not only because we have mixed our labor with it, but that by doing so we've added to the amount and distribution of abundance in the world. This public qualification is a vitally important check on the excesses of Locke's defense of private property, one too often overlooked. See chapter 5 of Locke's *Second Treatise on Government*.

41. Wallace, "Wants," 23. He goes on to add that "[h]e knows he cannot have such peace and happiness if the means of earning peace and happiness are denied to any man on the basis of race or creed." The emphasis on hard work is mine, and the significance of work in this formulation will be discussed in more detail later in the chapter.

42. Muncie newspaper editorial cited in Foner, *Liberty*, 151.

43. See Plotke, *Building*, chapter 4. Even amongst the rank and file, union leaders confronted a body of workers concerned primarily with advancing their own material interests rather than creating any kind of working class consciousness. See Nelson Lichtenstein, *Labor's War at Home* (Cambridge: Cambridge University Press, 1982), 13.

44. Fischer, *Liberty*, 475. And Patrice Higonnet's *Sister Republics* (Harvard University Press, 1988) and Larry Fuchs' *American Kaleidoscope* (Wesleyan University Press, 1991) locate its origins to the colonial era, especially in the Southern colonies.

45. Claude Fisher, *Made in America: A Social History of American Culture and Character*, (Chicago: The University of Chicago Press, 2010), 9 and 60.

46. Foner, *Freedom*, 147.

47. See Foner. Note too that the New Deal's emphasis on work as a right aims more at securing a meaningful life outside of work, ensuring that the presence of work granted dignity and the pay sufficient to provide security and happiness, but not autonomy.

48. Fischer, *Liberty*, 475.

49. Kenneth Goode quoted in Foner, *Freedom*, 147.

50. As McWilliams notes, while the language of choice was often employed by the New Deal, central to its philosophy and its temperament was that choosing between conflicting positions was rarely necessary, and always a less desirable option than reconciliation.

51. It was during the Progressive era that we saw the creation of the amusement park, the proliferation of vaudeville (and later movies) accompanied by a drastic reduction in the cost of admission (from two dollars to as low as ten cents). Trachtenberg, *Incorporation*, 253. If we were not exactly prepared to call entertainment a right, we were certainly working to democratize it.

52. Addams in McGeer, *Discontent*, 316. See also chapter 8 in McGeer for an extended discussion of the progressive era's uneasy relationship with leisure and pleasure.

53. Glickman, *Buying*, 178

54. Glickman, *Buying*, 192.

55. Glickman, *Buying*, 17.

56. Here the New Deal builds on the work of progressive economists like Simon Patten. See Foner, *Freedom*, 151.

57. What's more, this desire for comfort and material goods opened new avenues for participation in American society for women and played a major role in the movement for unionization, wages and hours, retirement security, and the regulation of the economy on behalf of the consumer. It is possible for the search for material comfort to lead to public participation rather than solely private pursuits, although how to keep that public participation publicly minded is another question entirely (and will be addressed later).

58. Abbot, *Exemplary*, 34.

59. Norton, *Signs*, 50.

60. Tocqueville, *Democracy*, 618-620.

61. As almost any advertisement, then and now, will make clear. The emphasis is never just on the utility of the product, but the emotions the products evoke in the user—the sense of fulfillment and satisfaction they generate and how they help us recreate our identity.

62. Norton, *Signs*, 55. It has also become a symbol of citizenship, as President Bush made it clear in the days after 9/11 that our primary obligation as citizens was to head to the malls and spend money.

63. Choices freely made in theory, at least. Obviously the presence of advertising is more than capable of manipulating consumers into purchasing products they do not need, and did not even know they wanted.

64. Arnold, *Fair Fights*, 41.

65. Note Wallace's series of speeches "America Tomorrow" on the importance of defining the post-World War II order. *Democracy*, 17-40.

66. And not coincidentally, the groups that also supported the New Deal, although to reduce this move to simple pandering for votes ignores the self-conscious attempts by Roosevelt and company to fashion the New Deal as a liberal party, not just an electoral coalition.

67. Eventually, in the case of Social Security. The regressive taxation that financed it has the opposite effects in the short term.

68. Thurman Arnold's explicit formulation of this philosophy is found in *Bottlenecks*, written while he was Assistant Attorney General.

69. Brinkley, *Reform*, 106.

70. Arnold, *Democracy and Free Enterprise*, (Norman: University of Oklahoma Press, 1942), 46.

71. As an individual thinker Arnold lacked the concern for the excesses of the con-sumerist approach that colored the work of the Roosevelts and Wallace.

72. Abbot, *Exemplary*, 34.

73. Tocqueville, quoted in Roger Boesche, *Tocqueville's Road Map*, (Lanham: Lex-ington Books, 2006), 45.

74. Even today, calls to citizenship, for voting and participation, are phrased in the consumer's language of choice, rather than the citizen's language of responsibility.

75. Tocqueville quoted in Boesche, *Map*, 46.

76. Jefferson quoted in Boesche, *Map*, 58.

77. Ray Stannard Baker cited in Otis Graham, "The New Deal and the Progressive Tradition," in Hamby, 193.

78. ER, *Moral Basis*, 56.

79. Mill, *Liberty*, 56-57.

80. Mill, *Liberty*,12,

81. Eldon Eisenach, "Introduction," *Mill and the Moral Character of Liberalism*, ed. Eldon Eisenach, (University Park: The Pennsylvania State University Press, 1998), 8.

82. Mill, *Liberty,* 61.

83. Mill cited in Fred Wilson, "Psychology and the Moral Sciences," in *The Cambridge Companion*, ed. John Skorupski, (Cambridge: Cambridge University Press, 1998), 238. Mill scholar Wendy Donner puts this argument forcefully in her essay "Mill's Utilitarianism. "People have a right to liberty of self-development and their rights are violated if their social circumstances bar them or do not provide adequate resources for them to attain and excise self-development." "Mill's Utilitarianism," Skorupski, 278.

84. Mill, *Liberty*, 60.

85. Mill, *Liberty,* 10.

86. ER, "Are We Overlooking the Pursuit of Happiness," *The Parents Magazine* 11 (September, 1936), *Leave Behind*, 62

87. Mill, *Liberty*, 56.

88. ER from "It's Up To Women" quoted in Cook, *II*, 72.

89. The New Deal resisted the mean-spirited tendency to deny that enjoyment is a necessity of life. For example, FDR insisted that the baseball season continue in 1942, and even urged more night games so that people working during the day had a chance to see a game.

90. ER, "Happiness," 62.

91. ER, " Happiness?" in *Courage*, 38.

92. FDR, "First Inaugural."

93. ER, *Moral Basis*, 48.

94.Tocqueville, *Democracy*, 340.

95. Quoted in Ryan, *Dewey*, 37.

96. The awareness of sin and human limitation informed the New Deal's theory of practice, but was, with rare exceptions absent from its theory of ends.

97. Informal Remarks to Visiting Protestant Ministers, 31 January, 1938. Quoted in Morone, *Hellfire*, 354-355.

98. Roosevelt exhorted clergy to emphasize the Sermon on the Mount during his second term. *New York Times*, 4th February 1938. Quoted in Ibid., 354.

99. ER, "What Religion Means to Me," *The Forum* 88 (1932), *Leave Behind*, 3.

100. ER, "What Religion Means to Me," *Leave Behind*, 3.

101. The Protestant roots of her religious principles (and political theory) are seen in the emphasis placed on the individual's relationship with god, himself, and with society.

102. Here, for a number of reasons, the New Deal breaks ranks with Mill, who was an implacable foe of institutional Christianity.

103. Wallace, *Statesmanship*, 8.

104. ER quoted in James Kearny, *Anna Eleanor Roosevelt: The Evolution of a Reformer,* (Boston: Houghton Mifflin Company, 1968), 68-69.

105. ER, "The Minorities Question," written for the Joint Commission on Social Reconstruction, (October 1945), *Leave Behind,* 169.

106. Found in his *A Letter Concerning Toleration.* For Locke a believer had to have a belief in a future state of divine rewards and punishments. Everything else was secondary.

107. She lists 13th Chapter 1st Corinthians, with its famous celebration of love, as her favorite Bible verse. Eleanor Roosevelt, *If You Ask Me,* (New York: D. Appleton-Century Company, Inc. 1946), 126.

108. ER, "12 February, 1937," in *My Day.* In this particular column ER is attacking the idea of definitive Constitutional interpretation, which Wallace and Arnold addressed more systematically in *Whose Constitution?* and *Symbols of Government.*

109. ER, *Moral Basis,* cited in Tamara Hareven, *Eleanor Roosevelt: An American Conscience,* (Chicago: Quadrangle Books,1968), 126.

110. ER, *Moral Basis,* 56-57.

111. ER, *Moral Basis* 57.

112. ER quoted Lash, *Eleanor and Franklin,* 285.

113. The derisive hostility with which Wallace's call to provide milk for the children of the world in his 'Century of the Common Man' speech demonstrates just how far we still had to come.

114. ER, "Religion," 5.

115. ER, "Religion," 3.

116. ER, *Moral Basis,* 14.

117. The assumption here, as is the case with most democratic theory, is that the process of democracy, irrespective of outcomes, is a positive one as it enables the participants to exercise the faculties that make them most human, and grant them a healthy sense of agency and autonomy, at least in the political world.

118. ER, *You Learn by Living,* (New York: Harper & Brothers, 1960), 40.

119. ER, *Moral Basis,* 72-74.

120. The most elegant formulation of this objection is made by William Graham Sumner in *What Do the Social Classes Owe Each Other.*

121. Happily enough for ER and FDR these religious beliefs were authentically held, which is one of the reasons why they were so effective in convincing the voting public to follow them.

122. ER, *Moral Basis,* 77.

123. ER, *Moral Basis,* 77.

124. ER, *Living,* 152.

125. Sidney Milkis and Michael Nelson, *The American Presidency,* (Washington, D.C.: CQ Press, 2003), 275.

126. This number averaged well over 100,000 the rest of her time in the White House, and all mail was answered by her or her staff. Frequently they contained pleas for help, full of heart-rending specifics, and ER was a sympathetic audience. Whenever possible funds were raised and letters referred to appropriate agencies. ER took her mail quite seriously, recognizing that as a symbol of the government, doing so humanized the presence of the government in the lives of millions.

127. Eleanor Roosevelt in a letter to Joseph Lash, cited in Winifred Wandersee's "ER and American Youth: Politics and Personality in a Bureaucratic Age," in *Without Precedent: The Life and Career of Eleanor Roosevelt*, ed. Joan Hoff-Wilson and Marjorie Lightman, (Bloomington: Indiana University Press, 1984), 72.

128. ER, "WPA Wages," *My Day*, (August 8 1939), *Courage*, 45.

129. Karl, *Uneasy*, 98.

130. FDR, "An Economic Bill of Rights" 11 Jan. 1944, *Chat*, 292.

131. ER quoted in Ruby Black, *Eleanor Roosevelt: A Biography*, (New York: Duell, Sloan and Pearce,   1940), 309.

132. See Lincoln's celebrated "The Perpetuation of Our Political Institutions," address to the Young Men's Lyceum in Springfield," 27 Jan. 1838.

133. ER, "Religion," 3.

134. FDR, "Government and Modern Capitalism," *Chat*, 62.

135. ER, "Religion,"5.

136. Wallace. "The Hard Choice," 1940, *Democracy*, 163.

137. Hiram Canton, "Progressivism and Conservatism During the New Deal," Eden, 187. Note that Canton is describing what he would call the more dynamic Federalist attitude about the role of the state, contrasting it to what he paints as an anachronism that endured due to material conditions that allowed six generations to experience the Jeffersonian promise of land and independence.

138. And even here harm was defined so narrowly as to exclude most forms of distress caused by industrial capitalism.

139. ER, "Helping Them to Help Themselves," *The Rotarian* (April 1940), *Leave Behind*, 370-371.

140. Morton Frisch makes this argument as well in *Franklin D. Roosevelt*, 65.

141. Wallace, "Capitalism," 142.

142. There is an obvious tension here between the New Deal's claim that certain goals are fundamentally a part of the social fabric of the society, while elsewhere claiming that each generation can define its social contract for itself. The New Deal never troubled itself with these tensions, probably because the meaning of these goals was to be contested politically, which eases the tension.

143. Wallace, *Constitution*, 11.

144. Kessler, "Public." Kessler's argument spends much more time on Wilson than it does on the New Deal.

145. FDR, "Third Inaugural Address," 20 Jan. 1941, *Speeches*, 103.

146. ER, *If You Ask Me*, (New York: D. Appleton-Century Company, Inc., 1946), 131.

147. Bernstein, *Caring*, 53.

148. Bernstein, *Caring,* 20.

149. Susan Faludi explores the social implications of masculinity, so bound up with the idea of being a provider, in an economy that increasingly offers neither security nor the ability to be a sole, male provider in *Stiffed: The Betrayal of the American Man*, (New York: Harper Collins, 1999).

150. Bernstein, *Caring,* 146.

151. Bernstein, *Caring*, 20-21.

152. FDR, fireside chat 5 July, 1933 in *Chat*, 19.

153. Quoted in Joseph Lash, *Dealers*, 331.

154. Roosevelt's response to a Canadian journalist asking him about the social objectives of the New Deal. Quoted in Abbot, *Exemplary*, 125.

155. FDR, "First Inaugural Address."

156. The author's favorite defenses of these values are found in John Locke's *Letter Concerning Toleration* and John Stuart Mill's *On Liberty.*

157. FDR, "The Four Freedoms: State of the Union Message to Congress," 6 Jan. 1941.

158. Coolidge quoted in *Who Built America, Vol. II* (New York: American Social History Productions, Inc.), 1992, 273.

159. Quoted in Phillips-Fein, *Invisible*, 3-4

160. FDR, "State of the Union Address," 11 Jan. 1944.

161. From the Liberty League's articles of incorporation. Quoted in Pietrusza. http://www.davidpietrusza.com/Liberty-League.html.

162. Roosevelt quoted in Burns, *Lion*, 208.

163. There were real political limits to the groups the New Deal was able to help. Organized interests fared better than unorganized groups, as they have throughout time. The inchoate nature of the federal state meant that programs were often administered locally, and reflected local prejudice. Southern influence in Congress was able to ensure that its hierarchical society suffered only minimal disruptions. Social Security originally excluded many forms of low-paying work, especially those dominated by women and blacks. However, the language of the New Deal was one that explicitly refused to draw distinctions between citizens, and its universal cast left the possibility of future expansion wide open. David Plotke observes, "If the administration rarely challenged images of the 'people' as white, openly racist themes declined...The severely discriminatory character of the racial order meant that when new Federal programs were not explicitly racist they put elements of that order into question...[opening] political space for challenges to conventional racial practices." Plotke, *Building*, 179.

164. FDR, "The Four Freedoms," *Speeches*, 99-99.

165. FDR, "The Four Freedoms," 98.

166. As Sunstein demonstrates in *The Second Bill of Rights*, this idea of economic rights had been in the works throughout the entirety of the New Deal, ranging from mentions of an economic declaration of rights in 1932, through the emphasis on rights to work and rights to live during the 1936 campaign, up to the Four Freedoms and the Atlantic charter during the 'Dr. Win the War' phase of the Roosevelt Administration. In fact, it was during the war that the New Deal, acting through the NRPB, began work on formally and explicitly institutionalizing the idea of economic rights.

167. For a superlative discussion of this see Cass Sunstein's *The Second Bill of Rights.*

168. FDR, "State of the Union Address," 11 Jan. 1944. Emphasis mine.

169 When the commissioner of baseball inquired whether the season should be canceled in 1942 FDR replied as follows.

> I honestly feel that it would be best for the country to keep baseball going. There will be fewer people unemployed and everybody will work longer hours and harder than ever before. Baseball provides a recreation which does not last over two or two and a half hours, and which can be got for very little cost. And, incidentally, I hope that night games can be extended because it gives an opportunity to the day shift to see a game occasionally.

The Sporting News 22 January, 1942, 1. Thanks to Jerome Mileur for passing this along.

170. FDR, "State of the Union 1944."

171. FDR, "State of the Union Address," 6 Jan. 1937. Emphasis mine.

172. FDR, "State of the Union 1937."

173. Sunstein, *Second.*

174. Until World War II less than 5 percent of the country went to college, with the cost equal to the average national wage. More than half of those who served in WWII took advantage of the GI Bill, and in 1947 half of the students enrolled in higher education were veterans.

175. See Paul Starr's *Social Transformation of American Medicine*, (Basic Books: 1982).

176. From *Security, Work, and Relief Policies.* Quoted in Brinkley, *Reform*, 252.

177. Foner, *Freedom*, 198.

178. Badger, *New Deal*, 41.

179. Marxists would argue that our dependence on work in order to feel valuable is an example of capitalism's pathological effect on a worker's sense of self. Roosevelt certainly would have rejected that critique, but as previously discussed, Roosevelt never critically questioned capitalism either. In this respect he was no different than most Americans. Even American labor unions during the 30's never challenged the connection between work and value in any serious way.

180. FDR, "State of the Union 1935," quoted in Sunstein, 18.

181. Faludi, *Stiffed*, 55.

182. Although as we shall see momentarily the New Deal, especially via ER, would argue that the need to work, to create, transcended traditional gender boundaries.

183. Programs like the NYA and CCC reflected those priorities.

184. Perkins, *Roosevelt*, 187.

185. Although much of this reflected the need to accommodate the dominant folklore about deserving/undeserving poor and the superiority of private employment to relief, the New Deal still shared these prejudices, even if not to the same degree as others.

186. Abbot discusses this trend on pp. 82-84.

187. Roosevelt's thinking here reflects his liberal biases. From a social democratic perspective one could easily challenge the idea that private employment is more liberating, but it should be noted that Roosevelt's thinking was already to the left of mainstream America in this regard. His support of private employment also always went hand in hand with proposals for stronger laws on wages, hours, and working conditions.

188. Brinkley, *Reform*, 250-251.

189. Brinkley, *Reform*, 255.

190. As we saw in the 2010 debates over extending the Bush era tax cuts.

191. A phrase Roosevelt claimed to have invented, and was subsequently annoyed when Beveridge 'stole' the expression from him. Bernstein, *Caring*, 50.

192. Mary Ross, "Why Social Security," Washington, D.C.'s Social Security Board, 1936, in Freidel, 80.

193. Brinkley, *Reform*, 258.

194. Brinkley, *Reform*, 259.

195. ER, "Good Citizenship," *Pictorial Review* (April 1930), *Leave Behind*, 292.

196. ER, "Good Citizenship," 289.

197. Black, *Biography*, 307.

198. Smith, *FDR*, 218.

199. ER certainly lived that philosophy. Even while she was First Lady of New York she continued to teach history and civics part time in NYC, and she would take her students to tenements so that they could experience what that life was like.

> To these children of the rich, I had to explain what it meant to sleep in a room which had no window, what it meant to pant on fire escapes in hot July with people draped on fire escapes all around you, what it meant for a woman with her husband and eight children to live in three rooms in the basement...

"Defense of Curiosity," cited in Kearney, *Reformer*, 20.
As First Lady she continued to try and educate everyone she came in contact with about the lived experience of those forgotten by society, taking potential donors to visit the poor, giving press conferences to address issues like poverty, sweatshop labor, etc. Bess Furman offered a comparison between the differing styles of FDR and ER: "At the President's press conference, all the world's a stage; at Mrs. Roosevelt's, all the world's a school." Lash, *Eleanor and Franklin*, 363.

200. ER, *This Troubled World*, (New York: H.C. Kinsey & Company, 1938), *Leave Behind*, 484.

201 FDR, "State of the Union Address 1944."

202 FDR, "State of the Union Address 1944."

203. It was simply safer for ER to advance radical causes than it was for FDR.

204. ER, "The Unemployed Are Not a Strange Race," *Democratic Digest 13* (June 1936), *Leave Behind*, 367.

205. Her friend Lorena Hick, on one of her assignments for Harry Hopkins, wrote to describe the conditions in one coalfield town.

> Morgantown was the worst place I'd ever seen. In a gutter, along the main street through the town, there was stagnant, filthy water, which the inhabitants used for drinking, cooking, washing, and everything else imaginable. On either side of the street were ramshackle houses, black with coal dust, which most Americans would not have considered fit for pigs. And in these houses every child went to sleep hungry, on piles of bug-infested rags, spread out on the floor.

Cited in Cook, *II* 130-131. Descriptions like this also remind one that there are worse things to value in a society than the democratization of comfort.

206. Henry Wallace, responding to a book on southern poverty called *Preface to Peasantry*, claimed that calling them peasants "really offends the peasantry of Europe." Cited in Patrice Sullivan, *Days of Hope*, (Chapel Hill: The University of North Carolina Press, 1996), 2.

207. Told in Black, *Biography*, 158. Of course this kind of response also highlights the real limitations of the appeals to interdependence, community, and brotherhood that permeate the New Deal. One can perhaps force recognition of a problem, but not meaningful personal engagement. When one creates a welfare state the conscience can, in fact, be bought off, although it isn't clear that any other set of principles could address this more effectively.

208. This story led to the donation of a one hundred dollar check so that the rabbit might be saved. Cook, *II*, 132.

209. ER, "The Unemployed Are Not a Strange Race," *Leave Behind*, 367.

210. In the experimental community of Arthurdale, people were reluctant to share their crops for fear that another's child might get too large a share. They were equally

suspicious of a cooperative dairy. "They trusted nobody, not even themselves. They had an eye out all the time to see who was going to cheat them next." ER quoted in Black, *Biography*, 248.

211. ER quoted in Black, *Biography*, 257.

212. At least broad attachments. A community can rally around shared depravations, but the attachments will be narrow and suspicious, if not openly hostile, to outsiders.

213. Badger, for instance, reports that it was largely FERA caseworkers that 'discovered' the problem of rural poverty. Badger, *New Deal*, 186.

214. ER quoted in Cook, *II*, 131.

215. This attitude carried over into ER's views on charity: "I have never felt that people should be grateful for charity, They should rightfully be resentful and so should we, at the circumstances which make charity a necessity." Quoted in Cook, *II*, 137.

216. ER, "Helping Them to Help Themselves," *The Rotarian* (April 1940), *Leave Behind*, 370. These are enormously provocative words from a sitting First Lady.

217. Kearney, *Reformer*, 23.

218. Lash, *Eleanor and Franklin*, 536.

219. The Civilian Conservation Corps was a product of famous 100 days of the first. New Deal. It was a reforestation program that was very popular with the young, as it was easier for them to move themselves to rural/wilderness areas. Cook describes the accomplishments of the CCC as follows.

> Ultimately, three million men, including 250,000 veterans, planted two billion trees, stocked millions of waterways with fish, and built 52,000 public camp grounds and 123,000 miles of roads. They connected twelve thousand miles of telephone lines, protected grazing lands, drained mosquito-infested marshes, fought fires, battled crop disease, preserved wildlife habitats and historic sites, built hiking and horse trails in the national parks. They were responsible for so many magnificent deeds that Grand Canyon park rangers asked if that great miracle of nature was a CCC project.

Cook, *II*, 88.

The National Youth Agency was a New Deal program designed for the young created by executive order in June 1935. ER's prompting played a major role in its creation. It created service camps, provided job training, money for education, community development, and job creation.

220. Quoted in Ronald Edsforth, *The New Deal: America's Response to the Great Depression*, (Malden: Blackwell Publishing, 2000), 137.

221. Smith, *FDR*, 321.

222. Betty and Ernest Lindley quoted in Bernstein, *Caring*, 163.

223. Lash, *Eleanor and Franklin*, 536.

224. ER, *Ask Me*, 48.

225. ER quoted in Black, *Biography*, 243.

226. Lash, *Eleanor and Franklin*, 549.

227. ER, "Facing the Problems of Youth" *National Parent-Teacher Magazine* (February 1935), *Leave Behind*, 303.

228. Eleanor Roosevelt. "Why I Still Believe in the Youth Congress," *Liberty* (April 1940), *Leave Behind*, 376.

229. At times this reached such ridiculous proportions that FDR's mother, a model of blue-blooded New York high society, was on a list of possible communist sympathizers.

230. ER in Black, *Biography*, 200.

231. Quoted in Bernstein, *Caring*, 291.

232. Quoted in Roger Biles, *A New Deal for the American People*, (Dekalb: Northern Illinois University Press, 1991), 194.

233. Bernstein, *Caring*, 290-292.

234. ER, *What Are the Motives for a Woman Working When She Does Not Have to, for Income*? Unpublished article, *Leave Behind*, 280.

235. ER, "Motives," 279. The existence of work is sufficient. The nature of that work, the ways in which certain kinds of work are dehumanizing, is not addressed, although the evolutionary nature of the New Deal certainly leaves room to answer these concerns once the people involved actually have work.

236. ER devoted time and energy defending the right of women to work and encouraging female professionals. She set up all-female press conferences in the White House to preserve jobs for female reporters, and when it became clear that FDR often used ER to float policy trial balloons, she greatly increased those reporters' importance and prestige.

237. ER, "*My Day*," 34 July 1937, 19.

238. The government could be a source of this exposure (and this logic can be used to justify programs like bussing) but it had to be careful not to push the electorate too hard or progressives would lose power.

239. Hareven, *Conscience*, 70. This statement was from an address on NBC radio.

240. "There must doubtless be an unhappy influence on the manners of our people produced by the existence of slavery among us. The whole commerce between master and slave is a perpetual exercise of the most boisterous passions, the most unremitting despotism on the one part, and degrading submission on the other. Our children see this, and learn to imitate it." Thomas Jefferson, "Notes on the State of Virginia," Query XVIII, 288.

241. ER, "Speech to the National Conference on Fundamental Problems in the Education of Negroes," *The Journal of Negro Education* (October 1934), *Leave Behind*, 143,

242. FDR's National Emergency Council's *Report on Economic Conditions of the South* made it clear that the South constituted the nation's top economic problem. Blanche Wiesen Cook summarizes the findings of the report. "While the South 'led the world' in cotton, tobacco, paper, and other products, it was a disaster area. The average per capita income was half the nation's; the poll tax limited voting rights to 12 percent of the population in eight Southern states, including Virginia; the region's children were being undereducated. The South was hampered by backward and colonial customs; and its entrenched leaders wanted no changes." Cook, *II*, 564.

243. ER quoted in Lash, *Eleanor and Franklin*, 525.

244. As well as one of the biggest causes of the black migration to the Democratic Party. Her example gave FDR cover when he had to backpedal on issues like lynching. Hareven, *Conscience*, 123-124.

245. Quoted in Kearny, *Reformer*, 73. Both the pictures and the White House picnic were campaign issues in 1936. Felix Frankfurter wrote to ER, praising her actions. "You render deep service to the enduring values of civilization by serving the nation as a historic example of simple humanity and true human brotherhood in the highest places." Quoted in Lash, *Eleanor and Franklin*, 520.

246. Harold Ickes, Secretary of the Interior and one of the most racially progressive members of FDR's Cabinet (he was the head of the NAACP in Chicago before coming to Washington) arranged for her to sing at the Lincoln Memorial, a far more fitting location.

247. This was during the 1938 Southern Conference on Human Welfare in Birmingham, Alabama. Bull Connor ultimately chose not to arrest her.

248. Lash, *Eleanor and Franklin*, 513.

249. Mileur, "The 'Boss.'"

250. Lash, *Eleanor and Franklin*, 522.

251. Dr. Carrie Weaver Smith quoted in Kearney, *Reformer*, 68.

252. Mary Stuckey, *Defining Americans*, (Lawrence: University Press of Kansas, 2004), 225-231.

253. ER, "Race, Religion and Prejudice," *New Republic* (May, 11th, 1942), *Leave Behind*, 159-160.

254. Plotke, *Building*, 179.

255. Edsforth, *New Deal*, 278.

256. "1936 Democratic Party Platform," The American Presidency Project. http://www.presidency.ucsb.edu/showplatforms.php?platindex=D1936

Part III: Means

Chapter 5
"All Armed Prophets Have Conquered":
A New Deal Theory of Agency

> Politics is always the art of exceptions. It seeks to know where custom must be violated, where human habits and institutions must be changed to guarantee the survival of what is most important, and where the ideal itself must be compromised or muted so that life itself may endure.
>
> —Wilson Carey McWilliams[1]

Normative political theory is abstract by nature, but it is not truly political without simultaneously addressing questions of practice. What is the institutional context of the subject or object of theory? How is power distributed in that context and how does it affect the agency of the actors involved? How does the context alter the theory? In political life, reality is a shadowy approximation of the normative ideal, but politics is always situated in the Cave. The practitioner engages theory not at the level of abstraction, but at the level of imperfect institutionalization. Political actors are forced to confront uncertainty and necessity under hostile circumstances. For the practitioner then, political theory must also be a theory of engagement, accounting for the political, structural, and psychic roadblocks that tarnish the normative ideal.[2]

The New Deal is often dismissed as a source of theory precisely because of its concreteness—it is easy to miss the theory amidst the practice because its theory was designed for practice. We have already explored the normative component of the New Deal's political theory. These next two chapters look at its theory of practice. Chapter 6 addresses the New Deal's institutional context.

Here we explore the nature of the New Deal's political pragmatism and its theory of symbolic politics—the connection between symbolic frames and political change. In particular we will examine the complicated relationship between the folklore of old and new institutions, and the ways in which the legitimacy of the new often depends on the appropriation of the old, especially for progressives looking to transform an ideologically conservative system.

New Deal "Pragmatism"

> There is nothing more difficult to handle, more doubtful of success, and more dangerous to carry through than initiating changes in a state's constitution.
>   —Niccolo Machiavelli[3]

Frances Perkins, charged with the unenviable task of building a welfare state for a nation conditioned to reject it, believed that "nothing in human judgment is final. One may courageously take the step that seems right today because it can be modified tomorrow if it doesn't work well."[4] There was a refreshing honesty that characterized the New Deal's experimental, incremental approach. Roosevelt freely admitted that he has "no expectation of making a hit every time I come to bat,"[5] and his second fireside chat warned Americans that some policies would fail.[6] It is common to describe this attitude, and the New Deal in general, as pragmatic, but we should be careful. All people, especially political people, make pragmatic judgments, weighing costs against benefits. Only the most committed ideologues refuse to ever bend. But then again, the New Deal existed in a time defined by ideologues and abstractions, and as Arthur Schlesinger has noted, "The distinction of the New Deal lay precisely in its refusal to approach social problems in terms of ideology. Its strength lay in its preference of existence to essence."[7]

Of course existence alone does not define reality. Some framework is needed to interpret, evaluate, and provide that reality direction. As Schlesinger goes on to argue, "Without some critical vision, pragmatism could be a meaningless technique; the flight from ideology, a form of laziness; the middle way, an empty conception....But at bottom [Roosevelt] had a guiding vision with a substantive content of its own."[8] That there was a guiding vision is clear. What differentiated the New Deal from other theoretical frameworks was not merely the content of that vision, but the way it thought about the very idea of vision. David Plotke summarizes its approach.

> In the quite different sense in which "pragmatic" usefully describes the new political order in the 1930s, the proper antonyms are "formalist" or "doctrinaire." The opposite of pragmatic is not principled. Without strong commitments to a distinctive set of views about politics and society, it is doubtful that a new political order would have been built.[9]

What made the New Deal both distinct and singularly effective was its willingness to avoid doctrinaire, a priori ideological commitments, to keep its focus on both the institutionalization of its principles and the immediate needs of its constituents, accepting the inevitably imperfect nature of the process. However, it might be better to steer clear of the word entirely, or at least further qualify it. Pragmatism, especially the pragmatism of a figure like John Dewey is a rigorous and sophisticated philosophy, one that privileges a scientific process of inquiry in which beliefs are corrected in light of experience. It is an epistemology more than a theory of power. It requires a degree of detachment and control unfeasible in democratic politics. Instead, the New Deal represented a goal-oriented approach that was remarkably flexible (some say too flexible)[10] about the methods used to pursue those goals, highly sympathetic to pragmatism, but ultimately something different from the philosophic school.[11]

Rather than looking to John Dewey, we can find the New Deal's political sensibilities reflected in Machiavelli's *The Prince*—an example of political theory in its purest *political* form, which is to say a form where political realities trump theoretical models and transcendent goals. More simply, politics, in all its forms, is about the acquisition and use of power. Obviously what one does with that power is an open question informed by normative theory, but for Machiavelli that question is secondary. Discussions of ends without reference to means may be diverting intellectual exercises, but they are not politics, as surely as talk of means without ends is not theory. Political theory must therefore be conversant in both the strategies necessary to acquire power and the factors (cultural, institutional, personal) that interfere with its acquisition.

The New Deal understood this. It possessed a theory of ends, but unless progressive Democrats (or failing that, the party as a whole) gained and maintained control of the government its theory of ends would remain theoretical. As Roosevelt reflected, "If I were now back on the porch at Hyde Park as a private citizen there is very little I could do about any of the things that I have worked on."[12] A private citizen can preach, an opposition party can obstruct, but it is difficult for either to create. Responding to the misery of the Depression and establishing the regulatory controls and safety net necessary to prevent its recurrence, let alone safeguarding and expanding rights to security and happiness, required the acquisition, maintenance, and expansion of power. In a constitutional democracy this meant holding together the massive coalitions of disparate interests necessary to win elections and pass legislation. It also required ugly compromises with the enemy and a tragic awareness of the limits of power—one will never have all the authority one needs to remake the world over, especially in a liberal democracy with numerous institutional choke points and (in the American case) a conservative electorate. Liberal reform requires three things from its practitioners: a theory of ends, so that we know the direction to shape our society; a faith in the mastery needed to remake, and in some ways refound political society; and an awareness of the limits of mastery so that ends do not run too far ahead of means, jeopardizing the entire project.

This is, in many ways, a fallen view of politics, reflecting the pessimism of Niebuhr despite the optimistic tone sounded in the speeches, pamphlets, articles, and books of the New Dealers. There is a tragic, perversely romantic element to this kind of politics; when justice is contingent on power and power is dependent on skill (*virtu*), mobilization, resources, and luck (*fortuna*). The effective prince will always be forced to deal with the Devil, to swallow pride, principle, and make the noxious compromises necessary to secure the power needed to (partially) achieve his ends. The prince is willing to make the sacrifices that fortune and necessity demand of him, even at the cost of his integrity (a word that for Machiavelli has meaning only in private morality). FDR realized this, and it is no coincidence that he found himself drawn to the tragic figure of Abraham Lincoln, who also understood.[13] Confronted with the human wreckage of the Depression and a disintegrating international community, FDR found himself forced to accept compromises he found distasteful and shy away from taking the stands he wished to take. For his critics on the left, these actions embodied failures of leadership and vision. From the standpoint of his governing philosophy, one he shared with Lincoln and Machiavelli, the willingness to compromise in service of larger ends is the essence of leadership, the embodiment of courage, sacrifice, and responsibility. It is the act of a statesman.

The New Deal's political theory, following Machiavelli, revolves around the limits of mastery, recognizing that the space where we can act is defined by fortune and necessity.[14] Political action will always be constrained by the facts on the ground, and despite our best efforts, our control over those facts will be limited. A virtuous leader (effective is a fair modern-day analogue) is one who understands the constraints under which they operate and works to carve out the maximum possible freedom of action within them. An effective prince (executive) has a keen understanding of the contingent nature of reality and is always prepared to react to fortune. Some of this involves diligent planning and an intelligent awareness of the structural forces at play in any given circumstance. It also involves exerting as much control over, and independence from, forces that prevent the prince from acting as necessity dictates. Many of these forces are external—the presence of reactionary Southern Congressmen in key committee positions, the sit-down strikes—and will be the subject of the next chapter. But this also involves freedom from the internal forces that limit our ability to act—freedom from the constraints that political, moral, and economic ideologies impose upon us. The prince is subjected to enough external checks on his agency; he need not add more himself. This means that the effective prince does not allow his expectations or analysis to be colored by a priori expectations and preferences. It becomes necessary to distinguish between, to use Thurman Arnold's language, creeds and ends.

Clarifying this distinction is useful. Arnold hesitated to provide precise definitions for the terms he used, but their meaning became clear from his usage.[15] Ends are the ultimate goals of a political actor—they are the reason he seeks power in the first place. Creeds are instrumental, the theories we use to govern our immediate choices and produce the morale necessary to sustain engagement. Central to the New Deal's political approach is a willingness to be flexible regarding its creeds, as FDR explains in his oft-quoted Oglethorpe address. "The country needs and, unless I mistake its temper, the country demands bold, persistent experimentation. It is common sense to take a method and try it: If it fails, admit it frankly and try another. But above all, try something." It is worth juxtaposing this attitude with that of Hoover, who, as Karl argues, "saw the needs, but the solutions terrified him," leaving him "stranded in a new and clamorous age."[16] The lines in FDR's Oglethorpe address speak to a profoundly undogmatic political theory, one that enabled the New Deal to act under the conditions that left Hoover paralyzed, and this quote is usually regarded as the definitive summation of Roosevelt's pragmatism. But, as Charles Kessler points out, we usually overlook the crucial context provided earlier in the Oglethorpe speech, where Roosevelt states "Let us not confuse objectives with methods."[17] Roosevelt calls for flexibility in our means, but the ends themselves are fixed. The New Deal's commitments to economic and psychic security are examples of ends. A belief that market economies with a minimum of regulation (or the opposite view) are the best way to achieve these ends is an example of a creed. For both Machiavelli and the New Deal, the effective prince will not let his own creeds, his own philosophic categories and theories, unduly limit his ability to act on behalf of those ends.[18] Our motivations can be absolute and unyielding, but our methods must always be governed by flexible, empirical standards of evidence, proof, and practicality.

This is most famously expressed (not by Machiavelli) in the oft-misunderstood phrase "the ends justify the means." We commonly interpret this to mean that any action is justifiable provided it "works," and while broadly true, the criteria for constituting what "works" is important. Once decided on an end, the virtuous/effective prince will pursue whatever avenues offer the greatest probability (nothing is ever certain in a contingent world) of achieving that end. Every option with a plausible chance of success must be considered, and dismissing them on purely ideological grounds marks a failure of leadership, the prince allowing himself to be ruled by creedal passions. If the end is something simple, like the acquisition of power for its own sake, the prince will find few means denied to him. But certain ends will exclude certain means, and political actors must watch to make sure that short-term victories do not undermine larger goals. Ends can all too easily be compromised right out of existence. Still, the fact that ends may limit means does not change the fact that no desired political end can be achieved without institutional power. As Machiavelli reminds us, "all armed prophets have conquered, and unarmed prophets have come to grief."[19] Princely virtue comes from learning how to prioritize and balance—discovering when compromise is necessary, and how much strain an end can endure.

For example, the New Deal's business policy alternated between the planning and industrial cooperation of the NRA and Thurman Arnold's anti-trust regime. Theoretically these two approaches to political economy are at odds with one another, and are often used to illustrate the schizophrenic, groundless, atheoretical nature of the New Deal. What this actually reflects is a purer political pragmatism.[20] The ultimate policy goal was an economy capable of providing for the basic needs of the American people. The means used should remain as flexible as possible, responsive to changing political realities and the continuing vagaries of fortune. As Barry Karl has argued:

> What seems clearest about the first phase of New Deal legislation is its need to use the largest structures capable of having an effect. That the New Dealers turned to big industry and farming was less a product of logic, progressive or nationalist, than of the need to stimulate the largest units of production and employment in the shortest possible time.[21]

As contexts changed, and as consequences became clearer, the New Deal shifted its approach. If a method proves unresponsive or threatens the possibility of future action, as the increasingly unpopular NRA experiment did, refusing to try another on the grounds of theoretical commitments is the height of political irresponsibility. An effective prince understands that there are no permanently right answers (or methods) in a contingent world, and is willing to embrace variability in order to respond to necessity. Policy is not to be judged according to abstract categories and creeds, but by the results it achieves.[22]

At the same time, effective political actors understand the limits of political possibilities. Creedal flexibility alone is not sufficient. Politics does not take place in a vacuum, and power is never absolute. As Machiavelli asserts, "[t]he wish to acquire more is admittedly a very natural and common thing; and when men succeed in this they are always praised rather than condemned. But when they lack the ability to do so and yet want to acquire more at all costs, they deserve condemnation for their mistakes."[23] Push too hard, compromise too little, and the rewards are electoral defeats and broken movements. Political mastery involves an appreciation of necessity—the external checks that limit the exercise of power. This moment is a great stumbling block for any political theory that strives for ideological purity, as it involves compromise and limits, concepts that, while anathema to the critic, are the reality of the political practitioner. A moral critique can involve a blanket condemnation of actors for failing to adhere consistently to creeds or keep perfect faith with a set of ideals, but a political critique must address the central question "what else is possible?"[24] At the same time, political actors must take pains to ensure that necessity does not become an excuse to abandon their commitments. The relationship between "radical goals and immediate demands, the exercise of freedom and the constraints of necessity" is a tenuous one, and true *political theory* requires a delicate balancing act.[25]

A brief look at Roosevelt's failure to campaign for an anti-lynching bill is instructive. The preservation of the New Deal coalition required noxious concessions to some of the most reactionary elements of the Democratic Party. Unrepentant racists in unassailable seats held key committees in Congress, and while FDR was able to break their stranglehold on the presidency with the repeal of the two-thirds rule on presidential nominations, he had little power to intervene here.[26] As FDR famously lamented to Walter White, head of the National Association for the Advancement of Colored People,

> I did not choose the tools with which I must work. Southerners, by reason of the seniority rule in Congress, are chairmen or occupy strategic places on most of the Senate and House committees. If I come out for the anti-lynching bill now, they will block every bill I ask Congress to pass to keep America from collapsing. I just can't take the risk.[27]

White primaries made it difficult to challenge conservative candidates. Poll taxes and intimidation kept voter turnout at 25 percent or less in the strongholds of conservative Democrats. Far more whites were disenfranchised than blacks, but the symbol of Reconstruction, and the terrifying threat of its renewal, gave the tax legitimacy, to the point that some states would not rescind it even for soldiers fighting in WWII.[28] Terrorism kept away blacks who were willing to pay. As one election official in Alabama proudly stated, "there ain't a fuckin' nigger in this end of the country who'd so much as go near a ballot box."[29] FDR believed he lacked both the constitutional authority and legitimacy to challenge these senators, and was reluctant to even take an open stand on race issues when he was planning his ultimately unsuccessful attempt to purge the most recalcitrant racists from the party in 1938.[30] This was compounded by the fact that many of these same Southern Democrats were among the strongest supporters of the New Deal's foreign policy. A critique of Roosevelt on race that ignores this context can be made from moral, but not political, grounds.[31]

Effective leadership is a combination of force and craft, the ability to know, in Machiavelli's celebrated phrase, when to act the part of the lion and when to play the part of the fox, as "the lion is defenseless against traps and a fox is defenseless against wolves."[32] Knowing which approach to use requires managing multiple centers of power and juggling competing interests. This is especially the case with the liberal democratic politics of the United States, which encourages the presence of competing interests and, in theory, refuses to legitimate some over others.

In the era of the New Deal, Machiavellian pragmatism found its most thoughtful and persuasive expression in the writings (and practice) of Thurman Arnold. For Arnold, like Machiavelli before him, politics is about the conflict between political will and institutional capacity. Given our productive plant, our triumph over scarcity, Arnold (and the New Deal) believed the primary limits to our mastery are the psychological roadblocks we voluntarily erect—our inability to overcome our own creedal limitations. His two primary works of theory, *The Symbols of Government* and *The Folklore of Capitalism*, represented at the time the clearest articulation of the approach towards institutional change (filtered through a Machiavellian psychology) that informed the practice, if not the ends, of New Deal theory. The rest of this chapter explores the nature of the New Deal's symbolic approach to politics.

Symbolic Politics

Let me designate the heroes of a nation and I care not who writes its
constitution.

—Thurman Arnold[33]

Machiavelli is noted for his characterization of humanity as "ungrateful, fickle,
liars, and deceivers," but as Bernard Crick[34] has argued, it is more accurate to
see Machiavelli speaking not of human nature, but instead of human tendencies,
susceptible to environmental cues. Machiavelli observes that the character of
citizens will affect (and in turn are affected by) the political regime that
constitutes them. The citizens of a republic will likely exhibit more virtue,
intelligence, and self-sacrifice than those simply being ruled. But as Walter
Lippmann argued at length, the republican citizen, the New Deal ideal, is
tragically the exception rather than the rule. Most citizens (perhaps subjects is a
better word) under most regimes are far less sophisticated, and the successful
fox has a clear understanding of the expectations and limitations of his subjects.
For Machiavelli this means *appearing* to posses whatever moral qualities the
population values, appearing to be a "man of compassion, a man of good faith, a
man of integrity, a kind and a religious man,"[35] but the attributes needed vary
depending on the people being ruled.[36] What matters is not the reality of these
qualities, but their appearance. As Machiavelli makes clear, "[M]en in general
judge by their eyes rather than by their hands; because everyone is in a position
to watch, few are in a position to come in close touch with you. Everyone sees
what you appear to be, few experience what you really are."[37] While the term
would be anachronistic, politics for Machiavelli is largely a form of
salesmanship, and the great leaders have mastered the art of advertising, selling
the people whatever it is they think they want (or what the leader convinces
them they want) in exchange for the currency of power.[38]

The New Deal understood this. Arnold gave it a theoretical voice. In both of
his major works, Arnold makes the argument that politics requires the
manipulation of the ideas and symbols that have existential value to their
audience. This folklore provides reality with shape and meaning. Republican
political theory is predicated on the belief that people can become educated
consumers of political information, inoculated against the fever spread by the
demagogue. New Dealers like Franklin and Eleanor Roosevelt were too devoted
to republican ideals of citizenship to ever publicly defend the less charitable
Machiavellian position. FDR and Eleanor saw themselves as political educators
as well as actors. They aspired to bring about a nation that could embrace ER's
rigorous definition of democracy, where "we sacrifice the privilege of thinking
and working for ourselves alone."[39] Such is the end, and the public language
used reflected both personal commitments and democracy's status as an
American creed. However, both Roosevelts were astute enough political actors
to intuitively grasp what Machiavelli and Arnold made explicit.

The republican ideal is an aspiration, not a description. The tendency of modern social organizations towards increasing size and complexity shuts the vast majority of people out of not only the decision-making process, but prevents them from comprehending the process in its entirety. Instead, as Murray Edelman argues, our "ideas about occurrences are shaped by memorable pictures, placed there by journalist accounts, everyday conversations, political oratory, or other sources of alleged information who devise striking images to win and hold audiences."[40] Accurate perception, if even possible, is now predominantly the province of the elite. The average citizen's understanding of political, social, or economic life becomes symbolic, filtered through the language, images, and ideas we use as heuristics. In this Arnold, his contemporaries like Walter Lippmann, and more recent theorists like Edelman and George Lakoff, place themselves firmly in this Machiavellian tradition.

Arnold, following Machiavelli, argues that change is not a product of educated choice. Instead it occurs through the subconscious habituation of symbols and myths that alter the character of the subject, and with it the political possibilities they can conceptualize. For most this is a passive process of absorption rather than an active process of education and engagement. As Edelman describes it, "[p]olitical actions chiefly arouse or satisfy people not by granting or withholding their stable substantive demands, but rather by changing the demands and expectations."[41] The only actors with true agency are the ones capable of controlling and manipulating the symbols that create demands. The public spokesmen of the New Deal, figures like the Roosevelts and Wallace, attempted to blur the line between political speech as education and political speech as advertisement: always with an eye to education, but realizing in the end that the consumer has to buy what they were selling. In practice the New Deal looked to craft a synthesis between the positions that Lippmann and Dewey staked out during their debates in the 1920s, embracing both a "cynical" realism and an 'idealistic' republicanism. Whether or not the synthesis is viable will be discussed in the final chapter.

Arnold's theory of symbolic politics (adopted in practice by the New Deal) argues that successful political change is dependent on a deep, anthropological understanding of the folklore or mythology (the terms are interchangeable for Arnold) of the relevant subjects.[42] The folklore of an institution represents the creeds, principles, and theories that people use to govern and legitimate their actions (for instance, capitalism), as well as the symbols (such as taxation or the small business) and ceremonies (occasional criminal trials for businessmen caught engaging in particularly egregious violations of the law) that dramatize those values and deal with contradictions between the principles and reality.[43]

Arnold rejects, with Lippmann, the possibility of the "omnicompetent" citizen. His theory revolves around the central importance of understanding and accommodating the ways in which people are at base irrational and passive— ruled by their emotions rather than their intellect, governed by habit rather than agency. In the arena of mass politics, appeals to symbols are always more persuasive than appeals to fact or theory.[44] Facts mean little without the context provided by a dramatic story; theory has power only when people are emotionally invested in its ideals. Therefore, the political practitioner must figure out a way to take advantage of our natural desire to fit ourselves into a narrative, to "reduce ambiguity to certainty."[45]

Political action requires understanding how to engage the folklore of the actors involved—to plug them into a compelling story. As Abbot argues, "[i]n a constitutional democratic regime the pursuit of these [political] activities requires at various points some deeper understanding of the nature of the regime in which they operate as well as the ability to convey that understanding to the citizenry."[46] When Abbot speaks of the nature of the regime he is not speaking of its infrastructure or the day-to-day functioning of its institutions. He refers instead to the actors' understanding of themselves and the various social relationships that bind them to their society. In short, what is needed is knowledge of their explanatory mythology—their folklore. We cannot ignore this folklore because it is a fundamental part of the actors' identity. As Robert Eden points out, the more radical members of the Roosevelt regime (and its critics on the left) who failed to appreciate this found themselves marginalized. In their zeal to build a new City on a Hill, they looked "on the city that happened to be on that hill—the liberal commercial republic and its representative institutions—as received historical material to be transformed or demolished."[47] Arnold's work is primarily addressed to, and a critique of, the principled but powerless stands of progressives like John Dewey, who refused to support Roosevelt (looking instead to third parties) and failed to recognize the progressive potential inherent in the executive centered approach of the Roosevelt administration.[48] Dewey's failure, by the standards of New Deal theory, was found not in his desire for transformation, but his inability to learn to work with the preexisting foundations of a city desiring neither transformation nor demolition.

We need to acknowledge the reality and the power of these foundations even as we attempt to alter them, Arnold argues. He is not concerned about whether an institution's folklore is true, as the truth of an idea is largely irrelevant from a political perspective.[49] Ideas are of political consequence only when they are concretely expressed through institutions. "Philosophies," Arnold asserts, "have no meaning apart from organizations."[50] What matters is the idea's ability to inspire its adherents—its success "in creating public demands which have to be recognized."[51] It is morale and organization, not truth, which determines the distribution of power. The more persuasive folklore wins, and we must not lose sight of the fact that in politics, being right rarely ends a conversation. As Betrand De Jouvenel reminds us, "[c]onstitutions may contrive admirable organs, but these get life and force only so far as they are filled with a life and force derived from a social power which it is not within the capacity of the constitution-makers to create."[52] The power of a social construction is dependent on the morale it generates.

Arnold is careful to draw a distinction between the empirical world and the mythological constructs that interpret it, although the two worlds share a complicated symbiotic relationship. While our folklore retains a political and interpretive primacy, it is normally reactive. Material circumstances necessitate institutions that organize life around those circumstances. These institutions (or their partisans) in turn generate the folklore needed to legitimate these institutions. Theory is (for Arnold) a reflection of material events, reacting to, rather than creating, existing social organizations.[53] Socialism is independent of Marx, liberalism independent of Locke, as these ideologies were necessary responses to failures of the existing institutional order. If they did not exist it would have been necessary for the institutions to invent them. The political significance of their work is not due to its truth content, but the morale it provided new social organizations, their ability to legitimate new institutional forms.

The first task of any political actor is to learn the folklore of their audience, to discover their symbols and stories. Next, Arnold urges the progressive reformer to realize the necessity of manipulating these symbols to advance their "humanitarian" objectives.[54] Truth is but one weapon, and a secondary one at that, in the battle for political influence. This can be a hard pill to swallow, especially for the committed democrat. The New Deal never embraced power as an end in itself, and its republican ideals meant that it was unwilling to reject the possibility of voter rationality, but it did recognize that reforms are far more likely to be successful when they are dressed up in the accepted symbols of the time.[55] Political actors must remember that theory exists to serve institutions and that the ultimate test of a theory's usefulness is empirical. Echoing Machiavelli's call to "represent things as they are in a real truth, rather than as they are imagined,"[56] Arnold argues,

> If you understand that human behavior is symbolic then you cease to look for the reality behind the symbols. You judge the symbols as good or bad on the basis of whether they lead to the type of society you like. You do not cling to them on general principles when they are leading in the wrong direction.[57]

As always, we must be careful to avoid the superficial accusation that this worldview is devoid of direction and commitment, interested only in power for its own sake. The argument here is not an argument against ends, but against dogmatic methodology that judges a practice by evaluating means without reference to ends. It was, in the end, a response to the apolitical pragmatism of Dewey that advocated voting for Norman Thomas and the dream of socialism instead of supporting Roosevelt and building a welfare state.

Arnold is responding to both critics and squeamish supporters of the New Deal who believed (sincerely) that any attempt to alleviate the distress of the Depression and reform the structures that produced it would undermine both the values and stability of our democracy.[58] The commitment to the creeds of laissez faire and rugged individualism was always ideological, and that is why it hindered recovery. It condemned policy in the realm of abstraction, and brushed aside immediate concerns in the interest of our future salvation. By promising the best of all possible worlds tomorrow, we abandon the one we inhabit today.[59]

> The quaint moral conceptions of legal and economic learning by which the needs of the moment could be argued out of existence were expressed by "long run" arguments. Such arguments always appear in religious thinking. From this point of view the future is supposed to be the only reality, just as Heaven in the Middle Ages was the only reality. All else is regarded as temporary, shifting, and ephemeral. This way of thinking allows men to ignore what they see before them in their absorption with the more orderly blueprint of the future.[60]

Therefore during the Depression the anti-New Deal reaction could justify their opposition to humanitarian public policy on moral, principled grounds.[61] Relief becomes shortsighted, hunger an inconvenience to be borne, all because of the conviction (an article of faith, lacking empirical evidence) that the welfare state today brings tyranny tomorrow.

But this dedication to principled abstraction was not simply a phenomenon of the right. Progressives like Senator Borah, at the forefront of reform in a previous generation, found himself in an increasingly anachronistic position, opposing the reach of both capital and the state when it was clear that the size of the former was not going to be reduced and that the size of the later was therefore necessary to restrain it. Further to the left, committed socialists argued that reform becomes a bar to the possibilities of future revolution, with the New Deal accused of undermining the possibilities (another article of faith) of more radical change. In both cases the critique is primarily based on abstractions that ignore the needs of the present.[62]

These beliefs about the price of reform were so firmly (and sincerely) held by the opposition because they and their institutions were surrounded by symbols and ceremonies designed to generate emotional attachments that are by their very nature and purpose irrational—inspirational, rather than descriptive. Our need for "religious" folklore is endemic to the human condition. Neither individual nor institution can function without them.

These mythologies require an extra-human force to legitimate them. In the past that force was God, who in turn was replaced by Nature. Today our gods are the law (in particular the Constitution) and especially the market. In practice they all act as a source of divine, transcendent inspiration for an institutional order. Regardless of their source, Arnold argues, founding myths tend to look the same. A long time ago, a group of gifted forebears created (or discovered) principles that contained the secret of successful social organization. These demigods were people of penetrating insight far beyond what we are capable of producing today. Hence the veneration. To question their principles is to question the absolute, which makes believers uncomfortable. A troubling by-product of these religious attachments is that these 'faiths' also create taboos that limit political possibilities when contexts change.

Scholars invent theories to justify these taboos (regulation undermines business confidence and delays recovery) in much the same way priests invented dogma to justify the social arrangements of the Middle Ages. Arnold sees little difference between the role of modern scholars and medieval priests. Both work to provide the mystic foundations for practical organizations. As long as these mythological, symbolic constructs enjoy legitimacy change is difficult, progress painful. Exceptionally large groups (like the business community or the federal government) develop particularly potent forms of mythology, like the ideal of the free market or sanctification of the Constitution. Often times these are intertwined to the point that you cannot talk about one without talking about the other. For Arnold, this is the "Folklore of Capitalism," and Wallace argues that our trust in laissez faire capitalism is grounded in a faith "which is as unreasonable, dogmatic and theoretical as any long-established theology."[63]

> The faith of business men in rugged individualism, in profits unlimited and in the divine right of big business to call on government for help in case of need, while at the same time government was to stay out of business under all other conditions, represent views so firmly held as to be beyond mere logic and in the realm of the transcendental."[64]

By restricting our ability to respond to necessity, this folklore has outlived its usefulness, but nonetheless remains a potent political force that must be addressed. Arnold's concern is the disconnect between the realm of scholarship—which legitimates the creed, and the realm of practice—which deals with the actual needs of people in concrete circumstances.[65] The extent that our scholarship takes place in an abstract world removed from practice is the extent to which creeds cease to describe reality and instead become a theoretical tool used by priests to punish heretics—those who question the legitimacy of the established order.

The fundamental principles established by the relevant founders determine the limits of acceptable discourse. Arnold argues that outside times of institutional collapse there is only agency within these boundaries (no serious American political movement can propose doing away with capitalism or argue that the Constitution lacks inherent meaning). To go outside of those prescribed bounds is heresy, and in most cases means marginalization at best, outright persecution at worst. Since political actors of all stripes share the same symbolic toolkit, these accepted symbols end up meaning all things to all people, which make them not only logically incoherent but psychically powerful and politically useful. Arnold observes:

> ...where the center of attention is abstractions rather than practical objectives all parties are bound to be alike. The creed of each must represent all the current conflicting ideals and phobias. Only minority parties which do not expect to get into power can write creeds without internal contradictions. Opposing parties which hope to win will necessarily worship the same gods

even while they are denouncing each other because they are talking to actual voters and not to some ideal society of the future. This is not something to complain about. It follows from the fact that every governmental creed must represent all the contradictory ideals of people if it is to be accepted by them.[66]

In order for a principle to unify a diverse collectivity that principle must be inconsistent. It has to be capable of appealing to multiple cognitive frameworks simultaneously.[67] In order to unify the United States, the Constitution must be able to appeal to both progressives and conservatives, to privilege federal power and state's rights, to protect the weak and serve the powerful. This enables one side to accept political defeat without becoming alienated from the larger community.

The need to appeal to these contradictory frameworks is a source of New Deal "inconsistency." Political commentator Dorothy Thompson cut right to the heart of the problem.

> Two souls dwell in the bosom of this Administration, as indeed, they do in the bosom of the American people. The one loves products of large-scale mass production and distribution…The other soul yearns for former simplicities, for decentralization, of the interests of the little man, revolts against high pressure salesmanship, denounces monopoly and economic empires, and seeks means of breaking them up.[68]

As long as the American people want both, a regime that hopes to bring about mass change in a democratic fashion will be forced to appeal to each perspective, even at the expense of theoretical inconsistency. If cognitive dissonance does not bother the voter, the theorist has to make space for it.

This theoretical inconsistency, Arnold argues, is not a problem when social conditions are static. When there is little meaningful challenge to dominant folklore contradictions can be resolved through ceremonial action and sub rosa institutions. But inevitably new institutions are needed to respond to changing conditions, and whenever new organizations arise, "respectable and conservative" people, fully raised and schooled in preexisting folklore, will oppose them.[69] We are, for the most part, psychologically incapable of making choices and decisions that fall beyond the limits of our familiar symbolic context.[70] It is why, Arnold argues, we enjoy social stability and lack agency.

> Their [conservatives] moral and economic prejudices, their desire for the approval of other members of the group, compel them to oppose any form of organization which does not fit into the picture of society as they have known it in the past. The principle is on the one hand the balance wheel of social organization and on the other hand its greatest element of rigidity.[71]

For Arnold, the logic of mass reaction is always the same, grounded not in economic self-interest, but in a sense of outrage over the existential violation of a worldview by new ideas and forms of organization that challenge the parts we play in a larger story.[72] This response is only natural, Arnold argues, given our psychic needs to believe in the purity and truth of existing arrangements that provide comfort and meaning. We see the same response to changing institutional contexts during the Reformation and the French Revolution. We see it as well in Herbert Hoover's response to New Deal programs. While "'National Planning' to preserve the initiative of men, etc, would be all right," Hoover objects to referring to organizations such as "NRA PWA, CWA, TVA as 'national planning' unless, of course, one is planning Fascism or Socialism."[73] The connection Hoover draws between relief and fascism seems overwrought, but is natural and inevitable according to Arnold.

Along with the human need to believe in the rightness of our institutions, we are naturally inclined to find heresy in our opposition, as the presence of heresies transform, to paraphrase John Stuart Mill, dead dogmas into living truths. Heresy affords us the opportunity to rejuvenate convictions that were habituated over time. It is a powerful tool of political mobilization. Note that this is not the sharpening of ideas that comes from the give and take of intellectual argument and debate that Mill argues for in *On Liberty*. Arnold speaks not of the rational act of clarification but the irrational act of building attachments through what is essentially fear. Arnold argues that all movements against heresy consist of the discovery of a devil, not all-powerful (otherwise resistance would be futile), but seductive enough to cause moral panic. Invariably a priestly class arises to legitimate (and lead) the battle against the heretics. During the Great Depression it was the priests of the established order—the conservative economists, lawyers, and scholars—who fought the devil of the welfare state and the impending loss of freedom and individuality that their folklore assured them it would inexorably usher it.[74] In this case, the devil manifested itself in the heart of anyone who suggested that market excess can undermine democracy, or that the government has a real interest in regulating that excess for the good of the nation. The profit motive is an axiomatic, religious proof—not to be questioned under pain of "financial death...political death and social ostracism."[75] Intolerance of heresy has always obstructed social reform; the 1930s being no different than the 1600s or 2000s. From the standpoint of the believer, change is necessarily immoral because our morals were formed in a time when current needs were not recognized as legitimate. Received wisdom can rarely look to the future, Arnold argues, because it is rooted in the past.

Today we are able to look back at the Middle Ages and recognize the mythology of that age for what it was. Although the people of that time believed the portrait painted by their priests reflected truth, subsequent generations can recognize it as ideology—a way of justifying and preserving a particular set of social arrangements. Every age has its folklore, but no age recognizes it as such. There is usually little to be gained by critically examining the myths of a stable order. Once you expose a myth as a myth it loses its force. "Nothing disturbs the attitude of religious worship so much as a few simple observations."[76] And of course the social structures of any society are organized to protect its myths from challenge. In every age the United States has had its own folklore and attendant heresies. In the past, heresy was a lack of faith. For Arnold, twentieth-century heresy was a lack of acceptance of "rational" and "scientific" doctrine and principle, especially the principles of established economic and constitutional law. Outside of religious opposition, Arnold argues, cries of heresy are comparatively uncommon in the hard sciences because it faces no crisis of legitimacy. There is no folklore trying to replace it. Instead experts are allowed to settle these issues themselves in a calm, deliberate fashion, with standards of evidence not linked to emotive stories.[77] Similarly, the folklore of capitalism allows for a business to invest and organize based on empirical expectations of profits, devoid of questions of character and morality—which is why that folklore is worthy of emulation and, prior to the Depression, possessed so much vitality.

In moments of institutional failure (like the Great Depression) the adherents of an old folklore are especially vigilant in their defense against heresy. The experience and needs of the 25 percent of the nation in distress had to be discounted by its opponents because their folklore could not make room for their suffering. Radicals and reformers are dangerous because they refuse to accept the received truth of the market. They look at empirical evidence and refuse to have faith in the natural laws that guarantee prosperity (just around the corner), if only the federal government would abandon its reckless desire to interfere in the natural unfolding of economic law.

All myths have their central characters, and one of ours, according to Arnold, is the rational thinking man—capable of looking past his immediate material circumstances to recognize the truth in abstract principles: capitalism, the Constitution, democracy, justice, the family, liberty—the ideals we use to orient our lives.[78] Education, a free press, and public discussion enable us to make unbiased and unemotional decisions about what is in our interest.[79] If we implement these ideas objectively and rationally, we will have a productive, orderly, society. Despite contrary evidence that people do not actually interact with the world in this fashion, we clung to our faith in our fundamentally rational nature, with the writings of economists and legal scholars serving to justify that faith. "Today, of course, we consider ourselves too rational to rely too much on the believer. Beliefs and faiths are all right in a democracy only after we have first *thought them out* or hired someone to think them out for us."[80] Likewise, Arnold argues, we believe that the rational thinking man possesses political agency, that the policies that govern our dominant economic, political, and social organizations reflect his will and are designed to serve him. The warnings of Lippmann go unheeded, and as Edelman declares, "The faith virtually all Americans profess that they live in a country in which the will of the people prevails is based on socialization, wishful thinking, and psychological need, not on everyday experience."[81] Our eyes may tell us one thing, but we have our heavy textbooks and weighty theorists to tell us something else.[82]

The combination of rationality and agency, Arnold argues, leads to a belief in free will, which enables individuals to overcome structural limitations and eliminates our need to confront them. All our actions are a product of choices, and if rational people simply choose to obey our natural laws we will end up with a prosperous and moral society. The same holds true for organizations. Market forces are benevolent and progressive, so choosing to surrender to them assures long-term prosperity and growth. Failures are never the fault of structural deficiencies but the necessary outcome of an individual's inability to follow clear-cut guiding ideals. They reflect a moral lapse. People unemployed during the Depression are unemployed due to poor choices or deficient character (or later, because of government interference in the economy). Corporate malfeasance is the product of immoral executives who refuse to play by the rules, not structural forces that reward certain behaviors. The process is the same for individuals and organizations.[83] As long as we can blame our social problems on bad men who refuse to follow reason and principle we do not need to question the principles themselves. The problem is the individual sinner, not a failure of the market or our system of distribution. This notion of freedom is inspiring, empowering, and psychically necessary but it is not an effective standpoint from which to solve problems.

> It is essential that the individual feel that he has free will and reason, as separate qualities, in order to conduct his affairs with dignity and force. It is equally necessary that he have the same feeling toward the institutions to which he is loyal. All the ceremonies of daily life are set in the confines of that stage. However for purposes of diagnosis or dissection of social institutions, it is necessary to realize that what we call free will, and sin, and emotion, and reason are attitudes which influence conduct and not separate little universes containing principles which actually control institutions.[84]

Our tendency to dramatize, to look for sin and heresy, to look at problems through a moral lens, means that we are unable to recognize the presence of structural causes, of necessity, and respond to them appropriately. If we cannot diagnose a problem we cannot address it.[85]

Institutional Change

> Social institutions require faiths and dreams to give them morale. They need to escape from these faiths and dreams in order to progress. The hierarchy of governing institutions must pretend to symmetry, moral beauty, and logic in order to maintain their prestige and power. To actually govern, they must constantly violate those principles in hidden and covert ways.
>
> —Thurman Arnold[86]

Arnold's theory is ultimately a theory of political agency, meant to facilitate a progressive transformation of a conservative society. This is no easy task. The deep roots of our folklore mean it cannot be categorically abandoned, even when necessity requires new stories for new institutions. Eden nicely summarizes the problem, "majorities do not knowingly vote for a moral revolution to be conducted against their own morality. The old individualism was the creed by which the majority of Americans lived and to which they subscribed. It was not an issue that could be decided favorably in a critical election or even by a gradual electoral realignment over several elections."[87] Outside of a revolution, new social arrangements can legitimate themselves only by connecting themselves to the symbols of the past, since socialization into new folklore takes so much time. Fortunately, Arnold argues, the elasticity of the human mind and the poorly defined nature of our symbols make this appropriation of the past possible. This process slows down the pace of reform, but it is necessary if we wish to confer legitimacy on new institutions. Roosevelt said as much himself.

> It is this combination of the old and new that marks orderly peaceful progress, not only in building buildings, but in building government itself. Our new structure is part of and a fulfillment of the old...All that we do seeks to fulfill the historic traditions of the American people.[88]

Legitimacy and stability are only conferred when they are grounded in habit and tradition, and reformers must direct their efforts at utilizing preexisting symbols and stories, our extant folklore, to facilitate this process.

In Arnold's view, changing a nation's psychology is like changing the habits and preferences of an individual. It takes enormous and sustained commitment. Usually the impetus for change is a response to outside pressures, when the individual's previous habits are no longer satisfying and organizations are no longer able (or appear to be able) to fulfill their established roles. This process takes time to play itself out, and happens largely as a result of tension between principle and practice. Creeds exist to provide organizations with morale, and effective principles are the ones that do not interfere with the actual running of the institution. Laissez-faire capitalism was the creed of the business community, and justified that community's privileged position in American folklore. By the time of the Depression, progressive economists had clearly demonstrated that the creed of capitalism in no way provides an accurate description of actual business practice. The United States has been a corporate welfare state from the moment Alexander Hamilton had the treasury pay off Revolutionary War debts purchased by speculators. But the point of the creed is to provide morale to the institutions it serves, not describe its practice. The gospel of laissez faire may not have resembled reality, but it sanctified the accumulation and concentration of wealth and power. An actual accounting of the way businesses functioned would undermine its morale by calling its folklore into question.

Descriptive accuracy is desirable only when designing new institutions. Because business managed to perform its function of making and distributing goods reasonably effectively, there was no psychic tension between creed and practice except in times of depression. Then calls for reform were heard and largely dealt with in a ceremonial fashion until the depression ended. The point of these ceremonies was not to actually address the issues at hand (which would require structural intervention and new institutions), but to reconcile the tension between theory and practice—to demonstrate that failures are a product of immoral, sinful choices born of free will, rather than a product of systemic failure. They also indicate that the actors responsible for addressing the problem are successfully performing their function, without actually requiring the institutional revision necessary to address the issue.

In *The Folklore of Capitalism* Arnold provides his famous analysis of the Sherman Anti-Trust Act as an example of ceremonial intervention in action (which made for some awkward moments during his confirmation hearings to run the anti-trust division at the Department of Justice).[89] Arnold was critical of the symbolically rich but substantively empty way the act had historically been used. Trust-busting paid big political dividends for Teddy Roosevelt, but did not limit the growth of concentrated economic power, because actually containing their growth was never the goal. There was a practical need to have large-scale organizations if we wished to enjoy the benefits of industrial capitalism, but those organizations had no place in the American folklore of the time. The few prosecutions Roosevelt made under the Sherman Act were ceremonial: intended to ease our moral concerns about economic consolidation; draw distinctions between 'good and bad' corporations; to provide cover for the growth of these organizations; and to assuage the Jeffersonian side of the American soul.

It was impossible for Roosevelt to destroy trusts because there were no existing organizations capable of handling large-scale manufacturing and distributional needs as effectively.

> The reason why these attacks always ended with a ceremony of atonement, but few practical results, lay in the fact that there were no new organizations growing up to take over the functions of those under attack. The opposition was never able to build up its own commissary and its service of supply. It was well supplied with orators and economists but lacked practical organizers. A great cooperative movement in America might have changed the power of the industrial empire. Preaching against it, however simply resulted in counter preaching.[90]

However, the act retained its symbolic value and its moral delegitimation of large corporations made it a potent weapon if the political will was ever found to actually propose new institutional arrangements to replace trusts.[91] Certainly Arnold felt that using the Sherman Act (albeit in new ways) would be more immediately effective than the formation of new regulatory institutions[92] that lacked legitimacy and would be subject to public challenge. As Arnold argued, "if you are going to make that adjustment [to increased regulation] easier and less painful, you must use methods which do not create fear and distrust by attacking revered traditions. And there lies the strength of the Sherman Act. It is a symbol of our traditional ideals."[93]

As we have discussed, the functionality of an organization or social structure is threatened when commitment to creedal principles ends up preventing an institution from performing its necessary functions. For instance, governments need to take care of the material needs of their people, but prior to the existence of the New Deal our political government largely ignored this responsibility. Our principles told us that the government administering welfare and regulating business would lead to socialism and the abolition of freedom. So the (public) government had to take a principled stand against its own responsibilities. This led to the development of what Arnold calls 'sub rosa institutions,' organizations that enable an institution to fulfill its practical functions in cases where its own principles prevent it from doing so. Arnold often used political machines to illustrate this point.[94] They never enjoyed public legitimacy, and progressive reformers bemoaned their existence as a blemish on the face of our democratic ideals.[95] Yet they performed a vital role, providing the necessary welfare services that the government could not furnish on principle.[96] So time and time again we went through the familiar ceremony of reformers promising to banish machines in order to save our government, passing laws and making speeches to that effect. Of course the machines never went away because they were actually integral for the survival of our governing institutions.[97] They performed necessary welfare functions the folklore of capitalism denied the state. However, the act of condemning them was itself a necessary ceremony designed to reaffirm our faith in the principles of good government.

Normally ceremonial intervention and sub rosa institutions are sufficient to maintain the balance between principle and practice. However, in times of crisis these institutions can be overwhelmed, as witnessed during the Depression. Arnold argues that by 1933 our "industrial feudalism" could no longer take responsibility for the millions of unemployed in America and ceased to act as a governing institution. America's networks of private charities and political machines lacked the resources necessary to cope with a sustained crisis of that magnitude. At this point, new institutions (in this instance, the welfare state) begin to form; designed to supplant older ones psychologically unequipped to deal with current problems.[98] At first these new institutions are persecuted by the priests of the old order, their practitioners condemned as heretics in the appropriate language of the period. As Arnold points out in his typically breezy fashion, we saw the Roman Catholic Church attack the reformation, we saw monarchists resist the rise of liberal democracies, and we saw New Deal reformers attacked by its opponents for engaging in practices that violated the sanctity of the Constitution and "sound economic thinking" (whatever abstractions are used to justify the status quo).[99]

This is inevitable, Arnold argues, because principles linger on long after their usefulness has ended.

> When the institutions themselves disappear, the words still remain and make men think that the institutions are still with them. They talk of the new

> organizations which have come to take the place of the old in terms of these old words. The old words no longer fit. Directions given in that language no longer have the practical results which are expected. Realists arise to point this out and men who love and reverence these old words (that is, the entire God-fearing, respectable element of the community) are shocked. Since the words are heavily charged with a moral content, those who do not respect them are immoral. The respectable moral element of society will have nothing to do with such immorality. They feel compelled to run the power over to non-respectable people in order to reserve the right to make faces at them.[100]

Many "well-meaning people," as Arnold frequently referred to the opposition, found they could not endorse the humanitarian ends of the New Deal because it violated their fundamental beliefs about the nature of the government's role in society.[101] Their commitments to theoretical principles paralyzed their ability to act in a humanitarian fashion. Welfare reform was opposed during the New Deal out of fear for our character. Many were convinced a welfare state would breed a nation of dependents who would prefer the dole to an honest day's work for an honest day's wage. Structural defects in the system were attributed to the personal habits of the poor. Unemployment and poverty were primarily moral issues because we had difficulty conceptualizing them in any other fashion, no matter how many people were unemployed.

Ideas change slowly and painfully, which is why reform is so slow and painful. New ideas have no established myths—they have no creeds and ceremonies that have been accepted by the public. What's more, these new organizations have to overcome all of the philosophy, scholarship, ceremony, and tradition that legitimated previous institutions. As such, new forms of organization will always be looked upon as illegitimate until they develop their own creed capable of winning widespread acceptance.[102]

> This can be observed in revolutions of all kinds, peaceful as well as violent. A ruling class ceases to perform the functions necessary to distribute goods according to the demands of a people. A new class appears to satisfy those demands. At first it is looked down on. Gradually it accumulates a mythology and a creed. Finally all searchers for universal truth, all scholars, all priests (except, of course, unsound radicals), all education institutions of standing, are found supporting that class and everyone feels that the search for legal and economic truth has reached a successful termination.[103]

Arnold argues that all periods of social change follow this pattern.[104] New folklore is born in the struggle that legitimates new institutions, themselves a response to the failures of the old order. As circumstances change new forms of ceremony rationalize inconsistencies between the creed and function of the institution, new sub rosa institutions develop as necessary and this process begins anew as reified principles once again begin to trump practice. But creating a new folklore takes time, and until an institution develops and establishes that folklore its legitimacy is in danger, which is why the reformer must work, when possible, to link new policies to old ideals.

The more a program violates prevailing folklore, the harder it is to institutionalize. The New Deal learned the lesson with the Arthurdale experiment. Ostensibly a relief program for destitute farmers, the project proposed to create a community based on a hybrid of subsistence farming and light manufacturing. Townspeople would grow their own crops and maintain a cooperative dairy. During off seasons they would operate a small factory to supplement their income. In time they would buy their land and home from the government.

The idea of subsistence farming was never meant to compete with commercial farming. Instead it was designed to offer (perhaps paternalistically) the rural poor a new opportunity to live simply and healthy. The idea was given a twenty-five-million-dollar budget for study and experimentation, as ER believed that "[i]t is from our rural home dwellers that we must hope for vision and determination to bring again contentment and well being into the homes of our nations."[105] It was a grand experiment in community building and an attempt to permanently deal with the problem of poverty in modernity, to help those whom the market had forgotten.

Resettlement has a rich history in this country, with roots in the agrarian nostalgia that accompanied industrialization, our communitarian heritage, and the safety valve theory of the frontier made popular by Frederick Jackson Turner. The New Deal saw Arthurdale as an experiment not only in alternative solutions to poverty, but as an exercise in establishing the standards by which all Americans were entitled to live. Basic human dignity and happiness do not have a price tag—or rather they have a price tag four times Arthurdale's allocated budget.[106] There was a fundamental disconnect between whether or not the project was intended as relief or an exercise in alternative ways of living, community building, and democracy.[107] For Arthurdale to achieve the goals set for it, the community would need to be seen as an investment, and as Arnold argues, we have a difficult time conceptualizing how to publicly budget human investment.[108] For the New Deal, the cost was defensible because it was an educational/experimental experience that would pay off huge dividends in the future. "This is pioneering. The first automobile and the first airplane cost a lot of money to make,"[109] ER argued. "The lesson learned as to character and cost and ability to obtain work and subsistence will be very cheap, because it will enable others to profit by this experience."[110] But for Congress, Arthurdale was overpriced relief, granting the undeserving poor a greater standard of living than other hard-working Americans. For the project to be successful there would need to be a cooperative factory, and private industry (and parts of Congress) revolted. This was seen as tantamount to communism, although, as ER pointed out, it was difficult to see how giving people a chance to buy and own their own houses was communistic.[111] Nevertheless, the ideological objection held, as ER and other New Deal partisans were never able to fully erase the stigma attached to relief, nor create widespread empathy for the dispossessed as a group.[112] One innovative New Deal program after another found that the more they challenged our public folklore the more difficult, if not impossible, it was to sustain both the public and political commitment necessary for legitimacy.

The Role of the Theorist

What is needed today is the kind of theory which will be effective both as a moral force and as an intellectual playground, yet which will permit politicians to come out of the disreputable cellars in which they have been forced to work. This kind of theory might make it possible for men with social values to cooperate with political organizations without the present disillusioning conflict between their ideals and necessary political practices. The reason that such a theory is needed is that political organization is the only tool which a government faced with practical problems can use. It therefore needs a respectable set of symbols.

—Thurman Arnold[113]

The failure of Arthurdale was due in part to what we would today call poor framing. The New Deal was unable to control the symbolic language used for understanding the project. It was perceived as radical and dangerous, when new social organizations are safest justifying themselves through language and ideas that are comfortable and familiar, drawing upon the past and interpreting it in new ways.[114] This means, as Abbot argues in *The Exemplary Presidency*, that

American political culture does indeed place severe restrictions on a president's speech. Not only are there entire vocabularies of politics unavailable to a president, but there are cultural beliefs, deeply held, that are radically inconsistent. Moreover, suspicion of elites and political authority in general as well as the creedal acceptance of individualism often requires a president to justify not only his administration but government itself.[115]

Elected officials in a democratic regime need to both demonstrate a sophisticated understanding of their society's folklore, and learn how to frame any and all policy innovations in terms of that folklore. Perhaps most controversially, this requires political theorists addressing an American audience to rethink the utility of Marxist categories from a political standpoint. If, as Lipset and Marks argue, there is neither institutional nor symbolic space for socialism in the United States, it becomes necessary to look to other, more authentically "American" traditions like the social gospel, economic populism, and (today) the New Deal and use their categories for selling (if not theorizing) the welfare state to the American people.[116]

The progressive reformer is put in a tricky position. As Machiavelli observes, "the gulf between how one should live and how one does live is so wide that a man who neglects what is actually done for what should be done moves towards self-destruction rather than self-preservation."[117] The unromantic nature of both Machiavelli and Arnold's worldviews make it easy to default to a position of cynicism.[118] Arnold, perhaps not quite fully understanding Machiavelli, responds:

> Machiavelli insisted that the world was run by knaves and therefore to be a good governor one must act like a knave. In this is a moral judgment which destroys the accessibility of his teaching. I would prefer to say that the world is run by very nice people of ordinary intelligence and therefore the governor must understand the limitations of nice people of ordinary intelligence and act accordingly.[119]

The limitations imposed by our existential need to be plugged into a story means that there is limited utility in the simple exposure of hypocrisy and false consciousness. "Man was born to be harnessed by priests," Arnold claims, and that is not a condition we are easily emancipated from. As a result;

> "Realism," effective as it is as a method of political attack, or as a way of making people question ideas which they had formerly considered as established truths, ordinarily winds up by merely making the world look unpleasant. Since, for most people at least, the world is actually not an unpleasant place, the realist remains in the sun only a short time...[120] Man can never escape from his moral self, and a cynical position brings the futility of disillusionment.[121]

The disillusioned make neither effective leaders nor followers, Arnold argues. If you cannot look at the Statue of Liberty, salute a flag, or sing the national anthem without irony or disgust you will not move masses. This, then, is the role of theory in political life. We require illusions, and prefer ones so familiar that we cannot identify them as illusions. Someone needs to be able to justify the symbols that the reformer wants to use, to write poetry for institutions.

Arnold draws a useful distinction between the anthropologist, diagnostician, and the advocate. The successful political actor must play all three roles. The anthropologist learns to recognize creeds as creeds—sources of morale, not truth. He catalogues the ceremonies, symbols, and creeds that make up the folklore of an institution. The diagnostician learns to see past them to view the world of necessity, and react to it empirically. The diagnostician crafts policy. But this is not sufficient. An advocate is needed to justify the proposals of the diagnostician. To be successful, the advocate needs to learn to utilize the cultural tools of the anthropologist to make the new seem old, the unpalatable palatable.

The move is trickier than it seems. In order to do more than simply pander, the advocate must simultaneously believe the folklore of the institution without becoming trapped by it. The flag cannot embarrass him, nor can he blindly salute it. The anthropologist must provide the advocate with his script, and effective advocacy requires commitment, rejecting the detached anthropological standpoint of the observer, while still appropriating his insights. The New Dealers who were effective advocates were those who spoke about American symbols with passion and conviction while still managing to keep the recommendations of the diagnostician firmly in hand.

David Plotke seems to recognize the implications of this when evaluating the New Deal as a body of theory. He argues, in regards to FDR, that while "his public discourse was often superficial as political philosophy, it was deep in its resonance, in its evocations of Christian and democratic themes from the American tradition...Roosevelt tapped the power of vocabularies that had been largely cast aside in the march of American individualism, materialism, and capitalism."[122] New Deal advocates had to take two steps to grant their institutions legitimacy. They had to weaken our attachment to the principles and folklore they sought to replace, and find a way to make the new order appear familiar. As FDR argued, "Our task of reconstruction does not require the creation of new and strange values. It is rather the finding of the way once more to known, but to some degree forgotten, ideals and values."[123] We must find our way back before we can rebuild.

Folklore Old and New

We are now struggling to formulate a philosophy which will give a more centralized power the freedom to learn from experience. This philosophy must be woven out of the terminology of the older way of thinking.
—Thurman Arnold[124]

New Deal institutions lacked an established folklore and the organic development of folklore takes time that any challenge to the established order may not have. Therefore, its supporters mined America's cultural history, reinterpreting and reinvigorating old symbols in the fight for legitimacy. The public writing of figures like FDR, Wallace, and ER were all in service of this goal, convincing Americans that radical changes were not so radical after all. And in large measure this is the goal of *political* theory—creating the poetry needed to justify a response to necessity, and linking this response to the deeper aspirations of a people otherwise suspicious of the response. On this score the New Deal's success was ultimately mixed. It failed to destroy the folklore of capitalism, but it did manage to legitimate what, for the purposes of this study, we can refer to as the folklore of the New Deal, creating a set of counter symbols and creeds for future American reformers. That Roosevelt and the New Deal is the default symbolic frame of reference for any reasonably progressive president speaks to the enduring weight of that folklore.

Both the folklore of capitalism and the folklore of the New Deal exist within a larger American folklore, the central tenet of which is the belief that the United States is a land of limitless, boundless opportunity, reflected in the breathtaking hubris of Manifest Destiny, the bootstrap pluck of the young boys populating the stories of Horatio Alger, Benjamin Franklin's homespun wisdom, and countless other sources. The New Deal, which assumed abundance even in a time of apparent scarcity, certainly accepted this basic premise—indeed, its theoretical viability may require this acceptance. It differs from the folklore of capitalism in the secondary myths drawn from this basic assumption, which Arnold lays out in *The Folklore of Capitalism*. We have already explored the New Deal's critique of the basic creeds and symbols of the folklore of capitalism: the private, rather than public, nature of economic power, the rational thinking man, the assumption of scarcity, and the myths of private property and free will. Now, with Arnold as our guide, we will explore the New Deal's critique of three more symbols of the folklore of capitalism, symbols that remain just as potent today as they were eighty years ago: the positive symbol of the businessman, and the negative symbols of government and welfare.

However, Arnold argued, it is never sufficient to just tear down. Something must be standing by to replace what is lost, and the New Deal had its own repurposed symbols they hoped could bridge the transition into its own folklore, "the social philosophy of tomorrow." The symbols were familiar, but given a new twist that made them acceptable metaphors in the New Deal's institutional poetry. This chapter concludes by examining the New Deal's appropriation of the symbols of religion, the frontier, and the Constitution.

The Businessman

> Entrepreneurs and their small enterprises are responsible for almost all the economic growth in the United States.
>
> —Ronald Reagan[125]

As Arnold argues, all nations (in fact all organizations of any kind) generate heroes appropriate for their folklore. Sometimes these are actual historical figures, but an abstract ideal works just as well (and seems more appropriate for a liberal society whose principles derive from a universal subject). Although we honor and build monuments to our greatest statesmen, Arnold claims in the end that they are minor characters in our pantheon of heroes. For generations, Americans had found politics to be a sordid, unwholesome enterprise, and while great leaders might inspire us, they are the exceptions that prove the rule. And as Tocqueville made clear, a socially egalitarian democracy, hostile to excellence, will require unexceptional heroes. In Arnold's view, therefore, the American hero is not the political operative but the industrial organization, formerly the small entrepreneur, which embodies all our consequential values, regardless of their contradictory nature. "The American industrial organization is a hard boiled trader, a scholar, a patron of modern architecture, a thrifty housewife, a philanthropist, a statesman preaching sound principles of government, a patriot, and a sentimental protector of widows and orphans at the same time."[126] Business thought of itself in this same lofty fashion. In the aftermath of Roosevelt's Four Freedoms address Armour and Company launched a series of ads establishing free enterprise as the fifth freedom, and reminded Americans that the corporate system "exalts the individual, recognizes that he is created in the image of God, and gives spiritual tone to the American system."[127]

The claim to exalt the individual may seem surprising coming from an organization that obliterates it, but it is necessary given the symbolic importance of the individual in American folklore. Long after the corporation became our dominant social actor our language continued to exalt the entrepreneur and the small business. Rhetorical support for the small businessman was a useful ceremony and reliable source of political capital.[128] The fact that these actors were increasingly marginal does not negate their existential importance in American folklore, so symbolic homage must be paid.

Like any piece of folklore, incompatible positions had to be resolved through ceremony, so despite all evidence to the contrary, the businessman, while acting selfishly, must benefit the collectivity in the long run through the wealth generated by his selfishness. As long as this is believed, interference by the government in economic matters damages the long-term welfare of the nation, even if that intervention is designed to protect the small businessman and entrepreneur.

The businessman embodies freedom. Therefore any attempt to govern him is by definition tyrannical. He only owes allegiance to the Constitution, which rewards him by protecting his right to do whatever it is he wants to do, unfettered by regulation or democratic accountability.

> As regulatory bodies expanded in power and influence, the weight of all our philosophy and our judicial drama was aimed at keeping them on a lower plane. Principles of freedom did not find their habitation in surroundings where man is being directed for his own good. The Lord in Milton's *Paradise Lost*, confronted by the same problem, decides it is better to allow man to fall than to take any active steps to help him out. He conceives his function to preserve man's free will by judging him only after he has sinned. To prevent sin by divine regulation would be to create a heavenly bureaucracy.[129]

Only the employer was granted this freedom, however. Employees remained subjected to his arbitrary control, and "[t]heir only freedom consisted in the supposed opportunity of laborers to become American businessmen themselves."[130] The businessman's privileged position as the incarnation of freedom meant that a free government necessarily served the interests of the business community and, as Hiram Canton observes, any political pursuit of social equality becomes fundamentally despotic.[131] Those who lacked this true freedom would have to trust that "the rights and interests of the laboring man will be protected and cared for—not by the labor activists, but by the Christian men to whom God in his infinite wisdom has given the control of the property interests in this country."[132] There is something medieval about this arrangement (and Arnold's characterization of it as industrial feudalism is apt), and it is telling that some of the earliest critics of 'wage slavery' came from Southern slaveholders who knew a feudal system when they saw one. It cannot be stressed enough, however, that unlike the slave system, the power of our folklore meant the majority of (politically active) Americans, outside of periodic moments of crisis, accepted the legitimacy of their industrial feudalism and were complicit in its perpetuation.

At one point this mythological hero existed in some capacity. Otherwise the myth would have no resonance. The poetry of John Locke and Adam Smith would not have been internalized if it did not speak to people's experiences. But the independent American businessman diminished with the advent of industrialization and the closing of the frontier. We still mourn when a big box chain destroys a mom and pop store, but these are nostalgic tears, reminders of a battle lost long ago. The middle class entrepreneur has been replaced by the corporation, the legal status of corporate personhood aiding the transition. American mythology is predicated on freedom and individuality, and so the personification of corporations became inevitable once the industrial corporation became a permanent fixture in our landscape.

Modernity defined itself in part by making the idea of a free man pursuing wealth something dignified, even noble, Arnold argues.[133] In fact, it was this idea that helped bring down the medieval social order by providing morale and legitimacy to a middle class whose wealth and power was based in commerce, rather than property. The idea lingered long after our industrial feudalism extinguished the reality. Under our system, a few men had become dictators and the rest, as Tocqueville predicted, were functionally closer to slave than master. A powerful ceremony was needed to square this circle. Not surprisingly then, the courts, one of our most exalted symbols, played a crucial role in legitimating this new order by turning corporations into pioneer farmers freely trading with one another. It is true, Ann Norton reminds us, that we have "forgotten not only that the founders of the regime once protested vociferously against [the corporation's] institutional establishment but also that people once found the possibility of the creation of fictive bodies, invested by the regime with rights, to be an effete fiction, an absurdity, or a fraud."[134] But as Arnold argues, when we became dependent on these organizations with no viable institutional structures available to replace them the legal concept of corporate personhood was not only necessary— it was inevitable. And once we saw industrial organizations as businessmen, it did not take much rhetorical sleight of hand to make an assault on a corporation an assault on our freedom. "So long as men instinctively thought of these great organizations as individuals," Arnold observes, "the emotional analogies of home and freedom and all the other trappings of 'rugged individualism' became their most potent protection."[135]

A central American creed has always been suspicion of power and privilege, but as we have seen, the folklore of capitalism tells us that the corporation is an individual acting in a marketplace, not an organization governing the lives of citizens. There are innumerable benefits that corporations derive from their classification as people (including the enjoyment of more rights than their organic counterparts), instead of organizations,[136] but for Arnold the greatest advantage was their freedom to experiment.

It was this identification of great organizations with the dignities, freedom, and general ethics of the individual trader which relieved our federation of industrial empires from the hampering restrictions of theology which always prevent experiment. Men cheerfully accept the fact that some individuals are good and others bad. Therefore, since great industrial organizations were regarded as individuals, it was not expected that all of them would be good. Corporations could therefore violate any of the established taboos without creating any alarm about the "system" itself. Since individuals are supposed to do better if let alone, this symbolism freed industrial enterprise from regulation in the interest of furthering any current morality. The laissez faire religion, based on a conception of society composed of competing individuals, was transferred automatically to industrial organizations with nation-wide power and dictatorial forms of government.[137]

American industry was so fantastically successful because we made an ethic of pragmatic mastery part of its creed, without incorporating concerns about morals and character. Only "private money" was lost in the event of failure, and in the long term (the preferred orientation of the folklore of capitalism) any inconvenience or hardship caused by experimentation would benefit everyone through the generation of new wealth (a position that the New Deal accepted as descriptively valid for much of U.S. history).[138]

The folklore of capitalism insists that we draw distinctions between what the New Deal identified as economic and political government— with the former much more powerful than the later.[139]

As business organizations grew after the Civil War, they gradually began to use for their support the ancient symbolism of freedom and liberty, until, in the quaint poetic fancy of our day, The United States Steel Company has become an individual whose powerful organization must be protected at all hazards from tyranny. The freedom of the press has come to mean the noninterference with great chains of newspapers, pouring out propaganda, even though under no stretch of the imagination can it be said to be the free opinion of those who actually write it. Liberty of individuals to live unmolested by the power of overlords has become confused with the liberty of great industrial overlords to hold in their uncontrolled discretion the livelihood of individuals. The very Declaration of Independence is now the symbol of great business organizations, who insist that every corporation is born free and equal, and that holding companies are entitled to life, liberty, and the pursuit of power. The ideal of free competition is used to stamp out competition. Thus great organizations became the actual government of the people in their practical affairs.[140]

Because the profit motive ensures the *long-term* welfare of the people as a whole, it had no particular obligations to workers, consumers, or society.[141] Since these responsibilities would only interfere with the laws guaranteeing our prosperity in the long run, this is really for everyone's benefit.

Meanwhile, Arnold continues, political governance is left to care for the souls of its citizens, leaving their bodies in the hands of the economic government. The state is to concern itself with questions of character, to protect us from our own sinful and shiftless tendencies, while preserving the purity of the law that sanctified private property. The state cannot address material issues because its folklore consists of creeds that constrain experimentation and distribution: symbols of taxation, incompetent bureaucrats, locating poverty and inequality in defects of character. Desirable programs would be generated by the market, which would manage them more efficiently. Any action taken by the public government was fundamentally wasteful, and always at the expense of the public it claimed to act on behalf of. Governments consume, rather than create, wealth. This fear of public spending could manifest itself in unusual ways. One young reporter recalled sharing a dining car with a businessman while Congress debated FDR's court reorganization plan.

> After two or three minutes paced only by the click of the car wheels, he banged down his paper angrily on the window ledge. He took out his pencil and figured lightly on the tablecloth for another minute or so. "Good Lord!" he volunteered in a loud voice. "Our taxes are going up still more. This Supreme Court plan of Roosevelt's will cost a barrel of money. Six new Justices at $20,000 a year each—that's $120,000 right there. Then they're going to let them retire at full pay. And the same thing with all the other federal courts. It's just another scheme to spend more money."[142]

The man's misplaced outrage is amusing, but it is indicative of a larger, overriding suspicion of government that enervates public possibilities.[143]

There is an oligarchic cast to the folklore of capitalism, its aristocratic implications softened by the creed of unlimited opportunity. Although the United States was ostensibly an egalitarian and middle-class society, in practice the wealthy enjoyed an honored place at the top of our social pyramid, not because of their money per se, but because wealth had long been equated with personal virtue. If the possession of wealth did not make you better, certainly the ability to acquire it testified to the quality of your character. The New Deal challenged this view, and elite hostility to it was a response to the existential threat that New Deal liberalism represented to the connection between wealth and worth. As Burns argues,

> The vehemence of the rightist revolt against Roosevelt can be explained only in terms of feelings of deprivation and insecurity on the part of the business community. Roosevelt had robbed them of something far more important than their clichés and their money—he had sapped their self-esteem. The men who had been economic lords of creation found themselves in a world where political leaders were masters of headlines, of applause, and of difference. Men who felt that they had shouldered the great tasks of building the economy of the whole nation found themselves saddled with the responsibility for the Depression.[144]

Once celebrated as the cornerstone of American prosperity, the businessman was now the cause of its greatest economic disaster. Our national heroes had become our great villains. One mill worker knew exactly what was at stake when he said "Mr. Roosevelt is the only man we ever had in the White House who would understand that my boss is a sonofabitch."[145] From the standpoint of Roosevelt's business opposition this attitude, apparently shared by the president, threatened to undermine the fabric of our social tapestry, the folklore of capitalism.

Welfare Is Theft

Unemployment insurance is a pre-paid vacation for freeloaders.
—Ronald Reagan[146]

American mythology had long taught that success in the United States was almost entirely a function of hard work, determination, and ingenuity.[147] The Horatio Alger myth, the legend of the self-made, "rags-to-riches," millionaire, while greatly exaggerated (the vast majority of millionaires came from privileged or upper-middle-class backgrounds), contained enough truth to legitimize the social standing of the powerful.[148] This was not merely a form of social control. It was something felt in an intensely personal, meaningful way.

The flip side of the myth was that those who did not make it could only blame themselves. In a land of unlimited opportunity, failure was a consequence of character rather than structure.[149] Legal equality and democratic institutions ensured that opportunity was fairly allotted. This is why the pursuit of happiness was so thinly protected for so much of American history. The people at the bottom authored their condition, and had no recourse to ask anyone, especially the government, for help. To do so was both economically irresponsible and morally illegitimate.[150] Governor Eugene Talmadge of Georgia could speculate that castor oil was the best cure for poverty and get reelected four times.[151] The poor earned their lot as assuredly as the rich earned theirs. The proper response to poverty is shame and guilt, not anger, and with the occasional exception the poor accept the legitimacy of this—the folklore of capitalism has socialized us into being passive and submissive in the face of poverty.[152]

Within this folklore class is a moral, rather than economic, category. Even the New Deal (and Roosevelt especially) could not fully embrace structural economic theories without introducing a moral component. Market forces might pressure a business to act counter to the public interest, but its owners could take an ethical stand against those pressures, and were worthy of praise or condemnation based on the choice they made. Nor was welfare a moral necessity. Undeserved poverty was temporary, permanent poverty deserved, and therefore no cause for public concern. Channeling Benjamin Franklin, deprivation is itself a sign of self-reliance and rugged individualism; too much aid makes people dependent and indolent. The president of GM prophesied that, "[w]ith unemployment insurance no one will work; with old age and survivor benefits no one will save; the result will be moral decay and financial bankruptcy." New Jersey Senator Harry Moore railed that social insurance, "would take all the romance out of life...we might as well take a child from the nursery, give him a nurse, and protect him from every experience life affords."[153]

Of course, what constitutes paternalistic handouts and what counts as legitimate aid is, as always, a question of symbolic construction and interpretation. The poor get welfare, but business gets subsidies.[154] As Edelman observes:

> Subsidies from the public treasury to help businessmen are justified not as help to individuals but as promotion of a popularly supported goal...The abstractions are not personified in the people who get generous depletion allowances, cost-plus contracts, tax write offs or free governmental services. To perceive the expenditure as a subsidy to real people would portray it as an iniquity in public policy. The word 'help' is not used in this context, though these policies make people rich and substantially augment the wealth of the already rich.[155]

The help given to the poor is framed as an act of charity, its beneficiaries frequently deviant and undeserving. But public funds transferred to business are investments, a word with only positive implications. As Albert Romasco points out, it is Jesse Jones, head of the Reconstruction Finance Corporation (whose $10.5 billion dollar budget equaled what was spent on all other relief programs combined), not Harry Hopkins, who was the nation's premier relief official—as RFC relief "effectively sustained the nation's property owners and its owners of capital.[156] The only ones excluded from these benefits were those who held no equity in anything, not even a job. These were the folks who were ministered to by Harry Hopkins."[157] The great irony here, of course, is that the people most against the dole were simultaneously on it, their opposition to welfare a ceremony to address the tension between their own creeds and practice.[158]

This careful construction of welfare is further supplemented by several strands of political theory that further legitimated not only the moral failings of welfare, but also the inevitability, even desirability, of poverty. Alexander Hamilton argued that inequality was an irremovable feature of commercial society, and that tax burdens should be shouldered by the poor (especially the agrarian poor) since taxing capital and wealth hinders investment and incentives.[159] There is something troubling about this acceptance of inequality, but as Michael Thompson argues, it did not require much rhetorical sleight of hand to make inequality natural in a nation that had to make its peace with slavery.

Social Darwinism helped take the moral sting out of this theory by teaching us that inequality and poverty, suffering and despair, were evolutionary growing pains, signs that society was shedding its unfit. Moral outrage was anachronistic—reflecting ignorance about social biology. The whole process was profoundly individualistic, with little room to conceptualize either community or solidarity. Forms of collective action were almost always seen as coercive, "A and B decide what C shall do for D," Sumner argued. The work of Sumner and others succeeded in purging "ethical and moral categories from social theory and analysis. They were able to reinterpret liberty and the entire American brand of liberalism itself as a radical individualism that was—when framed in the context of a capitalist economic framework—conducive to progress."[160] Therefore George Cutten, president of Colgate College, could argue, "Nothing could threaten the race as seriously as this [the New Deal]. It is begging the fit to be more unfit."[161] This understanding of Darwin jelled nicely with the claims of economists (priests of the folklore of capitalism) who argued that under capitalism short-term selfishness produces long-term prosperity. Americans believed this with a sincerity and fervor normally reserved for religion. In significant ways, as Arnold argues, it was their religion.

There were, of course, other traditions and creeds that interfered with the establishment of a welfare state. Convention insisted that local charities address social problems, and that family should look after its own. Certain figures in the union movement (Gompers, for instance) had long been insistent that workers should be dependent on their unions and bargain for private welfare programs, rather than enter into a partnership with the state. There was the unsettling notion that the ideas behind social security were foreign and alien, a continental concept that had no place here.[162] But of greatest import and significance was, as previously discussed, the conviction that the private economy was obliged only to produce profit. The private welfare provided by certain corporations was a boom time privilege, not an entitlement. Workers who lost (or never had) that privilege were simply left to their own devices, or looked to charity and the machines, as the folklore of capitalism prevented the national government from accepting responsibility for alleviating the economic distress of its citizens.

Government Is Incompetent

The best minds are not in government. If any were, business would steal them away.

—Ronald Reagan

American thinking about government had long been shaped by a unique combination of mutually reinforcing historical, intellectual, and geographical factors that made us hostile towards public inference in economic matters.[163] We could call ourselves free because America was not bound by necessity, and in a world without necessity government becomes a source of restraint,[164] a form of coercive power interfering with our freedom to pursue happiness (which was almost always conflated with making money).

With some notable exceptions, this view of American opportunity was accurate enough to serve as the foundation of our American gospel. However, material conditions always seem to change faster than our ability to make sense of them. As FDR made clear in the Commonwealth Club Address, ours was a reified understanding of government, frozen in a time that no longer existed. When Americans looked into the mirror, our reflections still showed a land of small farmers and independent shopkeepers, masters of our own fate, long after industrialization and the corporation, holding company, and trust subjected us all to the 'freedom' of wage labor.[165] Even those who felt the sting were reluctant to ask the government for help, since the version of classical liberalism worshiped in America taught us that the laws of capitalism are eternal and immutable. Any attempt by the government to interfere with those laws would damn our nation to economic hell.

As Arnold observed, the folklore of capitalism assures us that organizations are always run less efficiently in public, rather than private, hands.[166] Our economic theory tells us this must be true, and who are we to trust our eyes over the divinely inspired wisdom of our priests. Of course the priests have their proof, but, as is often the case, their arguments suffer from an acute selection bias, as we remove all instances of effective public management from consideration. Today the folklore of the New Deal conditions us to look to the government in times of distress, and so we feel these prejudices less strongly. Yet we still cling to the belief that private organizations are generally more productive and efficient than public ones (or somehow less coercive), even in cases where private organizations have proven to be abject failures. Government programs remain an evil, just one we have accepted as necessary.[167] Here we see the power of Hartz's liberal consensus, that despite the presence of alternative traditions in American life, the boundaries of the liberal ideal and the power of the Horatio Alger story prevent us from ever fully abandoning the folklore of capitalism.[168]

> This folklore colors the way we look at what the government can legitimately do for us, and the explanation for the way institutions are created and justified. In this mythology are found the psychological motives for the decisions of courts, for the timidity of humanitarian action, for the worship of states' rights and for the proof by scholars that the only sound way of thinking about money is a fiscal way of thinking...So long as the American Businessman maintains his present place in this mythological hierarchy, no practical inconvenience is too great to be sacrificed to do him honor—every humanitarian impulse which goes counter to the popular conception of how the businessman should act is soft and effeminate.[169]

The contemporary conservative success with defining the terms of public debate reflects the continued power of this folklore, as we remain psychologically incapable of treating infrastructure as an investment or distribution primarily as a question of capacity.[170] Despite attacking popular programs and advancing aims demonstrably against the general economic interests of many of its supporters, the Republican Party has successfully manipulated our suspicions of government to legitimate its agenda. This is hardly a new development. FDR's calls to raise the purchasing power of the forgotten man during the 1932 election led formerly progressive Democrats like Al Smith to accuse Roosevelt of fomenting demagogic class war.[171]

Our suspicion of government was abetted by a creeping wariness of the growing centralization and standardization of American life, a recognizable threat to our individual liberty. The dominant source of this centralization was the corporation, but since those are just individuals writ large, the folklore of capitalism could not acknowledge it as the source. Instead it plays off our fear of 'socialism,' and locates the threat in the state. David Lilienthal, a director of the TVA, offers a wry description of the phenomena.

> A wondrous state of confusion arose in the minds of men…they ate food bought at a store that had its replica in almost every town from coast to coast; they took their ease in standard chairs; they wore suits of identical weave and pattern and shoes identical with those worn all over the country. In the midst of this uniformity they all listened on the radio to the same program at the same time, a program that bewailed the evils of "regimentation," urging them to vote for a candidate who said he would bring an end to centralization in government.[172]

Our folklore, which sanctifies the businessman, offers us the perfect devilish foil. Arnold identifies him for us.

> Our Devil is governmental interference. Thus we firmly believe in the inherent malevolence of government which interferes with business. Here are people who are not to be trusted—they are the bureaucrats, the petty tyrants, the destroyers of the rule of law.[173]

The faceless public bureaucrat is a particularly powerful negative symbol, rivaled only by the specter of socialism. Arnold describes the image of the bureaucrat in his typical sardonic style:

> These men [bureaucrats] were really incredible individuals. They had three main objectives. Their first was to waste all of the taxpayers' money they possibly could. The second was to perpetuate their wasteful organization and increase it as quickly as possible. The third was to interfere with business and cause businessmen to lose confidence. How and why these bureaucrats sink to such low estate is a mystery. There must be some poison gas distilled in government offices. For the plain and simple fact is that the moment an individual is employed by the government he becomes a bureaucrat, contumacious to all holy men, and someone geared to run this country down the road to hell.[174]

As long as this Devil torments us, the symbols of government inefficiency, socialism, and bureaucracy will remain powerful symbolic weapons for anyone opposed to a regulatory welfare state.

Of course, as a symbolic construct, this image of the bureaucrat need have no relationship to reality. Given the scope of social services provided by the government, its performance has been remarkably efficient. The accomplishments of the New Deal alone are staggering. Starting essentially from scratch, the CCC had over two and a half million people engaged in environmental projects, and the output of the WPA makes the fate of post-Katrina New Orleans even more striking. In its eight years it built or improved 670,000 miles of road, street, and sidewalk; 122,000 bridges and 1,000 tunnels; 1,050 air fields and 4,000 airport buildings; laid 24,000 miles of sewers, built 4,000 wells, and 3,000 water treatment plants; 20,000 stadiums and playgrounds; 38,000 schools and libraries; 7,000 hospitals, firehouses, armories, and prisons; and 20,000 other government buildings.[175] And these are just several New Deal organizations.[176] But the folklore of capitalism judges the government by impossible standards of perfection, with every misstep pilloried and their most unpleasant incarnations, such as the Department of Motor Vehicles, serving as its public face.[177] Long lines, unhelpful service people, and confusing paperwork are hardly limited to the government. Yet the image of the public bureaucrat, alternately sinister and incompetent, has been cunningly exploited by enemies of reform for as long as large government organizations have existed. When a program cannot be attacked on the grounds of its merits the mere mention of bureaucracy's ominous shadow is enough to make people cautious.

The problem runs deeper than just hostility towards government. Any opposition to business is a threat to liberty, and so the union movement has long been hampered by the same negative mythology. Opposition to the Wagner Act was grounded in the folklore of the time, rather than any real empirical discussion of the economic effects that unionization would have on the economy. Plotke offers a brief summation of the opposition. Unions would interfere with the rights of owners and managers. Unions (unlike capital) reflect narrow self-interests. They would act coercively against their members and their rule would be arbitrary and inefficient. Above all else, they represent an unwanted intrusion into private matters, violating the sanctity of a contract entered into by two equal, consenting individuals.[178]

The effects of the Depression, the New Deal's rhetorical onslaught against corporate greed, and a political commitment towards collective bargaining helped clear the space needed to establish a powerful union movement in the United States. But their good will was lost when the sit-down strike confronted the folklore of capitalism. While half of the people polled in 1936 favored unions, that number had dropped to 17 percent during the United Auto Workers strike.[179] Tactically the sit-down strike proved very effective,[180] and there was public support for the right to unionize (the strikes were primarily to win union recognition). Nevertheless, in the eyes of the public the seizure of private corporate property amounted not only to theft, but a threat to the free enterprise system itself. New Jersey Governor Harold Hoffman argued that "A labor union has no more right to take possession of a factory than a band of gangsters has to take possession of a bank...There is no difference between the two, either in principle or in degree."[181] Unlike Michigan Governor Frank Murphy, a strong New Dealer who refused to order Michigan's militia to expel the strikers, Hoffman declared that "The avoidance of the possibility of bloodshed is, of course, desirable, but not at the expense of surrender to or compromise with or toleration of those guilty of such criminal acts."[182] When pressed further Hoffman argued that the sit-down strike was "a symbol of communism" that has "as its basic principle a deliberate disregard for what we have always regarded as hallowed property rights and it is inevitably followed by contempt for honorable judicial proceedings."[183] As Robert Shogan argues, the sit-down strikes cannot be understood outside the context of the court battle (and vice versa). The two controversies fed off each other, creating tangible fear that the New Deal was seeking to unravel the bedrock principles (free enterprise and the rule of law) of the United States (and the folklore of capitalism). As such the opposition to them was as much existential as it was based on interest. Hostility towards the New Deal and the American welfare state has to be seen from this perspective, based less on self-interested opposition to policy than its assault on a powerfully held mythology.

New Symbols for a New Folklore

The architects and builders are men of common sense and of artistic American tastes. They know that the principles of harmony and of necessity itself require that the building of the new structure shall blend with the essential lines of the old. It is this combination of the old and the new that marks orderly peaceful progress—not only in building buildings but in building government itself.
—Franklin Roosevelt[184]

In order to enact a positive agenda, the New Deal had to oppose this mythology on all fronts. Much of the work was an act of deconstruction, with Arnold's *The Folklore of Capitalism* the most theoretically compelling tool in that arsenal, aided by the (more politically significant) public writings of Wallace and the Roosevelts denouncing the human costs and arbitrary power of the market. But destruction alone is not sufficient, and so New Deal simultaneously sought to establish a new folklore for its new order. The reformist, rather than revolutionary, nature of this order ensured that the new symbols, at least for the short term, would be drawn from the old.

Arnold found much to admire in the folklore of capitalism, and wanted to appropriate its strengths for the folklore of the New Deal. We have previously discussed a number of these in greater detail, and will only review them quickly here. Of particular value was the ability of business to experiment and conceptualize human and capital development as investing in, rather than squandering, the future. Business was allowed to focus on the production and distribution of goods rather than the content of character. It interacted with the world empirically, rather than morally. Now a government is not a business. Its primary concerns are fundamentally moral, but as we have seen, there is a distributional component to New Deal morality, and a more effective governing folklore can enhance the state's ability to minister to our physical needs. But Arnold was less effective as an advocate than as an anthropologist.[185] It was the other New Dealers in this study, Wallace most of all, who self-consciously set about reconstructing old symbols for a new mythology.

Religion

> It happens, fortunately, it seems to me, that the Biblical record is heavily loaded on the side of the Progressive.
>
> —Henry Wallace[186]

Today religious symbols and religious sanction is almost the exclusive possession of conservatism, but the New Deal found it natural to make use of religious imagery, given its central importance in American history, as well as the sincere faith of figures like FDR, ER, and Wallace. Wallace's arguments in particular often took on a millennial edge, and his words in *New Frontiers* are emblematic of his general approach.

> What we approach is not a new continent but a new state of heart and mind resulting in new standards of accomplishment. We must invent, build and put to work new social machinery. This machinery will carry out the Sermon on the Mount as well as the present social machinery caries out and intensifies the law of the jungle.[187]

Elsewhere, channeling an earlier Roosevelt, he proclaims, "the people's revolution is on the march, and the devil and all his angels cannot prevail against it. They cannot prevail, for on the side of the people is the Lord."[188] References to the Sermon on the Mount and intimations of Armageddon were not uncommon. Wallace cast himself in the role of the biblical prophet, charging the government "to devise and develop the social machinery which will work out the implications of the social message of the old prophets."[189]

In *Statesmanship and Religion* Wallace draws parallels between the American experience and the stories of the Old Testament, since "the prophets were the first people in recorded history to cry out in a loud clear voice concerning the problems of human justice."[190] And with enthusiasm, if not subtlety, Wallace draws parallel after parallel between progressive liberals and those who opposed Baal, who of course represented corporate interests and argued that the biblical prophets (who were as unpopular as Progressives during the Coolidge administration) were bad for business.[191]Amos is not an economist or philosopher, but someone disgusted by the way his civilization exploits its farmers. While opponents of the New Deal's economic reforms draw sustenance from their faith in the laws of supply and demand, Wallace gives progressivism the righteous sanction of scripture. Amos becomes a Roosevelt voter, Isaiah a public intellectual, advocating international cooperation.

These moves, while crude at times, are designed to highlight that the "essential problem of social justice has changed scarcely at all since the time of Amos."[192] We can read the prophets to understand ourselves, and give reform a powerful legacy both familiar and sacred. "The great lesson of the prophets...is their intensity of conviction that behind the material there is something supremely worthwhile which guides us in our handling of material things."[193] Wallace and other New Dealers had no shortage of economic theory with which to explain the depression, but this gave them a compelling set of symbols to buttress that theory, and FDR uses similar language in his First Inaugural Address when he declares "[t]he money changers have fled from their high seats in the temple of our civilization. We may now restore that temple to the ancient truths."[194] This is not just pandering. While Wallace and the Roosevelts had unorthodox or simple faiths, the strength of that faith gave this tactic an authenticity that was difficult to call into question, and was one reason why they were successful advocates.[195]

Beyond references to the Sermon on the Mount serving as our social ideal (and Eleanor Roosevelt's writings, especially *The Moral Basis of Democracy*, are full of comparisons between the life of Jesus Christ and the life of the democratic citizen), Wallace ignores the New Testament in *Statesmanship and Religion*. He does, however, spend a great deal of time on the Protestant Reformation, drawing parallels between the assumption of infallibility that legitimated religious repression and the hysterical opposition to New Deal programs.

Wallace, paralleling Roosevelt's liberal history in the Commonwealth Club Address, acknowledges that we owe a debt to the heirs of the Reformation, since their struggles resulted "in the generation of tremendous material power which expressed itself first in the creation of democratic institutions and secondly in science and the production of great capitalistic wealth."[196] But its historical moment has ended. Just as the prophets of the Old Testament and the Reformation ultimately ushered in new eras of history that partially fulfilled the promise of the Sermon on the Mount, we find ourselves at the dawn of the next great era of reform, what Wallace would elsewhere call a New Frontier.

We are now ready for another step; the impetus of the reformers of the sixteenth century has failed us. The Century of Progress has turned to ashes in our mouths. Is it possible that the world is finally ready for the realization of the teachings of Jesus the appreciation of the Sermon on the Mount, the beginning of the kingdom of heaven to earth?"[197]

At any rate, Wallace reminds us that if we do not embrace the spirit of love and possibility that animates Christianity, the forces of reaction will prevail.

> Until recently this generation has been too immersed in the greed of capitalism, the spiritual sloth of ever-increasing material pleasures and the humanistic agnosticism of men who drew their inspiration from the superficial scientists and economist of the nineteenth century.[198]

The priests of Baal are still with us, and they are voting against the New Deal. The repressive spiritual hegemony of Luther and Calvin lives in any who puts the need of class or nation over the needs of humanity. They are, fundamentally, anti-Christian.[199] "Any religion which recognizes above all the fatherhood of God and the brotherhood of man must of necessity have grave questionings concerning those national enterprises where the deepest spiritual fervor is evoked for purely nationalistic, race or class ends."[200] We can fulfill our destiny and become a City on a Hill, but only if our aim is universal brotherhood, rather than oligarchy or American aggrandizement.

The Frontier

> The frontiers that challenge us now are of the mind and spirit. We must blaze new trails in scientific accomplishment, in the peaceful arts and industries. Above all, we must blaze new trails in the direction of a controlled economy, common sense, and social decency.
>
> —Henry Wallace[201]

Another important symbol in the rhetoric of the New Deal was the symbol of the frontier and its conquering pioneer, one of FDR's most commonly used symbols.[202] He embodies the sense of independence and individualism that defined our rugged individualism. The frontier, in turn, carries with it a sense of limitless potentiality. As Anne Norton observes, our folklore teaches us that creation is an act of will divorced from restraint. Horatio Alger's characters make their fortunes (or achieve middle-class respectability) from humble origins. Lincoln learns to read by firelight on a dirt floor and becomes president. Our Manifest Destiny is to subdue the entire continent and then send Lindbergh across the ocean and put a man on the moon.[203] The frontier means anything is possible, and being an American means mastering the impossible, the pioneer's sacred duty to God and country. As long as we face a perpetual frontier, waiting to be tamed through infinite acts of individual conquest, we can avoid any serious confrontation with divisive political, social, and economic questions. "Carefree exploitation without thought of the consequences is, of course, delightful to the American temperament,"[204] Wallace reminds us. The presence of the frontier and the promise of its possibilities meant that Americans could always respond to tension by escaping and starting over.

There is an affinity between the symbol of the frontier and what Richard Hofstadter termed the 'agrarian myth.' "The United States was born in the country and has moved to the city," Hofstadter tells us, and its romantic defenders were "drawn irresistibly to the noncommercial, nonpecuniary, self-sufficient aspect of American farm life."[205] Hofstadter rightly observes (as did Wallace) that the ideal of Jefferson was not shared by the farmer himself, who focused more on making money than preserving "his honest, industry, his independence, his frank sprit of equality, his ability to produce and enjoy a simple abundance."[206] Nevertheless, the spirit of rural independence carried with it an air of authenticity that had a powerful hold on the mind of the American people during the Depression, the minds of FDR and Wallace included.[207]

Since the pioneer is a significant character in our folklore, writing him into the New Deal's social order became an important political project. Lilienthal equates the TVA engineer and administrator with the pioneer settler of old, who accomplish 'impossible things...armed not with the ax, rifle, and bowie knife, but with the Diesel engine, the bulldozer, the giant electric shovel, the retort—and most of all with an emerging kind of skill, a modern knack of organization and execution."[208] FDR would pepper his speeches with references to the "pioneer spirit," reinterpreting the lone individual into a champion of cooperative communities. "It is true that the pioneer was an individualist but, at the same time, there was a pioneer spirit of cooperation and understanding of the need of building up, not a class, but a whole community."[209] The emphasis is no longer on the lone settler braving the elements, mastering the wild with his rugged individualism. Instead we see the pioneer, a member of a cooperative community, recognizing that the pacification of any frontier reflects an act of communal, not individual will. The pioneer understood that he must surrender some of that individuality to the needs of the larger community—out on the frontier the preservation of his individuality would require a social network of support. The cowboy, alone on the range, could survive in but not master his environment. It was the founding of new villages and towns, connected via railroad and telegraph to the rest of the nation, that finally subdued the west.

However, the most systematic reinterpretation of the pioneer and frontier symbols was found, as usual, in the work of Henry Wallace—in particular his first major work, *New Frontiers*. Like the Roosevelts, Wallace was an effective advocate because he was also an anthropologist, capable of dissecting his own cultural convictions. He appreciated the power of frontier myth because he sincerely believed it. But he also recognized that there was a fundamental immaturity about the pioneer dreams of the United States. Just as children eventually outgrow childhood games of cowboys and Indians, Americans too must grow up and accept our adult responsibilities. Our old solutions will no longer work. No longer can depressions be "be cured by the pioneer virtue of optimistic grab and toil."[210]

We educated our children—among them, millions of unemployed young—in the belief that the United States was still a pioneer country where the rugged, individualistic virtues of hard work and saving would inevitably bring success. We did not tell our sons and daughters that they were caught between two worlds, and that in the new world it will take more than hard work and saving to insure salvation.[211]

Like Eleanor Roosevelt, Wallace feared the creation of a lost generation, one that would be left either enervated or radicalized by the Depression, but alienated from American society regardless. Either possibility threatened the stability, integrity, and future of the United States. In order to save this generation, and preserve our future, we must figure out where the boundaries of the old world end, and where our new frontier begins.

One possibility is found in the imperialism of Henry Luce's "American Century." But the New Deal rejected that vision. Instead of seeking new land, we must explore, discover, and unlock new possibilities of the human heart in a world that can conquer scarcity. Ours is no longer a problem of necessity. It is a problem of will. Can we change our social institutions, and ourselves, to adapt to a world of abundance? The next great frontier is found within ourselves.

Wallace was a scientist, and he shared the New Deal's faith in the power of experts to reorder the world. But he also understood, following Tocqueville, that new institutions are not sufficient.

> This vague new world has thus far been approached chiefly by restless, romantic men who feel that the vast riches of a cooperative good life can be attained suddenly by making a speech on the New Deal, by electing someone to Congress, by writing a book, or by passing a law. All these things may be a part of the necessary pioneering but the work that finally counts will be slower, less romantic and infinitely more difficult.[212]

Only by changing ourselves, laboring in the long abandoned frontier of the soul, can we erect permanent foundations in our new world. It is a daunting task, but possible, provided we can commit for the long haul. Wallace is not advocating that we wait for changed hearts before we act. If we build institutions to cope with abundance and end artificial scarcity our habits would change over time. The shifts will be subtle, "literally of a million different kinds,"[213] but we will gradually come to realize that the grasping selfishness that subdued the world and conquered scarcity is now preventing us from enjoying the fruits of that conquest.

One of the great difficulties we will face is the fact that the gateway to this frontier is difficult to find. The existential shock of the Great Depression, the realization that our heritage is "rather bitter—a rich land racked and mismanaged, with huge accumulations of goods and wealth, yet with millions of our people deprived and helpless"[214] created a brief opportunity for progressives to change an otherwise a conservative people. Wallace notes that "[t]he New Deal sprit ebbs and flows. Ordinarily the progressive liberals get a real opportunity to change the rules only about once in a generation." The rest of the time we are just too complacent. "Most people resolutely refuse to think politically if they have jobs, a place to sleep, and something to eat and wear."[215] As long we are comfortable we will not take a critical look at the foundations of that prosperity. For Wallace, abundance undermines its own possibilities. Progress requires privation. There is no millennium without apocalypse.

The potential cost of the social discipline required to subdue this new frontier asks a great deal of Americans. The aftermath of a struggle often poses a greater challenge than the struggle itself. Constructing a new state may be even harder than fighting a war for independence. Pacifying the continent will prove to be less difficult than learning to cope with our success.

> When everyone began to realize finally that the country was really filled up, that there were no more good homesteads and no frontiers to flee to in times of depression, there was great uneasiness. The day which we feared had come upon us. At last we had to learn to live with each other.[216]

The old frontier united us. Its dangers were very real, and its possibilities defined our identity. But that frontier is closed—its promise has finally arrived. It will not be easy to abandon the pioneer individualism that absolves us of the obligation and responsibilities that arise from confronting each other as citizens in a community instead of isolated individuals in an empty landscape. The potential benefits are staggering, but the first tentative steps towards them will be among the most difficult we have ever taken. It will be like learning to walk again as we come to learn that people supporting our weight are not just competitors, but friends and neighbors. This, Wallace tells us, is our new frontier.

The Constitution

> To interpret the Constitution in the light of the spirit of its framers is one thing. To interpret it in the light of the economic conditions as they were in 1787 when the Constitution was draw up is another.
>
> —Henry Wallace[217]

We have previously discussed the New Deal's reinterpretation of the Declaration of Independence, but the Constitution, and the idea of constitutionality, remained a powerful weapon in the opposition's symbolic arsenal. Indeed, Roosevelt himself compared the Constitution to the Bible, as both foundational texts and works of spiritual importance. Therefore it was necessary for the New Deal to not only justify itself in terms of the spirit of the Declaration, but to demonstrate that it was not actively undermining the Constitution in the process.

The New Deal's pragmatism, suspicious of formal liberal constitutionalism that made no space for power and context, influenced its Constitutional interpretation. Our folklore teaches us that "[t]he faith that dignifies the Supreme

Court is the belief that through logic and reason it may discover impartial principles of law that are independent of the whims, prejudices, or the economic philosophy of the justices."[218] Aided by a long legal history of controversial 5-4 decisions that "suggested that constitutional interpretation was decidedly uncertain,"[219] The New Deal rejected that folklore, denying that the Constitution embodied unchanging legal truths, even if it did embody, through the preamble, an eternal promise. As Karl argues, "[i]t was not the literal statement of an interpreted past nor a detailed map for the future."[220] Instead, the Constitution was a living document, responsive to the needs of the people. It was a gift from our founders, but we were gifted a useful tool, not a divine mandate. "The Constitution itself was not to be worshipped; it was to be used in worshiping the quality of life it was intended to promote."[221] This attitude towards the Constitution explains in part why FDR reacted so strongly to what he saw as the Supreme Court's obstruction of popular will and abuse of the framers' intent.[222] The courts were flouting the general desires of the people in the name of narrow and selfish interests at worst, an attachment to paralyzing folklore at best. The battle over constitutional interpretation loomed large over Roosevelt's second inauguration, and when reflecting on his oath to uphold the Constitution he later remarked to speechwriter Sam Rosenman "I felt like saying; 'Yes but it's the Constitution as I understand it, flexible enough to meet any new problem of democracy—not the kind of Constitution your court has raised up as a barrier to progress and democracy.'"[223]

In *Symbols of Government* Arnold systematically destroys the idea of reified legal 'theory,' and attempts to supplant rule by the courts with rule by administrative elites. But here Arnold miscalculates, overlooking the importance of the Constitution as a symbol. It was Henry Wallace who again offers the most systematic reinterpretation of Constitutional intent as a buttress for New Deal social policy, this time in his 1936 work *Whose Constitution?* His central argument is that the Declaration of Independence and Constitution (filtered through the Preamble) must be read as the two halves of a greater whole. We find our spirit of liberty and independence in the Declaration, moderated by the Preamble's "doctrine of unity and interdependence."[224] The tension between these two ideals is responsible for the dynamism at the heart of American greatness. But Wallace places particular emphasis on the Preamble's call to create a more perfect union. Within this line we find the logic behind both the legitimacy and the necessity of the welfare state.

Of special importance, Wallace argues, is the way that the Preamble makes clear the intergenerational nature of our social compact. Even if Jefferson is right and every generation should rewrite the rules that govern it, those new rules should never undermine the freedom and possibilities of those who will follow. Our obligation to future citizens may even be greater than our obligations to each other, since our descendents have no voice in the creation of the world they will enter. As such, we have a duty to future as much as to the present to address the systematic inequalities that keep certain classes, ages, races, and regions in perpetual poverty.

The spirit of this Preamble's mission remains the same. It is the material conditions, the context, that have changed. Today we must apply it to a world of corporations, unions, and commercial farmers instead of plantations, small farmers, and shopkeepers. "Today, the States mark no economic boundaries that make sense, and they provide only limited instruments for action to meet modern problems."[225] He notes that "were agriculture truly a local matter in 1936, as the Supreme Court says it is, half of the people of the United States would quickly starve," and similar parallels can be drawn in the industrial world.[226]

Simply observing that conditions have changed is not sufficient, nor is arguing that the Founders would support a welfare state. The argument must be made that the Supreme Court's decision to return the country to the 'horse and buggy days' is constitutionally wrong—that it is bad theology. Wallace is prepared to make this case, claiming that "National power to solve national problems was intended by the Founding Fathers...What the national problems might be a generation hence, a century hence, no man could say. The power had to be created, to be utilized by future generations as they required."[227] We find support for this in the writings of Alexander Hamilton, who argued in *Federalist 31* that

> A government ought to contain in itself every power requisite to the full accomplishment of the objects committed to its care, and to the complete execution of the trusts for which it is responsible, free from every other control but a regard to the public good and to the sense of the people.[228]

Therefore, a broad view of Constitutional interpretation is in fact the original intent of the Framers, especially in regards to the changing dynamics of economic life.

We must be reminded of our fundamental principles, enshrined in our great texts: the spirit of unity, the commitment to social justice, and the insistence that being an American obligates you to the future as well as the present. This is the central truth of the Constitution. Aggressive use of our founding texts reminds opponents of the New Deal that before the folklore of capitalism, we were ruled by a much nobler mythology. This is what the New Deal hoped to restore.

Conclusion

The so-called demagogue has an advantage because he does not view the
control of human institutions under the illusion that men in groups are
composed of so-called thinking men, to whose knowledge of fundamental
governmental principles he must appeal.

—Thurman Arnold[229]

The New Deal's theory of practice is in the end a theory of agency, at least
agency for the political actor who can penetrate the folklore of an institution,
attach himself to an organization, and be fortunate enough to live in a time of
institutional collapse. Transformative agency is normally limited to these brief
periods—old symbols are vulnerable for only a short time, and so the actor must
be prepared to make the most of those fleeting opportunities to lay the
foundations of an alternate order.

For a new institution to be viable it needs to respond to a specific material
need of the moment. It must address an issue of (perceived) necessity. Theory
provides that organization with its legitimacy and the morale its members need
to function, but our tendency as human beings is to reify dynamic principles,
fixing them in a particular moment of time and preventing them from
responding to new material conditions. It is at the moment where sub rosa
institutions can no longer counter the paralysis of static folklore, when necessity
overwhelms ceremonial interventions—in short, times of institutional collapse,
when the reformer has the greatest possibility of actually affecting the structure
of his society.

But old folklore dies hard, and almost always remains a potent weapon of
reaction. This is why the New Deal argued that a new social philosophy must
connect itself to the old folklore it hoped to supplant. This addresses our fear of
the new, and blunts one of the most valuable tools of the opposition. This is
especially true in the early stages of new institutions, when they lack the
legitimacy born of repetition and continued existence. And this is why being
able to navigate the symbols, ceremonies, and creeds that make up the old
mythology is so important for the progressive reformer. He must learn which
symbols have emotional resonance.

Therefore the first lesson to be learned by the objective student of
governmental theory is that, when he desires to step into the moving stream of
events as an actor, he must accept the legal and economic theories of his time
just as he accepts the language of his time. He will find, in the vocabulary of
current theory, principles though which he may support any cause.",...His
choice of theories cannot be made on any other ground than that of expediency
in gaining the ends he desires. [230]

We must never forget, Arnold cautions us, that creeds need to serve the
institution, not the other way around. "You judge the symbols as good or bad on
the basis of whether they lead to the type of society you like. You do not cling to

them on general principle when they are leading in the wrong direction."[231] Successful reformers, Arnold argues, have to be politicians before philosophers. They must concern themselves less with theoretical consistency and purity, and more with figuring out how to manipulate and control symbolic language to create political possibilities for the New Dealers of their era.

Philosophy needs to conceptualize our ends, but equally important is its ability to create political space for pragmatic action. "In Arnold's view, people acted upon their beliefs, and these beliefs became real in the consequences of that action; what they believed was what was important. As far as action was concerned, their beliefs were the operative reality."[232] Arnold argues for, and the New Deal largely followed, a Machiavellian conceptualization of the relationship between theory (as traditionally understood) and practice. The purpose of constructive theory is to build morale for political actors, not to discover transcendent truths that constrain our ability to act. The point of destructive theory is to weaken existing ideals, clearing space for new ones.

The pure theorist has the luxury of ignoring politics because theory is accountable to nothing but its own ideals. Princes are willing to make the emotional (demagogic) pleas necessary to accomplish their goals. They are willing to sacrifice principle to engage in the horse-trading that forms the core of political action. "They [politicians] lack social values, their aims are imperfect, but society clings to them rather than to the occasional reformer who does not understand its emotional needs, and tries to fit it into some procrustean bed made in the world of his own dreams."[233] Theorists expect their principles to conform to practice, and get discouraged when they do not. Princes know better, and minimize internal checks on their ability to respond to necessity and fortune. The fact that they choose to use principles as weapons is particularly infuriating for those who put principles before practice. But the practical politician knows what Machiavelli knows, that moral commitments, taken too far, makes compromise and experimentation difficult. Honest people who refuse to accept the presence of shadows in the Cave are unable to make the compromises that are at the heart of politics.

> A most significant effect of our scholarship and learning about government today is to remove from active participation in governing most of the kindly and tolerant people who might otherwise be a more important factor...The reason is that our students of governmental problems consider politics a low and unworthy purist. They think that sincerity and candor can be used in a political campaign. They feel a sort of spiritual trouble when confronted with the realities of a political institution, which makes them confused and ineffective. Unscrupulous persons who do not feel the same spiritual trouble when confronted with things as they are naturally become more proficient.[234]

Not only does the progressive need to engage in the "demagogic" practice of appealing to people's emotions and utilizing popular symbols to accomplish practical political ends, he needs to be willing to accept that it is more important to make dirty changes in the real world than possess clean hands in an ideal one.[235]

In the end the New Deal's theory of practice challenges the progressive to accept our world of necessity, and engage the possible in the hopes of someday transcending it. This involves a realistic assessment of the institutional options available for reform, and is the subject of the next chapter. But the truly bitter pill is the one that forces the theorist to confront the limits of human rationality, our fundamentally religious nature, and our squeamishness about engaging that nature tactically. In order to achieve the power needed to move society forward, a degree of manipulation is necessary. In order to free people as subjects a certain degree of instrumental thinking is necessary. A dangerous concession, but as Arnold reminds us, the progressive's refusal does not stop the reactionary from exploiting the same human vulnerabilities. A principled refusal to win keeps the actors hands clean, while leaving those he would help at the whims of the less principled opposition. Treacherous waters, but the New Deal demonstrated that they are possible to navigate, especially if the leaders involved are animated by both a clear sense of ends, and an understanding of which means so severely compromise ends that they cannot be considered. This in turn creates an enormous responsibility on behalf of citizens to police those leaders, and to ensure that the best ones assume positions of power. We may not get it right every time, but as Henry Steele Commager reminds us, the ugly side of democracy is the right to be wrong.[236]

Notes

1. McWilliams, *Fraternity*, 26.
2. Parts of the argument in this chapter were previously published in Brian Stipelman, "The New Deal's Theory of Practice," *New Political Science* 32, no. 2 (June 2010): 237-260.
3. Niccolo Machiavelli, *The Prince* (trans. George Bull. London: Penguin Books, 2003), 21.
4. Frances Perkins, describing Roosevelt. She goes on to note, "it was this faculty which released him from the driven, frightened, psychosis of the period." Perkins, *Roosevelt*, 164.
5. Quoted in Goldman, *Destiny*, 324.
6. Although Paul Conkin has pointed out it was rare that FDR would "frankly admit the failure of one of his policies." *The New Deal* (Arlington Heights: AHM Publishing, 1975), 11.
7. Arthur Schlesinger, "FDR: Pragmatist-Democrat," in Hamby, 114-115.
8. Schlesinger, "FDR," 118.
9. Plotke, *Building*, 165.
10. As Burns describes it, "Roosevelt's mind was attuned to the handling of a great variety of operational and tactical matters, not to the solving of intellectual problems." This was a problem Roosevelt was able to ignore in part due to the staggering ignorance

of so many of his critics, "slaves to the theories of defunct economists, and Roosevelt could puncture their pretensions with his knowledge of their own business and its relation to the rest of the world." Quoted in James MacGregor Burns, "FDR: Unsuccessful Improviser," in Hamby, 130-131.

11. Charles Eden in particular is a harsh critic of Deweyan pragmatism, or at least a harsh critic of its political significance. "Prior to the New Deal, pragmatism had exercised considerable influence within the world of reform, especially over intellectuals and academics. But it had otherwise remained at the margins of American political life. The New Deal put pragmatism on a firm institutional footing in the American constitutional order; it set in motion a regime of long duration, capable of executing a pragmatic liberal program over several decades." Eden in "Origins," 75. Eden later argues that whatever cache Dewey's pragmatism has was earned by the institutional success of the New Deal. "[T] he extent that pragmatism ever held a powerful fascination for men of intellect it was because it could take credit for the intellectual energy the New Deal released and channeled. It could also, of course, trade upon the vast political capital the New Deal laid up." Eden, "Origins," 101-102.

12. Samuel Rosenman, *Working with Roosevelt*, (New York. Da Capo Press, 1972), 30. Roosevelt understood what had to be done to get elected, ranging from comparatively innocuous compromises like having Jack Garner serve as Vice President to ensure his nomination on the fourth ballot of the 1932 convention; or in 1928 watching Tammany Hall's Ed Flynn threaten upstate Republicans with investigations if they did not speed up sending in their ballot totals.

13. At least the Lincoln presented by Carl Sandburg, which was the one that FDR found most compelling. One can also imagine the political costs of capitulation on slavery weighed heavily on Hamilton and Jay, both members of the New York State Abolitionist Society. Canton, "Progressivism," 184.

14. Looking at fortune, one can look at, for instance, the Great Depression and the rise of fascism in Europe. Both happened independent of any action taken by FDR, and his ability to act was aided by the dislocation created by these events. Likewise, President Bush had two great moments of national desolation (the 9/11 terror attacks and the destruction of Hurricane Katrina) where he had the chance to remake the world over, and will be remembered as either a great leader or a spectacular failure based on how history judges his response. Necessity refers to the fundamental concerns a leader must address to maintain power and/or preserve the state, as well as the context in which he confronts them. So for Roosevelt necessity dictated that he respond to the economic dislocation of the Depression, and determined the political and institutional factors that shaped his response.

15. He believed that precise definitions robbed words of flexibility and utility, and that words, like people and institutions, cannot be understood outside of their context. "[I]f you ever define a term carefully, it loses all meaning." Arnold, "Letter to Willmott Lewis," 27 Feb. 1936, *Voltaire*, 223.

16. Karl, *Uneasy*, 75. Pages 74-75 contain an efficient and effective overview of the constraints Hoover's ideological commitments imposed on his practice.

17. Kessler, "Public," 160.

18. Again, it should be pointed out that FDR was not always a consistent New Dealer, and his a priori commitment to balanced budgets arguably handicapped the New Deal's response to the Great Depression.

19. Machiavelli, *Prince*, 21.

20. And one that reflects the general lack of consensus about causes of, and solutions to, the Depression—amongst both FDR's advisors and the economic community at large.

21. Karl, *Uneasy*, 125.

22. We see a similar move made after World War II. As Badger observes, "[w]ith the unprecedented success of the post-war American economy, it was not long before liberal economists once again abandoned their anti-trust prescriptions, accepted the inevitability and desirability of large corporations, and advocated instead the concept of countervailing power to sustain their goal of social justice." Badger, *New Deal*, 108.

23. Machiavelli, *Prince*, 14.

24. Although the New Deal is not one of his explicit cases, see Stephen Bronner's *Moments of Decision*, (New York: Routledge, 1992) for a detailed look at this approach to political theory and practice.

25. Stephen Bronner, *Imagining the Possible: Radical Politics for Conservative Times*, (New York: Routledge, 2002), 2.

26. A democratic presidential nominee needed the support of 2/3rds of the delegates, granting the South a veto over any racially progressive candidate. FDR was able to eliminate this rule in 1936.

27. Lash, *Dealers*, 415.

28. See Sullivan, *Hope*, 106-107, for a discussion of how the poll tax played out in practice.

29. McMahon, *Race*, 160.

30. The purge itself was understood as an attempt to change the nation's racial order, as we shall see in chapter six.

31. A critique of Roosevelt's sometimes tepid support of labor needs to be subjected to the same contextual overview—not only in terms of what the New Deal had done compared to past regimes, but also how far support could have been politically extended. While unions enjoyed a 50 percent approval rating during 1936, sit-down strikes dropped that number down to 17 percent. As Robert Shogan notes in *Backlash*, "As the sit down strikes proliferated, more and more Americans and their representatives in Congress had lost sympathy with labor. Most Americans did not know and many no longer cared who was to blame for the wave of labor agitation that plagued the country. But they did know they wanted it stopped" 55. See *Backlash* for a detailed look at the public reaction to labor agitation and the political difficulties it created. Shogan also argues that Roosevelt, who was pushing his court plan at this time, was trying not to take two controversial stands at the same time. This is not to say that Roosevelt should not have been more supportive, just that there is a context behind his timidity that must be accounted for. Robert Shogan, *Backlash: The Killing of the New Deal*, (Chicago: Ivan R. Dee, 2006).

32. Machiavelli, *Prince*, 56. Not coincidentally, the title of one of the most influential comprehensive looks at the Roosevelt administration is Burns' *The Lion and the Fox*.

33. Arnold, *Folklore*, 34.

34. Machiavelli, *Prince*, 54. See Crick's introductory essay in the Penguin Classics edition of *The Discourses*.

35. Machiavelli, *Prince*, 58. It is also worth noting that for Machiavelli, the actual presence of these attributes poses a risk to the prince's ability to act (genuine personal moral standards are a form of restraint) but as long as the subjects value these attributes it is important to pay lip service to them. That will be sufficient. The New Dealers profiled here, even ones as "Machiavellian" as Arnold, would balk at this. They follow

Machiavelli far enough to concede the primacy of power, but as we've discussed, power is a means to an end, not an end in itself.

36. Americans, for instance, increasingly look for their leaders to have business experience, so they manage the 'business' of government like they would a company, which also goes to show how little Americans understand how the government actually works.

37. Machiavelli, *Prince*, 58.

38. President Bush summed this up nicely when he noted, "You can fool some of the people all the time, and those are the ones you want to concentrate on."

39. ER, *Moral Basis, Leave Behind*, 87-88.

40. Murray Edelman, *The Politics of Misinformation*, (Cambridge: Cambridge University Press, 2001, 11.

41. Murray Edelman, *Politics as Symbolic Action*, (Chicago: Markham Publishing Company, 1971), 7.

42. One could easily substitute ideology or culture here as well. Arnold uses the terms interchangeably, occasionally missing subtle but importance nuances between them. Parallels can be drawn between Rousseau's discussion of civil religion, Tocqueville's talk of habits and mores, or Burke's reverence for tradition. However, the concept that it most closely parallels is Marx's notion of the superstructure, especially with its close connection between ideas and institutions.

43. Edelman offers us a more precise definition of symbol than Arnold. "Symbols become that facet of experiencing the material world that gives it a specific meaning." Murray Edelman, *Constructing the Political Spectacle*, (Chicago: The University of Chicago Press, 1988), 8. One can witness the trials of Bernie Madoff or Jack Abramoff as contemporary examples of ceremonial intervention. Jail time enables us to believe that our basic institutions function well, and that isolated bad apples receive their just dessert, rather than having us confront the existence of systemic flaws within American capitalism and democracy.

44. In fact, "the very concept of 'fact' becomes irrelevant because every meaningful political object and person is an interpretation that reflects and perpetuates an ideology." Edelman, *Spectacle*, 10.

45. Edelman, *Spectacle*, 3. "Only man among living things reconstructs his past, perceives his present condition, and anticipates his future through symbols that abstract, screen, condense, distort, displace, and even create what the senses bring to his attention...It...facilitates firm attachments to illusions, misperceptions, and myths and consequent misguided or self-defeating action." Edelman, *Spectacle*, 2.

46. Abbot, *Exemplary*, 13.

47. Robert Eden, "Introduction: A Legacy of Questions," in Eden, 11.

48. Eden, "Origins," 75.

49. This should not be taken too far. As Mill points out in *On Liberty*, the advantage that truth has over error is that even when suppressed it is likely to rise again (although there is certainly no guarantee of this happening, and the suppression always comes with costs). Likewise, institutions are bound to necessity, and one built on faulty empirical premises will eventually find itself overwhelmed by that empirical reality. But even then the interpretation of institutional collapse is an open political question. As David Plotke argues, we should not forget that the New Deal was not the only possible response to the Depression.

50. Quoted in Edward Kearney, *Thurman Arnold Social Critic*, (Albuquerque: University of New Mexico Press, 1970), 63.

51. Arnold, "Letter to Oliver Thomason" 19 June, 1936,*Voltaire*, 231.

52. Jouvenel, *Power*, 331.

53. In a letter to Jerome Frank, 18 June, 1945, Arnold remarked, "I had a hard time adjusting myself to your emphasis on writers, economists, and philosophers as motivating forces in the development of social organization. Personally, I think they had very little to do with it and you would have just as much socialism if Karl Marx had never lived as you have today." *Voltaire*, 358.

54. Arnold envisions a process more akin to advertising than brute propaganda.

55. So, for instance, the TVA was set up as a corporation, because, as Lilienthal notes, "There was a psychological advantage in using the corporate device since by established practice and custom the corporation has come to embody in people's minds this idea of managerial responsibility." Lilienthal, *TVA*, 173.

56. Machiavelli, *Prince*, 50.

57. Thurman Arnold, "Letter to Sam Bass Warner," 26 April, 34, *Voltaire*, 200.

58. The attitudes of former Progressives regarding the New Deal is instructive here. Otis Graham studied 105 former progressives who were still alive after the first term of the New Deal. He found that five were more radical than the New Deal, forty generally supportive of it, and over sixty found themselves in opposition. Typically from the Jeffersonian wing of the movement, they found themselves unwilling to adjust Progressive concerns to new institutional realities. "In an era when institutions and social patterns are transformed every generation, it is not just the ordinary, conservative citizen who finds himself and his standards outmoded by the arrival of the next generation with its new problems and its inevitable irreverence. Such is the pace of change that the greatest losses of liberalism are by defection." Graham, "Tradition," 200-201.

59. This is not to say that progressives should abandon principle, or that wholesale compromise with our creeds for any political end is justifiable. Any potential gains always need to be measured against the potential damage that compromise will do to the symbolic value of the principle—its ability to inspire others and keep them politically engaged. New Deal pragmatism seeks to balance principle and interest—this is what gives it its political character.

60. Arnold, *Folklore*, 96.

61. Of course, there is a certain simplicity found in simply not caring. See, for instance, a 1964 comment by Ronald Reagan. "We were told four years ago that seventeen million people went to bed hungry every night. Well, that was probably true. They were all on a diet."

62. Figures like Zinn, Piven, and Cloward are amongst the more prominent names who argue that the New Deal prevented more radical possibilities, but as Anthony Badger observes, New Deal programs like the WPA, rather than co-opting worker agitation, tended to stimulate it. Beyond that, the protest movements that formed in the thirties did not focus enough on the political education and consciousness raising needed to pursue a more radical politics. Surges in membership tended to be temporary, and movements spent their time occupied with more material issues. Badger, *New Deal*.

63. Wallace, *Statesmanship*, 83.

64. Wallace, *Statesmanship*, 83

65. Arnold uses scholarship broadly to refer to any formal defense of a particular order, although when he uses it pejoratively he refers in particular to instances where the institution's creeds block practical action.

66. Arnold, *Folklore*, 31-32.

67. Murray Edelman, *Political Language: Words That Succeed and Policies That Fail*, (New York: Academic Press, 1977), 19.

68. Quoted in Eads, "Airliner," 70.

69. Arnold uses the word conservative in the sense of having a stake in the established order, not conservative in terms of necessarily leaning towards the Right.

70. We have seen this in the Middle Ages, Arnold argues, with the need for a banking industry that the current social hierarchy could make no room for—therefore only the Jews, who existed outside (or underneath to use a term Arnold would prefer) this established order could engage in banking. The church was brought in as an authority to justify this prevailing order and to declare that a violation of it was a sin against God. We saw a similar reaction during the depression when FDR attempted to regulate banks. The move was opposed in the same moral language of the Middle Ages, because this new technique again fell outside of accepted channels of action. Arnold, *Folklore*, 2-3.

71. Arnold, *Folklore*, 3.

72. Arnold fills his books with examples of people outraged over New Deal policies that are actually in their material interests but because they seem 'socialistic' or 'bureaucratic' they violate their principled commitment to 'limited government' and 'capitalism.' The hostility and loyalty given to these respective terms is one grounded in an emotional commitment, not any objective understanding of what these terms and policies actually mean and do. See chapter 4 of Edelman's *Politics as Symbolic Action*, for further discussion.

73. Herbert Hooverm "Letter to Wesley Clair Mitchell," 26 Oct. 1934, in Patrick Reagan, *Designing a New America: The Origins of New Deal Planning 1890-1943*, (Amherst: University of Massachusetts Press, 1999), 183.

74. Of course this is not to say that other groups were not opposed to Roosevelt, but Arnold is less interested in the militant opposition of the racist or hopelessly reactionary. He focuses instead the fierce condemnation of Roosevelt by the educated middle and upper classes.

75. Wallace, *Statesmanship*, 86. Conveniently, this devil, as Wallace reminds us, is easy to spot because of the 'red' company he keeps, and Wallace provides a quick test to tell if someone has been corrupted by its false theology. "Anyone who is further to the Left than you are—and whom you don't like—is a communist." Quoted in Culver, *Dreamer*, 415.

76. Arnold, *Folklore*, 30.

77. Although the dependence of research on capital does serve to undermine Arnold's assumption, and many scientists will be quick to point out the hostilities to change existing in their own area of study.

78. The fact that no two people have the same views on what these words actually mean is not a problem because other than scholars, people take them on faith. The whole reason (in Arnold's eyes) that scholarship is publicly supported is because people assume that somewhere experts are producing literature that settles these questions and justifies our beliefs in these principles. Of course no one will bother to read that literature. They just want to know that it is there. Arnold would certainly point out that the dry style of much academic writing does much to contribute to this state of affairs, but in many ways that is desirable. If people actually read they would learn that these fixed principles we orient our lives around are far from settled, and our role as social priests would be greatly diminished. The Catholic Church knew what it was doing when it refused to translate the Bible out of Latin.

79. The problem, of course, is that the free press and education only present ideas accepted by our current mythology, and public discussion usually consists of rallying cries designed to inspire the faithful more than any considered debate. That can only happen in smaller, intimate settings—at least for Arnold. In his eyes public debate consists of demonization and sloganeering. He had as little patience for deliberative democracy as he did for most forms of scholarship. Abstract scholarship is only capable of following, and public deliberation is so riddled with misinformation and political manipulation that it can never live up to its promise. Innovation comes from the actions of managers responding to practical needs, which theorists will then justify.

80. Arnold, *Folklore*, 8. Italics his.

81. Edelman, *Misinformation*, 109.

82. Or, in times defined by a populist hostility to expertise, we have the common sense and wisdom of average Americans to help us make sense of the world, shunning the advice of the expert and his research.

83. Recall again that Arnold conflates the two.

84. Arnold, *Folklore*, 9.

85. Edelman is again instructive on this point. "A focus on individuals rather than on social structure as the causes of political developments is a major and chronic reason for distorted analysis because it highlights personality and good or evil intentions rather than the social and economic grounds for conditions that might be changed if they were adequately recognized as influential." Edelman, *Misinformation*, 109.

86. Arnold, *Symbols*, 229.

87. Eden, "Origins," 99.

88. FDR, "Answering the Critics," 28 June 1934, *Chat*, 51-52.

89. Including critical remarks on the way Senator Borah gained political capital through moralistic enforcement of the act that accomplished nothing in terms of practical policy. Needless to say, when Borah showed up to Arnold's confirmation hearing with a copy of the book tucked under his arm, Arnold was a bit nervous.

90. Arnold, *Folklore*, 220.

91. "For forty years we have been just about ready to enforce the law. We have written books; we have passed supplemental legislation; we have preached, we have defined, we have built a great system of legal metaphysics; and we have denounced. Indeed, we have done everything except to get an organization together and do an actual job of policing." Arnold, *Bottlenecks*, 70.

92. Arnold faced a great deal of hostility from liberals and other reformers who did not trust the Sherman Act, who were suspicious of the courts, and preferred some form of administrative tribunals. Much of Arnold's *The Bottlenecks of Business* is aimed at assuaging their fears, or at least reminding them of the practical restraints that prevented critics from putting their theories into practice.

93. Arnold, *Bottlenecks*, 92.

94. Another example he liked was the existence of bootlegging during the prohibition. Our folklore would not allow us to drink, but of course there was a real material need for alcohol, and bootlegging provided this function without ever being legitimized.

95. As did FDR in the early stages of his legislative career, until he learned to appreciate their value both as a political tool and a provider of services the state was not prepared to handle.

96. There is some evidence that the machines themselves understood the vital role they played in our broader democratic process. H.W. Brands quotes Tammany chief Richard Croker at length.

> Consider the problem which every democratic system has to solve. Government, we say, of the people, by the people, and for the people. The aim is to interest as many of the citizens as possible in the work—which is not easy work, and has many difficulties and disappointments—of governing the state or the city...We have thousands upon thousands of men who are alien born, who have no ties connecting them with the city or the state. They do not speak our language, they do not know our laws. They are the raw material with which we have to build up the state.

Brands, *Traitor*, 51.

97. Another example Arnold frequently refers back to is the idea of anti-trust legislation. Our economic folklore, which privileged the idea of the individual economic man in control of his production, at the time could not make room for big corporations. Yet they were essential to progress. So laws were passed that were largely ceremonial condemning trusts. Occasionally there were trials of specific companies, utilizing another form of ceremony. But eventually the contradiction is resolved to the point that the corporations can perform their vital function and the principle can remain pure. Arnold. *Folklore*, 211.

98. Interestingly enough, as Arnold predicted, it was the welfare state that really destroyed the dominance of the local machine in American politics. There was no longer a vital function for them to perform because the new folklore of government made space for its welfare functions.

99. This is laid out wonderfully in *The Folklore of Capitalism*. See especially 46-83.

100 Arnold, *Folklore*, 121.

101. "Respectable people are not as bad as reformers would paint them. They are only caught in ideals which happen to have, at the time, no emotional relevance to the complaining reformer." Arnold, *Symbols*, 216.

102. It is the failure to do this that threatens the accomplishments of the New Deal. It is not that the New Deal failed to legitimate itself, but that "the ancient symbols and traditions have never been deserted by even the most radical of those who have exercised power during the depression. We have not witnessed a revolt of the down trodden, but a panic on the part of the well to do." Arnold, *Symbols*, 107. Because the old symbols were never fully replaced, they remained available as a source of morale and political manipulation for future opponents of the welfare state. We will explore this idea in more detail later.

103. Arnold, *Folklore*, 38. The rise of a commercial class against feudalism is one of Arnold's examples of this phenomena.

104. Here he misses the great insight of the modern conservative movement—that one can, through sufficiently ruthless manipulation of folklore, create the appearance of collapse and the demand for change regardless of actual material conditions.

105. ER quoted in Kearney, *Reformer*, 156.

106. The homes were budgeted at 2,000 dollars but due to a number of administrative errors (such as ordering houses designed for Massachusetts summers instead of West Virginian winters, as well as what some saw as too many luxuries for

people on relief, the total cost per home ballooned to 8,000 dollars and contained conveniences the middle class might envy.

107. Some of which can be attributed to a failure by FDR to clarify the real nature of the project.

108. Arnold, *Folklore*, 311-332. Black, *Biography*, 254-255.

109. Black, *Biography*, 254-255.

110. Hareven, *Conscience*, 105.

111. Lash, *Eleanor and Franklin*, 400.

112. It should be noted that the dispossessed themselves had no desire to participate in a grand experiment in new ways of living. Their primary concern was to earn enough money to purchase enough land to return to for-profit farming.

113. Arnold, *Symbols*, 237.

114. For instance, FDR appropriated the term *liberal*, which enjoyed great legitimacy, for welfare state progressivism, saddling laissez faire liberalism with the term *conservatism*. Even programs like Social Security were dressed up in the symbols of the corporation.

115. Abbot, *Exemplary*, 9

116. See Lipset and Marks, *It Didn't Happen Here* for a cultural, institutional, and historical look at why socialism has failed to gain political traction in the United States

117. Machiavelli, *Prince*, 50.

118. Which was the experience of progressives like Walter Lippmann after the catastrophe of WWI.

119. Arnold, "Letter to Felix Frankfurter," 11 June, 1934, *Voltaire*, 203. He formulated a name for this position, coming up with 'neo-positivistic-semi-realistic-post-Machiavellistic.'

120. Arnold, *Symbols*, 6.

121. Arnold, *Symbols*, 125.

122. Plotke, *Building*, 244.

123. Quoted in Plotke, *Building*, 245.

124. Arnold, *Symbols*, 100.

125. Ronald Reagan, "Moscow's Spring," 31 May 1988. http://www.nationalreview.com/document/reagan_moscow200406070914.asp

126. Arnold, *Folklore*, 34.

127. Cited in Nace, *Gangs*, 39.

128. Jim Heath, "American War Mobilization and the Use of Small Manufactures, 1939-1943," in Himmelberg, 94.

129. Arnold, *Symbols*, 188-189. Laid out principally in *Symbols of Government*, Arnold makes a fascinating argument that the legal system is constructed to be a rational morality play, a form of ceremony designed to resolve contradictions via the idea of combative jury trials—which in fact is a terrible way to discover the truth.

130. Arnold, *Folklore*, 35.

131. Canton, "Progressivism," 180.

132. George Frederick Baer, quoted in Downey, *Perkins*, 198.

133. An idea that the New Deal always embraced, as the New Deal remained a product of the folklore it was trying to overcome.

134. Norton, *Signs*, 25.

135. Arnold, *Folklore*, 190.

136. Nace, *Gangs*, 70-86.

137. Arnold, *Folklore*, 188-189.

138. It is not surprising that the currency of our business elite is stock. We think of stock as private property and as such there is no real sense of public responsibility or obligation. Failed corporations like Enron consisted of a collection of shares, not a mass of workers, families, and shareholders whose livelihood depended on the success of the company. Likewise, since corporations are individuals, our first instinct when scandals (a word choice that implies individual misbehavior instead of systemic faults) break is to seek criminal penalties instead of government control. "Since the organizations were persons, they should be treated as if they had free will and moral responsibility. Regulation was bureaucracy and tyranny over individuals." Arnold, *Folklore*, 215.

139. Somewhat surprisingly, Arnold does not allow for independent spiritual forms of government. The spiritual aspect is always attached to an organization with material commitments.

140. Arnold, *Symbols*, 238-239.

141. Which is to say, any current shortcomings are not an indictment of the overall system. This argument was first made by Mandeville in *The Fable of the Bees*. Adam Smith, to whom this logic is also credited, argued that legislation would be necessary to prevent radical inequality.

142. Richard Neuberger, "America Talks Court," *Current History* (June 1937), in Freidel, 106.

143. There are perhaps many reasons to oppose Roosevelt's court reorganization plan, but the cost of the judges' salaries should probably not rank too high on that list.

144. Burns, *Lion*, 240.

145. Goldman, *Destiny*, 345.

146. Ronald Reagan, *Sacramento Bee*, 28 Apr. 1966.

147. And, when we are being honest with ourselves, a bit of luck.

148. Zinn, *People's*, 188.

149. Or possibly bad luck, but if it was just a question of luck you could always start over.

150. It cannot be overstated how prevalent this belief was in the United States when Roosevelt took over, especially amongst elite opinion makers. That the government could not hope but fail if it engaged in economic functions that private industry could provide was an article of faith believed with the same sincerity with which Christians believe in the divinity of Jesus. And, like all forms of faith, contradictory evidence (such as the performance of the War Industries Board in World War I that inspired so many New Dealers) was ignored or dismissed, the exception rather than the rule.

151. Badger, *New Deal*, 194.

152. This is reinforced by the public stigmatization of relief, guaranteeing that, as Edelman puts it, the "poor are therefore inundated with cues from reference groups and from government defining them as personally inadequate, guilty, dependent, and deserving of their deprivations." Edelman, *Symbolic*, 55. Edelman goes on: "The American poor have required less coercion and less in social security guarantees to maintain their quiescence than has been true in other developed countries, even authoritarian ones like Germany and notably poor ones like Italy; for the guilt and self-concepts of the poor have kept them docile. That such violence as has occurred has been localized, sporadic, limited to small groups in special circumstances, and rarely perceived by participants as am movement for purposeful institutional change but rather as despairing protest, is further evidence for this conclusion." Ibid., 55. And, as Goodwyn argues in *The Populist Moment*, an organized, combative response to privation has

always been the exception rather than the rule. Privation in the United States tends to breed passivity.

153. Smith, *FDR*, 352.

154. In 1887, for example, President Cleveland vetoed a bill to give $100,000 in aid to drought-stricken Texas farmers. Cleveland argued that "Federal aid in such cases encourages the expectation of paternal care on the part of the government and weakens the sturdiness of our national character." Instead, the national treasury, flush with cash, was used to give bond holders a twenty-eight-dollar bonus on hundred dollar bonds. Cited in Zinn, *History,* 191-192.

155. Edelman, *Language*, 73.

156. Miroff, *Icons*, 258.

157. Romanasco, *Recovery*, 64.

158. This aspect of our folklore is alive and well today. Just one day before the government fronted the money to bail out Bear Stearns, President Bush argued that "If we were to pursue some of the sweeping government solutions that we hear about in Washington, we would make a complicated problem even worse—and end up hurting far more homeowners than we help." Terrance Hunt, "Avoid Overcorrecting Economy Bush Warns," Associated Press, 15 March 2008, http://ap.google.com/article/ALeqM5j057jB-ReERcsFFcZRSWe0hlgaXQ D8VDU1A80?

159. Michael Thompson, *Politics of Inequality: A Political History of the Idea of Economic Inequality in America*, (New York: Columbia University Press, 2007), 78.

160. Thompson*, Inequality*, 124-125.

161. Fischer, *Liberty*, 491.

162. Bernstein, *Caring*, 46-47.

163 This is not the place to discuss them in any great detail; suffice it to say the presence of our frontier offered the appearance of limitless opportunities necessary to justify laissez faire capitalism, and the comparative ease with which (white men at least) were able to secure their political rights prevented the rise of class-based movements found in Europe, where the fight for economic and political democracy were inextricably linked.

164. Since, for Locke and especially Hobbes, we form governments out of necessity—and ONLY out of necessity for Hobbes. Locke concedes there are other benefits.

165. Ironically, Southern apologists for slavery picked up on the brutal nature of this freedom, noting that a slaveholder at least had a vested interest in making sure their workers don't starve. There was an investment in a particular body that was missing in a system of wage labor. A dead slave was expensive to replace, whereas wages could go to whatever body was present on a particular day.

166. *Efficiency* is an example of what Arnold calls polar words, words that are defined only by what they oppose, lacking any essential meaning. Efficiency and inefficiency are value judgments that reflect the personal preference of whoever is using the word. Arnold will still use the word, but his measure of efficiency would privilege distribution, as opposed to maximizing profits.

167. And our first CEO president tried his hardest to bring us back to the mentality of the 1920s. Of course, like the 1920s, this hostility to government spending is disingenuous. Hundreds of billions of dollars are still spent every year. The question is whether it goes to provide social programs, the military or corporate welfare. The folklore and symbols of the 1920s legitimate the later and challenge the former.

168. Although, as Hartz would likely (correctly) argue, this is inevitable since the folklore of the New Deal starts from the same Lockean assumptions.

169. Arnold, *Folklore*, 36.

170. Although we are less paralyzed by fear of debt and balancing the budget than we were in Arnold's time.

171. Hamby, "Historians," 14.

172. Quoted in Abbot, *Exemplary*, 95.

173. Arnold, *Folklore*, 36-37.

174. Arnold, *Fair Fights and Foul*, 89-90.

175. Edsforth, *New Deal*, 226.

176. Abbot, *Exemplary*, 80.

177. Feminists, hardly enjoying an excess of public good will, are typically judged by its most strident and radical adherents, yet few people judge Christianity by the standards of the Westboro Baptist Church, and their charming website, www.godhatesfags.com.

178. Plotke, *Building*, 95.

179. Shogun, *Backlash*, 55. Support was possibly higher as polling data tended to skew towards middle- and upper-income families.

180. They invalidated most traditional strikebreaking tactics—which is to say that violence visited against striking workers could be countered by damaging corporate property.

181. Shogun, *Backlash*, 141.

182. Shogun, *Backlash*, 141.

183. Shogun, *Backlash*, 141.

184. FDR, "Answering the Critics," 28 June 1934, *Chat*, 51.

185. His primary work of advocacy was *The Bottlenecks of Business,* a defense of his anti-trust philosophy which was fairly well received.

186. Wallace, *Statesmanship*, 22.

187. Wallace, *Frontiers*, 11.

188. Wallace, "Russia," *Address at Congress of American-Soviet Friendship*, 8 November 1942. *Democracy*, 196.

189. Wallace, *Statesmanship*, 8.

190. Wallace, *Statesmanship*, 18.

191. Wallace, *Statesmanship*, 22-23.

192. Wallace, *Statesmanship*, 33.

193. Wallace, *Statesmanship*, 37-38.

194. FDR, "First Inaugural," 30.

195. Although Wallace, whose Christianity was highly unconventional, was often accused of being a dreamy mystic incapable of seeing the real world.

196. Wallace, *Statesmanship*, 71.

197. Wallace, *Statesmanship*, 71.

198. Wallace, *Statesmanship*, 79. Provocative words from a member of the presidential cabinet.

199. Although Wallace, like Eleanor Roosevelt, was quick to point out that any religion that embraced these ethical principles was functionally Christian. It was the ethics, and not the cosmology, that truly mattered.

200. Wallace, *Statesmanship*, 81.

201. Wallace, "A Declaration of Interdependence" 13 May. 1933, *Democracy*, 45-46.

202. Stucky, *Defining*, 237.
203. Norton, *Signs*, 102.
204. Henry Wallace, "Technology," 128,
205. Hofstadter, *Reform*, 23.
206. Hofstadter, *Reform*, 23.
207. Although both of them, Wallace especially, were keenly aware of that fact that farm products were ultimately a commodity, and that the continuation of the agrarian lifestyle required making it economically viable, even at the expense of much of the farmers 'independence.'
208. Lilienthal, *TVA*, 3.
209. Abbot, *Exemplary*, 73.
210. Wallace, *Frontiers*, 3.
211. Wallace, *Frontiers*, 5.
212. Wallace, *Frontiers*, 10.
213. Wallace, *Frontiers*, 11.
214. Wallace, *Frontiers*, 9.
215. Wallace, *Frontiers*, 16.
216. Wallace, *Frontiers*, 251.
217. Wallace, *Constitution*, 92.
218. Arnold, *Fair Fights Foul*, 72.
219. McMahon, *Race*, 50.
220. Karl, *Uneasy*, 151.
221. Karl, *Uneasy*, 151.
222. Some members of his administration, like Arnold, went a step further and took the position of the legal realist: The Constitution has no inherent meaning, and its interpretation is subjected to the arbitrary whim of the judge doing the interpreting. They will find what they want to find—what their background has encouraged them to find.
223. Shogun, *Backlash*, 86.
224. Wallace, *Constitution*, 8.
225. Wallace, *Constitution*, 93.
226. Wallace, *Constitution*, 96.
227. Wallace, *Constitution*.
228. Hamilton, quoted in Wallace, *Constitution*, 205, interestingly enough for a Secretary of Agriculture, Hamilton is quoted more often than Jefferson in Wallace's major works.
229. Arnold, *Folklore*, 87.
230. Arnold, *Symbols*, 103-104.
231. Arnold, "Letter to Sam Bass Warner," 26 April 1934. Quoted in "Legal Realism and the Burden of Symbolism: The Correspondence of Thurman Arnold," 13 *Law & Society*, Summer 1977, 1006.
232. Samuels, "Realism," 1005.
233. Arnold, *Symbols*, 21.
234. Arnold, *Folklore*, 87.
235. FDR went through a similar education. His early political career in New York was marked by an anti-Tammany, anti-corruption standpoint that ignored the role of interest in society, the fact that these organizations were important political coalitions, and the role they played in providing necessary civil services. But by 1924 he was eulogizing Tammany captain Charles Murphy for his leadership and service. In the end the decline of political machines can probably be traced not to the corruption crusades,

but the rise of a central state willing to provide the social services once offered only by Tammany and the other machines. Arnold offers a detailed account of this in *Folklore of Capitalism.*

236. Henry Steele Commager, *Majority Rule and Minority Right.*

Chapter 6
The Third New Deal: The Institutional Context of Reform

[P]rogrammatic rights, such as Social Security and collective bargaining, would not amount to anything unless new institutional arrangements were established that would reorganize the institutions and redistribute the powers of government.

—Sidney Milkis[1]

Fortune and necessity cannot be conquered, Machiavelli argued, only contained. The New Deal took this lesson to heart, and drew the appropriate consequences. First, political theory must account for the presence of necessity in its evaluation of the possible. The imaginative, transcendent moment is needed to orient the direction of political behavior, but as a guide, not an absolute standard that negates the possibility of action in the name of utopia. Second, the effective political actor must learn how to respond to fortune and necessity in a way that maximizes his own potential for action. Political life exists in the realm of necessity, but within that realm there is considerable room to determine how necessity shapes our lives, for "imagining the possible." We must learn to maximize our agency in a bounded world.[2]

Thus far we have explored the symbolic constraints on action—the way an institution's folklore determines the limits of political action, and how that folklore can be adapted to serve new institutions. Here we examine the New Deal's political context, and conclude with a look at the New Deal's theory of change. [3] Ultimately, the limits of the New Deal, both in terms of the breadth of its vision and what it was able to institutionalize reflect a realistic assessment of necessity—what was possible within the New Deal's political context.

The Forces Against Reform

No leader is a free agent...[Roosevelt] was captain of the ship of state, but many hands reached for the tiller, and a rebellious crew manned the sails.
—James MacGregor Burns[4]

The New Deal confronted both a conservative folklore and severe institutional limits that constrained almost all attempts at thoroughgoing reform.[5] The purpose of this section is not to provide an exhaustive look into any of these areas, nor is it to issue an apology for the Roosevelt administration's failures. Instead I wish to introduce an informal set of 'Machiavellian' criteria for making normative judgments of political acts. Given the constraints the New Deal operated under, *could* it have done a better job mastering its conditions, and to what degree? These judgments cannot be rendered without first looking at the institutional framework in which political decisions are made. What other choices were available? Were they viable? What might their consequences have been? The empirical context has to be carefully considered before the normative evaluation is made. In the face of missed meaningful possibilities, the normative critique is valid as political critique. In the absence of meaningful choice, the normative critique devolves into the apolitical moralizing Arnold cautioned against. Although this list is hardly exhaustive, we will examine the conservative coalition in Congress, the Supreme Court, the sit-down strikes, and the fundamentally weak nature of the U.S. state, and in doing so begin to unpack how circumscribed the politics of reform can be.

The Conservative Coalition

Somewhat counter intuitively, the vast majority of the New Deal's reforms preceded Roosevelt's landslide 1936 victory. James Patterson, one of the first historians to trace the rise of the conservative coalition that successfully stymied the New Deal after 1936, is clear that its strength was not a direct response to leadership failures on the part of New Dealers.[6] The coalition owes its vitality to a potent combination of FDR's court plan, his failed purge, hostility towards a labor movement that its detractors identified with FDR (or at least with FDR's refusal to suppress it), the 1937-1938 "Roosevelt Recession" (never mind that the recession seemingly validated the successes of the New Deal measures under attack), a rural reaction against the increasing visibility of the Democrats' urban coalition, Southern fears of a civil rights agenda, the common loss of influence that accompanies a second term president, and the decreased sense of urgency borne of the New Deal's very success. By the end of the 1930s this coalition had come to thoroughly dominate Congress, rolled back progressive measures during World War II, and has wielded considerable influence since.[7]

The elements of this coalition were always there, a reflection of deep antagonisms rendered temporarily dormant, but not resolved, by the gravity of the Great Depression and the momentum of the New Deal. Its roots were in the Solid South, built around principled support of Jim Crow, which had long served as a bulwark against any progressive change that might disturb southern racial hierarchies. In the South the category of class paled in comparison to the category of color. As Carol Horton notes, "Segregation, like disenfranchisement, reinforced the dominance of conservative elites by crushing all politically salient divisions among whites under the overwhelming weight of racial hierarchy."[8] Class divisions and economic concerns were subordinated to issues of race, and memories of Reconstruction were powerful symbols justifying the massive disenfranchisement of poor whites—probable allies of the New Deal—provided this also kept blacks from voting. This block became increasingly capable of holding the New Deal hostage, especially on policy issues touching on race. Given the New Deal's color-blind, universal language, this ultimately covered a great deal of legislative territory.

Senator Jimmy Byrnes, usually a stalwart Roosevelt ally, gives voice to the palpable Southern fear that thanks to the New Deal, "the Negro has not only come into the Democratic Party, but the Negro has come into control of the Democratic Party."[9] In particular, Southern congressmen feared the passing of an anti-lynching bill in 1938. Byrnes comment is noteworthy for its comparatively moderate tone, compared to the dire prophecies of Senator Bilbo (the Platonic form of a fire-eating Southern populist, and normally a friend of the administration) that "upon your [supporters of anti-lynching legislation] garments...will be the blood of the raped and outraged daughters of Dixie, as well as the blood of the perpetrators of these crimes that the red-blooded Anglo-Saxon white Southern men will not tolerate."[10] The emotional salience of race, combined with the wholesale abandonment of the region by Republicans, meant that the seats of reactionary congressmen, especially those representing rural areas, were safe (as FDR discovered during the failed purge).[11]

Of course in the early stages of the New Deal many of these congressional figures voted in tandem with the New Deal. But the increasingly anti-business, pro urban, (which of course is not the same thing anti-rural), racially inclusive face of the New Deal was creating new tensions that a decreased sense of crisis could not paper over. Roosevelt's insistence on legislation breaking up utility trusts (the death-sentence bill), even in its final, moderate form, awoke within previously sympathetic members of Congress a desire to reassert institutional prerogatives and once again let ambition counteract ambition. Roosevelt expended a great deal of political capital getting the bill passed, forcing many recalcitrant congressmen into compliance, which led to ill feelings resurfacing during the court fight—an important reminder that political capital is finite, and victory in one battle may spell defeat in another. More importantly, as Shogan observes, the fight showed opposition moderates within the party that "they could resist the New Deal and survive to fight another day,"[12] especially with FDR's expected retirement in 1940.[13]

Opposition to the New Deal could also take on subtle forms, hidden from larger public scrutiny. When they lacked the votes to kill a bill members of the opposition, especially southerners, would avoid committee meetings to prevent a quorum.[14] Similarly, opposition Democrats could use their positions on committees to force concessions into bills they opposed before they made it to the floor, changing the nature of the bills under consideration. As Eliot Rosen argues, roll calls do not show the full picture of democratic obstruction.[15]

It was difficult to oppose the coalition in part because it was not a fixed entity. Patterson notes that while its members shared common characteristics—they were Democrats from safe (often rural) districts where FDR had limited influence—their membership changed from issue to issue. The hostility of Byrnes to race legislation is instructive here, as he was one of FDR's leading supporters during the court-packing debate, and generally one of his most stalwart congressional allies. However, certain prominent conservative Democrats were in frequent opposition, which grew increasingly strident when the Supreme Court finally embraced Roosevelt's constitutional vision and ceased to function as a check on New Deal power.

Here the New Deal was partly a victim of its own success. Roosevelt warned that "[p]rosperity already tests the persistence of our progressive purpose."[16] The American middle class, upon losing its fear, quickly returned to its characteristic inwardness and simply forgot (or stopped caring) about the $1/3^{rd}$ of the nation still "ill-housed, ill-clad, ill-nourished." Likewise, moderates in Congress, no longer ruled by fear or cowed by crisis, were increasingly inclined to oppose New Deal policies they felt were too radical, or that concentrated too much power in the hands of the executive. Roosevelt had managed to paper over tensions by focusing on the temporary nature of relief programs.[17] As it became clearer that the New Deal would reflect a new, permanent order, Democrats became far less deferential to the administration. Having banished the looming sense of fear and catastrophe from the nation (generally considered to be the one unqualified success of the Roosevelt administration) it was much easier for the old folklore, whose Constitutional fetishism often worshiped at the altar of business confidence, to reassert itself.

The Courts and the Sit-Down Strikes

The fear of centralized executive power was once a cornerstone of American folklore, still powerfully felt at the time of the New Deal. It is telling that Roosevelt's comparatively modest plan for executive reorganization was pejoratively referred to as the "Dictator Bill" which intended, in the words of Massachusetts Senator David Walsh (a Democrat) to plunge "a dagger into the very heart of democracy."[18] Even if the accusations of Roosevelt being a dictator are nonsensical (with the advantage of hindsight or even with measured reflection at the time), the rise of totalitarian governments worldwide made this fear understandable. During the first six years of the Roosevelt administration there was little serious congressional resistance to New Deal programs and the rapid expansion of federal (and especially executive) power.[19] Its opponents instead had to look to the sometimes careful, sometimes tortured reasoning of the Supreme Court in order to check an immensely popular president ruling (as they saw it) in the name of the democratic mob.

The court represented a powerful bulwark against the expansion of federal power, the last check in a time of crisis. Southern Democrats, especially following the loss of the two-thirds rule in the 1936 Democratic National Convention,[20] worried (presciently) that liberals would use the courts to push civil rights legislation. Felix Frankfurter warned FDR that the sit-down strikes emphasized amongst many voters the need for "law and order," which would heighten the prestige of the court and make the electorate more suspicious of tampering with the institution.[21] As columnist Dorothy Thompson observed, "Cleverness and adroitness in dealing with the Supreme Court are not qualities which soberminded citizens will approve."[22]

While there is not necessarily consensus on the popularity of FDR's court reorganization plan outside of elites,[23] it is generally conceded that its failure marks the end of FDR's dominance over Congress, the end of the active New Deal agenda. But the fact that FDR failed does not mean that action against the court was unnecessary. The court's opposition to government intervention in the economy was ideological in the worst sense of the word—so divorced from empirical circumstances that even action aimed at bolstering free enterprise was out of bounds. Shogan captures what was at stake when he notes that no matter how much power Congress handed to FDR, "he could count on wielding that power effectively only at the sufferance of the Supreme Court."[24] The *Morehead v New York* (1936) decision demonstrated the bind in which the courts placed the New Deal. Previously in its *Adkins* decision (1932) the court denied the federal government the authority to establish minimum wages. The *Morehead* decision (by a divided 5-4 court that highlighted the ideological nature of the ruling) overturned the rights of states to declare their own minimum wage laws, jeopardizing the very idea of worker protections and functionally denying citizens the possibility of even marginal agency in the face of arbitrary economic power.

Roosevelt has been criticized for his handling of his court plan on a number of levels—for pursuing it at all (Brandeis and others argued that the problem was the ways the laws were written, not their substance), for insisting on it even after the Court's famous Switch in Nine, for the way it was framed, and for the secrecy surrounding it.[25] Some, like Jean Smith in an otherwise sympathetic biography, argue that this was pure hubris on the part of FDR, a sentiment echoed by Bruce Miroff, "the work of a president whose normal political acumen had been supplanted by the over confidence of the resplendent ego."[26] But as always, criticism of Roosevelt must keep in mind the surrounding political context. For example, knowing the superheated atmosphere surrounding the court, FDR believed that any proposal would be second-guessed from the start. "The danger he faced would be that his proposal would be so battered that by the time he sent it to Capitol Hill it would be dead on arrival."[27] Keeping it secret, FDR believed, was essential to its survival.

Joseph Lash argues that opposition to the plan was inevitable, that Congress was looking for a chance to reassert itself and defend its institutional prerogatives.[28] He recounts an exchange between Senator Wheeler and Tom Corcoran, a member of Roosevelt's inner circle. "I've been watching Roosevelt for a long time. Once he was only one of us who made him. Now he means to make himself the boss of us all. Well he's made the mistake we've been waiting for a long time—and this is our chance to cut him down to size. Your court plan doesn't matter: he's after us."[29] Again, the characters involved here are significant. Senator Wheeler was a mainstay of the progressive movement, even leaving the Democratic Party to run as LaFollette's vice president on the Progressive Party ticket in 1934, and was an ardent support of FDR prior to the court plan.[30] The congressional hostility to the comparatively innocuous proposal is a reaction to Roosevelt's executive centered approach to governance as much as it was any substantive reflection on its content.

As Robert Shogan argues in *Backlash*, the court plan cannot be made sense of without also considering the rise of the sit-down strike and a more militant labor movement.

> The court fight and the sit down strikes were two great political dramas that played out simultaneously on the national stage in the winter, spring, and early summer of 1937 and transformed the balance of power in the country. Taken together, the two controversies became a whole far greater, and more devastating to the New Deal, than the sum of its parts. [31]

Although the New Deal administration was sympathetic and supportive of labor (with the caveat that unions were valuable primarily as a form of worker representation and a means to raise purchasing power), during the era of the sit down strike even modest support came at a cost, leading in the end to Roosevelt's Shakespearean condemnation of both labor and capital ("a plague on both your houses") and John L. Lewis's marvelous rejoinder.[32] Although labor would ultimately stay loyal to Roosevelt, the decision of Roosevelt and fellow New Dealers like Michigan's Governor Murphy to avoid cracking down on the strikers helped pave the way not only for Roosevelt's defeat on the court packing plan, but also the conservative takeover of Congress in 1938.

In the first three months of 1937 the number of sit-down strikes jumped from 25 to 170, leading the *Detroit News* to remark "[s]itting down has replaced baseball as a national pastime."[33] There was a lighter side to the strikes, including children in Illinois engaging in a sit-down strike at a drugstore to assert their right to free candy.[34] But most of the incidents were far more serious, especially when it was clear that strikers were prepared to try and hold the plants by force. The Roosevelt administration and its allies refused to use state violence to break the strikes, a tremendously *unpopular* decision.[35] The President Emeritus of Harvard commented that thanks to the "sit-down revolt" "freedom and liberty are at an end, government becomes a mockery, superseded by anarchy, mob rule, and ruthless dictatorship."[36] By and large the American people shared this assessment. A poll taken in July 1937 indicated that two-thirds of the public felt that sit-downs should be made illegal and favored using force to eject the strikers. Eight in ten favored laws regulating the conduct of strikes, and a two-thirds majority found AFL president William Green (who rejected the use of sit-down strikes) to be a more responsible political leader than John L. Lewis.[37] Perhaps most damaging to the New Deal coalition was the opposition of farmers, who were amongst the most vociferous opponents of the sit-down strikes. Gallup also indicated that 40 percent of the people voting for Roosevelt self-identified as conservatives and disagreed with one or more of his policies. While they may not have yet been ready to break with the President, they were more than willing to punish his party.[38] The Senate, trying to stave off an electoral backlash, passed a non-binding resolution condemning the strikes 75-3. But it was not sufficient, and not even Roosevelt's intervention could prevent the conservative coalition from asserting full control over Congress after the 1938 midterm election. In the end, the court plan, alongside the purge and reorganization failures spelt the end of the New Deal as the embodiment of the Democratic Party. After that it became a movement within the party, reacting to, rather than controlling, a national agenda.

The Weak Central State

As Bernstein notes in *A Caring Society*, our modern state "lodged power not in a bureaucratic elite, but in patronage based political parties, local governmental units, and a strong judicial system. As Badger argues in *The New Deal*, the state lacked the infrastructure to create a bureaucracy capable of managing a national welfare system or implementing a centrally planned economy (and by the time it could develop the governing infrastructure the political opportunity, if it had ever existed, was no longer present).[39] Modern bureaucracy had emerged primarily in the private, rather than public sector. As a result, the New Deal could institutionalize itself imperfectly at best, and this helps to explain the urgency, experimentalism, and willingness to accept the compromises necessary for getting a policy or program off the ground. Future reformation was desirable but impossible until something, however flawed, was in place in the present. The dominant impulse in the New Deal was to act now and perfect it later. In the end the New Deal was animated simultaneously by the hope that anything was possible, and the realization that its possibilities were highly constrained, its incrementalism a balance between these poles.

The Federal Emergency Relief Administration (FERA) tried to make the distribution of relief as professional as possible, but the need for speed, lack of funds, pork barrel approaches to local relief, and differing state standards made this impossible for a fledgling organization.[40] While those in distress were supposed to receive food, fuel, shelter, utilities, clothing, and medical care they rarely received much beyond food. The goal was to dispense relief in cash grants (for the dignity of the recipients), but this was not viable in practice. This was an issue of state capacity, which was itself related to larger issues of federalism. While the town meeting may have been an excellent vehicle for democracy, it proved to be a poor vehicle for distribution. The problem the programs ran into (besides finding funding at the federal level) was their local implementation. As Walter Davenport reported for *Collier's* magazine, "We do know that some farmers refused to serve on the committee [AAA], saying that if they were strictly honest in their appraisals they would lose some of their friends."[41] In addition, the AAA had to rely on the cooperation of the major southern planters, who exercised enormous control over tenant farmers. In a famous incident early in the administration, Wallace was forced to fire Jerome Frank and a number of high profile New Dealers who, in his view, refused to recognize that the state simply lacked the infrastructure to bypass these farmers.[42] "The farm people are just too strong."[43]

The lack of national institutional capacity was doubly hampered by the general failure of the states to successfully implement their own reforms. Most attempts at providing adequate state-level welfare were short-lived, financed by regressive consumer taxes, lacking the infrastructure and personnel necessary for effective implementation, and quickly met their demise at the hands of local conservatives uninterested in relief. Lorena Hickock observed the implementation of New Deal programs throughout the country, chronicling the unrelenting disaster that so often was local relief. In order to qualify in Maine, "a family has got to measure up to the most rigid Nineteenth Century standards of cleanliness, physical and moral...and Heaven help the family in which there is any 'moral problem"; In Texas she reported, "If I were twenty years younger and weighed 75 pounds less I think I'd start out to be the Joan of Arc of the fascist movement in the United States," and by the time she reaches California she was ready to can the entire enterprise. "I think we ought to let Japan have this state. Maybe they could straighten it out."[44] While Hopkins never did suggest that FDR turn California over to the Japanese, he did have to federalize relief in 6 states, and Patterson believes he would have preferred to nationalize it in many more.

When it was not the politicians, conservative courts and static constitutions were even more imposing obstacles to reform, and far more difficult to address. The funding cuts that accompanied Roosevelt's ill-conceived attempt to balance the budget in 1937 exacerbated what was already a dire shortage of funding. Patterson concludes that with only a handful of exceptions (FDR's New York being one of them) by the 1930s states had long ceased being laboratories of social reform, and there was little the New Deal could have done in the short term to address the "limited nature of pre depression state progressivism and the bitter resentment of outside interference,"[45] a lesson FDR learned firsthand in his purge. Patterson ultimately concludes that

> [t]he most striking feature of federal-state relations during the 1930's was not the failure of New Dealers but the limits in which they had to operate. Time was short, the need for immediate action great, courts hostile, state institutions blocked progressive reforms, and state parties were often divided, conservative or concerned with patronage instead of policy.[46]

As a result, Patterson argues, the New Deal could only function federally, with its power centered in Washington.[47] The question then becomes where to situate that power? This is at the heart of the New Deal's efforts to center national power around the presidency, rather than in Congress or with the parties.

The President and the Party

> The purpose of the New Deal institutional program was to force Congress to relinquish its control over national administration, which was becoming the center of political life in industrial societies.
>
> —Sidney Milkis[48]

Machiavelli warns of the risks of dividing power in *The Prince*, lessons the New Deal absorbed as it set out to not only build a national bureaucracy capable of administrating a welfare state, but to control both an increasingly hostile Congress not structured for national leadership, and a Democratic Party unsure of its identity.[49] Addressing these limitations would require, as Milkis argues, the creation of the modern presidency, which "emphasized executive administration with limits on partisanship and rhetoric...emancipat[ing] the president from the constraining influence of American political parties, which made national administrative power chimerical."[50] The institutionalization of the New Deal social contract would prove to be impossible without first greatly expanding the nation's capacity for what FDR referred to in his Commonwealth Club address as "enlightened administration"—governance (not necessarily rule) by experts.[51] It was the effort to permanently strengthen this enlightened national administration that Milkis refers to as the Third New Deal.

> It marked an effort to transform a decentralized polity, animated by localized parties and court rulings that supported property and states' rights into a more centralized, even bureaucratic, form of democracy that could deliver the goods championed by New Dealers.[52]

Thus, while democracy as an act of citizen self-creation remained an important part of New Deal theory (both as a check on materialist excess and as a moral ideal) the process of governing took on a decidedly more managerial tone.

The Brownlow report served as the basis for this reorganization.[53] Although its recommendations (expanded support staff and increased presidential control over the executive branch) were comparatively modest, the aim was clearly to establish permanent institutional mechanisms for reform, so that progressives could act outside of episodic moments of crisis. This required making the president the central actor in our political system. As John Rhor notes, "The Brownlow Report prepared us to accept President Truman's description of his office—"the buck stops here." Before Brownlow we might have thought the genius of American government lay in the fact that the buck stops nowhere."[54] Brownlow envisioned the president and his advisors as both the primary source of public policy and the people most responsible for its implementation.

The original recommendations of the Brownlow report were defeated in April of 1938, due to massive party defections inspired by opposition to the Court plan and sit-down strikes. It was this combination of defeats that led Roosevelt to attempt his ill-fated 'purge' of conservatives from the Democratic Party. FDR's logic was Jacksonian—an appeal to the people over the heads of the reactionaries and their sheltering institutions, a method made viable by the existence of direct primaries and modern media. While the purge was technically unsuccessful, it did scare enough recalcitrant Democrats to get a more modest reorganization bill through Congress in 1939, establishing the Executive Office of the President and increasing his formal control over the bureaucracy, institutionalizing a relationship that previously had been dependent on FDR's leadership.[55] This increase in centralized power helped to emancipate presidents from their parties, as parties were no longer as essential for logistical or electoral support, policy formation, and interest group contacts. It also, as Milkis points out, facilitated ideological patronage, whereas prior patronage was almost solely a form of spoils. Thanks to the Ramspeck Act of 1940, which granted civil service protections to New Deal appointees, the New Deal would be able to maintain its presence in the federal bureaucracy long after FDR left the White House.[56]

The Democratic Party

The New Deal was not synonymous with the Democratic Party, as David Plotke makes clear.

> The Democratic Party was not the leading agent in those efforts [at progressive reform]; it was not powerful or coherent enough to create the New Deal. Parts of it flourished in a political bloc that cut across institutions – in this bloc the Roosevelt administration and new state agencies exercised more political leadership than the Democratic Party.[57]

Roosevelt's impressive electoral victory in 1936 was self-consciously framed as a referendum on his leadership, rather than the party.[58] His public statements made little mention of the Democrats, "nor did he credit his accomplishments to the party. He offered a national, progressive, and popular-democratic program and vision, always trying to attract Republicans and independents."[59] Voters tended to mirror Roosevelt's thinking. They were for FDR first, administration second, and party third, in an increasingly derivative fashion. Roosevelt was fine with this. While he desired an ideologically coherent Democratic Party, this vision was always second to the implementation of the New Deal. As such, he was prepared to work with the Democratic Party as it was, and bypass it when needed, instead of trying to simultaneously reform the party and build a welfare state. Party reform would always be a means, not an end, one to be abandoned when preferable options presented themselves.

To understand the New Deal's attitude towards parties we must remind ourselves that the Democratic Party of the 1930s was hardly a monolithic organization with ideological coherence (nor, for that matter, were the Republicans). Instead it was a massive coalition of state and local organizations, harboring within its borders both the New Deal and Conservative coalitions, with some members of Congress existing in both camps simultaneously. As Albert Romasco observes,

> [i]t would be more precise to speak of the Democratic parties, for the party label was a convenient umbrella covering a congeries of large and small factions representing different regions, diverse and conflicting interests, and the entire political spectrum from left to right. All these unwieldy components were held together under one designation, mainly by the uncertain glue of tradition and party loyalty.[60]

The new groups brought into the party by Roosevelt reflected its expansion more than its reformation, a reformation desired by neither the party leadership nor the rank and file. The Democrats simply contained too many divisions guaranteed to "undermine any attempt to make the party a coherent and autonomous center of power."[61] This lack of coherence is one reason why Roosevelt, as opposed to a progressive like Wilson, chose to distance the executive branch from the party, rather than unite them under a banner of presidential leadership.[62] Whereas Wilson saw parties as a way to integrate the different branches of government, the New Deal simply doubted that the Democrats could demonstrate the kind of independent agency needed to serve as the heart of the movement. As Jerome Mileur put it, "In governing, a leadership of principle and national purpose could frame issues more effectively and produce change more quickly, but not so with party leadership, in which old habits and localism held sway."[63]

FDR's efforts at party reform were sporadic, in part because of the limited institutional power he possessed as party leader. He had no formal disciplinary power, and Congress is not constitutionally responsible to him. He reformed the presidential nomination process (the significance of overturning the two-thirds rule for presidential nominations must not be understated) and the Jacksonian appeal to the public was a useful weapon, but as the purge demonstrated, it often faltered in the black box of local politics. The fact that Roosevelt could claim to speak for all the people did not necessarily help when speaking to a particular people, especially when local laws and customs silenced huge swaths of potentially sympathetic voters. His control was over the national, not the local party. As Hamby argues,

> Unable to control the constituencies of these congressmen, Roosevelt could not wield effective power as a party leader. He could and did continue to dominate the Democratic 'presidential party,' the coalition that controlled the Democratic nominating conventions and provided the margin of victory in presidential elections. However, he could not control the Democratic 'congressional party'; after 1938 he could hope to achieve legislation only through the weak and largely ineffective method of persuasion.[64]

Therefore, simply bypassing the party was often preferable to directing it, since party reform was not an urgent priority.

The idea of giving the party coherence nevertheless remained appealing to the New Deal, and part of FDR's ambiguous legacy on parties is his attempt to create a national liberal party while simultaneously undermining its importance by transferring power to executive institutions. "Once the administrative state he envisaged was in place," Mark Landy argues, "such grand partisanship would no longer be either necessary or even possible... Administration would replace partisanship as the defining force in public affairs."[65] Nevertheless, there was still a role for parties, especially ideological parties, to play in a new institutional order dominated by the executive.

Although fiercely loyal to the Democratic Party, FDR wanted to see the country move away from a party identification that reflected ancestral loyalties and accidents of birth. A party should be more than a sports team. He desired ideological parties and sought to be the architect of a new liberal party.[66] This was on his mind as early as the 1932 campaign, where he prophesized to Tugwell that "I'll be in the White House for eight years. When those years are over, there'll be a Progressive party. It may not be Democratic, but it will be progressive."[67] Having a 'liberal' and 'conservative' party, the New Deal believed, would enhance participation, citizenship, and accountability—that thick definition of citizenship advocated by the New Deal. Ideological parties ensure that something is at stake in every election and give voters the chance to send clearer signals to Washington about the desired direction of the national agenda. Roosevelt was frustrated by the fact that, as Frisch observes, "the liberal principles embodied by the New Deal were so little ingrained in the rank and file of the Democratic Party in 1937-1938 that it was difficult to tell what the party stood for, especially in view of the widespread cleavage between the New Deal and conservative democrats."[68] Ideological parties both address this confusion and serve to make the government more efficient, ideally minimizing the friction existing between the executive and legislative branches.

The base of that party would be found in its urban coalition as urban immigrants, blacks, and working-class whites were drawn into the Democratic fold, a movement begun by Al Smith and consolidated by Roosevelt. As Samuel Lubell argues, "Roosevelt did not start this revolt of the city. What he did do was to awaken the climbing urban masses to a consciousness of the power in their numbers,"[69] and the tangible presence of New Deal programs in their lives "gave a clearer content to partisan preferences than had previously been the case."[70] Roosevelt sought to use their strength to impose his own vision onto the Democratic Party, justified by the Jacksonian legitimacy conferred by his office. This link with the public was in the end more important than party, as it enabled him to govern on behalf of a liberal ideology as the head of the entire nation, rather than as the leader of a coalition of factions.

FDR was clear about this from the beginning, and in his 1932 speech accepting the Democratic nomination he warns

> nominal Democrats who squint at the future with their faces turned to the past, and who feel no responsibility to the demands of the new time, that they are out of step with their Party. Ours must be a party of liberal thought, of planned action, of enlightened international outlook, and the greatest good of the greatest number of our citizens.[71]

The presence of Republican (at the time) progressives like Henry Wallace and Harold Ickes in his cabinet emphasizes his desire to make the Democratic Party (or failing that, the Roosevelt administration) the primary voice of the mainstream American left. FDR would endorse prominent liberal Republicans like Senator George Norris over conservative Democrats, and in 1944 was discussing with Wendell Willkie (at this point a committed internationalist and arguably the nation's most prominent liberal Republican) the possibility of a mass migration of liberal Republicans into the Democratic Party alongside a new purge of its conservative wing.[72] The death of both Willkie and Roosevelt within a few months of each other obviously put an end to this possibility, but it demonstrates that Roosevelt continued to entertain this notion years after the purge attempt that Burns marked as "the bankruptcy of his party leadership."[73]

By almost any standard the 1938 purge has to be judged a failure, and Burns' assessment is common. He is particularly harsh in his appraisal of Roosevelt's performance, arguing that he never made a commitment to building up the party rank and file. Frisch agrees, arguing that organizational reform was secondary to ideological reform for Roosevelt.[74] Burns concedes that our political system contains numerous constitutional blocks designed to prevent the emergence of the majorities that Roosevelt sought, that the third term taboo lessened his influence, and that recovery made the New Deal less urgent and strengthened the opposition. Nevertheless, Burns' accusation that Roosevelt failed to build a coherent party at least partly misses the mark. Roosevelt's short-term failure was not found in neglecting party infrastructure, but by attempting to give the Democratic Party an ideological coherence that would have alienated huge swaths of the party (and in many cases the fact of intervention itself became a major campaign issue, demonstrating the intensity of parochial politics even in a time of national depression),[75] threatening the entirety of Roosevelt's recovery program. The sheer audacity of the President of the United States intervening in local politics was a bold, controversial, seemingly unprecedented stroke. The fact that the press labeled it a "purge" with all the fascist and Stalinist connotations the word evokes, is itself significant.[76]

While he desired an ideologically liberal party, Roosevelt was clear that he was prepared to ignore the party when he had to, especially if it threatened recovery and reform. Obviously a fully liberal Democratic Party eliminates constitutional roadblocks, but the attempt at creating one would have absorbed vast amounts of political capital with an uncertain prospect of success. It would have required simultaneous action at the federal, state, and local levels, and given the ways in which state constitutions and voting laws were often roadblocks to voter enfranchisement and liberal politics, this would have been an enormous undertaking in the midst of the twin goals of recovery and reform, with war on the horizon. Burns argues that a more developed and organized, long-term purge could have been successful, given the fact that its few successes came when Roosevelt was supporting established figures in well-organized campaigns.[77] But in his ultimate indictment of FDR he attributes the failure of the purge to "[Roosevelt's] unwillingness to commit himself to the full implications of party leadership" which "would have demanded a continuing intellectual and political commitment to a set strategy—and this kind of commitment Roosevelt would not make."[78] For Burns this is due to a failure of vision on Roosevelt's part, the fact that he was "less a great creative leader than a skilful manipulator and a brilliant interpreter."[79] What Burns misses is that Roosevelt in fact had a 'creative' vision for the role of president in American political life. It just did not center around the president's role as party leader.

The Centrality of the Executive

Much has been made of the alleged Jeffersonianism of the New Deal, which following in the tradition of Teddy Roosevelt's New Nationalism, sought to fuse Jeffersonian ends (democracy) with Hamiltonian means (state power). While it is certainly true that FDR was sympathetic to aspects of Jeffersonian thought, in particular his romantic agrarian streak, FDR's leadership owes much more to Jackson than it does Jefferson, especially given the centrality of the executive in the political life of the New Deal. It is with Jackson that we first start to see the president conceptualized as the tribune of the people, the most democratic, rather than the aristocratic, element of the federal government. Congress is demoted, embodying factionalism and localism, devoid of any unified vision or purpose. The presidency, on the other hand, personifies democratic legitimacy, as it is the only branch of government capable of articulating a common, rather than aggregate, good.

Beyond the moral legitimacy conferred upon the voice of all the people (as opposed to the narrower, factional representation embodied by Congress), there was a tactical consideration involved in the New Deal's Jacksonianism—namely that the nature of our Constitution virtually ensures that programmatic leadership and accountability has to come from the executive branch.[80] As Milkis argues, Roosevelt offers a strong executive as an alternative to the collective responsibility of the Congress.[81] Rather than concern himself with full-fledged party leadership, the New Deal sought to emancipate the presidency from the shackles of party government.[82] Roosevelt makes clear his intentions during his first inaugural address when he declared:

> I shall not evade the clear course of duty that will then confront me. I shall ask the Congress for the one remaining instrument to meet the crisis—broad Executive power to wage war against the emergency, as great as the power that would be given to me if we were in fact invaded by a foreign foe.[83]

It is the president's job to lead. The initiative and responsibility clearly lie here, and it is the job of Congress to facilitate the president's leadership, not to act as an equal partner.

As diminished as the role of Congress becomes, the role of the party is even more reduced. "I do believe in party organization." Roosevelt claims, "but only in proportion to its proper place in government....Parties are good instruments for the purpose of presenting and explaining issues, of drumming up interests and elections, and, incidentally, of improving the breed of candidates for public office."[84] And in that same speech Roosevelt talks about both the rising importance of independent voters not bound to traditional party loyalties, and the increased recognition that "the great public is interested more in government than in politics,"[85] politics, of course, being synonymous with parties.

The content of FDR's address declining the 1940 presidential nomination (written when Wallace's vice presidential confirmation looked doubtful) expressed similar sentiments.[86] We may never have a moment when the entire country shares an ideology, but the party differences should reflect principled disagreements about the proper role of the state in people's lives, rather than shifting, arbitrary loyalties that only serve to hinder voter accountability by making the parties interchangeable.

In the New Deal's formulation, the president becomes not only the voice of the people, but the central actor in the process of governance. The president is both the tribune of the people and their chief administrator. The later function is particularly vital as governance increasingly means discretionary mandates interpreted and implemented by appointed, rather than elected, officials.[87] This is why the idea of executive reorganization was as important to Roosevelt as the purging of the Democratic Party and the liberalization of the

Supreme Court. All three were roadblocks preventing the implementation of executive leadership.

The New Deal's abandonment of party government rejects the Democratic Party's Jeffersonianism and attempts to make the welfare state a constitutional issue, a permanent fixture of our social contract, rather than a set of programs whose basic stability is threatened with each election. Roosevelt made clear in the Commonwealth Club Address, and throughout his presidency, that modern social conditions require an enduring alteration in our constitutional order. Joseph Harris, the director of the research staff on the President's committee on administrative management, sums up what is at stake.

> We must consider a planning structure in light of expansions of functions occurring in collectivist periods like the present and in periods of reaction during contracting phases marked by the dominance of rugged individualistic views. We must assume, however, that these contradictions will always be less in fact than in profession. We may assume that the nature of the problems of American life are such as not to permit any political party for any length of time to abandon most of the collectivist functions which are now being exercised. This is true even though the details of policy programs may differ and even though the old slogans of opposition to governmental activity will survive long after their meaning has been sucked out.[88]

Ultimately the administrative welfare state becomes a permanent institutional arrangement, where the parties (ideally liberal and conservative) can debate its size and scope, but not its existence. The recommendations of the Brownlow report call for centralizing the actual process of governance, the effective delivery of social services, in the executive branch. The role of Congress is limited to establishing broad mandates, and exercising accountability via impeachment, appropriations, and oversight.[89] Small surprise then, that Congress ultimately balked at the committee's recommendations.

Milkis is correct. There was a "third" New Deal, although that third New Deal did not represent a departure as much as it did a recognition that institutional reform would be required to make the New Deal's Social Contract a permanent fixture of American life. And Burns is wrong when he argues that there is no larger vision animating the enterprise. The New Deal sought to transform the executive into the centerpiece of an administrative state, whose priority was ensuring the delivery of necessary services to the American people. The role of Congress and the parties were necessarily diminished in this new arrangement, the parties serving as a tool of the executive, and Congress engaging primarily in oversight. Citizens would have to look to external organizations if they wished to participate in democratic politics beyond the broad accountability and agenda setting that occurs with elections.

Organization

The President wants you to join the union.
—Union rallying cry[90]

FDR began his political career running on an anti-Tammany, clean government platform. His opposition was largely based on aesthetics, resentful of political machines, ignorant of their importance as governing institutions providing necessary services neglected by formal government. A description of FDR and his political priorities circa 1911 "the silly conceits of a political prig [devoid] of human sympathy, human interests, human ties" encapsulates this quite nicely.[91] It was under Secretary of the Navy Josephus Daniels that FDR learned of the Democratic Party, its diversity, the importance of small favors, and the need to accommodate regional political balances of power. By 1924 he is honoring Charles Murphy, the recently deceased leader of Tammany Hall, and the 'political prig' learned that one must work with whatever organizations present themselves in the process of institutionalizing a vision, even if they are a little dirty.[92]

The New Deal was always shot through with the primacy of politics. On the surface this gives the New Deal a Niebuhrian coloring—a sense that humanity has fallen and its organizations will always reflect our lack of grace—but the rhetoric of the New Deal is one of uplift, of the belief that, through democratic action, we can save ourselves. Thus we have the complicated relationship between New Deal democracy and political organization. The New Deal has a clear theory of political ends, and among those ends is an adherence to democratic practice and procedure—that giving people a direct voice in the laws that govern them is a positive good in itself, even if they do potentially destructive things with it. Autonomy is arguably the principle virtue of democracy. However, the reality of political life is that the voice that shouts the loudest is the most likely to be heard, no matter how numerous the silent majority, no matter how just their cause. Intensity is the practical arbiter of democracy, and unfortunately for the New Deal the loudest voices in American life were frequently the reactionary ones.[93] Therefore, the New Deal always recognized the central importance of organization, and the steps that had to be taken to organize the groups that needed to be heard. The New Deal's leftward shift after the failure of the NRA is a response to the increasingly vocal presence of that constituency, but ending the discussion here misses an important point. These groups were pushing the New Deal where it wanted to go, giving it the political cover it needed to make those moves, and in some cases the groups talking found their voices, or had them amplified, through the New Deal.[94]

This is why organization was such a fundamental part of the New Deal's theory of practice. In a healthy democracy those in power have no choice but to listen to the demands of the people, so the more organized a particular people are, the more likely their voices are to be heard above the din of competing interests. Organizational pressure cleared the space necessary for the government to act, and both Roosevelts were talented organizers. ER especially worked hard on behalf of unions, civic organizations, and any group capable of aggregating those in need of help. Pluralism and factions are a political reality, so it was necessary to make sure that the most vulnerable are sufficiently organized. The New Deal understood that justice is unlikely to inform public policy unless the votes line up that way. And so government and politicized groups enjoy a symbiotic relationship. Social movements and their attendant organizations provide political cover for the administration, and it becomes the job of the government to empower those movements. The relationship is symbiotic; each generates the conditions under which the other can act, and neither can effectively act without the other. Harry Hopkins and Aubrey Williams, facing a constant Congressional and public backlash against their relief programs encouraged the organized coalitions of the unemployed "always to ask for more"[95] to provide the kind of countervailing pressure that could preserve and expand New Deal programs.

Like education, organization was a constant process. Eleanor Roosevelt understood that in a democracy the campaign is permanent, and under her leadership in the 1920s the Women's Division of the New York Democratic Party was transformed into arguably the most effective political organization in the United States. But any group so organized must always keep their particular interests in line with the interests of the nation as a whole. The New Deal advocated more than basic pluralism. ER's advice to the American Youth Congress sums up nicely both the importance of organization and the ways in which it fits into the New Deal's democratic theory.

> Organize first for knowledge, first with the object of making us know ourselves as a nation, for we have to do that before we can be of value to other nations of the world and then organize to accomplish the things that you decide to want. And remember, don't make decisions with the interest of youth alone before you. Make your decisions because they are good for the nation as a whole. [96]

In a democracy, you cannot acquire political power without first making yourself heard, which requires power and a message. Most will find that power within organizations. However, there is a moral obligation not to abuse the power that follows mass, and to always keep the common good (ideally as defined by the New Deal and ratified by the electorate) of the nation at heart.[97] As always, the New Deal sought to achieve a balance the reality of interest, the necessity of countervailing power, and the hope of republican dispassion and eventual unity.

Organization becomes even more important as the power of the state expands and centralizes, as exclusion becomes more probable and the costs of nonparticipation that much higher. Beyond the obvious representation of their welfare, without organizational participation it will become more and more difficult for individuals to play some kind of role in their government.[98] An increasingly powerful state requires an increasingly well-organized electorate to ensure accountability and avoid the type of administrative despotism Tocqueville warned about—both within the state and within its political organizations. Active citizen participation (usually filtered through organizations) also serves to soften the elitism that inevitably flows out of an administrative state. Even if there is little room for the citizen to manage policy, they can at least determine the principles and goals that drive the policy itself, and make their leaders accountable to that vision.

Pluralism is not inherently democratic in a substantive sense, and when necessary, it becomes the obligation of the state to make it so, to organize the unorganized, or facilitate their self-organization. One thinks of the relationship between organized labor and the New Deal. Clearly the surge of unionization helped provide the political capital necessary to advance the "second" New Deal, as well as ensure Roosevelt's continued reelections. But the New Deal also played a major role in the resurgence of union organizing. As Badger argues, labor activism was a necessary but not sufficient condition for labor advances. A sympathetic administration that protected the membership during economic downturns and ensured a more protective environment for organization was also essential.[99]

The onset of the Great Depression obliterated a union movement already in steep decline from its previous highs, and restricted to a few major industries. By early 1933 fewer than three million workers were unionized, and those workers who remained had become understandably reluctant to strike given the glut of available labor, even in the face of very real grievances. It was section 7a of the NRA which seemed to elevate labor to a status equal to that of capital, promised government protection against business reprisals, and made the very process of unionization, for perhaps the first time, an act of patriotism rather than subversion.[100] When the country began its rightward turn in the late 1930s, with the House Un-American Committee's search for labor radicals in the Roosevelt administration supplanting the LaFollette Committee's reports on industrial violence in the headlines, labor leaders now saw 'a close alliance with the Roosevelt wing of the Democratic party...essential to shield the union movement from the new power of big business and the aggressive anti-union politics of the congressional and entrepreneurial right wing."[101] The New Deal seemed to be the catalyst for the revival and protection of an aggressive labor movement which would in turn push national policy to the left.

Of course, this emphasis on organizations did not mean that the New Deal saw itself as the administrative arm of labor. The New Deal approached the labor movement as a set of organizations that could advance the aims of workers, but the aims of workers did not trump the larger goal of maintaining a peaceful, stable community of varied interests.[102] That the New Deal ultimately ended up privileging arbitration as the preferable way to adjudicate labor grievances, bureaucratizing industrial conflict in a way that some have argued (unintentionally) privileges management, speaks to that.[103]

Organization did not start and stop with the union movement, and the efforts made by New Dealers to encourage rising black political activism are often overlooked. This was both a moral obligation and, as Sullivan notes, part of a deliberate strategy of using blacks to act "as catalyst in a long term effort to institutionalize the democratic aspirations of Roosevelt's recovery program by appealing to expectations of groups long on the margins of southern politics."[104] Likewise, the creation of the Southern Tenant Farmers Union prompted the New Deal to explore the economic and political handicaps facing black farmers, and Philip Randolph got the defense industries desegregated when the strength of his organization was capable of overcoming existing institutional roadblocks.[105]

There is a dark side to this process, one that reflects the realities, rather than the aspirations, of democracy. The code-making process of the NRA was perfectly democratic, which is to say that it reflected the massed strengths of the interests involved, and those with the best organization were the most successful. While organized business was held in low esteem at the time of the first inaugural, this did not reflect their actual power, economically or politically. As Bernstein notes in *A Caring Society*, it is not surprising that the New Deal's minimum wage law had the gaps in coverage that it did, especially in the South, as "the prospective beneficiaries of such a law, the most exploited persons in the employed labor force, were unorganized and many, probably most, did not even vote.[106] Since they did not speak, no one heard them."[107] In the end the Roosevelt administration did pay the most attention to the groups who talked the loudest. That is the reality of political life, and of formal democracy. However, this reality should not undermine the New Deal's call for a more democratic and just conversation. Everyone needs to be given a voice, and even more radically, it is the obligation of the state to help citizens acquire that voice.

Change in a Liberal Democracy

> To remove the rag bag of phobias, prejudices, principles, and ideas that condition the reactions of the human computer to new data is a long and painful process...But gradually the change comes about, principally through the substitution of new words, words that have a different emotional content from those previously used.
>
> —Thurman Arnold[108]

Both supporters and critics of the New Deal on the left found themselves frequently frustrated by the pace of reform. Regardless of how radical many changes were, there was always so much more that could have been done.[109] We have examined thus far some of the external forces that checked the depth and breadth of reform. But as Arnold argued in the last chapter, institutional checks can be exacerbated by the internal ideology of the regime, and a liberal regime will by its nature be inclined to move slowly. If Arnold is right, and our folklore determines the boundaries of possible action; if Louis Hartz is right, and we are a liberal nation to the core, then this pace is inevitable. Different regimes require different political practices, and generate different political possibilities. A liberal representative democracy is no different. If anything, it is an especially limiting form of government, as a democratic prince has less recourse to the lion and must make do with the fox. What's more, a liberal democratic government headed by a philosophically liberal prince creates even more constraints. Liberalism, at least the Lockean strain that influenced the United States, is grounded in a skeptical modesty about ends, which in turn leads to a tolerance of other views, and grants them access to the machinery of government. We've seen this play itself out not only in the New Deal's positive insistence on an inclusive common good, but also in its emphasis on organization and the importance of giving all interested parties a voice in their government—and that the government's legitimacy is dependent on the presence of that voice. Violence is not (theoretically) a legitimate form of political authority to be used against the citizens of the state. Power is contested in freely (perhaps not fairly) fought elections where both sides engage in persuasion (the demagogue is effective, but illegitimate), and the winner must respect the rights and interests of the loser. Leaders are bound by the rule of law, which trumps the rule of man and the passions of the moment. Liberals can fight to win but they cannot fight to destroy.

The emphatic protestations of the Liberty League to the contrary, FDR was an authentic liberal democrat. While New Dealers like Eleanor Roosevelt were more staunchly committed to the idea of politics as education, FDR was enough of a believer to ensure that his salesmanship usually lacked some of the more demagogic, nakedly manipulative appeals to passion, and certainly his policy proved more temperate then his strategically inflammatory electoral rhetoric. Roosevelt could claim, as he did on the eve of the 1936 election, "I should like to have it said of my first Administration that in it the forces of selfishness and of lust for power met their match. I should like to have it said of my second Administration that in it these forces met their master."[110] Nevertheless, these voices were never shut out of the legislative process, as much a matter of liberal commitment as necessity. While Roosevelt greatly expanded the power of his office and at times had a hostile relationship with both the courts and the conservative Democratic/Republican congressional opposition, he accepted the legitimacy of checks on his power as well as the right of the opposition to exist. Not only that, he was also willing to concede that they in turn represented interests entitled to a voice in government (the source of many accusations of New Deal schizophrenia).

This adds up to a tolerance for divided government and willingness to rule in the name of all, which runs counter to the Machiavelli of *The Prince*. Mill's great fear was that democracy confers a breezy sort of legitimacy onto the actions of the state and threatens minorities. But as the Roosevelt administration folded ever more power into the executive, the New Deal began to fear that minorities could use this new power to impose its will upon majorities, especially when those majorities stand in the way of policy. The coercive power of government *must* be limited. We cannot force anyone to be free. "Unless you are Mr. Hitler you must not lead where your responsible following is not ready to uphold you."[111] Respect for the autonomy of others means you must also respect their right to dissent, their freedom to be stubborn, and their right to be wrong.[112] The process of educating the electorate, exposing them to new ideas and new

experiments in living is a gradual one, and the liberal democrat must resign himself to the frequently glacial pace of reform.

If one is to remain a liberal it requires moving liberalism to the top of the
hierarchy of ends, with a respect for due process and the recognition of legitimate dissent topping even the humanitarian goals of the New Deal. Justice is
served when all people have a substantively fair chance at playing the game, not
in forcing a particular outcome. For Machiavelli there is no such thing as legitimate power (or rather all power is functionally legitimate), whereas for the New
Deal there is. [113] Questions of justice, law, tolerance, and obligation have intrinsic, not just instrumental value. Machiavelli argues that leaders must stand outside both history and morality and cannot be judged by either. The liberal democrat must reject that stance on moral grounds.

The recognition of legitimate independent interests and respect for the democratic process also means that the American prince will be dependent on others,
limiting his freedom to act. Roosevelt was willing to concede that the Democratic Party had interests and goals independent of his ideological policy preferences. Likewise, the nature of a democracy itself means that the prince will be
as dependent on the interests of the coalition voting for him as much as that coalition is dependent on the prince. He will never be able to wean himself from his
dependence on the arms of others, even if steps can be taken to minimize their
importance (party reformation, executive reorganization). In a democracy the
prince will always rule at the sufferance of others, which in turn brings us back
to a basic Machiavellian principle. The election must come first. Without office
there is no institutional vehicle through which the democratic leader can achieve
his political goals. The only choice available is picking which mercenaries to
use, be they the Hearst newspaper chain during the 1932 campaign or the southern Democrats prepared to obstruct any and all attempts to challenge the racial
and economic status quo of the South. While a progressive coalition strong
enough to be the entirety of New Deal support was the ideal, it was neither numerous nor influential enough in practice to be the sole basis of its support. And
even if it was, victory does not grant the moral authority to silence other voices.
The New Deal is ultimately a liberal movement more than a democratic one,
tempering its tyrannical possibilities with a healthy dose of modest liberal skepticism.

These liberal commitments place reformers in a difficult position. Ideological purity demands commitment to principle. Democratic power requires compromise. To not give ground on the issue of lynching means surrendering both
the expansion of the New Deal in other areas (and blacks did benefit from its
protections and programs, as their political leaders recognized)[114] and the possibility of arming the nation to meet fascist aggression, as some of the same
southern Democrats were strong supporters of FDR's foreign policy.[115] Individual political decisions can be called into question empirically. Maybe FDR could
have endorsed the lynching bill without tearing apart what was left of his coalition. The historical record gives us the data necessary to make an educated
guess, but for Machiavelli, for Arnold, and for Roosevelt the larger necessity of

compromise is never called into question. The political leader, responsible for the welfare of the electorate, does not have the same luxury of the principled stand that the extra-institutional actor enjoys.

Conclusion

There is nothing more difficult to handle, more doubtful of success, and more dangerous to carry through than initiating changes in a state's constitution.
—Niccolo Machiavelli [116]

Arnold concludes *The Folklore of Capitalism* with what he calls his theory of political dynamics, a first attempt at systematizing the theory of institutional change implicitly accepted by the New Deal. While his version contains twenty-three separate points we can simplify the argument down to six.

1. Organizations, in order to meet specific goals, require morale—a belief in the rightness of their project and the appropriateness of their methods. In the process of acquiring this morale institutions develop folklore, a set of symbols, ceremonies, and creeds.
2. This folklore determines the limits of what sorts of actions are legitimate, or even possible. Most forms of folklore lead over time to a reification of principles that limit the adaptability of the organization to new challenges and conditions.
3. Because practical needs have to be met, sub rosa institutions develop to address new challenges, with ceremonial action taken to mask the disconnect between principle and practice.
4. In times of crisis, sub rosa institutions get overwhelmed and old institutions break down. It is in this moment that fundamental political change is possible, through the development of new institutions. "The failure of older social organizations to act leaves a vacuum into which some new organization is bound to follow."[117]
5. As these institutions are new, and are frequently in conflict with older folklore (which Arnold argues maintains its psychic value long after it ceases to provide an accurate reflection of reality), they are often seen as illegitimate.
6. The crafting of new folklore takes time. During the transition period, before new folklore has acquired legitimacy, it is important to reinterpret older forms of folklore to lessen the existential shock that comes with change. As Arnold argues,

> When you are marching under a banner of reform or revolution you can accomplish great things, but you cannot keep marching forever. Sooner or later you have to stop, and only when you can stop and know peace have you been successful. This is best accomplished by making sure that "the

ancient habits of thought are preserved while molding them to new needs."[118]

The primary moment of agency comes at point four, the moment of institutional collapse. However, the largely inescapable symbolic limitations of the human mind mean that it is difficult to fully break with the past, even in the face of clear failure. The effective political actor is the one who best knows how to navigate this moment, to recognize the psychic and institutional forces that prevent change (the anthropologist) and neutralize them through a simultaneous process of co-opting old symbols while creating new ones.

An illiberal ideology will likely find the possibilities of action less constrained, given that liberalism is self-conscious of its limits. The liberal progressive is always trapped in a null space between reform and revolution. The old forms have a degree of legitimacy beyond their instrumental value that precludes them from ever fully being challenged (the New Deal was attempting to preserve, not undermine constitutional governance, and FDR always saw his mission as saving capitalism). Yet the New Deal could also be considered a real American revolution that drastically redefined our understandings of the relationship between government and citizen no less than the first founding or Civil War. The principality is both new and old, a founding and a renewal of a previously established regime.

The failure of the New Deal reflects in part its failure to establish a new form of folklore capable of completely vanquishing the old. This is not surprising. Given the liberal restraints New Dealers operated under, they were in fact creating a counter-tradition to be appropriated when needed, a set of competing symbols rather than an entirely new creed. The old order can be discredited for a time, but never fully purged. Doing so would have required a genuine refounding, an exercise of princely power not achievable through liberal means.[119]

And so the reformer must be prepared to accept two things. The first is the slow, measured pace of change. FDR reminds us that "governments such as ours cannot swing so far so quickly...They can only move in keeping with the thought and will of the great majority of our people. Were it otherwise the very fabric of our democracy—which after all is government by public opinion—would be in danger of disintegration."[120] The New Deal was committed to the process of liberal democracy. One can plead with, cajole, manipulate, and hopefully educate the people. But in the end the President can only point the way to go. The people must choose to follow, and they are a long time in choosing. If they reject your direction, you are obligated to accept their judgment. This principled respect for autonomy buttresses the willingness of people like FDR and ER to accept compromise and take the ideas of the opposition seriously. The government must serve all the people, and those who oppose you still have a claim on your leadership. In order to be a liberal and a democrat, one must maintain their ethical and political commitments without letting those commitments become imperial. This is a difficult tightrope to walk. On the one hand the president is the instrument chosen by the people to do their bidding and on the other hand he has an obligation to enlighten and lead.

In criticizing FDR's second term performance, Burns argues, "During his second term Roosevelt seemed to forget the great lesson of his inaugural speech of 1933—that courageous affirmation in itself changes the political dimensions of a situation."[121] Burns offers us an important check on the seductive complacency of any political theory that gives pride of place to compromise—that surrender is not only easier than fighting, but easy to justify. But we must still remember at all times there are limits to what can be done, even as we work to redefine what those limits are. Even when a movement has its moment, it will be difficult to sustain. As FDR reflected on the failures of Woodrow Wilson, he observed that "[p]ublic psychology and, for that matter, individual psychology, cannot, because of human weakness, be attuned to a constant repetition of the highest note on the scale."[122] Learning to manipulate that scale, to control when and how each note is sounded, becomes essential to any kind of political agency. And it is here that Arnold offers his most important advice to progressive reformers, advice that FDR, ER, and Wallace embodied in their public writings and public actions. The progressive reformer in a liberal democracy must never forget that his ability to affect the changes he wants depends on his ability to make the electorate desire those changes. Theory plays an important role here—it acts as institutional poetry, reminding us why change is desirable and perhaps inevitable. It gives an otherworldly beauty to an otherwise empirical politics. "Accurate detailed photographs never bring out that blurred beauty which thrills us at twilight. To the artist, the human body is a far more poetic and beautiful symbol than it is to the physician, who is interested in it chiefly because of its disease."[123] But Arnold also reminds us of the need to avoid mistaking poetry for truth. Successful politicians must be prepared to use theory instrumentally, as a form of manipulation as much as education, in order to secure the power necessary to institutionalize change.

The act is certainly distasteful, and perhaps offensive, but this is why politics is the realm of fallen angels. The actor must be willing to make the emotional (demagogic) pleas necessary to accomplish their goals. Princes are willing to sacrifice principle to engage in the horse-trading that forms the core of political action. "...They [politicians] lack social values, their aims are imperfect, but society clings to them rather than to the occasional reformer who does not understand its emotional needs, and tries to fit it into some procrustean bed made in the world of his own dreams."[124] Without recourse to the destructive power of the lion, the role of the fox becomes more important than ever. If Machiavelli and Arnold are right, political change in the short term results from habituation and manipulation, not education. Power is acquired through the emotive appeals of the demagogue and the effective use of folklore tied to viable political organizations. If anything, Arnold underestimates the power of these appeals, missing (as conservatives later demonstrated with the successes of the Reagan and Bush II presidencies) that with sufficient framing and first-rate storytelling one can delegitimate a functioning institutional order.

'Respectable people' Arnold argues, expect their principles to conform to practice, and get discouraged when they do not. Politicians know better, get things done, and are condemned for it. The fact that they choose to use principles as weapons is particularly infuriating for those who put principles before practice. But the practical politician knows that moral language, once reified, makes compromise and experimentation difficult. Honest people who privilege the world of principle over the world of politics are unable to compromise those principles, and are therefore uncomfortable making truly political decisions.

> Our students of governmental problems consider politics a low and unworthy pursuit. They think that sincerity and candor can be used in a political campaign. They feel a sort of spiritual trouble when confronted with the realities of a political institution, which makes them confused and ineffective. Unscrupulous persons who do not feel the same spiritual trouble when confronted with things as they are naturally become more proficient. The so-called demagogue has an advantage because he does not view the control of human institutions under the illusion that men in groups are composed of so-called thinking men, to whose knowledge of fundamental governmental principles he must appeal.[125]

Not only does the progressive need to engage in the "demagogic" practice of appealing to people's emotions and utilizing popular symbols to accomplish practical political ends, he needs to be willing to accept that it is more important to make dirty changes in the real world than keep clean hands in the ideal one.

> Therefore the first lesson to be learned by the objective student of governmental theory is that, when he desires to step into the moving stream of events as an actor, he must accept the legal and economic theories of his time just as he accepts the language of his time. He will find, in the vocabulary of current theory, principles though which he may support any cause....His choice of theories cannot be made on any other ground than that of expediency in gaining the ends he desires. Legal and economic theory, whether radical or conservative, can never make him a prophet. They may, however, make him a successful advocate.[126]

While this manipulative frame may be necessary for advocacy, at the same time we should recall the simple truth that in order to advocate one needs a set of goals to advocate for. And here we must not lose sight of the fact that the New Deal advocates this particular theory of means in the pursuit of a particular theory of ends, namely the creation of a society in which, in the poetry of Eleanor Roosevelt, "we maintain a standard of living which makes it possible for people really to want justice for all, rather than to harbor a secret hope for privileges because they cannot hope for justice."[127]

There is much the New Deal took from Machiavelli, and its method can in the end be called Machiavellian. Of primary importance is an awareness of the intersection between power and theory, and the way that democratic power limits theoretical possibilities. The democratic prince is forced to lead and follow at the same time. What can be accomplished is bounded by the realities of institutional arrangements and the imagination of the electorate (the ultimate source of democratic authority and power). In order to act effectively in the interests of reform, the prince requires an understanding of the forces that check him. Some are beyond mastery, but Machiavelli and the New Deal both argue that if one understands and utilizes the folklore of their audience that audience can usually be convinced to follow at least part of the way. This requires not just appeals to logic and rationality, but to emotion and passion that are both familiar and existentially satisfying. The basis of democratic political power is found in education *and* manipulation, and it is the instrumental, rather than ontological, value of theory that should serve as the basis for its adoption. In politics truth is what works, and what works is what the electorate will accept. The New Deal will not go as far as Machiavelli—it never questions the legitimacy of the ends of the welfare state, and limits its means by those ends. The New Deal embraces the possibilities of meaningful citizenship, and retains the liberal commitment to constraining arbitrary power. However, if the progressive desires a society defined by Arnold's humanitarian ideal, namely that "it is a good thing to make people comfortable if the means exist by which it can be done,"[128] he must learn to emancipate himself from the creedal aspects of those ends, to grant himself the flexibility to confront necessity and fortune with the greatest possible internal freedom of action. The inability to do so marks a failure to take seriously the real responsibilities of political leadership.

Notes

1. Milkis, " Economic," 41.
2. Parts of the argument in this chapter were previously published in Brian Stipelman, "The New Deal's Theory of Practice," *New Political Science* 32, no. 2 (June 2010): 237-260.
3. Unlike its positive political theory, a great deal of excellent work exists on the New Deal's relationship to the institutional structure of the United States. As a result, this chapter will focus more on the theoretical implications of the New Deal's response—the way these structures affected its theory of practice, more than the nature of the structures themselves.
4. Burns, "FDR: Unsuccessful Improviser," in Hamby, 137.
5. Anthony Badger's *The New Deal* is a particularly good single-volume study of how the external constraints facing policy makers impacted the depth and breadth of the New Deal.
6. James T. Patterson, "The Conservative Coalition," in Hamby, 165.
7. For example, the conservative coalition in Congress was successful in beating back attempts to expand social security (the 1943 Wagner-Murray-Dingell Bill), restricted union activity with the 1943 Smith-Connally Act, rejected FDR's proposed caps on salaries (wage caps were acceptable), overrode FDR's attempt to veto a regressive tax bill in 1944. Jeffries, 157.

8. Carol Horton, *Race and the Making of American Liberalism*, (Oxford: Oxford University Press, 2005), 114.

9. Quoted in McMahon, *Race*, 117. This was not just pandering. McMahon notes that lynching was receiving new support from southerners who supported it as a means to keep the Negro in his place. McMahon, *Race*, 164.

10. McMahon, *Race*, 117.

11. Of course one could blame the New Deal for not fighting harder for the bill, for not making the undeniably courageous decision of an LBJ to sign civil rights legislation even if it costs the Democrats the South for a generation (or more). But with World War II on the horizon, and Southern congressmen amongst FDR's strongest foreign policy supporters, the benefits of the legislation have to be weighed against the possible costs.

12. Shogan, *Backlash*, 117.

13. "While the Big Four [Senate Majority Leader Robison, Senator Byrnes, Senator Pat Harrison, and Vice President Garner] had been loyal to Roosevelt during his first four years, with their terms presumably extending beyond his, they now figured to be much less reliable in their support for his plans." McMahon, *Race*, 80.

14. Bernstein, *Caring*, 139.

15. Eliot Rosen, *Roosevelt, The Great Depression, and the Economics of Recovery*, (Charlottesville: University of Virginia Press, 2005), 198.

16. Abbot, *Exemplary*, 133.

17. Karl, *Uneasy*, 122.

18. Burns, *Lion*, 344. These accusations were taken seriously enough to prompt FDR to make an announcement helpfully confirming the following:

> A: I have no inclination to be a dictator.
> B: I have none of the qualifications which would make me a success-
> ful dictator.
> C: I have too much historical background and too much knowledge
> of existing dictatorships to make me desire any form of dictatorship for a
> democracy like the United States of America.

Quoted in Burns, *Lion*, 345-346.

19. Adam Cohen's description of the congressional debate over the Emergency Banking Act (the first major piece of legislation considered in the famed One Hundred Days session of Congress) captures the deferential mood inspired by the crisis of the Great Depression, and is worth quoting at length.

> Most members of Congress knew that they were being called in to vote on a banking act, but little more. Steagall, the chairman of the House Banking an Currency Committee, who had the only draft of the bill, one with pencil corrections scrawled on it, walked down the aisle of the House chamber, waving it overhead and shouting, "Here's the Bill; lets pass it. "The debate was over in forty minutes. Bertrand H. Snell, the House Republican leader, urged a 'Yes' vote even though he had not been able to read the bill. Snell conceded that it was "entirely out of the ordinary " to vote on a bill that had not even been printed yet, but he said that "there is only one answer to this question, and that is to give the President what he demands and says is necessary to meet the situation." The bill passed without a recorded vote.

Cohen, *Nothing to Fear*, 79.

20. The two-thirds rule insisted that any Democratic nominee for president have the support of two-thirds of the delegates. In practice representing a Southern veto on presidential nominees, FDR's successful campaign to change that rule was an enormously important institutional victory.

21. Lash, *Dealers*, 310.

22. Shogan, *Backlash*, 122.

23. Shogan cites that the mail coming into the White House was 9-1 against the plan, while Patricia Sullivan points out that a Gallup poll showed that the South especially was in favor of FDR's plan, and that Lyndon Johnson made his support of it as an issue in his 1937 congressional campaign. Shogan, *Backlash*, 123, and Sullivan, *Hope*, 61. That support did not extend to most of the entrenched Southern leadership, another example of their comparative safety and the extent of Southern disenfranchisement.

24. Shogan, *Backlash*, 14.

25. Regarding the framing, FDR's initial claim was that it was designed to help justices deal with overwork and advanced age, a claim the Chief Justice famously and publicly demolished. Jean Smith argues, for instance, that FDR should have framed his attack on the court as their own failure to follow judicial precedent. Smith, 379. Frank Freidel argues that he would have been better off approaching it openly as an obstruction issue, believing that the subterfuge conjured up unfavorable comparisons to fascist Europe and communist Russia. Frank Freidel, "The New Deal in Historical Perspective," Hamby, 24.

26. Miroff, *Icons*, 237.

27. Shogan, *Backlash*, 85.

28. Something it seems far less interested in doing in an era of ideological parties.

29. Cited in Lash, *Dealers,* 98.

30. Afterwards he became John L. Lewis' choice to lead a third party to oppose Roosevelt, before sadly deciding to endorse Willkie.

31. Shogan, *Backlash*, 239.

32. "It ill behooves one who has supped at labor's table and who has been sheltered in labor's house to curse with equal fervor and fine impartiality both labor and its adversaries when they become locked in deadly embrace. " John L. Lewis, "Labor and the Nation," 3 Sept. 1937. Lewis ultimately backed Wendell Willkie in the 1940 election, and when labor did not follow his lead he resigned as head of the CIO.

33. Shogan, *Backlash*, 138.

34. Shogan, *Backlash,* 138.

35. And one that begs the question, what sorts of reactionary responses might a mainstream movement to the left of the New Deal have called into existence. While the New Deal arguably co-opted the possibility of more radical reform, it similarly co-opted what would likely have been an even more potent right-wing reaction.

36. Shogan, *Backlash,* 177.

37. Shogan, *Backlash,* 210.

38. Shogan, *Backlash,* 223.

39. Badger, *New Deal*, 306. See also Rosen, *Roosevelt*, 157.

40. Bernstein, *Caring*, 30.

41. Walter Davenport, "Money in the Mailbox," *Colliers* (10 Feb. 1934), in Freidel, 56.

42. Sullivan, *Hope*, 57.

43. Quoted in Culver, *Dreamer*, 156.

44. Quoted in Patterson, *Coalition*, 209.

45. Patterson, *Coalition*, 214.

46. Patterson, *Coalition*, 217.

47. And, as Karl argues, the necessity of power being located in Washington does not mean that there would be public acceptance or legitimacy conferred upon that power.

> To argue that new machinery for managing the country would have been accepted requires one to argue that the Depression itself had created an acceptance of a national industrial state that had not existed before and convictions strong enough to obliterate memories of wartime controls and strong enough also to produce a major intellectual reversal or regionalism and localism, both of which had experienced a vigorous rebirth in the 1920s.

Karl, *Uneasy*, 119-120.

48. Milkis, "Economic," 45.

49. As Karl argues, Congress was poorly set up for national leadership, and it became the responsibility of the president to construct from the individual members of Congress a working majority capable of supporting his particular vision. Karl, *Uneasy*, 160. And as Morton Frisch argues, party leaders like Jim Farley "failed to recognize that parties require principles or doctrines as well as organizations, that is, that interests cannot be held together if they are not held together by a principle." Frisch, *Franklin Roosevelt*, 79.

50. Milkis, "Economic," 32.

51. The distinction being that the bureaucracy took its cues from mandates furnished by the people. Although, as Milkis notes, the end result was "a more active and better equipped state, but one without adequate means of public debate and judgment. " Milkis, "Economic," 33.

52. Milkis, "Economic," 42

53 . The Brownlow Committee, formed in 1937 and consisting of Louis Brownlow, Charles Merriam, and Luther Guilick, was tasked with proposing a reorganization of the executive branch in light of its new (and permanent) administrative responsibilities. The Executive Office of the President is the major legacy of that committee's report.

54. "We might have said it floats freely among such competing institutions as the Senate, the House, the courts, the presidency, the bureaucracy, the states, our allies, our enemies, and a host of private organizations blessed with either fat coffers or righteous fervor or both." John Rohr, "Constitutional Legitimacy and the Administrative State: A reading of the Brownlow Commission Report," in Eden, 95.

55. Milkis, "Economic," 46.

56. Although, as Milkis points out, it is likely that this bill would not have passed had FDR not declared he would run for a third term, which he in turn would not run for if not for the presence of Fascism and Japanese imperialism.

57. Plotke, *Building*, 129.

58. Karl argues that it was the public's attachment to the person and personality of Roosevelt that sustained the New Deal, rather than the Democratic Party (or even an initial acceptance of the various programs themselves). Karl, *Uneasy*, 110.

59. Plotke, *Building*, 135.

60. Romasco, *Recovery*, 34.

61. Plotke, *Building*, 138.

62. Sidney Milkis, "New Deal Party Politics, Administrative Reform, and the Transformation of the American Constitution," in Eden, 126. Milkis argues that whereas Wilson reconciled himself to the splits in his party, Roosevelt tried to either govern through progressives or bypass the party in its entirety.

63. Mileur, "The Boss," 103.

64. Hamby, "Historians," 6.

65. Marc Landy, "Presidential Party Leadership and Party Realignment: FDR and the Making of the New Democratic Party," in Milkis and Mileur, *New Deal*, 74.

66. Miroff, *Icons*, 250. Miroff argues that Roosevelt was too timid to make the commitment to full-fledged party reform, although he admits that the local roots of the parties were extremely strong, and he does not really address the question of priorities— did Roosevelt have the political capital and capabilities to simultaneously address the Depression and reform his party.

67. Quoted in Brands, *Traitor*, 272. Brands goes on to argue that FDR centered his campaigns around himself so that he could eclipse the Democratic party and make it easier to set a progressive agenda.

68. Frisch, *Franklin Roosevelt*, 18-19.

69. Lubell, "Coalition," 145.

70. Miroff, *Icons*, 250.

71. Smith, *FDR*, 276.

72. Rosenman, *Working*, 463. Of course this obscures the very real policy differences between figures like Willkie and Roosevelt. *Liberalism* and *conservatism* are broad covering terms, capable of endless variation.

73. Burns, "Improvisor," 133.

74. Frisch, *Franklin Roosevelt*, 79. It should be noted, however that Frisch, unlike Burns, believes that Roosevelt's emphasis on ideology over organization was more important for the long-term health and survival of the Democratic Party.

75. Smith, *FDR*, 411-414.

76. Milkis, "Reform," 131.

77. Burn, "Improviser," 136.

78. Burn, "Improviser," 136.

79. Burn, "Improviser," 140.

80. Miroff, *Icons*, 251.

81. Milkis, "Reform," 134.

82. The source of some New Deal hostility from progressives like Borah and Wheeler. McMahon, *Race*, 77.

83. Quoted in Smith, *FDR*, 302.

84. FDR, Jackson day speech, 1940, quoted in Milkis "Reform," 140.

85. Jackson day speech, 1940, Milkis "Reform," 140.

86. The Democrats "must go wholly one way or the other. It cannot face both directions at the same time. By declining the honor of the nomination for the Presidency, I can restore the opportunity to the convention. I so do." FDR quoted in Culver, *Dreamer*, 222.

87. Milkis and Nelson, *Presidency*, 279.

88. Milkis, "Reform," 141.

89. Rohr, "Legitimacy," 97-101.

90. The standard organizing speech in the aftermath of section 7a of the NRA began "The President wants you to join the union." Abbot, *Exemplary*, 102.

91. Smith, *FDR*, 78.

92. Therefore, Roosevelt ultimately accepted the need for political machines, at least until the final institutionalization of a welfare state. Arnold captures why this is necessary.

> The political machine as an institution separate from recognized government thrived in the United States as in no other country in the world. It was called in whenever the Government, bound by its ideals to stay aloof from reality, was compelled to enter into the affairs of an everyday world. We were always just about to get rid of it, but we never did. The reason of course was that we refused to permit recognized government to become a practical force.

Arnold, *Symbols*, 239-240.
As long as the machine remains the only organization willing to address the practical needs of its constituents they will remain an important and necessary part of the political process.

93. For instance, Badger notes that "some of the most effective grass-roots political pressure during the Depression came from organizations of taxpayers anxious to cut government spending in order to relieve their own tax burdens...[putting] far greater pressure on politicians than did unemployed groups who demanded greater local spending for relief." Badger, *New Deal*, 56.

94. Badger argues that it was the rising expectations of relief workers that helped radicalize them to the point of engaging in strikes against wage reductions and lay-offs. "Disorder did not frighten the New Deal into a more generous welfare policy; disorder was an unavailing effort to keep New Deal relief at existing levels of generosity." Badger, *New Deal*, 56 202.

95. Badger, *New Deal*, 202-203.

96. Lash, *Dealers*, 554.

97. This was one of the reasons why the New Deal did not fear labor radicalism, as these were seen as growing pains in a new organization, and as it matured it would come to see its place in a larger web of interdependence.

98. Although hardly a New Dealer, de Jouvenel expresses this concern in *On Power*. 365-366.

99. As Badger argues, labor activism was a necessary but not sufficient condition for labor advances. A sympathetic administration that protected the membership during economic downturns and ensured a more protective environment for organization was also essential. Badger, *New Deal*, 134-143.

100. Roy Rosenzweig, ed. *Who Built America: Working People and the Nation's Economy, Politics, Culture, and Society Vol. II* (New York: Pantheon Books, 1992), 354-355.

101. Lichtenstein, *Labor*, 6, 19.

102. Nor is it clear that rank-and-file labor saw itself as anything beyond a mechanism to improve wages and working conditions for the particular people who happened to be in a union. Lichtenstein, *Labor*, 13.

103. Lichtenstein, *Labor*, 179-180.

104. Sullivan, *Hope*, 43.

105. Sullivan, *Hope*, 56, 136.

106. This could also reflect a lack institutional capacity. For instance, while Perkins argued to include Agricultural and domestic workers in Social Security the Treasury Department insisted collecting their taxes would be too difficult. Downey, *Perkins*, 241.

107. Bernstein, *Caring*, 135.

108. Arnold, *Folklore*, 285.

109. For example, the original Social Security act was funded through a regressive tax and largely excluded women and minorities out of a desire by Congress to reinforce traditional gender roles and by Southern congressmen in particular to not have government money undermining racial hierarchies. It excluded domestic laborers and agricultural workers (fields where minority workers and women were overrepresented), public employees, and often teachers, medical professionals, and social workers (traditionally female areas of employment).

110. FDR, "Campaign Address," 31 Oct. 1936.

111. ER quoted in Kearney, *Reformer*, 263.

112. Both Roosevelts thought people should be allowed to make their own mistakes and learn from them—the job of parents is to provide them with the support they need while they make those mistakes. See "Mother to a Generation," in Kearney, 3-56.

113. Although, as Leo Strauss has noted, ideas of conscience and the common good appear in Machiavelli's *The Discourses*, in addition to a distinction between princes and tyrants.

114. Keller reports that by the mid-1930s 40% of blacks were getting some kind of federal aid. Keller, *Regimes*, 210.

115. Karl, *Uneasy*, 127.

116. Machiavelli, *Prince*, 21.

117. Arnold, *Folklore*, 388.

118. Arnold, *Symbols*, 247.

119. It is worth noting that the previous moment of refounding, the birth of the Union after the Civil War, represented a failure of liberal politics, not its triumph.

120. FDR quoted in Smith, *FDR*, 465. This particular quote was in reference to the possibilities of a draft.

121. Burns, "Improviser," 138.

122. Milkis, "Economic," 32.

123. Arnold, *Symbols*, 229.

124. Arnold, *Symbols*, 21.

125. Arnold, *Folklore*, 87-88.

126. Arnold, *Symbols*, 103-104.

127. ER, *The Moral Basis of Democracy, Leave Behind*, 89.

128. Arnold, *Symbols*, 236.

Part IV: Conclusion

Chapter 7
"A Living and Growing Thing": Appropriating New Deal Liberalism

Ideas are practiced by and upon human beings, who fulfill them only more or
less workably, never perfectly.

—Franklin Roosevelt[1]

No theoretical framework will ever negate the need for politics. There can be no
political change without struggle and no struggle without organization, all of
which happen in contexts that constrain the choices actors can make.
Transformative organizations need a theory that can both generate morale and
create new partisans without interfering with its ability to function effectively,
and this book argues that progressives looking to move the country forward
should look backwards to the insights of New Deal theory. But while the theory
provides us with a compelling framework for progressive politics, it is not
without its own tensions. This final chapter has two purposes. First we will
discuss the relevance and value of New Deal liberalism for progressives in
search of a theoretical frame capable of generating internal morale and building
external legitimacy within America's political context. The second half of the
chapter begins (but hardly exhausts) a critique of the theory itself, highlighting
its limitations while looking to see if these limitations can be addressed from
within the framework of the theory.

The critique focuses primarily on five areas of tension. The first highlights
the New Deal's privileging of the consumer as the central agent in its theory of
the common good. This is followed by a look at the nature of citizenship in the

modern welfare state. What sorts of attachments can we create? How much space is there for democratic participation? From there we will briefly explore the limits of the interest group liberalism that emerged from the New Deal. Underpinning all of these questions is the New Deal's decision not to openly engage the structure of capitalism. The practical and theoretical consequences of that philosophic and political choice are critical to understanding how the New Deal has both contributed to the current crisis in American politics and has the potential to address it. Finally we examine the New Deal's theory of political practice—the dangerously seductive appeal of compromise and manipulative politics.

There are a number of consequential issues not addressed in this chapter. Of particular import is further theorizing about the strengths and weaknesses of liberal universalism. How do we go about making space for advancing the claims of clearly disadvantaged groups without alienating other components of a progressive coalition?[2] I am not sure we have a better option than linking liberal rights to a framework that acknowledges both the moral obligation to protect those rights and our own interdependent interest in a rising standard of living for all of our citizens, but of course this argument has to go hand in hand with an attack on the economic theories and structures that orient us towards scarcity.

Possibly even more troubling is the New Deal's assumption of abundance, one political traditions on the left and right (but particularly the left) need to seriously engage. What if our environment simply cannot sustain the standard of living we are accustomed to? Progressives assume abundance to avoid having to make hard choices, and in a world increasingly likely to be defined by the scarcity of essential raw materials (oil, water, etc.) we need to reorient people towards standards of value that privilege time, leisure, and self-development over conspicuous abundance as the marker of wealth, success, and self-worth. True, the New Deal sought to limit the excesses of consumption-oriented liberalism, but in a world increasingly likely to be defined by the limits of our mastery over nature this is an aspect of the theory that needs a much greater emphasis than it was given during the 1930s.

At the risk of giving away the ending, most of the objections to New Deal theory reflect problems inherent in the corporate form of organization (if not capitalism in general), liberalism, and the nature of modernity. Absent any immediate mechanism for challenging these deeply imbedded ideological and structural frameworks, the New Deal offers us a viable theory for addressing these larger concerns within an American context. The New Deal is an imperfect theory, but the weaknesses in the theory reflect the limits of our citizenry and institutions. These limits can be overcome, but as our history has made clear, even incremental advances require great care and enormous effort. Nonetheless, even small changes are capable of making a measurable difference in the lives of millions of American citizens, and perhaps laying a foundation for something even more profound.

The Value of New Deal Liberalism

Man's capacity for justice makes democracy possible; but man's inclination to injustice makes democracy necessary—Reinhold Niebuhr[3]

The New Deal understood the delicate balance of darkness and light that is at the heart of the American, and the human, experience. It crafted a political theory that accounted for the worst in us while striving for the best. It is an imperfect theory, but it was constructed amidst an imperfect world, and that is its value—it speaks to the tensions at the heart of democracy and takes responsibility for reforming what cannot be redeemed.

We should not look to the New Deal for particular policy prescriptions. Every generation must confront its particular institutional context with its own set of proposals, and reflexive loyalty to old forms represents precisely the kind of dogmatism the New Deal opposed. We are no longer a country whose economic strength derives principally from industry. A welfare state designed for a service economy will look different than one intended for an industrial economy. We are no longer employed for life, and our benefits and protections will need to be more portable, or guaranteed by the state rather than employers. But these are questions of empirical policy, open to debate and experimentation, and contemporary figures like Robert Reich deserve credit for challenging the old dogmas without abandoning their aims.[4]

What the New Deal does offer us is a justification for the welfare state that speaks to American categories and the American experience. By articulating the theory of the New Deal we can tell a story capable of preserving and expanding the welfare state. In fact, much of the necessary groundwork has already been laid. Morton Frisch argued in 1975 that the "New Deal so completely set the tone for the politics of succeeding generations that we still think and act largely in the broad lines of the liberal doctrines articulated during that period."[5] Thirty-five years later the New Deal's opposition is certainly emboldened, even dominant, but that opposition still defines itself in contrast to the values and policies of the New Deal. The New Deal remains a powerful, inspirational moment in American history, and FDR is the Reagan of the Left, a weapon to be cultivated in the battle for the hearts and minds of the electorate. The Right has been working to delegitimate (or co-opt) the New Deal as a symbol for over thirty years precisely because it understands its power. The New Deal speaks to the promise of our founding principles and highest ideals, and grounds a welfare state within the American political tradition. It challenges us to aspire for more, without undermining what we already have. And the importance of this cannot be stressed enough. While we can cite statistics demonstrating that our institutions no longer serve our interests, or point to the self-help section of Barnes and Nobles as evidence of dissatisfaction in American society, no matter how much we are plagued by a nagging sense that somewhere along the way we have gone terribly wrong, there is no evidence that Americans are prepared to reject America. As was the case in the 1930s, we see our distress as a perversion of our ideals, rather than a refutation of them.[6] We want continuity. We do not want a new government—we want the government we have to work. We look for the restoration of America's traditional promise: not a new game, but a new deal.

This is why the ability of the Left to tap into our traditions, to craft new policy out of old language, is so important. Wallace is right—a truly new order will require that elusive "quarter turn of the human heart." And ER is also correct—we cannot effect that quarter turn without education, without helping Americans learn to see the structures of power that undermine opportunity, the artificiality of privation, and our fundamental interdependence. But this educational process can take years, a generational attempt at socialization, and by itself is not sufficient. This transformation needs to be grounded in a new institutional order, and these new institutions require legitimacy in order to survive and thrive. Education and socialization can provide them with legitimacy over time, but they cannot help us overcome our existential attachment to the old order, even when its principles have long since failed to map onto our lived experience. This is why, the New Deal argues, the reformer of any age needs to learn to tap into the stories and language relevant to the electorate. They need to learn to ground new ideas in old values, so that the old story can protect new institutions while they develop their own legitimacy. Much of the truly difficult work is already done. Today we have a powerful tradition capable of competing with the (weakening) hold that laissez faire individualism has over the public mind. It is the tradition of the New Deal.

So what does this tradition offer us? The New Deal's critique of unregulated capitalism provides an effective platform from which to challenge its dominance. The New Deal understands the arbitrary nature of private economic power; the way in which it is in fact a form of government with the same capacity for tyrannical abuse as its political counterpart. This formulization of economic power speaks to the distrust of power so deeply rooted in American culture without engaging the contradictions within capital itself, which the American electorate has made clear time and time again that it has no interest in doing. It reminds us that the market is as likely to threaten our rights as protect them. It enables us to confront capitalism as a structural institution without having to radically rethink our fundamental values—making it a far more effective strategy for promoting institutional reform.

The same can be said of the New Deal's focus on consumption as the basis of our collective common good. If it was true of the 1930s it is certainly true of today—for most Americans the act of consumption defines our experience of freedom. It is the place in our lives where we feel ourselves most capable of acting as agents. The fact, as Benjamin Barber argues in *Consumed*, that this may be a false agency, that we are prisoners of planned obsolescence and an economic structure that conceptualizes freedom by negating our identities as citizens does not change the fact that this is the frame Americans have adopted (or been forced to adopt). A frontal assault on this position is almost certainly doomed to fail as long as capitalism remains capable of providing a decent quality of life for a majority of Americans, and we remain socialized into thinking that consumption is both a legitimate exercise of freedom and that the shortcomings of capitalism reflect human failings.[7] The New Deal embraces the inevitability of consumption while seeking to move away from it. It subverts, rather than confronts. It understands the value of comfort while refusing to end the conversation there. Higher quality food, access to entertainment, a washer and dryer in every house, high speed Internet access on every computer—these are positive outcomes in and of themselves, but they also provide the building blocks that enable us to potentially transcend consumption. We will not suddenly transform into a nation of ascetic luddites even if it is good for us (and the author would miss his ipod, Internet message boards, and World of Warcraft too much to endorse this position). But while a strong case can be made (and the New Deal makes it) for the fact that citizenship and self-development represent higher ends than consumption, it highlights them as a refinement of our consumerist impulses, rather than standing in opposition to it. It attempts to integrate all three, alongside concerns for time and leisure, into a broader understanding of liberty, security, and happiness.

The New Deal rejects substantive equality as an end in itself, as one fundamentally foreign to our identity as Americans. Our understanding of equality has always been primarily formal—equality of opportunity in a land where everyone had an equal chance to craft a decent, self-directed life for themselves. But the New Deal manages to preserve much of the robust commitments and obligations found in substantive equality by emphasizing the obligation of society (via the state) to furnish the preconditions of liberty and the pursuit of happiness. Liberty and happiness may require broad, and reasonably equal, distributions of fundamental resources, privileges, and opportunities.

Of course it is vital in all of this to address our narrow interests. While the hope is that suspicion borne of privation will gradually turn into a warmth and generosity borne of abundance, this transformation is in the future. It must be made clear that the welfare state, which promises freedom, reflects more than special interests capturing the machinery of government for their own advantage. The New Deal's emphasis on community and the collectivity as the source of individualism grants the welfare state legitimacy that can only come from an appeal to solidarity—even if it is a thin solidarity—and our self-interest rightly understood. It is possible to prioritize disadvantaged groups without the groups themselves becoming a narrow interest by emphasizing our interdependence—it is in all of our interests to develop the human capital of the nation, to remind us, as Benjamin Franklin once did, that "[w]e must all hang together, or assuredly we shall all hang separately."

The New Deal supported a greatly empowered national state—only as a last resort in the face of capital's abdication of its governing responsibilities, but since that abdication seems complete (and likely necessitated by its structure), in practice this calls for a permanent expansion of the state. The attendant risk is that the institutions the state needs to regulate can capture and pervert the regulatory function they were founded to serve. Much, if not all of the leadership in our regulatory bureaucracy under the Bush administration was firmly in the control of the industries they were created to police, and there was not a wholesale rejection of this approach under President Obama. There is, unfortunately, no way to ever eliminate this risk—only reduce it. But reduce it we must. Given the ever-increasing global challenges we face, we will only grow more dependent on Federal oversight. Many of the problems facing Americans vastly overwhelm the capacities of local governments to effectively address them. This regulatory welfare state is a necessity, despite the possibilities of co-option. The reduction of that risk requires first of all accepting the permanency of politics, the fact that the threat of co-option is ever present and only preventable via the vigilance of citizens and their organizations. This is one of the primary roles that the citizen must play in modern democratic politics. We can no longer think of ourselves as administrators, or even legislators other than in the broadest possible sense of declaring or ratifying national priorities. Our role instead must privilege holding the state accountable to the common good, to ensure that it serves the interests of the collectivity.

This can best be accomplished, the New Deal argues, through the aggregation of citizens into groups, capable of providing the pressure necessary to overcome the various institutional roadblocks in the way of reform. The state, at the same time, has an obligation to empower those groups that are unjustly underrepresented within our institutional structure. There is, in that sense, a symbiotic relationship between state and organization. The state needs to give political cover to progressive organizations, and these groups in turn must work to strengthen the bargaining power of progressives within government.

All this presents difficulties as pure political theory. There are tensions and cross-purposes running through much of the New Deal. It is more schizophrenic than elegant. But we are a schizophrenic people who recognize our need for government while resenting ourselves for needing it. The United States has long been a land of contradictions, contradictions that we have been fortunate (or unfortunate) enough to avoid having to confront outside of moments of crisis and collapse. Arnold argues that when considering politics, the truth of a theory matters less than its ability to inspire. An unnamed aide of President Bush derided progressive critics of the administration as members of the 'reality based community' and argued that they failed to account for the way in which political reality is symbolic and constructed by elites.[8] And he was right, to a point. Symbolic reality can only hold for so long. Eventually our institutions will buckle under the strain. The aftermath of the Iraq invasion has demonstrated this with perfect clarity. The long run may have vindicated the progressive critique, but this did not keep us out of the war. Bush told the better story, had the better outlet for it, and got his war. As long as we believe our contradictions and illusions, any attempt at engagement will need to find a way to embrace those contradictions even as it tries to eliminate them. This is what makes reform politics so slow, its theory so blurry, and ultimately so frustrating to those who, in the interest of purity and in the name of transcendent justice, excise the political moment out of political theory. The question is whether or not these contradictions are fatal to New Deal theory.

The Limitations of New Deal Theory

The New Deal was tentative, cautious, bold enough to shake the pillars of the system but not to replace them.

—Howard Zinn[9]

Thus far this project has been a work of synthesis, attempting to build a unified theory of the New Deal from its disparate parts. Now that we have that theory in front of us, it is time to turn a critical eye towards it. A critique of New Deal theory is in large measure a critique of eighty years of welfare state liberalism as practiced in the United States, and there has been no shortage of works across almost every theoretical tradition participating in every aspect of the critique. As such this section does not propose to be comprehensive. Instead this section offers a preliminary examination of some of the more significant potential weaknesses of New Deal theory, as well as the ability (or inability) of the theory to respond.

There are a few standard arguments from the right and left that I am going to ignore, as they are either almost entirely disingenuous or they have already been addressed in previous chapters. Hiram Canton provides a useful overview of five standard conservative critiques of the New Deal (and progressive politics in general).[10]

1. That the New Deal's goal of social equality is not achievable except through despotic means: This line of argument involves either a blind or ideologically willful misreading of how the New Deal understood equality, what the New Deal was attempting to do, and sees the specter of communism in child labor laws and minimum wages. It is a powerful political critique insofar as it has a lot of public traction and falls squarely within the folklore of capitalism, but it is substantively empty.

2. The government consumes but does not produce wealth so whenever it spends money it is spending 'the people's' money:[11] Both the acontextual individualism present in this critique (we see individuals removed from any discussion of the institutional structures that impose limits and obligations or create opportunities) as well as Arnold's effective rejoinders in chapter 3 effectively negate it. As with the first argument there is a tactical need to respond, but it poses few theoretical difficulties.

3. Wealth created by deficits leads to inflation, the collapse of credit, etc.: The economic viability of deficit spending may in fact be an argument worth addressing, but it needs to go hand in hand with a discussion of national priorities that rarely accompanies the critique.

4. The New Deal exhibits contempt for the separation of powers and concentrated too much power in the hands of the executive: The key to making this argument responsibly, which New Deal critics from the right and Jeffersonian left often fail to do, is to simultaneously address the obligations of society to provide its citizens with security, not only from external threats of violence, but from economic coercion at home. The framers constructed the Constitution to fulfill the promise of its preamble. Is there another viable set of institutional arrangements that can manage this without expanding executive (or state) power?

5. The very idea of welfare is offensive: This is an ideological and aesthetic critique grounded in laissez faire dogmatism rarely attached to intelligent discussions of the structural location of capital in our society, the potentially tyrannical realities of economic power, and the like. One can make a very compelling case that welfare is in fact offensive, but it would have to be done from the standpoint of Eleanor Roosevelt—that it is offensive because it is a clear indictment of the failure of our civilization to provide for the basic needs of its members. But that is not what usually happens here.

These arguments are not worth visiting largely because this entire project is meant as a refutation of them. Similarly, there are critiques from the Left that also fail to engage the New Deal on its own terms. Howard Zinn's introduction to his New Deal reader is typical of this. He attacks Roosevelt and the New Deal for not utilizing Marxism, for not putting nationalization on the table, and for not replacing liberty with equality in our hierarchy of values. For a historian normally so cognizant of the presence of power in political life he is surprisingly generous in his assessment of the agency available to the New Deal, and seemingly assumes that FDR could have effected an even more radical sea change in American political culture, negating its folklore through an act of political will. Zinn laments that "The New Dealers moved in an atmosphere thick with suggestions, but they accepted only enough of these to get the traditional social mechanisms moving again, plus just enough more to give a taste of what a truly far-reaching reconstruction might be."[12] The implicit assumption is that if FDR had embraced the Marxism "in the air all around him"[13] the United States would have transitioned into a full-fledged social democracy during the Great Depression. Bracketing whether or not this would have been an improvement, it certainly was not likely to happen.[14] There was no mass base for socialism, and the fates of programs like TVA expansion and the Federal Theater, and the extent to which even their comparatively modest aims were too radical for Americans, speaks to that.

Still, from the perspective of the Left, Zinn's broad assessment is accurate.

[W]hen it was over, the fundamental problem remained—and still remains—unsolved: how to bring the blessings of immense natural wealth and staggering productive potential to every person in the land. Also unsolved was the political corollary of that problem; how to organize ordinary people to convey to national leadership something more subtle than the wail of crisis (which speaks for itself); how to communicate the day to day pains felt between emergencies, in garbage-strewn slums, crowded schools, grimy bus stations, inadequate hospital wards, Negro ghettos, and rural shacks—the environment of millions of American clawing for subsistence in the richest country in the world.[15]

The test of New Deal welfare state theory is whether or not it is capable in practice of addressing this fundamental problem better than any other politically viable alternative. The experience of the Great Society is instructive here. As Morton Keller notes, "The Great Society legislation of the 1960s was the fulfillment of much that was implicit in the New Deal: it was an extension of its predecessor rather than a distinctively different political movement."[16] At the same time, its failures highlight important deviations from the New Deal's theoretical frame, failures New Deal theory addresses.

It did not take long for the American people to turn against the Great Society. By September 1966 Gallup polls reported that over half of the people surveyed thought integration was being pushed too fast, a number that had almost doubled from the previous year. Support for the war on poverty had dropped over the same period from 60 percent to 40 percent. 46 percent of the people identified 'big government' as the "biggest threat to the country in the future," twice as many as selected labor and four times as many as had selected big business. Perhaps most telling was the loss of support of working-class whites, as almost two-thirds felt that liberals had been running the country for too long.[17]

Why was the country so hostile to the continued expansion of the Great Society? Clearly the Vietnam War was divisive and drained important resources, but this does not tell the entire story. We must also look towards where the Great Society differed from the New Deal. Alonzo Hamby highlights the shift from economic issues (income, corporate power, social welfare) to cultural issues, as well as the sense of disillusionment that followed from promising more than could be delivered, the overreach Machiavelli warns against. He believes that there was too great an emphasis placed on equality of outcomes rather than opportunity, which cuts against the grain of American folklore.[18] This is a fairly standard interpretation and not too controversial in and of itself.

What Hamby does not adequately spell out is the way in which the Great Society, at least in practice, lost track of the need to articulate a broader vision of the common good in which disparate groups could press legitimate claims (simply denying the urgency of the long overdue cultural reforms pushed in the Sixties is not an option) as part of a framework that highlighted the essential interdependence of working- and middle-class white males, women, and blacks.

Instead these groups were treated as discrete interests competing with one another for scarce resources, and ultimately built interest groups instead of coalitions, advancing individual rights claims without situating them in an inclusive overarching vision that can ground the attendant obligations and sense of reciprocity that rights require.[19] Legitimate cultural concerns were not persuasively unified with questions of economic interest and a broader sense of shared community and inclusive justice. Easier said than done perhaps, but possible. Part of the problem was that the New Left, with its emphasis on participation, localism, and a suspicion of New Deal liberalism ironically shared with conservatives, meant that movements were also denying themselves the tools required to build both the organizational, coalitional, and administrative infrastructure needed to achieve their broader ends and sustain a long-term integrated movement, mistakes the New Deal (and the labor movements of the 1930s) did not make. Of course the New Deal had its own tensions that need to be addressed, and we turn now to that.

The Consumer and the Common Good

> Privatization turns the private, impulsive me lurking inside myself into an inadvertent enemy of the public, deliberative we that also is part of who I am. The private me screams "I want!" The privatization perspective legitimizes this scream, allowing it to trump the quiet "we need" that is the voice of the public me in which I participate and which is also an aspect of my interests as a human being.
>
> —Benjamin Barber[20]

Prior to the New Deal, our right to property enjoyed an unmatched dominance in our hierarchy of political goods, and property itself was in practice narrowly defined as the opportunity for the individual to earn as much as he could, independent of any larger social considerations. It was an atomistic, isolating, and narrow conception of rights. Social Darwinism and laissez faire liberal economic theory provided a profoundly, almost pathologically anti-social framework both a moral and pseudo-scientific legitimacy. The courts blessed it with constitutional sanction. Although modern variants are stylistically different, modern conservatism still clings to the broad outlines of this theory, and anyone wishing to challenge this position needs to offer a larger collective vision—a common good that trumps (while not negating) individual rights claims in the name of both rights expansion and a broader exercise of the rights we possess. Without this standpoint the welfare state is vulnerable to charges that redistributive policies, even a basic safety net, are a form of theft. There is no response to William Graham Sumner's accusation that the redistribution is almost always coercive; A and B deciding what C shall do for D. In order to grant social legislation legitimacy there needs to be some larger framework that enfolds within it all facets of society, in which the redistribution of resources from C to D serves a larger moral and social purpose all (or at least most) citizens can agree to. Without this vision Sumner's formulation holds, and the welfare state becomes legalized theft against which individual citizens have no recourse.

The pronounced streak of anti-statism running throughout the American mind means that, other than in brief periods of national unity brought on most frequently by war (whose symbolic language Roosevelt would often appropriate) we cannot use the idea of the state as a proxy for the common good. Nor, as thinkers like Randolph Bourne have made clear, is that kind of sublimation of individuality to the state something to be encouraged. War is the health of the state, but that health is a source of sickness within civil society. Similarly our long-standing national hostility to class as a category eliminates it as a possibility.[21] Americans, as Tocqueville makes so clear, have long thought of themselves as a middle class (which is to say, largely classless) nation, where disparities in wealth are not commonly seen as reflecting injustice, and where inequality is felt more in terms of exclusion than privation.[22] The New Deal settled ultimately on the category of consumer, using it as a substitute for class or state when theorizing the common good. What are the consequences of that "choice?"

To complicate this question, there were not really any other choices available to the New Deal. Whether through preference, coercion, or simply due to the closing of other options,[23] Americans identified themselves as consumers first and citizens second long before the New Deal openly embraced that formulation. The promise of abundance and economic opportunity defined Americans as a people from the very beginning. Tocqueville observed, "In democracies nothing is greater or more brilliant than commerce. It attracts the eyes of the public and fills the imagination of the crowd."[24] This orientation caused him to fear for the future of American democracy. As the small independent producer became increasingly anachronistic in a corporate economy, Americans challenged that decline only periodically and imperfectly. Instead of splitting with their old folklore they, following the Arnold logic lays out, celebrated the ceremonial process of consumption as a way to resolve the tension between ideals and reality. We became a nation of consumers rather than producers. Thinkers like Thorstein Veblen were highly critical of this new emphasis on consumption, but his was never a voice that held sway over popular imagination. As Alan Brinkley notes:

> [T]he idea and reality of mass consumption were gradually supplanting production as the principal focus of popular hopes and commitment. In an economy driven by consumer spending, and in a culture increasingly dominated by dreams of consumption, it is not surprising that political thought began to reflect consumer-oriented assumptions as well.[25]

The New Deal embraced this new orientation, seeking only to reign in its worst excess rather than replace it with something new. Any open challenge to that consumer consensus would likely have been politically unsuccessful. Even during the worst of the Depression the vast majority of Americans sought restoration, not revolution, and our post-war economic boom was driven by sixteen years of consumer impulses checked by depression and war. We were prepared to tweak our fundamental assumptions, but unwilling to abandon them.

The New Deal could not easily have avoided privileging the consumer in its political order, but its acquiescence had consequences nevertheless. First of all, the New Deal was ultimately unsuccessful in achieving the goal it set for itself. The New Deal hoped to instill a collective consumer consciousness within the nation, using the consumer as a universal category that could occupy a political position normally belonging to class. In the formulation of the NRA, the consumer was theoretically given a voice in the construction of industrial codes equal to that of both capital and labor. If anything, their position occupied a moral high ground as it was the only universal perspective in that triumvirate. But consumption remained an individual, rather than a collective process, private and divorced from the public implications necessary to connect it to citizenship.[26] Although there have been fitful moments of consciousness, the consumer movement never materialized.[27] It never found a constituency, and therefore never found a voice.[28] And unlike the case of farmers and unions, the New Deal largely failed to organize Americans as consumers. While "the Depression decade witnessed...the first, halting attempts by the federal government to represent the consumer interest (in the Consumers' Division of the National Recovery Administration and the Consumers' Counsel Division of the Agricultural Adjustment Administration)" a broad-based consciousness never appeared.[29] Consumption remained, and still remains, a fundamentally private act, the groups that speak for consumers acting as reflections of particular private interests rather than a common good, or reflecting what Lawrence Glickman calls 'gyp consciousness,' with its concerns about maximizing the quality of products, rather than the social implications of how and what we consume.

As a result, the interests of capital (and occasionally labor) would come to set the boundaries for policy discussions. As Stephen Bronner argues in *Imagining the Possible*, "Where the collective capitalist concern will define the general or 'national' interest, all other interests will necessarily appear as subordinate or 'special.'"[30] We see this reflected not only in the oft-quoted GM CEO who claimed "what was good for the country was good for General Motors *and vice versa*" but even earlier in a remarkable 1919 Supreme Court case, *Dodge v. Ford Motor Co.*, where it was ruled that Henry Ford could not choose to reinvest his profits in his workers rather than pay out dividends to his shareholders.[31] The court ruled that

> A business corporation is organized and carried on primarily for the profit of stockholders. The powers of the directors are to be employed for that end. The discretion of directors is to be exercised in the choice of means to attain that end, and does not extend to a change in the end itself, to reduction of profits, or

to the nondistribution of profits among stockholders in order to devote them to other purposes.[32]

The consistent public acceptance of the right of a business to pass along increased costs to consumers, rather than have them eat into profits, similarly reflects the weakness of consumer consciousness in the United States.

But there are deeper, more theoretically troubling concerns. The emphasis on consumption feeds the worst excesses of our individualism, as we came increasingly to define ourselves, our freedom, and our happiness through our possessions, rather than through our work, our personal development, or our relationships to a larger community.[33] Likewise we equated the act of consumption with the celebration of autonomy, again removing the public component of consumption (the economic, environmental, and social consequences) from our thinking and discourse. The New Deal was aware of and hoped to mitigate these tendencies as best it could. Following Tocqueville and Mill, it emphasized the need for a richer conception of citizenship, and an elevated understanding of individualism grounded in self-development—of satisfying the soul as well as the body—as necessary checks on an enervating individualism. There was clearly an awareness that the idea of consumption has no natural sense of obligation—it would have to come from outside our consumer instincts, as Reich argues in *Supercapitalism*. No viable theory of the common good is possible without some recognition that we owe something to the social system and its members that provide us with our individual benefits.

For all its imperfections, the New Deal believed that we were stuck with this consumption framework, and that we must aim at damage control, rather than look for alternatives. Even critics like De Jouvenel conceded that at best we can struggle to remember that "our wealth-mindedness brings us into conflict with many values which deserve respect."[34] Wilson Carey McWilliams agreed with that assessment, arguing that the New Deal sought to have it both ways, to demonstrate that "Americans need not choose between the relations of men as citizens and the affluence of men as private individuals."[35] However, the New Deal did not seem to appreciate exactly how destructive the emphasis on consumption could be to citizenship. Wallace spoke at length about the need for a quarter turn of the human heart, but there was a simultaneous conviction, shared by almost all prominent New Dealers, that the narrowness of consumption-oriented individualism was a reflection of a fear of privation, that upon the achievement of abundance and security our natural inclination would be to soften this acquisitive edge. It misses Tocqueville's insight about the perpetual, totalizing nature of the desire for consumption, what Leo Strauss called our "joyless pursuit of joy." Indeed the nature of capitalism is such that it depends on planned obsolescence and the creation of new desires to maintain itself. The point of equilibrium where we might call ourselves satisfied and think of other things remains perpetually fixed on the horizon.

If we cannot reach a stopping point naturally, then a much greater effort needs to be made to highlight the social side of consumption. Here I think there is potential to develop this kind of consumer-oriented consciousness, even if the Roosevelt administration failed to do so. We have seen the role that economic boycotts have played in attacking Jim Crow at home and apartheid abroad, as well as ending sweat-shop labor and challenging destructive environmental practices. Perhaps the most promising arena for fostering this kind of consciousness is found in the food industry with newfound concerns over organic food, the health content of the fast food industry, and the like. There is no reason the impulses that are made manifest in these isolated instances cannot be fostered into a general movement that insists the government enforce public concerns for quality of life over the profit motive.

We have a right to healthy food, clean air, and reasonable working conditions. The New Deal framed the welfare state as a question of rights, and given the absolute nature of a rights claim and our historical affinity to them, this was probably the right way to go. But, as Jerome Mileur argues, FDR frequently downplayed the collectivist implications of rights, the fact that the public good (understood here as the greater expansion of individual rights) will sometimes trump individual rights claims. The implications were there, and at times, especially in response to the overblown attacks of the Liberty League and their exaltation of property, the New Deal could be quite clear. But the Roosevelt administration did not embrace that line of argument with consistent emphasis. A people oriented towards individualism require a constant reminder of the public foundation of their individual rights, of the fact that the Declaration of Independence argues that rights are held collectively by a people. This reminder needs to come from the government when possible, and from progressives constantly (especially as their work will provide the mandate the government needs to institutionalize policies that look beyond the right to profit through exploitation and predation).

Without a public orientation, our evaluation of social, political, and economic institutions are based not on whether or not they meet the needs of everyone, but whether or not they meet my individual needs. It is difficult from this perspective to make space for the regulation of markets or the redistribution of wealth outside moments of market failures, when enough individuals feel shortchanged that they manage to respond as an accidental collectivity. Given that one of the aims of the New Deal was to make the national state proactive, rather than reactive, this has to be accounted a failure of the Roosevelt administration.

Similarly, a consumerist orientation removes from the individual the burden of thinking about the broader implications of our habits of production and consumption. How are goods produced? What sacrifices do others have to make in the name of Wal-Mart's low prices? How does the convenience of fast food distort the agricultural and environmental priorities of the country? What does it do to the structure of our family life? Do workers in service industries make enough to sustain themselves as consumers and citizens? A consumer perspective may be, as the New Deal hoped, liberating, but we must have a robust understanding of consumption. A true vision of the common good needs to be totalizing—not totalitarian insofar as it needs to provide answers to every question, but possessing a perspective that enables it to view the totality—to see the impact of policy not only on our lives as consumers, but to measure the effect it has on the environment, on our social institutions, on our fellow citizens at worst, and fellow human beings at best. Justice and a vision of the common good requires that we make space for the idea of reciprocity, that we recognize ourselves as individuals situated in a larger context where every action affects others, and so we must make space for them in our own choices. This is a theme progressives need to advance at every opportunity if they want to make it possible to build a movement capable of electing (outside of crisis) and holding accountable leaders who will advance these aims.

Nothing said here contradicts the theory of the New Deal per se. Its universalism, its willingness to expand, however imperfectly, the rights of citizenship to previously marginalized groups, and the space made in the theory for the recognition of interdependence and "higher" articulations of individualism point the way towards addressing these concerns. The problem, as previously argued, is that these aspects of the theory need to be given much greater emphasis in public framing. The New Deal's approach centered on the idea of human decency, that in the end the just society is one in which people are able to live dignified lives. Such a life requires a basic level of security and an expanded realm of personal choice. The focus on consumption makes sense in this larger framework, as material comfort offers the security needed to pursue self-development, and is not a terrible final destination in its own right. The restless nature of capitalism certainly militates against the kind of equilibrium (personal and social) needed to advance beyond a basic materialism. But capitalism is the dominant governing institution in the United States and the New Deal had no real opportunity to replace it with something fundamentally different, regardless of how desirable such an outcome may have been.

A *political* rather than strictly normative theory will have to accept these constraints. The focus instead should be on mitigating its worst excesses. The New Deal was right to recognize that at the time the only symbol capable of unifying Americans was the ideal of consumption. Space was made in the theory to dull its enervating qualities. The NRA's Blue Eagle linked the act of consumption to patriotism and the development of the common good by identifying what businesses were supporting the New Deal's recovery efforts. More importantly, the New Deal reminded Americans that material security was the place where our development as citizens and individuals begins, rather than ends. Where it failed was in not appreciating just how overwhelming the appeal of consumption, narrowly defined, would be within an institutional structure that naturally privileges it. Perhaps this was a reflection of the Depression and the administration's desire to get the economy moving again, but appeals to citizenship and self-development, to replace consumption with leisure and time, were never at the forefront of New Deal discourse.

For the New Deal, consumption was invariably linked with indicators of economic growth. Even though the last forty years have demonstrated that there is no necessary connection between the generation and distribution of wealth, we still look at stock prices and the Gross Domestic Product as absolute measures of the nation's economic well-being. Challenging the conceptual dominance of Wall Street and the GDP would make it easier to call for Americans to move beyond a narrow focus on consumption and the simple generation of goods. As Arnold argued, we have no way of quantifying value outside of monetary terms. We have difficulty placing a value on public parks, leisure time, clean water, and good health. But in the intervening seventy years economists have begun developing ways to measure what we could broadly term quality of life, such as the recent construct of the Redefining Progress think tank—the Genuine Progress Indicator.[36] GPI incorporates personal consumption but accounts for income distribution and factors in the value (positive and negative) of community service, leisure time, hours spent commuting, pollution, crime, and the like. The GPI indicates that our overall well-being has remained stagnant (or fallen) ever since the mid 1970s. A focus on GDP tells citizens that the country is wealthier than before, that their experience of discontent or privation is isolated, an exception to an otherwise prosperous rule, and no doubt a reflection of personal failure. A focus on GPI gives progressives a chance to reframe our well-being in ways that could have far-reaching policy implications. At the very least it gives progressives the opportunity to introduce standards of well-being into our normal definition of consumption as quantity, where my happiness is measured by the sum total of my stuff.

This is an encouraging development because it does not ask Americans to abandon their self-interest. In that it probably reflects a more promising way forward than the emphasis on citizenship and sacrifice. ER was the New Deal's principle advocate of the obligations of citizenship, but her democratic theory is exhausting, her vision of citizenship unachievable to all but political martyrs. While she acknowledges that it is an ideal to be worked toward, she is a bit too comfortable holding up the life of Jesus (a symbol of a life freely given in service to others) as the model for democratic citizenship. The exchange between ER and Harry Truman after FDR's death is illuminating. Hours after news of Roosevelt's passing, Truman asked "Is there anything I can do for you?" Her answer: "Is there anything *we* can do for *you*? For you are the one in trouble now."[37] It is a remarkable response, one that illustrates both ER's deep commitment and the near impossibility of matching it. Any political theory that requires this much self-sacrifice may simply be too demanding to serve as a practical guide. ER's personal tastes ran towards the ascetic side. She wore nice clothes (the way she saw it, the First Lady was something of a public monument and had to be dressed that way) but beyond that her needs were fairly simple (although hers was an aristocratic simplicity) and the sacrifices she demanded of people in the name of democracy were comparatively easy for her to make. For ER public service was truly a vocation, but this is the exception rather than the rule. She never explores what happens to her theory if the rest of America cannot match the example of Jesus (or Eleanor Roosevelt).

The way our individualism narrows our social focus has been a problem in the United States long before the New Deal. This problem is exacerbated by the fact that a large administrative state discourages the kinds of deeper attachments and opportunities for participation required to move people past a narrow, consumer-oriented self-interest. But the fact that the deck is stacked against reintroducing a public component into our private lives only underscores the necessity of working to bring that about. It will not happen on its own.

Bloodless Liberalism

We all begin in a world of particulars, from which the human spirit ascends, on any account only slowly and with difficulty.
—Wilson Carey McWilliams[38]

The New Deal was able to institutionalize an abstract concern for the nation's citizens, but legitimacy requires something more concrete. The issue is whether or not it is possible to truly think of the nation as a 'great community.' Can we form the necessary attachments needed to grant the welfare state legitimacy when the vast majority of one's fellow citizens remain an abstraction? McWilliams argued that one of the great failures of the New Deal was its inability to make the idea of a great community into something personal. "Almost universally inclusive, the good will of the New Deal was radically impersonal, comprehending masses and not men. It was distant, outside the lives of most Americans, a condescending sentiment which, while it felt for the suffering of others, only rarely felt it with them in their travails."[39] The state was useful, but useful in the way that going to the dentist is useful. There was enormous gratitude towards the person of FDR (here he serves a ceremonial role), with the resentment towards the state transferred to the impersonal bureaucracy. We were unable as a public to see the state as the embodiment (or tool) of a great community, even if the president could embody a people.

The New Deal recognized the need for these attachments within its theory, arguing beyond the fact of interdependence and asking instead that its citizens open themselves up to one another, allowing affection to ultimately replace interest as the bond that unites us as a people. But, as McWilliams notes, love and attachment are intimate and personal feelings. The more impersonal the object of love, the less strongly it is felt. The New Deal's theory is universal, but love is local and provincial, and attachment often defines itself in opposition to an 'other' that universalism demands we include. Love is always felt most powerfully at home, and the politics of the small community can be reactionary. It prioritizes the needs of those in proximity, and is prepared to sacrifice those farther away. It privileges the familiar against the alien. It defines itself in the name of tradition, and these traditions can (but obviously do not have to) embody racism, sexism, xenophobia, and hostility to change. These local values certainly blunted the impact of New Deal reforms. As Suzanne Mettler notes, the states frequently softened the universal implications of the New Deal, creating in the end two tiers of citizenship. "National government incorporated citizens within a liberal realm of rights, where they were regarded as free and equal citizens, States made social provision conditional upon meeting obligations that pertained to hierarchical, status-bound definitions of gender norms and other societal roles."[40] The more political autonomy and power given to local government, the more that power may buttress the forces of reaction.

This is a real problem, and the New Deal's primary solution was education. Meaningful attachment can only really begin in the home, so we must focus our efforts on enlarging our understanding of what the home is. But there is also a sense in which the emphasis on education is a dodge, a catchall response to an intractable problem. The New Deal may also be asking our educational system to lift too heavy a burden. A true liberal arts education can make people more cosmopolitan and generate broader (if still impersonal) attachments, but such an education is notoriously expensive, the cost increasing far more rapidly than our ability to pay. The New Deal looked to our public schools to make citizens, but our modern educational system was modeled (and largely still is) to service the needs of capitalism. Children were educated to become workers, or perhaps professionals, and the increasingly common perception of students as consumers purchasing an education (which is itself a gateway to more money and increased consumption) makes it difficult to prepare them for cosmopolitan citizenship. What little citizenship training we receive (our exposure to history, civics, literature) frequently remains focused on indoctrination rather than critical self-reflection or political engagement.

Outside of formal education thinkers like ER placed a premium on travel and new experiences (since we cannot love what we cannot understand), and while this is a great way to learn, our culture's emphasis on work and material markers of success ensure that enormous cultural and structural forces conspire against this kind of continuing education. A true cosmopolitan education may not be possible without moving leisure and time up in our hierarchy of values.

New Deal theory assumes that progressive change will come incrementally as a result of education, The hope is that with the right kind of lifetime schooling (formal and experiential) we can educate into our national consciousness cosmopolitan conceptions of love, and use this as the basis for a just and equitable state. This is, without a doubt, an ambitious, arguably utopian, set of expectations. However, this may be less a critique of the New Deal, and more a recognition of how difficult progressive change really is. As McWilliams concedes, "under modern conditions, general political fraternity is impossible."[41] The universalism of the New Deal will remain bloodless, and this makes it difficult to form meaningful attachments. But this reflects a larger concern with modernity and alienation. "The defect lies in the philosophy of the liberal Enlightenment itself, and the New Deal may be the best and most humane of all the reflections of that philosophy. Modern society, indeed, may not be able to do better."[42] And even within these limitations the New Deal still recognizes that affection is not only desirable, but essential for granting legitimacy and loyalty to the welfare state beyond a vague respect for the law or the power of self-interest. It may never be fully achievable, the hopes of Henry Wallace to the contrary, but it still marks the place where we need to begin (aided of course, by the happy coincidence that our interdependence links our interests to the welfare and well-being of others).

The Problem of Democratic Citizenship

> From a humanitarian point of view the best government is that which we find in an insane asylum...Their aim is to make the inmates of the asylum as comfortable as possible, regardless of their respective moral deserts.
>
> —Thurman Arnold[43]

The New Deal made space within its theory for both democratic participation and the sort of Jeffersonian localism celebrated by Tocqueville, but in both cases these were secondary concerns, designed to serve as partial correctives to the excess of the main theory. The New Deal privileged administration over participation, universalism over particularism. Its commitment was to justice over democracy (as participation), even if democracy was a component of justice. There are important consequences that stem from the New Deal's focus on centralized administration, notably the alienation of people from politics, and the soft despotism of the state. While both are to be regretted, neither one poses an irresolvable problem.

Eileen McDonough measures democratic reform along a participatory and institutional axis, and the New Deal was clearly more successful along its institutional axis.[44] It democratized the state in terms of the interests it served, expanding the possibilities of average citizens to exercise meaningful choices and providing security from the vagaries of chance and market. However, in doing so it moved far from a local, participatory understanding of citizenship towards something much more akin to Arnold's facetious vision of the ideal government as an insane asylum, where we judge the government primarily on its ability to care for its charges, not for their participation in their treatment. Of course Arnold's formulation leaves little space for the fact that the patient's involvement in his treatment may be the only way to ensure the asylum keeps his interests in mind. The moment of accountability that comes from participation and organization is understated in his work, although Eleanor Roosevelt gave it due consideration in her writing. The tension between administration and participation is not easily reconcilable, and Jim Morone frames it well in *The Democratic Wish*, when he wonders how Americans can "reconcile their expanded bureaucracy with their notions of democracy," what he calls their 'democratic wish.'[45]

This is an old problem, one eloquently addressed by Tocqueville and his concern about the soft "democratic despotism" engendered by commercial democracies that "debase men without tormenting them."[46] As it remains one of the most compelling articulations of this fear to date, it is worth quoting at length.

> I wish to imagine under what new features despotism might appear in the world: I see an innumerable crowd of men, all alike and equal, turned in upon themselves in a restless search for those petty, vulgar pleasures with which they fill their souls. Each of them, living apart, is almost unaware of the destiny of all the rest. His children and personal friends are for him the whole of the human race; as for the remainder of his fellow citizens, he stands alongside them but does not see them; he touches them without feeling them; he exists only in himself and for himself; if he still retains his family circle at any rate he may be said to have lost his country.
>
> Above these men stands an immense and protective power which alone is responsible for looking after their enjoyments and watching over their destiny. It is absolute, meticulous, ordered, provident, and kindly disposed. It would be like a fatherly authority, if, father like, its aim were to prepare men for manhood but it seeks only to keep them in perpetual childhood; it prefers its citizens to enjoy themselves provided they have only enjoyment in mind. It works readily for their happiness but it wishes to be the only provider and judge of it. It provides their security, anticipates and guarantees their needs, supplies their pleasures, directs their principle concerns, manages their industry, regulates their estates, divides their inheritances. Why can it not remove from them entirely the bother of thinking and the troubles of life?[47]

Tocqueville's prescient fear was that our desire for material comfort would lead us to privilege equality over liberty—that our comfort was more important than our participation in political life. In fact, as we saw, the need to participate at all became less troubling as we came to identify freedom with consumption, folding both liberty and equality into our identities as consumers. Tocqueville anticipated a state in which its members spent their times in private cocoons, emerging periodically not to metamorphose into citizens but simply to choose new masters, the election ceremonially addressing the tension between democratic theory and practice. The ceremony is not entirely empty, as Tocqueville concedes. "Creating a national representative system in a very centralized country is thus to lessen the damage extreme centralization can produce but it does not entirely destroy it."[48] But, of course, the more vacuous the electoral process becomes, the less effective a bulwark against democratic despotism it is.

Tocqueville's concern is that the rule of the petty bureaucrat saps us of our political will, our love of liberty. No doubt he is correct, as the enduring power of the bureaucrat as a negative symbol attests to. But perhaps without realizing it, elsewhere in *Democracy in America* he points to the necessity of the governmental bureaucrat, as the threat posed by an 'aristocracy of manufacturers' is surely the cause of as much, if not greater, indignity and alienation, with fewer possibilities for the widespread exercise of liberty. Capitalism, if left to its own devices in a culture that places consumption and the creation of wealth at the top of its hierarchy of values, will result in a social arrangement where in the name of efficiency work becomes specialized (or scarce) to the point that it interferes with our self-development. Liberty becomes identified with consumption—we end up celebrating our freedom by shopping because our working lives are uncertain, constrained, and confined. At the same time, increasingly reified workers become utterly dependent for their livelihood in a system that has little vested interest in whether or not the worker lives or dies, let alone thrives. "As "the industrialist only asks the worker for his labor and the latter only expects his wages the one is not committed to protect, nor the other to defend; they are not linked in any permanent way, either by habit or duty."[49]

If the decentralized semi-agrarian localism of a Jefferson and Tocqueville is lost to us (and if it was in 1932 it certainly is today) the state represents what may be the most effective response to the petty tyranny of the manager, the landlord, and the reification of both worker and consumer. The state may be in the thrall of capital, and we may surrender to a soft despotism, but that despotism is still superior and likely more humane than the freedom to starve, and as long as our system remains democratic there is always the possibility of change and the redress of grievances. There is potential for direct accountability in the state that is simply not available in the corporation. As Wallace argued,

> I am well aware of the sins of bureaucracy, its occasional pettiness and red tape. The bureaucracy of any country cannot be much better than the human beings of that country. But I am convinced that governmental bureaucracy, from the standpoint of honesty, efficiency and fairness compares very favorably with corporation bureaucracy....This is not because human beings in government bureaus are so much finer as individuals than human beings in corporation bureaucracies, but because continuous public scrutiny requires a higher standard.[50]

In fact, using the state to oppose our industrial aristocracy likely represents the most promising way forward towards a newer, more meaningful form of citizenship, since it is capable of restoring a sense of agency frequently overwhelmed by the political power of capital. And this is what Tocqueville seems to miss in his own critique of democratic despotism. The regulatory welfare state is paternalistic only if we think of it as the place where liberty ends, rather than the point at which it begins.

The tradition of Jeffersonian localism is largely anachronistic, as the New Deal understood (hence the need for Hamiltonian means). As problems become national (let alone global) larger aggregations of authority are necessary to address them. Of course local civic engagement can play an important role in this, but it is vital that it reflect an awareness of the scope of the problem in play, and local solutions need to be plugged into larger strategic visions, many of which will involve surrendering local autonomy to increasingly powerful and expansive organizations.

Despite the genuine efforts of New Dealers to promote an active and energetic conception of citizenship, the New Deal governing ideal was always the administrator (although not the sole ideal, as he is checked by the organization and there were efforts to incorporate local decision making whenever possible).[51] The individual citizen, through the election of their representatives and especially the president, sets long-term goals and establishes a broad 'throw the bums out' kind of accountability. Through their organizations they could wield considerably more power and influence, helping to set agendas and write laws, but the day-to-day process of administration was (ideally) to be based on expertise and sheltered from the inevitable political infighting as much as possible. It was believed that only the president could shield administrators from congressional meddling, and that the role of Congress would increasingly focus on budgetary oversight and investigation rather than active policy construction. Ideally these administrators would themselves be politically neutral, but of course this was never the case, even when ideology was held constant. Progressives with impeccable credentials like Wallace and Ickes were consistently at one another's throats, and Wallace's experiences with the AAA demonstrated that even technical administration could not escape the all too political questions about what constituency particular programs should serve.

Nevertheless, an institutional arrangement that concentrated decision-making authority in the bureaucracy was deemed necessary by the New Deal. While Roosevelt may have lacked some of Lincoln's humility and trepidation about an expansive state, he took pains to ensure that his bureaucracy remained in contact with the people, interjecting democracy into the system when possible. However, the executive-centered infrastructure outlasted his tenure in the office, and as Miroff notes,

> Unelected power brokers and zealous loyalists would from the glamorous vantage point of the White House, exercise vast influence in the president's name. Constructing an institutionalized presidency to make democratic government more efficient, Roosevelt may in the long run have made democratic leadership from the White House more difficult.[52]

And even Roosevelt's efforts at keeping the process democratic were necessarily limited. As the people's "true representative" FDR inadvertently encouraged a sort of passivity amongst his supporters, as it is far more difficult to interact with and influence a president the way one could influence a representative or a party. "A president in the Roosevelt mold might make occasional gestures of sponsorship for citizen participation, but his underlying message was that he was the people's surrogate, the practical embodiment of their theoretical sovereignty."[53] This tendency would only become more pronounced as modern media encouraged a presidency grounded in spectacle, where citizens were expected to be passive observers, participating primarily through their applause and financial generosity. Too much participation would interfere with the act of administration, and as McWilliams argues, there was "a general willingness of the New Deal to sacrifice human participation for technical efficiency where ever the two seemed to be in conflict, to prefer production of goods to the development of men."[54]

Here sympathetic critics like Milkis worry about FDR's devaluation of political parties, seeing them as an important vehicle for developing citizenship beyond voting.[55] Certainly the presence of ideological parties would make it easier for people to exercise a more coherent voice, and the New Deal aimed for the ideological realignment Reagan ultimately achieved, but the conversation need not and should not stop at parties. The larger concern here is with citizen passivity, and others, like Piven and Cloward, argue persuasively for the importance of citizen movements existing outside of parties to provide pressure and direction to our governing institutions. The New Deal recognized the importance of external organization as a vehicle for the mobilization of interest and opinion—as a liberal check and a source of democratic legitimacy. Probably party and movement are needed in conjunction with each other, as it is far easier to think of a social movement as a "special interest" than it is a political party, which by its nature represents a wide range of interests and people. Without a broad range of competing outside pressure, parties will gravitate towards the maintenance of the status quo. Without the existence of the broad coalitions engendered by parties the welfare state is vulnerable to the charge that its programs represent special interests rather than the public good.[56] The existence of parties gives the welfare state a potentially broad popular mandate. One of the factors leading to the New Deal coalition unraveling was, as Eden notes, its increased use of the courts rather than the process of coalition building and majority consensus. Doing so turned the welfare state built by the New Deal and expanded by its followers into a program without a party, without representation beyond the interests involved in the lawsuits.[57]

Again, simply making the state more democratic in the manner of Tocqueville, Jefferson, and the Anti-Federalists, or even in the vein of a New Freedom style progressivism is no longer an option. The New Deal recognized that modern capitalism creates a state of permanent crisis, and the role of government is to manage that crisis; to prevent collapse and shield citizens from its excess and failures. And for the most part the American people have a grumbling, incoherent acceptance of this fact that comes into sharp relief in the face of a Hurricane Katrina or economic recession. The New Deal also argued that the primary source of concrete policy direction has to come from a centralized executive—and that even if one concedes greater decision making power to Congress the administrative work involved is still centered in the bureaucracy. Clearly the risk of centralization under these circumstances is very real. Mileur captures what is at stake.

> For a public schooled in the idea of democracy as majority rule, the expansion of rights and entitlements diminishes popular control of government, erodes the idea of popular sovereignty, and encourage a sense of powerlessness in the public as well. In a regime that defines politics and democracy in terms of power, understood as the successful exercise of individual will, nothing is more debilitating for citizens and public alike than the sense of powerlessness as the present cynicism of Americans about their government and politics would seem to attest.[58]

Arnold argued that we need ceremonial intervention to address tensions between theory and practice, and for a variety of reasons many Americans no longer feel that their government actually represents them. The old ceremonies have failed. It is hard for many of us to believe that this is in fact a democracy if any part of the definition involves the people both ruling and being ruled.[59] And cynicism about the state of our democracy is not healthy, especially if, as the New Deal believed, a sense of public-spirited citizenship is necessary to mitigate the excesses of consumerist individualism.

It is necessary for people to cede power to the state to address the complications of modern capitalism. However, it is equally important for people to demand that the power given be used responsibly, that our administrators be held accountable. Modern democracy in an administrative state requires a dynamic tension between the people and the state, where we constantly threaten to take away what is given if not used appropriately. Grants of power are never absolute, never unconditional. The mark of democracy therefore becomes not participation, but accountability. And it becomes the obligation of the state, according to the New Deal, to empower the groups and organizations needed to demand that it both act and police its actions. Doing so requires a great commitment to the ideal of democracy, to realizing that the administrative state is a response to necessity, but that there is still room to determine how necessity plays out. The New Deal has this commitment in theory, and to a considerable degree the Roosevelt administration exhibited it in practice, organizing farmers and labor as well as laying some of the institutional and social groundwork for the civil rights movement.

In the end we are forced to choose between democracy (narrowly defined) and social justice. Both are desirable, but we must privilege one. The New Deal privileged social justice (although it privileged liberalism above both), arguing that it marks the place where a more substantive form of democracy begins. And this in turn requires that we accept a large, organized state. If we accept that there needs to be some form of safety net and public control over capital this can only happen via the federal government, however aesthetically displeasing this may happen to be. Any discussion focused on getting rid of government, especially by someone ostensibly progressive, misses the point entirely. "The issue," Bronner reminds us "is not the concentration of power, but its accountability."[60] Can we figure out ways to make institutions responsive to citizens—figuring out how to provide direction from below to the necessarily centralized administration above? The answer, for New Deal theory, is found in organization and mobilization, relocating the act of citizenship away from administration and towards a type of extra-governmental agenda setting. State and citizen enter into a symbiotic relationship where they each take responsibility for the other's flourishing. But, without fostering a deeper movement culture capable of sustaining interest, this may not be enough. People have to be given something to participate in, even if it is not direct political power. The New Deal understood this at the margins, but it must become a far more prominent part of any welfare state theory going forward.

Interest Group Liberalism

By a faction I understand a number of citizens, whether amounting to a majority or minority of the whole, who are united and actuated by some common impulse of passion, or of interest, adverse to the rights of other citizens, or to the permanent and aggregate interests of the community.

—James Madison[61]

Central to the New Deal's theory of practice is its insistence that a democracy is safeguarded by its organizations. Given the necessity of an administrative state, in which active citizen participation is problematic, the ability of citizens to organize, to influence the direction of the administrative state, becomes the primary moment of participation and accountability.[62] New Deal theory differs from the thin interest group liberal pluralism that evolved from it, where the common good is a simple aggregation of private preferences (or, worse, the common good is an ideological justification for policies that benefit whatever group currently has power) as the New Deal reflects something closer to the Madisonian ideal. A common good exists, and we can use it as a standard to evaluate whether or not an organization represents a narrow, factional interest, or serves a larger public purpose. There are obviously drawbacks to organizations serving as our primary vehicle for participation. There is the possibility of institutional capture by stronger groups, as well as a pressing need to empower weaker ones—especially those that can plausibly claim to speak on behalf of a public interest. There is the tendency of organized interests to ossify and lose their democratic character, to fail to provide a meaningful political experience capable of fostering agency. Some of these concerns can be addressed institutionally; others are dependent on the vigilance of the citizens themselves. However, the fact that interest group liberalism carries with it a high probability of abuse reflects the limits of democracy in a modern administrative state, something to be mitigated, rather than overcome, and the New Deal was largely aware of and responded (albeit sometimes inadequately) to its shortcomings.

What has come to be known as pluralism or interest group liberalism is commonly traced back to the New Deal. This assessment is not entirely accurate. Interest and interest groups have been a part of the American political system since the very beginning. The New Deal, however, sought to help empower the groups that had previously been at the margins. It would be more accurate to say that the New Deal fostered countervailing forms of power—it helped establish a competitive system of interest groups.

Regardless, as McWilliams notes, the reliance on these kinds of organizational structures reflects a failure of elite mastery, the inability of the administrative state to successfully plan. It defaults instead to a faith in interest groups somehow balancing each other out, which is to say a hope that it all works out all right in the end. "Redefined in terms of "groups," the market mechanism became once again the master concept of political thought."[63] But here McWilliams may overstate his critique. Organizations had intrinsic value as vehicles of countervailing power and democratic accountability. Although not a New Dealer by any means, De Jouvenel highlights that "[t]his spontaneous formation of society into syndicates of interests, secret or professed, has been denounced and damned, but in vain. It is a natural phenomena, acting as a corrective to the false totalitarian conception of the general interest."[64] He goes further than the New Deal while at the same time reflecting its liberal modesty. The New Deal had a theory of the general interest, but an open political process offered a check against it—a way for society to intervene if it disagreed. While I argued earlier that the New Deal was more concerned with social justice than democracy, it was a liberal movement before either, and this liberalism, the belief that the state cannot categorically insist on coercively defining the good for its citizens, demands a check even on the New Deal's best intentions.

Interest group liberalism was inevitable in a commercial democratic society, as Madison makes clear in "Federalist 10." As the government expands its operations it is only natural that self-interested citizens would try to capture that neutral machinery for their own ends. The obligation of the government, the New Deal argues (following Madison), is to ensure that we empower the disparate groups in society to check one another. The hope is that in this process a policy approximating the common good emerges (Madison) or that a preexisting vision can be ratified or rejected (New Deal). In particular we need to focus on the groups whose exclusion undermines the common good, a need that injects normative judgment into what is otherwise a neutral system. We must recognize and take steps to rectify what Eric Schattschneider identified as the primary flaw in the pluralist heaven, namely that "the heavenly chorus sings with a strong upper-class accent." Of course these steps are complicated in practice, maybe even impossible. Groups lose track of the larger good, identifying their own narrow interests with the interests of the whole, and with this newfound sense of legitimacy, justify the extraction of as many public resources as they can as quickly as they can (or, alternately, they can abandon any claim to speak for the public and approach common resources from a position of power in a state of nature). As E. Pendelton Herring notes, "The voice of the people sometimes suggests the squeal of pigs at a trough."[65] Democracy, left to its own devices, is no different than any other system of organization. The powerful (organized) will exercise greater influence, or capture the machinery outright, and there is not really any space for citizens who cannot aggregate themselves.

This happened in the early stages of the New Deal. The NRA was supposed to accord an equal voice to labor and consumer in the writing of its codes. But as Clarence Darrow's National Recovery Review Board discovered:

> In virtually all the codes we have examined one condition has been persistent, undeniable and apparent to any impartial observation...The code has offered an opportunity for the more powerful and more profitable interests to seize control of an industry or to augment and extend a control already obtained.[66]

In fact, in a few key industries like cotton and sugar, the codes themselves were actually written during the Hoover administration, and tenant farmers were written out of the AAA entirely. George Peek's reflections on the AAA make abundantly clear the nature of the problem.

> I learned that Americans think of their government as something above and beyond the people of the United States, as something which can control groups at its will. The truth is that no democratic government can be very different from the country it governs. If some groups are dominant in the country, they will be dominant in any plan the government undertakes.[67]

There is an inevitability to Peek's speculations that the New Deal simultaneously challenges and accepts. The New Deal understood that within a democracy the groups with power will always effectively influence, if not outright drive, public policy. Nevertheless, a democratic government, organized around a theory of the common good, is capable of empowering new groups, of challenging the face of dominance. It is difficult, short of repression, to eliminate the power of the powerful, but it can give new groups the tools to resist it in their own right. If it cannot cast down, it can at least elevate.

This is the key to the success of liberal democracy in an administrative state. It needs to ensure that worthwhile interests (those whose empowerment will expand the possibilities of security, happiness, and self-development to more citizens) are given the institutional support they need to influence policy— to push the government in the direction it wants to go (when liberal commitments will not allow government to push ahead alone). What's more, taking steps to ensure that disadvantaged groups can act with force within the political process is likely more conducive to the long-term legitimacy, expansion, consolidation, and protection of their rights than relying on a paternalistic bureaucracy. Here the New Deal enjoyed only partial success. Hence Zinn is right to argue that

> Humanitarianism pure and simple can only go so far, and self-interest must carry it further. Beyond the solicitude felt by the New Dealers for the distressed, beyond the occasional bold rhetoric, there was not enough motive power to create a radically new economic equilibrium; this would have to be supplied by the groups concerned themselves.[68]

The poor, the unemployed, and tenant farmers were told of the importance of organization, but they lacked preexisting structures like unions, and the Roosevelt administration could have done more to aid in creation of new organizations. Without that help, the likelihood of these groups getting adequate representation in democratic politics is slim. Of course they can organize themselves, and groups like the Southern Tenant Farmers Union represented an important step in that direction, but in the face of the resources that can be brought to bear by an entrenched opposition, it is asking a great deal, perhaps too much, to insist these groups go it alone.

The relationship between the state, its governing philosophy, and the people it aims to serve is complicated. The state is a neutral piece of machinery—liberal theory insists that it cannot be otherwise. But there can (and should) be a common vision existing independent of that machinery (this vision should inform the content of national elections), and its partisans must ensure that the machinery is used to empower the groups that support it, giving the state a democratic legitimacy it can only have through the mass participation of citizens in the democratic process— not just as voters, but as organized groups capable of pressuring the government to do the right thing.

But the state's neutral machinery does not exist in a neutral environment. Instead it operates in an atmosphere drenched in power, and this is an essential complication of the liberal welfare state. The institutions designed to help those who need it are vulnerable to capture by those it is supposed to regulate, and the more power we grant the state to address social problems, the greater the incentive to both capture and abuse that machinery. There is no way around this except having a state committed to resisting that capture, and this in turn is much more likely to happen through the counter-organization of those who can plausibly claim to represent the common good.[69] Given the overwhelming power of capital in the American system, this will involve first and foremost empowering workers. As Bronner argues:

> Generally, however state intervention has occurred most successfully under conditions in which the organizational and ideological unity of workers was strongest. Distribution of wealth is, in short, dependent not merely on productivity and economic growth but on the political power exercised by workers.[70]

But of course this need not be understood only in terms of class. To the extent gender, race, religion, sexual orientation, or any other category is a marker of privilege or exploitation those groups affected need to organize themselves and the state needs to foster that organization through moral support, legal protections, or whatever appropriate methods can be brought to bear. But the groups also need to police themselves. The burden is on the organization's members to maintain internal accountability and responsiveness, and above all to be clear how their own interests reflect a greater national interest, especially when competing for scarce resources like time, money, and legitimacy.

The union movement during World War II is instructive in this regard, highlighting the ultimate failures of the government to maintain this equal organizational playing field.[71] Labor leaders agreed to a 'no-strike' pledge and wage freeze to avoid accusations they were obstructing the war effort. Tactically this may have been necessary, as anti-labor sentiment was high. Capital, on the other hand, was not similarly bound, and this is one of the great failures of the Roosevelt administration during World War II—the presence of dollar a year men and the general influence of laissez faire 'free enterprise' conservatives throughout the war bureaucracy (800 in the Office of Production Management alone) ensured that business stood to make enormous profits off of the war and control production in the subsequent peace.[72] While laws limiting wages for workers were acceptable, attempts to limit maximum salaries at $25,000 a year were defeated (although they were proposed).[73] The public was clearly on the side of capital. Gallup Poll surveys during 1942 and 1943 found 81 percent of respondents favored a law forbidding strikes in war industries, and 78 percent favored laws requiring war industry employers to work forty-eight hours (instead of forty) before receiving overtime. The most common answer given as to the cause of strikes was "the unjust demands of workers, followed by labor leaders seeking personal power. Under these circumstances there was little chance for labor to maintain its position as a countervailing power. Perhaps there was little the administration could have done to preserve a greater parity between labor and capital. Conservatives were relentless in their critique of the welfare state, despite FDR's efforts at unity. But it also seems that the administration offered token resistance at best to the dominance of capital within the administration, when it was not actively aiding it. Roosevelt, suspicious of the dollar a year men, still allowed their entry into the bureaucracy, assuming that capital would be more likely to take marching orders from its own than from New Dealers. And pro-business reactionaries were appointed to key positions within the economic war bureaucracy. This helped ensure that the possibilities for a transformative post-war reorganization were not limited. The consequences are still with us today.

And that is the risk of liberal democracy. Despite the best (or not so best) efforts of the parties involved there is never any guarantee that we can retain a countervailing balance among interests. Some will have more power, others more legitimacy in the public eye and through these advantages they can control both discourse and policy. This is why it is so important for progressives to focus on the question of organization in total—to highlight the need for groups to organize, to ally with one another to counter the influence of capital, to work on crafting a message capable of building bridges and framing interests. Likewise, they need to prioritize investing what political capital they have in finding ways to expand it further, to increase their access to power and their ability to organize. How loud you can shout is as important as the content of what you're shouting. This is not necessarily an argument for the increased professionalization of interest groups. Certainly the maintenance of a movement culture is a critical form of power, and it is the fostering of a movement culture that has helped make the cultural right so effective over the last thirty years. Instead it is a reminder that the public good in practice will always be a political construction—a reflection of the interests of the groups most effective at selling their position to the public and figuring out ways to organize and access political power. The New Deal understood that all unarmed prophets fail, and that institutionalizing a progressive agenda requires arming your warriors before going to war, especially when the primary tool available to combat the power of money is the power of mass.[74]

Engaging Capitalism

There are three orders in society—those who live by rent, by labor and by profits. Employers constitute the third order...the Proposal of any new law or regulation which comes from this order ought always to be listened to with the greatest precaution and ought never to be adopted till after having been long and carefully examined, not only with the most scrupulous but with the most suspicious attention. It comes from an order of men whose interests are never exactly the same with that of the public, who have generally an interest to deceive and even oppress the public.

—Adam Smith[75]

Given the centrality of capital within American democracy, any political theory applied to the American case has to address the place of capital within the system. There is a sense in which the conventional socialist critique is moot as political critique. There was simply not a mass base ready to abandon capitalism in favor of something more radical, and the populist pseudo-fascism of figures like Father Coughlin had more traction than any left alternative. At any rate, the administration was not prepared to advance socialist claims, nor would the electorate have accepted them. The language of Roosevelt's early speeches, or even the more militant moments of the 1936 campaign, indicate that Roosevelt (and the American people, to the extent they accepted FDR's narrative) blamed the depression on short-sighted corporate leadership or, less charitably if not less accurately, economic oligarchs—not capitalism itself, which Roosevelt himself was always quick to reaffirm. And even figures like Wallace, the great liberal standard-bearer of the late New Deal, would argue, "There is something wooden and inhuman about the government interfering in a definite, precise way with the details of our private and business lives. It suggests a time of war with generals and captains telling every individual what he must do each day and hour."[76] In private, when railing about what he saw as the obstructionism of capital, Roosevelt's arguments (he was not alone here amongst New Dealers) showed a greater awareness of capitalism as a structure, rather than a collection of individual capitalists, but he still never fully grasped the implications of this.[77] While more reflective and less dogmatic than most, even the most liberal of New Dealers could not fully shake off the power of their folklore. In this they were no different than the people they represented. Capitalism may have needed protection from its own worst excesses, but they never doubted that it was capable of salvage, if not salvation.

As such the effort was always pitched at the level of taming or humanizing capital—to draw new attention to the fact that unreconstructed capitalism was unwilling or unable to accept its responsibilities as a governing institution. As long as that responsibility was abdicated it was the job of a democratic government to ensure that its obligations were met by grafting a regulatory welfare state onto a capitalist economic structure. Early New Deal efforts aimed at making that engagement as cooperative as possible, and after a brief flowering of anti-trust activity, World War II forced questions of economic reorganization to the back burner, where they never reemerged. A new engagement with the power and influence of capital was necessary given the increasing prominence of interest group liberalism. That engagement never happened, although there is room for it within the boundaries of New Deal theory. In fact, it requires returning to the New Deal imperatives that were buried by the war and never recovered after Roosevelt's death.

The NRA phase of the New Deal was characterized by an experimental volunteerism in regards to the possibilities of a socially responsible capitalism. The New Deal had hoped to unite all facets of society into a community capable of achieving social justice without excessive class tension. From Roosevelt's perspective, government was "the outward expression of the unity and leadership of all groups" and therefore his role as president was to find ways to nurture and foster that unity.[78] Clearly that was optimistic at best, assuming both a farsightedness and uniformity amongst business that did not exist. It assumed that the business community could speak with one voice and engage the government in a discussion of grand policy, ignoring differences across region, sector, and capitalization.[79] Still, the New Deal never abandoned the hope for an eventual understanding, even as it came to believe that cooperation would only come about incrementally, through socialization out of an economy of scarcity into one of abundance, where we could treat one another as citizens rather than competitors in a Hobbesian state of nature.

The TVA, laboring under less ignorance about the structural imperatives of capital, represented a more promising way forward, demonstrating the very real possibilities of how government intervention in the economy could both protect consumers, spur competition, increase demand, and through that aid private enterprise.[80] Of course Congress later resisted attempts to expand the TVA into other areas of the country, the hostility towards one of the most unalloyed successes of the New Deal demonstrating the sharp anti-New Deal turn that characterized much of the post-1936 political landscape.

The New Deal, frustrated with business intransigence even in the face of successful policy, and responding to the pressures of new political organizations, moved after the failure of the NRA to both limit the privileged position of business in policy formation and create forms of countervailing power and more equitable progressive taxation. If cooperation was not to be voluntary, the New Deal showed a willingness to engage in the utilitarian calculus that justified mild coercion in the name of greater freedom, subject to the limits of the democratic process. At least for a while. In the name of wartime unity Roosevelt made his peace with capital, abandoned Arnold's anti-trust program, and with it the last real effort within mainstream American politics to seriously confront the power of capital. Roosevelt was skeptical about the presence of dollar a year men, but was unwilling to challenge their presence.[81]

That Roosevelt thought this step necessary to maintain unity (as well as the comparative hostility of the American people towards strikes but not profiteering during the war) points to the deep roots of the folklore of capitalism. Never fully vanquished, it roared back to power in the wake of New Deal reforms and wartime profits and productivity, which "prompted much boasting about the virtues of private enterprise [and] restored public esteem for big business."[82] In fact, the remarkable productive capacity of the United States during the war seemed to demonstrate to the American people that the system of corporate capitalism was not only sustainable, but could more than meet the needs and expectations of the American system. As Brinkley argues,

> The wartime experience muted liberal hostility to capitalism and the corporate world. It challenged the commitments of liberals to a powerful centralized state and turned their efforts into less direct, less confrontational channels. And it helped legitimize both Keynesian fiscal policies and the idea of expanded social welfare commitments.[83]

Given that context, the move by the New Deal towards mitigating the sting of the market, rather than openly challenging it, focusing on fiscal policy, monetary policy, and welfare reforms rather than industrial planning, makes sense politically. The red hysteria of Martin Dies and the House Un-American Committee only made this policy of non-engagement more attractive.

Even if there were no other viable political options available, the consequences of this position are clearly severe. In a capitalist system benefits for workers (and consumers) are dependent on growth and innovation, which in turn is dependent on the right of capital to make a profit, and as Arnold made clear, our folklore does not enable us to adequately theorize public investment and innovation. As long as this is the case the needs of business will always have priority. Arnold's reconceptualization of anti-trust activities as looking to remove checks on productivity, innovation, and competition offers a way to attack certain concentrations of power, but still sacrifices the interests of workers in the name of the consumer, and both in the name of profits. We can see the economic consequences of this perspective in the Wal-Martization of contemporary America. In his focus on restraints of trade Arnold moves forward from anachronistic concerns with size as size, but still fails to consider the place of capital structurally.[84]

Still, the New Deal was right to highlight that not even unions are necessarily entitled to a privileged place within our economic structure, and that in the name of protecting their members they can stand in the way of greater prosperity and socially necessary legislations and reforms.[85] No organization is entitled to a position of absolute privilege. All public policy needs to evaluate its rights within the context of a larger utilitarian framework, although this may involve a certain degree of consideration for groups like unions that are asked to apply countervailing pressure against vastly more powerful organizations. It becomes the obligation of the state to ensure that all relevant parties are sufficiently empowered so that a Madisonian balancing can succeed where public spiritedness fails. This is by no means a perfect system, but it did demonstrate real promise during the 1930s, and may be our only realistic way forward as long as Americans reject a Manichean understanding of the tensions between labor and capital.

While contemporary progressives are understandably discouraged about the comparative political strength of capital, they should also recall their history. While our current political climate is often hostile (at least in boom times), by the 1930s the 14th amendment had invalidated about 200 statutes aimed at increasing the democratic accountability of the corporation.[86] The success of the New Deal, which built a regulatory state almost from scratch while lacking strong pre-existing public and constitutional legitimacy, demonstrates that while the American people may not be prepared to abandon capitalism, they are willing to give a hearing to populist critiques challenging corporate accountability and its exclusionary character. They are willing, when presented with the right message, especially in the face of institutional failure, to reengage the question of power in our economy. Americans may not be prepared to endorse substantive equality, but they are willing to challenge arbitrary privilege, and as Berle and Means argued, there is no more arbitrary form of organizational power than the corporation, where owners do not make decisions, decision makers are not owners, and layers of legal protections obfuscate any meaningful sense of responsibility and accountability.[87]

The interest group liberalism that emerges out of World War II refused to engage these questions in a meaningful way. Brinkley provides an efficient summary of their position, which adopts the New Deal's focus on consumption without its concerns about power and access.

It rested on the belief that protecting consumers and encouraging mass consumption, more than protecting producers and promoting savings, were the principal responsibilities of the liberal state. In its pursuit of full employment, the government would not seek to regulate corporate institutions so much as it would try to influence the business cycle. It would not try to redistribute economic power and limit inequality so much as it would create a compensatory welfare system (what later generations would call a 'safety net') for those whom capitalism had failed. It would not reshape capitalist institutions. It would reshape the economic and social environment in which those institutions worked.[88]

The use of the word *compensatory* is appropriate. Rather than challenge the presence of power it seeks to compensate for its shortcomings. In the end this is a necessary move, as wholesale abandonment of our economic and social institutions is not possible short of revolution, nor necessarily even desirable, since we lack certainty that what replaces it will mark an improvement. But without recognition of capital's superior agenda setting abilities, political influence, and arbitrary control over people's lives, in short, its privileged position as the dominant governing institution in our lives, there is no way we can even effectively soften its impact.

FDR said as much in his Commonwealth Club Address when he argued that America's industrial plant has been built—that the great question of the age was one of distribution, of democratizing and taming capitalism. FDR was not entirely correct, as we have learned since then that capitalism is always prepared to exploit new developmental opportunities. The industrial age is replaced by the information age, which no doubt will be supplanted by new environmental technologies. There will always be room for expansion—the plant may never be finished. But there will also always be a need to democratize it, and this was the great failing of the Roosevelt administration in practice during the Second World War, the post-war reconversion to peacetime production, and subsequent periods of deregulation in later administrations. This is a mistake we cannot afford to keep repeating. There is space in the New Deal theory to reject the absolute connection between the "free market" and a substantive, moral conception of democracy and freedom. The market is a tool to be used in the service of higher ends—and as long as it proves to be an effective tool it should be utilized. However, its position is to be one of service, not dominance. It is to be held accountable to the goals of the nation since its natural inclination to expand and accumulate without reference to larger questions of the common good is harmful, if not self-destructive (to say nothing of the forgotten fact that corporations are chartered by the public for the purpose of serving a public good). New Deal theory possesses the counter-symbols, heroes, and folklore necessary to make that case—that even if we accept the presence of capital in our lives, it need not be the subject of that system.[89]

The Theory of Practice

When leaders seize power by a virtue of a philosophy of disillusionment, they become lost in that greatest of all illusions, the beauty and sanctity of the bold exercise of power, unhampered by humanitarian or other contradictory ideal.

—Thurman Arnold[90]

The New Deal's theory of practice has important anti-democratic elements, and can perhaps best be considered a theory of manipulative, rather than deliberative democracy. In this it is at odds with its more rigorous republican ideals. On the one hand, meaningful citizenship, education, and participation offer a way out of both a vacuous consumerism and the dominance of capitalism. On the other hand, while ideals need to set directions, they cannot serve as an empirical guide, especially when the reality is so far removed from the ideal. This is as true of democracy as it is of anything else. And the New Deal understood that without power progressive ideas cannot be institutionalized. Of course we must not lose sight of our ends in the pursuit of power, and it is important that we identify boundaries we refuse to cross. Likewise it is vital that we learn to identify when compromise is necessary and when it will set back a goal or movement. But keeping our hands "clean" and refusing to recognize the presence of necessity, the price politics forces us to pay, carries with it a great cost—it hands the field over to the enemy, negating a progressive vision and enabling the alternative. The costs of failure are extraordinarily high, too high to justify the refusal to engage.

When it comes to winning elections and acquiring power the Arnold strain in New Deal thought comes to the fore (although not exclusively, as figures like Wallace, ER, and even FDR never stopped looking at elections as an educative moment). The political debate central to a healthy democracy has less to do with discovering an objective common good than with inspiring your own side to action. Education is a less effective electoral technique than manipulation. Citizens should be approached as irrational human beings in search of a good story, not rational calculators of objective interests. Sometimes the only difference between a demagogue and statesmen is whether or not you agree with their politics. In this regard the New Deal is situated in a long tradition running through figures like Walter Lippmann to contemporary figures like George Lakoff and Drew Westin.

But while the New Deal advocates a more Machiavellian conception of politics, the Machiavellian attitude is at bottom a cynical one, rejecting principles and replacing them with the glorification of power, and this is a position the New Deal does not embrace. While Arnold perhaps overstated his case when he argued that the folklore of America makes totalitarianism impossible, it is worth remembering that the New Deal comes firmly out of the enlightenment tradition that tempers its pursuit of mastery with limits imposed by human rights, human decency, and modesty. Skepticism about truth claims has been built into the liberal tradition since at least Locke's *Letter Concerning Toleration.* The major difference between Arnold and previous thinkers is his anthropological tone. Most of the great liberal theorists were writing works of political advocacy. Locke, Bentham, Paine, the Federalists, Jefferson, and Mill were all publishing texts designed to actively influence public debate, not provide a textbook analysis of the way politics actually functioned. Principle is not given pride of place for the anthropological observer of human institutions, but it is of great consequence for the advocate. Arnold is no different here. He has been criticized for his instrumental approach to theory, but in practice the only difference between Arnold and the thinkers mentioned above is the transparency of his motives. *Political* theory is not only a diagnostic tool. It is also a form of propaganda, of advertisement. We need to have theory because it provides the romance that motivates and inspires. "Men do not fight and die except for extremes...Men cannot fight over practical things. They do not march and parade and develop their heroes in a common-sense atmosphere."[91] If the progressive does not deliver the marching orders the reactionary will.

It is the job of the observer to strip himself of illusions, but the advocate needs to believe in symbols in order to exercise leadership. People need to be preached to, and in order to preach you need a message. The message may be the most valuable weapon available to reformers, and so theory, Arnold argues, needs to be a weapon through which we accomplish practical goals—not a God to bow down before.

> [T]he belief that there is something peculiarly sacred about the logical content of these principles, that organizations must be molded to them, instead of the principles being molded to organizational needs, is often the very thing which prevents these principles from functioning. The greatest destroyer of ideals is he who believes in them so strongly that he cannot fit them to practical needs.[92]

Principles must not prevent us from making intelligent political decisions. Reformers must allow compromises with the Devil, and they must have the courage to allow for experimentation—to try new methods and be willing to abandon old ones no longer effective. "They [principles] must be supports and defenses; they cannot be guides."[93] Theory can serve as a regulatory ideal, but we must take pains to make sure it does not become reified.

Given the utterly functional nature of this view of politics it is of great importance to learn when not to compromise, when to take the principled stand. In part this is a question of art—of learning to sense the long-term effects of a decision on an organization, a movement, a constituency, or a cause. People wielding political power are bound to the short term by necessity, but masterful princes will also learn how to craft a larger vision out of an immediate moment, to give direction to the necessity that controls us. Any ideology making space for compromise must have this view at heart. As Bronner reminds us, "[t]he compromises involved in bringing the welfare state into existence were less simply concessions to the existing order than part of an overriding attempt to change it."[94] This is a test that, from a progressive standpoint, FDR's regressive social security tax passes, as it led to the expansion of a program that became the backbone of our welfare state.

The New Deal argued that the progressive had to take the political moment seriously—that they had to recognize the constraints imposed by necessity, and the costs of ignoring those constraints. It asks them to walk a very narrow tightrope, where principled commitments inform their actions without letting ideological purity (especially romantic attachments to the ideal of democratic engagement interfere with the need to win elections and institutionalize reforms. If that meant prioritizing what can be accomplished, so be it. If it requires working with political machines, greasing the wheels with patronage and pork, so be it. An overriding emphasis on purity becomes the worst kind of selfishness, as clean hands can carry an enormous social cost. But at the same time reformers must avoid being seduced by the power that they seek. They have to learn to resist making power an end, rather than a means to an end. They must always be aware of when the means utilized become destructive of the goals pursued. But above all else they have to learn that politics has no endpoint, that any moment of rest is time in which the enemy is regrouping. While the Left slept and fought amongst itself the Right rearmed. The price progressives have paid has been severe.

Conclusion

Progressive Government, by its very terms, must be a living and a growing thing, that the battle for it is never ending and that if we let up for one single moment or one single year, not merely do we stand still but we fall back in the march of civilization.

—Franklin Roosevelt[95]

The conservative assessment of the New Deal proved to be more accurate than the more critical view of the New Left. The later saw the New Deal as a moderate, limited program—reformist and essentially conservative. This is true only insofar as we forget just how radical the founding enlightenment ideals of the nation are, and that the New Deal represented not only the conservation of those values, but actually attempted to bring them into a fuller existence. As such, the conservative fear of the New Deal as "inherently expansive and potentially unlimited"[96] turned out to have a clearer sense of the logic of the New Deal and its concerns for security and happiness than many of its left-leaning critics.

It is true that its logic has had unforeseen consequences. As Miroff observes, "An authentic democratic leader, Roosevelt nonetheless fostered a number of developments that would plague modern American democracy, an overweening presidency, a massive bureaucratic state riddled with special interests fiefdoms, a military leviathan."[97] These are serious problems, and represent a practical failure on the part not only of the New Deal, but also of progressive reformers, conservative reactionaries, and the American people. They reflect a failure on the part of our leaders to articulate the necessity of institutional structures that can protect the meaningful exercise of liberty and the pursuit of happiness, a failure on the part of the people to demand them, and a failure of both to police them.

What is lost by many progressives at every point in history is the reality that politics is a permanent condition, especially in a democracy where the overwhelming majority of people cannot be expected to comprehend the totality of their system, whether due to a lack of ability, education, focus, or time. If citizens cannot be relied on to have a rational understanding of their interests, progressive elites need to recognize and accept that it is necessary to engage in a permanent war, fought in part by finding and utilizing emotionally resonant symbolic language, persuasive frames, and effective storytelling capable of generating enthusiasm, relevance, and existential attachment. Today the United States possesses one history but two well-developed sets of interpretive folklore, and the successful reformer must constantly update and utilize those categories in order to frame their policy preferences in a compelling way. There are many competing visions of the national interest. It can be grounded in social justice, free markets, exclusive purity or inclusive development. Any one of these is capable of capturing the national imagination, precisely because that imagination lacks fixed meaning. The development of a common good, of a unifying vision, is something that must be constructed, contingent on political choices and political realities, not something ontologically present within a social order just waiting to be discovered.

The Right came to learn this lesson much more effectively than the Left, and its remarkable success over the last forty years, both in terms of framing policy discussions and developing the institutional infrastructure to transmit that message, has been well documented. The sheer disconnect between their theory and reality speaks to their skill at framing, at utilizing their folklore to obscure the divide. The Left, constantly swimming upstream in an ideologically conservative country, could not afford to cede that ground that it did. Part of the problem is that for many of its leaders politics was subsumed under the moral ideal of democracy, in the desire to have a "true" politics somehow devoid of interest, pandering, and electioneering.[98] But this separation has always been an abstraction—interest and power exist whether or not space is allotted for them in theory. What the New Deal understood is that ideal of democracy can only be approached through the medium of politics. We must think of political life as something to navigate, rather than rail against.

Burns' portrait of Roosevelt is clear on this. The title *The Lion and the Fox*, with its echoes of Machiavelli, was aptly chosen.

> Roosevelt was not an absolute moralist about means because, whatever his
> hopes or illusions about man's possible redemption and ultimate goodness and

reasonableness, he had few illusions about man's nature...The practical statesman or man of affairs encounters ambitions and passions in his daily experience that put man in a strong, harsh light...Roosevelt overcame these men because he liked and wanted power and, even more, because he wanted to defend the position of strength from which he could lead and teach the people. To seize and hold power, to defend that position, he got down into the dusty arena and grappled with rival leaders on their own terms. So sure was he of the rightness of his aims that he was willing to use Machiavellian means; and his moral certainties made him all the more effective in the struggle. To the idealists who cautioned him he responded again and again that gaining power—winning elections—was the first, indispensable task.[99]

There is, ultimately, no way around this. While there is an important place for abstraction—any movement needs ends to strive for and poetry to inspire it—that theory must enter into a conversation with politics. Abstraction must always be contextualized, and the fact that the context is frequently frustrating and distasteful means the political actor has to be prepared to get his hands dirty, to lower his expectations about what is possible, even while pushing the boundaries of the possible ever closer towards the ideal. It asks a great deal of our political leaders, which is why great leaders are so rare.

We live in a democracy, however imperfect, which means some of the failure of the Left to build a more just social order needs to be placed on the backs of the American people. The problem with democracy is that people can always choose the regressive option, and liberal democrats are bound to honor that decision. While the political structures that exist militate against progressivism, those structures themselves reflect political choices made and ratified by the American people. There is a certain degree of path dependency here, but this does not tell the whole story. We are constrained by the decisions of the past, but no door to public action is ever fully closed. That is the promise of democracy—the realization that justice is ultimately an act of collective will. And we have failed to will it. We have in important ways authored our own political alienation by refusing to hold our leaders accountable, by not challenging the presence of interest in the system, by rejecting the narratives and frames that offer a more abundant world.

In this respect the old progressive catch all, education, turns out to be the answer, as flawed an answer as it is. Or, more accurately, education in conjunction with a manipulative politics. True democracy will only come with education, but true democracy also cannot wait for citizens to be educated. Achieving democracy will take organization, electioneering, and all the rest. Without this we'll be trapped on our front porch in Hyde Park chatting with our neighbors about how much better things would be if we were in charge—self-righteous and impotent. It can be argued that endorsing a *political* political theory is dangerous, and of course it is. Politics is fundamentally about the distribution of power, and power is dangerous. Politics is war by other means. And so we need to ensure that our leaders are sufficiently liberal (in the modest, limited, skeptical sense) to know the limits of their own power, skillful enough to master their environment, committed enough to do what is necessary, wise enough to be able to navigate the short term without abandoning a broader vision, and finally, that we are collectively vigilant enough to hold them accountable when they fail. It is a tall order, but such is the reality of political life, and ignoring this simply cedes terrain to the enemy. The New Deal fought to hold that line and there is much we can learn from it.

The Founders argued that with good institutions politics becomes automatic, that in essence institutions negate politics by turning it from art to science. The Progressives privileged the need for good men and tried to craft a system capable of producing good men. They concerned themselves with "cleaning up" politics and taking steps to make sure that "the people" ruled. The New Deal, building on these insights, understood that a just society requires all this and more; good men leading good institutions checked by good organizations, alongside a definition of good elastic enough to account for political life and strong enough to not snap under the pressure. Our house has always divided against itself, and the protestations of Lincoln to the contrary, it always will. As Madison reminds us, this is the nature of a free society. Conflict is a symptom of liberty. The health of our nation and its governing theory is the ability of its foundations to hold against the strain, to embrace the political and the good at the same time, to build institutions that are strong enough to endure and dynamic enough to change.

Notes

1. Attributed to FDR.
2. Conventional wisdom holds, after all, that the rise of identity politics and the claims of previously marginalized minority groups and women played a major role in the unraveling of the New Deal coalition, driving socially conservative but economically liberal working people into the arms of conservatism.
3. Reinhold Niebuhr. Quoted in Young, *Liberalism*, 182.
4. See Reich's *Supercapitalism* for an excellent discussion of the limitations of traditional progressive policies like minimum wages and employer provided health insurance in our contemporary service economy. Reich never abandons the end those policies serve, but confronts head-on their limited applicability with our current economic structures.
5. Frisch, *Franklin Roosevelt*, 16-17.
6. As Barry Karl argues, "The heated language from both left and right in the years 1931-1933 did not reflect Middle-American opinion. Middle America was solidly behind the establishment of some sense of continuity, and control of American economic life by a strong central government not part of the useable past." Karl, *Uneasy*, 120.
7. Our economy fails us because of greedy CEOs, not the structure of corporate capitalism. Our political system fails to represent us because of crooked politicians and overreaching bureaucrats, not the way our institutions are currently structured.

8. The aide said that people like him were "in what we call the reality-based community," which he defined as people who "believe that solutions emerge from your judicious study of discernible reality...That's not the way the world really works anymore," he continued. "We're an empire now, and when we act, we create our own reality. And while you're studying that reality—judiciously, as you will—we'll act again, creating other new realities, which you can study too, and that's how things will sort out. We're history's actors...and you, all of you, will be left to just study what we do." Ron Suskind, "Faith, Certainty, and the Presidency of George W. Bush," *The New York Times Magazine*, 17 Oct. 2004.

9. Howard Zinn, "Beyond the New Deal," *The Nation*. 7 April, 2008, http://www.thenation.com/doc/20080407/zinn.

10. Canton, "Progressivism,"179-181.

11. The logic behind Bush's 2001 tax rebates—his attempt to return the 'people's money' to them.

12. Howard Zinn, "Introduction" in Zinn, xvi. Zinn himself has come to look more favorably upon the New Deal in the intervening years. While still cognizant of its limitations, he argued recently "in today's climate of endless war and uncontrolled greed, drawing upon the heritage of the 1930s would be a huge step forward." Zinn, "Beyond."

13. Zinn, "Introduction," xxviii. Others, like Barry Karl, argue (correctly, I think) that whatever radical potential was present during the early years of the Depression was born more of self-defense than a desire for transformation.

14. See Lipset and Marks, "*Here*," 205-235. Michael Harrington concluded that had the Socialists abandoned electoral politics and focused on unions the movement would have had far more staying power. The communists were more influential than the socialists by largely avoiding the sectarianism that kept the Socialists out of the Democratic Party, and embracing the Popular Front organizational principle, but again their efforts were primarily successful to the extent to which they acted as a reformist organization, a left-wing constituency within the Democratic Party. At their peak they claimed only one hundred thousand members. The fact that the turnover rate was as high as 30 percent indicated a high degree of dissatisfaction amongst new members as well.

15. Zinn, "Introduction," xvi.

16. Morton Keller, "The New Deal and Progressivism: A Fresh Look," in Milkis and Mileur, *Great Society*, 317.

17. Jerome Mileur, "The Great Society and the Demise of New Deal Liberalism," Milkis and Mileur, in *Great Society*, 441.

18. Alonzo Hamby, "Progressivism: A Century of Change and Rebirth," in Milkis and Mileur, *Progressivism*, 70.

19. Some of these splits reflect failures within the primary movements to not make space for new groups within the movement. Stokely Carmichael's response to the question 'what is the proper place for women in the civil rights movement?' (his answer—on their backs) makes the desire to separate understandable.

20. Benjamin Barber, *Consumed: How Markets Corrupt Children, Infantilize Adults, and Swallow Citizens Whole*, (New York: W.W. Norton & Company, 2007). 128-129.

21. In theory, if not in practice. In fact the wealthy display a great deal of class consciousness (in terms of voting for and supporting politicians and policies that support their class interest) in practice, even if it is not necessarily recognized for what it is.

22. Remember that the most successful reform movements of the past sought to reintegrate Americans into this middle-class order. The serious challenges to its fundamental structure were always found at the margins.

23. The central point here is that this is how Americans identified themselves. Why they chose that formulation is less important politically (at least in the short term) than the fact that the New Deal (or progressives today) was forced to confront the reality of that choice. Of course the presence of coercion in that choice may indicate that we will be receptive to other options if they become available.

24. Tocqueville, *Democracy*, 643.

25. Brinkley, *Reform*, 4.

26. Lawrence Glickman discusses this connection at length throughout *Buying Power*.

27. Ralph Nader led a rising consumer consciousness movement, but it was crushed by a rising business consciousness that opposed it through the courts, through political contributions, and all the usual methods. Any emerging group is more likely to succeed when the government protects its ability to organize, and unlike with labor in the 30s, that failed to happen here. Nace, *Gangs*, 142-143. The most promising arena today for consumer consciousness is found in calls for 'greener,' more environmentally sustainable forms of consumption, but there seems to be little mass movement to institutionalize this beyond individual consumer preferences.

28. Bernard Sternsher, *Rexford Tugwell and the New Deal*, (New Brunswick: Rutgers University Press, 1964), 161.

29. Glickman, *Buying*, 192.

30. Bronner, *Possible*, 155.

31. GM President Charlie Wilson (nominated by Eisenhower for Secretary of Defense) testifying before the Senate Armed Services Committee in 1953. Emphasis mine.

32. Nace, *Gangs*, 222.

33. Although, as Claude Fisher argues, all that really changed was that it became easier for Americans to indulge in what was a tendency to celebrate consumption that had been a part of America since the beginning. What we see in the late 19th and 20th century is a democratization of consumption—the expansion of a preexisting desire. Fisher, *Made*, 8-9 and 60.

34. Daniel Mahoney, *Bertrand de Jouvenel: The Conservative Liberal and the Illusion of Modernity*, (Wilmington: ISI Books, 2005), 130.

35. McWilliams, *Fraternity*, 551.

36. Robert Costanza, "Our Three Decade Recession," *LA Times*, 10 March 2008, http://www.latimes.com/news/opinion/la-oe-costanza10mar10,0,5656929.story

37. Lash, *Eleanor and Franklin*, 721.

38. McWilliams, *Fraternity*, 26.

39. McWilliams, *Fraternity*, 547.

40. Mettler, Suzanne, "Social Citizens and Separate Sovereignties: Governance in the New Deal Welfare State" in Milkis and Mileur, *New Deal*, 233.

41. McWilliams, *Fraternity*, 622.

42. McWilliams, *Fraternity*, 555-556.

43. Arnold, *Symbols*, 232-233.

44. McDonagh, Eileen, "Race," 262.

45. Morone, *Wish*, 130.

46. Tocqueville, *Democracy*, 804.

47. Tocqueville, *Democracy*, 805-806.

48. Tocqueville, *Democracy*, 807.

49. Tocqueville, *Democracy*, 648.

50. Wallace, " Choice," 172.

51. Badger notes that the New Deal bureaucracies were highly open and accessible to both their clients and their critics. Badger, *New Deal*, 304.

52. Miroff, *Icons*, 253.

53. Miroff, *Icons*, 253.

54. McWilliams, *Fraternity*, 550.

55. Although as James Patterson notes, 'Roosevelt's policies seemed at the time to strengthen the foundations of the Democratic Party. The social welfare policies of the New Deal attracted to the party millions of working-class people and minorities who had earlier voted Republican or (in most cases) had not voted at all. New Deal patronage strengthen Democratic urban machines that stimulated larger turnouts in many cities. James Patterson, "The Rise of Rights and Rights Consciousness," in *Contesting Democracy*, ed. Byron Shafter and Anthony Badger, (Lawrence: University Press of Kansas, 2001), 206.

56. Clearly social movements can bring together disparate organizations in a manner similar to parties, although it is not clear they would enjoy the same legitimacy.

57. It is not my purpose here to dispute the tactic of using the courts to effect social change, especially when the courts often represent a last resort response to the failure of the democratic process to bring about justice, but this approach certainly marked a change in the tactics and perhaps even the nature of social movements and interests.

58. Mileur, "Legacy," 278.

59. See McWilliams, "Democracy and the Citizen: Community, Dignity, and the Crisis of Contemporary Politics in America" in *Redeeming Democracy in America*, ed. Patrick Deneen and Susan McWilliams, (Lawrence: University of Kansas Press, 2011)

60. Stephen Bronner, *Socialism Unbound*, 2nd ed., (Boulder: Westview Press, 2001), 168.

61. James Madison, "Federalist 10," *The Federalist Papers*, ed. George Carey and James McClellan, (Dubuque: Kendall/Hunt Publishing Company, 1990), 43-44.

62. Figures like Theodore Lowi, in his seminal *The End of Liberalism: The Second Republic of the United States*, (New York: W.W. Norton & Company, 1979), argues that interest group liberalism is incapable of establishing justice and securing the long-term goals at the heart of New Deal theory. He rejects that such a system can be self-correcting and is uncomfortable with its adversarial posture. He sees the bureaucratization of government that it entails as undesirable, even harmful, the source of much of the modern alienation we feel towards our government. It is a damning, and powerful critique, although one focused more on the New Deal's descendents than the New Deal itself. My response to Lowi, following Madison in "Federalist 10" and Thurman Arnold more generally, is that in the absence of other forms of political organization capable of governing a global, interdependent economy and welfare state, our focus needs to be on democratizing as much as possible the structures that already exist. I also question (as would the New Deal) his assertion that interest group liberalism makes "no formal specification of means or of ends" (Lowi, *End*, 63). The way the New Deal understood its relationship to interest groups was sometimes adversarial, sometimes sympathetic, and sometimes symbiotic, but they checked, ratified, or contested a public vision of the good, rather than supplanting it. Likewise, his concern that "modern law has become a series of instructions to administrators rather than a series of commands to citizens" is well taken, but it certainly is not clear that Congress or other bodies would be capable of writing law that was up to the challenges faced by modern bureaucracies, nor is it clear that the public would accept them, since the length of a Congressional bill is frequently held up as an

evidence of the government's sinister motives. Nevertheless, his call for more juridical democracy, with an increase in transparency, the sunsetting of grants of power, and more formalized rule making, are all well taken, and not necessarily incompatible with the New Deal's understanding of interest group liberalism.

63. McWilliams, *Fraternity*, 558.

64. De Jouvenel, *Power*, 291.

65. Quoted in Morone, *Wish*, 132.

66. Quoted in Goldman, 347.

67. Goldman, 351.

68. Zinn, "Intro," xxii.

69. Of course this in turn is a product of political calculation and manipulation, but New Deal theory assumes every moment is contestable.

70. Bronner, *Possible*, 153.

71. Although Roosevelt did veto the 1943 Smith Connally Bill, which was written to curb labor's right to strike. Nevertheless, he was overridden by a Congress no longer interested in New Deal aims. Brand, *Traitor*, 757.

72. Lichtenstein, *Labor*, 82.

73. Similar efforts to allow smaller businesses to reconvert back to the production of civilian goods before the end of the war (granting a competitive advantage for the peacetime conversion) were also beaten back by big business.

74. For instance, FDR's success in the 1936 election was derived primarily from mobilizing new voters, those previously alienated from the political process, rather than convincing old partisans to chance their loyalties. Keller, *Regimes*, 208.

75. Adam Smith, *The Wealth of Nations*, 310.

76. Quoted in Brinkley, *Reform*, 47.

77. Burns, *Lion*, 48. Not that there were necessarily other alternatives available to him if he had.

78. Burns, *Lion*, 481.

79. Brinkley, *Reform*, 90.

80. Goldman, *Destiny*, 465.

81. Miroff, *Icons*, 268-269. Although a hostile congress greatly limited the authority of his office, Wallace's appointment to secretary of commerce for Roosevelt's final term indicated a willingness on the part of FDR and the New Deal to challenge the wartime dominance of the corporation, but the possibilities of that challenge died with Roosevelt.

82. Jeffries, *War*, 55.

83. Brinkley, *Reform*, 7-8.

84. Brinkley, *Reform*, 122. Although there was no real desire amongst the electorate or the government to engage these questions when other methods of dealing with the consequences, rather than the cause, of capital's power were available.

85. And this is not the same thing as Chief Justice Taft arguing "We have to hit [labor] hard every little while, because they are continuously violating the law and depending on threats and violence to accomplish their purposes." Nace, *Gangs*, 130.

86. Nace, *Gangs*, 130. 50 percent of 14th amendment cases involved corporations. One half of one percent involved blacks.

87. Nace, *Gangs*, 171.

88. Brinkley, *Reform*, 268.

89. Bronner, *Unbound*, 155.

90. Arnold, *Symbols*, 250.

91. Arnold, *Folklore*, 336.

92. Arnold, *Folklore*, 393.
93. Arnold, *Symbols*, 232.
94. Bronner, *Unbound*, xv.
95. FDR's renomination speech for the Governorship of NY. Quoted in Burns, *Lion*, 119-120.
96. Robert Eden, "Introduction: A Legacy of Questions," Eden, 4.
97. Miroff, *Icons*, 233.
98. Mileur, "Legacy," 273.
99. Burns, *Lion*, 476-477.

Selected Bibliography

Abbot, Philip. *The Exemplary President*. Amherst: University of Massachusetts Press, 1990.

Arnold, Thurman. *Symbols of Government*. New Haven: Yale University Press, 1935.

———. *The Folklore of Capitalism*. Washington, D.C.: Beard Books, 2000 (reprinting 1937).

———. *The Bottlenecks of Business*. New York: Reynal & Hitchcock, 1940.

———. *Democracy and Free Enterprise*. Norman: University of Oklahoma Press, 1942.

———. *Fair Fights and Foul*. New York: Harcourt, Brace & World, Inc., 1965.

———. *Voltaire and the Cowboy: The Letters of Thurman Arnold*, ed. Gene Gressley. Boulder: Colorado Associated University Press, 1977.

Badger, Anthony. *The New Deal: The Depression Years, 1933-1940*. New York: Hill and Wang, 1989.

———. "The Limits of Federal Power and Social Politics, 1910-1955," in Shafer and Badger, *Contesting Democracy: Substance & Structure in American Political History: 1775-2000*.

Barber, Benjamin. *Consumed: How Markets Corrupt Children, Infantilize Adults, and Swallow Citizens Whole*. New York: W.W. Norton & Company, 2007.

Bernstein, Irving. *A Caring Society: The New Deal, the Worker, and the Great Depression*. Boston: Houghton Mifflin Company, 1985.

Biles, Roger. *A New Deal for the American People*. Dekalb: Northern Illinios University Press, 1991.

Black, Ruby. *Eleanor Roosevelt: A Biography*. New York: Duell, Sloan and Pearce, 1940.

Boesche, Roger. *Tocqueville's Road Map*. Lanham, M.D.: Lexington Books, 2006.

Brinkley, Alan. *The End of Reform*. New York: Vintage Books, 1996.

Brands, H.W. *Traitor to His Class: The Privileged Life and Radical Presidency of Franklin Delano Roosevelt*. New York: Doubleday, 2008.

Bronner, Stephen Eric. *Ideas in Action: Political Tradition in the Twentieth Century*. Lanham, M.D.: Rowman & Littlefield, 1999.

———. *Socialism Unbound*. 2nd ed. Boulder: Westview Press, 2001.

————. *Imagining the Possible: Radical Politics for Conservative Times*. New York: Routledge, 2002.

————. *Reclaiming the Enlightenment*. New York: Columbia University Press, 2004.

Burns, James MacGregor. *Roosevelt: The Lion and the Fox*. New York: Harcourt Brace & World, 1956.

————. "FDR: Unsuccessful Improviser," in Hamby, *The New Deal: Analysis and Interpretation*.

Canton, Hiram. "Progressivism and Conservatism During the New Deal: A Reinterpretation of American Political Traditions," in Eden, *The New Deal and Its Legacy: Critique and Reappraisal*.

Clarke, Jeanne Nienaber. *Roosevelt's Warrior*. Baltimore: The Johns Hopkins Press, 1996.

Cohen, Adam. *Nothing to Fear: FDR's Inner Circle and the Hundred Days That Created Modern America*. New York: The Penguin Press, 2009.

Coleman, Robert. "The World of Interventionism, 1880-1940," in Eden, *The New Deal and Its Legacy: Critique and Reappraisal*.

Commager, Henry Steele. *The American Mind*. New Haven: Yale University Press, 1950.

Conkin, Paul. *The New Deal*. Arlington Heights: AHM Publishing, 1975.

Cook, Blanche Wiesen. *Eleanor Roosevelt: Volume I 1884-1933*. New York: Viking, 1992.

————. *Eleanor Roosevelt: Volume II 1933-1938*. New York: Viking, 1999.

Culver, John and John Hyde. *American Dreamer: A Life of Henry A. Wallace*. New York: W.W. Norton & Company, 2000.

Davenport, Walter. "Money in the Mailbox." *Colliers* (10 Feb. 1934) in Freidel, *The New Deal and the American People*.

Dawson, Nelson Lloyd. *Louis D. Brandeis, Felix Frankfurter, and the New Deal*. Hamden: Archon Book, 1980.

Dewey, John. *The Public and Its Problems*. Athens: Swallow Press, 1927.

————. *Individualism Old and New*. Amherst: Prometheus Books, 1999.

Dickstein, Morris. *Dancing in the Dark: A Cultural History of the Great Depression*. New York: W.W. Norton & Company. 2009

Doenecke, Justus D. and Mark A Stoler. *Debating Franklin D. Roosevelt's Foreign Polices, 1933-1945*. Lanham, M.D.: Rowman & Littlefield Publishers, Inc., 2005.

Donner, Wendy. " Mill's Utilitarianism," in Skorupski, *The Cambridge Companion*.

Downey, Kirstin. *The Woman Behind the New Deal: The Life of Frances Perkins, FDR's Secretary of Labor and His Moral Conscience*. New York: Doubleday, 2009.

Eads, George. "Airliner Competitive Conduct in a Less Regulated Environment: Implications for Antitrust," in Himmelberg, *Business and Government in America Since 1870: The New Deal and Corporate Power*.

Edelman, Murray. *Politics as Symbolic Action*. Chicago: Markham Publishing Company, 1971.

————. *Political Language: Words That Succeed and Polices That Fail*. New York: Academic Press, 1977.

————. *Constructing the Political Spectacle*. Chicago: The University of Chicago Press, 1988.

————. *The Politics of Misinformation*. Cambridge: Cambridge University Press, 2001

Eden, Robert, ed. *The New Deal and Its Legacy: Critique and Reappraisal*. New York: Greenwood Press, 1989.

————. "Introduction: A Legacy of Questions," in Eden, *The New Deal and Its Legacy: Critique and Reappraisal*.

———. "On the Origins of the Regime of Pragmatic Liberalism: John Dewey , Adolf A Berle, and FDR's Commonwealth Club Address of 1932." *Studies in American Political Development.* Spring 1993, p. 74-150.

Edsforth, Ronald. *The New Deal: America's Response to the Great Depression.* Malden: Blackwell Publishing, 2000.

Eisenach, Eldon J. *The Lost Promise of Progressivism.* Lawrence: The University Press of Kansas, 1994.

———, ed. *Mill and the Moral Character of Liberalism.* University Park: The Pennsylvania State University Press, 1998.

———. "Introduction," in Eisenach, *Mill and the Moral Character of Liberalism.*

Faludi, Susan. *Stiffed: The Betrayal of the American Man.* New York: Harper Collins, 1999.

Fischer, Claude. *Made in America: A Social History of American Culture and Character.* Chicago: The University of Chicago Press, 2010.

Fischer, David Hackett. *Liberty and Freedom.* New York: Oxford University Press 2005.

Foner, Eric. *The Story of American Freedom.* New York: Norton, 1998

Freidel, Frank, ed. *The New Deal and the American People.* Englewood Cliffs: Prentice-Hall, Inc., 1964.

———. "The New Deal in Historical Perspective," in Hamby, *The New Deal: Analysis and Interpretation.*

———. *Franklin D. Roosevelt: A Rendezvous with Destiny.* New York: Little Brown and Co, 1990.

Frisch, Morton. *Franklin D. Roosevelt: The Contribution of the New Deal to American Political Thought and Practice.* Boston: Twayne Publsihers, 1975.

———. "An Appraisal of Roosevelt's Legacy: How the Moderate Welfare State Transcended the Tension between Progressivism and Socialism," in Eden, *The New Deal and Its Legacy: Critique and Reappraisal.*

Glickman, Lawrence: *Buying Power: A History of Consumer Activism in America.* Chicago: University of Chicago Press, 2009.

Goldman, Eric. *Rendezvous with Destiny: A History of Modern American Reform.* Chicago: Knopf, 1952.

Goodwyn, Lawrence. *The Populist Moment: A Short History of the Agrarian Revolt in America.* Oxford: Oxford University Press, 1978.

Graham Jr., Otis. "The New Deal and the Progressive Tradition," in Hamby, *The New Deal: Analysis and Interpretation.*

Hamby, Alonozo, ed. *The New Deal: Analysis and Interpretation.* New York: Longman Inc., 1981.

———. "Historians and the Challenge of the New Deal," in Hamby, *The New Deal: Analysis and Interpretation.*

———. *Liberalism and Its Challengers: From FDR to Bush.* New York: Oxford University Press, 1992.

———. "Progressivism: A Century of Change and Rebirth," in Milkis and Mileur, *Progressivism and the New Democracy.*

Hartz, Louis. *The Liberal Tradition in America.* San Diego: Harcourt, Brace, and Co., 1955.

Hareven, Tamra. *Eleanor Roosevelt: An American Conscience.* Chicago: Quadrangle Books, 1968.

Hawley, Ellis. "The New Deal State and the Anti-Bureaucratic Tradition," in Eden, *The New Deal and Its Legacy: Critique and Reappraisal.*

————. "The New Deal and the Problem of Monopoly," in Hamby, *The New Deal: Analysis and Interpretation.*

Heath, Jim. "American War Mobilization and the Use of Small Manufactures, 1939-1943," in Himmelberg, *Business and Government in America since 1870: The New Deal and Corporate Power.*

Himmelberg, Robert, ed. *Business and Government in America since 1870: The New Deal and Corporate Power.* New York: Garland Publishing, Inc., 1994.

————. *The Great Depression and the New Deal.* Westport: Greenwood Press, 2001.

Hoff-Wilson, Joan and Marjorie Lightman, eds. *Without Precedent: The Life and Career of Eleanor Roosevelt.* Bloomington: Indiana University Press, 1984.

Hofstadter, Richard. *The Age of Reform.* New York: Vintage Books, 1955.

Horton, Carol A. *Race and the Making of American Liberalism.* Oxford: Oxford University Press, 2005.

Humphrey, Hubert. *The Political Philosophy of the New Deal.* Baton Rouge: Louisiana State University Press, 1970.

Jefferson, Thomas. *Thomas Jefferson: Writings*, ed. Merrill D. Peterson. USA: Library of America, 1984.

Jeffries, John. *Wartime America: The World War II Home Front.* Chicago: Ivan Dees, 1996.

Jouvenel, Bertrand de. *On Power.* Indianapolis: Liberty Fund, 1993.

Karl, Barry. *The Uneasy State: The United States From 1915-1945* Chicago: The University of Chicago Press, 1983.

Kearney, Edward. *Thurman Arnold: Social Critic* Albuquerque: University of New Mexico Press, 1970.

Kearny, James. *Anna Eleanor Roosevelt: The Evolution of a Reformer.* Boston: Houghton Mifflin Company, 1968.

Keller, Morton. "The New Deal and Progressivism: A Fresh Look," in Milkis and Mileur, *The New Deal and the Triumph of Liberalism.*

————. *America's Three Regimes: A New Political History* (Oxford: Oxford University Press, 2007).

Kessler, Charles. "The Public Philosophy of the New Freedom and the New Deal," in Eden, *The New Deal and Its Legacy: Critique and Reappraisal.*

Kiplinger, W.M. "Why Business Men Fear Washington." *Scribner's* (October 1934), in Freidel, *The New Deal and the American People.*

Kleinman, Mark L. *A World of Hope, a World of Fear: Henry Wallace, Reinhold Niebuhr, and American Liberalism.* Columbia: Ohio State University, 2000.

Kramnick, Isaac and Theodore Lowi. *American Political Thought.* New York: Norton, 2009.

Landy, Marc. "Presidential Party Leadership and Party Realignment: FDR and the Making of the New Democratic Party," in Milkis and Mileur, *The New Deal and the Triumph of Liberalism.*

Lash, Joseph. *Life Was Meant to Be Lived: A Centenary Portrait of Eleanor Roosevelt.* New York: W.W. Norton & Company, 1984.

————. *Dealers and Dreamers: A New Look at the New Deal.* New York: Doubleday, 1988.

————. *Eleanor and Franklin.* New York: History Book Club, 2004.

Lasser, William. *Benjamin V. Cohen: Architect of the New Deal.* New Haven: Yale University Press, 2002

Lawson, Alan. *A Commonwealth of Hope: The New Deal Response to Crisis.* Baltimore: The Johns Hopkins University Press. 2006.

Lichtenstein, Nelson. *Labor's War at Home: The CIO in World War II.* Cambridge: Cambridge University Press, 1982.

Lillenthal, David E. *TVA: Democracy on the March.* New York: Harper & Row, 1944.

Lippmann, Walter. *The Phantom Public.* New Brunswick: Transaction Publishers, 1999.

Locke, John. *Two Treatises of Government,* ed. Peter Laslett. Cambridge: Cambridge University Press, 1988.

Leuchtenburg, William. *Franklin D. Roosevelt and the New Deal: 1932-1940.* New York: Harper Torchbooks, 1963.

Leuchtenburg, William. *The FDR Years: On Roosevelt and His Legacy.* New York: Columbia University Press, 1995.

Lipset, Seymour Martin and Gary Marks. *It Didn't Happen Here: Why Socialism Failed in the United States.* New York: W.W. Norton & Company, 2000.

Lowi, Theodore J. *The End of Liberalism: The Second Republic of the United States.* New York: W.W. Norton & Company, 1979.

Lubell, Samuel. "The Roosevelt Coalition," in Hamby, *The New Deal: Analysis and Interpretation.*

Machiavelli, Niccolo. *Selected Political Writings,* trans. David Wooton. Indianapolis: Hackett Publishing Company, Inc., 1994.

———. *The Prince,* trans. George Bull. London: Penguin Books, 2003.

Madison, James, et al. *The Federalist Papers.* Eds. George Carey and James McClellan. Dubuque: Kendall/Hunt Publishing Company,1990.

Mahoney, Daniel. *Bertrand de Jouvenel: The Conservative Liberal and the Illusion of Modernity.* Wilmington: ISI Books, 2005.

Markowitz, Norman. *The Rise and Fall of the People's Century.* New York: The Free Press, 1973.

McCormick, Ann O'Hare. "Vast Tides That Stir the Capital," in Freidel, *The New Deal and the American People.*

McDonagh, Eileen. "Race, Class, and Gender in the Progressive Era: Restructuring State and Society," in Milkis and Mileur, *Progressivism and the New Democracy.*

McGraw, Thomas K. "Business and Government: The Origins of the Adversary Relationship," in Himmelberg, *Business and Government in America Since 1870: The New Deal and Corporate Power.*

McGreer, Michael. *A Fierce Discontent: The Rise and Fall of the Progressive Movement in America 1870-1920.* New York: Free Press, 2003.

McMahon, Kevin J. *Reconsidering Roosevelt on Race.* Chicago: The University of Chicago Press, 2004.

McWilliams, Wilson Carey. *The Idea of Fraternity in America.* Berkeley: University of California Press, 1973.

———. "Standing At Armageddon: Morality and Religion in Progressive Thought." in Milkis and Mileur, *Progressivism and the New Democracy.*

———. *Redeeming Democracy in America.* Ed. Patrick Deneen and Susan McWilliams. Lawrence: University of Kansas Press, 2011.

Mettler, Suzanne. "Social Citizens and Separate Sovereignties: Governance in the New Deal Welfare State," in Milkis and Mileur, *The New Deal and the Triumph of Liberalism.*

Mileur, Jerome. "The Legacy of Reform: Progressive Government, Regressive Politics." in Milkis and Mileur, *Progressivism and the New Democracy.*

———. "The 'Boss': Franklin Roosevelt, the Democratic Party, and the Reconstitution of American Politics," in Milkis and Mileur, *The New Deal and the Triumph of Liberalism.*

———. "The Great Society and the Demise of New Deal Liberalism," in Milkis and Mileur, *The Great Society and the High Tide of Liberalism.*

Milkis, Sidney M. "New Deal Party Politics, Administrative Reform, and the Transformation of the American Constitution," in Eden, *The New Deal and Its Legacy: Critique and Reappraisal.*

———. *The President and the Parties.* USA: Oxford University Press, 1993.

———. "Franklin D. Roosevelt, the Economic Constitutional Order, and the New Politics of Presidential Leadership," in Milkis and Mileur, *The New Deal and the Triumph of Liberalism.*

———. "Lyndon Johnson: The Great Society, and the "Twilight" of the Modern Presidency," in Milkis and Mileur, *The Great Society and the High Tide of Liberalism.*

Milkis, Sidney and Jerome Mileur, eds. *Progressivism and the New Democracy.* Amherst: University of Massachusetts Press, 1999.

———, eds. *The New Deal and the Triumph of Liberalism.* Amherst: University of Massachusetts Press, 2002.

———, "Introduction: The New Deal, Then and Now," in Milkis and Mileur *The New Deal and the Triumph of Liberalism.*

———, eds. *The Great Society and the High Tide of Liberalism.* Amherst: University of Massachusetts Press, 2005.

Milkis, Sydney and Michael Nelson. *The American Presidency: Origins and Development, 1776-2002.* Washington D.C.: CQ Press, 2003.

Mill, John Stuart. *On Liberty.* Indianapolis: Hackett Publishing Company, 1978.

Miroff, Bruce. *Icons of Democracy.* Lawrence: University Press of Kansas, 2000.

Morone, James. *The Democratic Wish.* New Haven: Yale University Press, 1998.

———. *Hellfire Nation.* New Haven: Yale University Press, 2003.

Nace, Thomas. *Gangs of America.* San Francisco: Berrett-Koehler Publishers, Inc., 2005.

Neuberger, Richard. "America Talks Court." *Current History.* June 1937, in Freidel, *The New Deal and the American People*

Norton, Ann. *Republic of Signs: Liberal Theory and American Pop Culture.* Chicago: The University of Chicago Press, 1992.

Patterson, James T. "The Conservative Coalition," in Hamby, *The New Deal: Analysis and Interpretation.*

———. "The New Deal and American Federalism," in Hamby, *The New Deal: Analysis and Interpretation.*

———. "The Rise of Rights and Rights Consciousness in American Politics, 1930s-1970s," in Shafer and Hamby, *Contesting Democracy: Substance & Structure in American Political History: 1775-2000.*

Perkins, Frances. *The Roosevelt I Knew.* New York: Viking Press, 1946.

Phllips-Fein, Kim. *Invisible Hands: The Businessmen's Crusade Against the New Deal.* New York: W.W. Norton, 2009.

Piven, Frances Fox. *Challenging Authority: How Ordinary People Change America.* New York: Rowman & Littlefield Publishers, Inc., 2006.

Piven, Frances Fox and Richard A. Cloward. *Poor People's Movements: Why They Succeed, How They Fail.* New York: Vintage Books, 1979.

Plotke, David. *Building a Democratic Political Order: Reshaping American Liberalism in the 1930s and 1940s.* New York: Cambridge University Press, 1996.

Radosh, Ronald. "A Radical Critique: The Myth of the New Deal," in Hamby, *The New Deal: Analysis and Interpretation.*

Rahe, Paul, ed. *Machiavelli's Liberal Republican Legacy*. Cambridge: Cambridge University Press, 2006.

Rauch, Basil. *The History of the New Deal 1933-1938*. New York: Creative Age Press, 1944.

Reagan, Patrick D. *Designing a New America: The Origins of New Deal Planning 1890-1943*. Amherst: University of Massachusetts Press, 1999.

Rohr, John. "Constitutional Legitimacy and the Administrative State: A Reading of the Brownlow Commission Report," in Eden, *The New Deal: Analysis and Interpretation*.

Romansco, Albert. *The Politics of Recovery*. New York: Oxford University Press, 1983.

Roosevelt, Eleanor. *The Autobiography of Eleanor Roosevelt*. Boston: G.K. Hall & Co., 1937.

————. *The Moral Basis of Democracy* New York: Howell, Soskin & Co, 1940.

————. *If You Ask Me*. New York: D. Appleton-Century Company, Inc., 1946.

————. *This I Remember*. New York: Harper & Brothers, 1949.

————. *You Learn by Living*. New York: Harper & Brothers, 1960.

————. *My Day: The Best of Eleanor Roosevelt's Acclaimed Newspaper Column 1936-1962*, ed. David Emblidge. Da Capo Press, 2001.

————. *What I Hope to Leave Behind: The Essential Essays of Eleanor Roosevelt*. ed. Allida Black. New York: Brooklyn, 1995.

————. *Courage in a Dangerous World: The Political Writings of Eleanor Roosevelt*, ed. Allida Black. New York: Columbia University Press, 1999.

Roosevelt, Franklin. *FDR's Fireside Chats*, eds. Russell Buhite and David Levy. New York: Penguin Books, 1993.

————. *Great Speeches*, ed. John Grafton. New York: Dover Publications, 1999

Rosen, Elliot A. *Roosevelt, The Great Depression, and the Economics of Recovery*. Charlottesville: University of Virginia Press, 2005.

Rosenman, Samuel. *Working With Roosevelt*. New York. Da Capo Press, 1972.

Rosenof, Theodore. *Dogma, Depression, and the New Deal*. Port Washington: Kennikat Press, 1975.

Rosenof, Theodore. *Economics in the Long Run: New Deal Theorists and Their Legacies, 1933-1993*. Chapel Hill: The University of North Carolina Press, 1997.

Rosenzweig, Roy ed. *Who Built America: Working People and the Nation's Economy, Politics, Culture, and Society Vol. II* New York: Pantheon Books, 1992.

Ross, Mary. "Why Social Security?" Washington D.C.'s Social Security Board. 1936. Freidel.

Ryan, Alan. *John Dewey and the High Tide of American Liberalism*. New York: W.W. Norton & Company, 1995.

Reich, Robert. *Supercapitalism: The Transformation of Business, Democracy, and Everyday Life*. New York: Vintage Books, 2007.

Samuels, Warren. "Legal Realism and the Burden of Symbolism: The Correspondence of Thurman Arnold." 13 *Law & Society*, Summer 1979, 997-1011.

Shafer, Byron and Anthony Badger. *Contesting Democracy: Substance & Structure in American Political History: 1775-2000*. Lawrence: The University Press of Kansas, 2001

Scharf, Lois. *Eleanor Roosevelt: First Lady of American Liberalism*. Boston: Twayne Publishers, 1987.

Schlesinger Jr., Arthur. "FDR: Pragmatist-Democrat." Hamby.

Schwarz, Jordan. *Liberal: Adolf A Berle and the Vision of an American Era*. New York: The Free Press, 1987.

Shales, Amity. *The Forgotten Man: A New History of the Great Depression*. New York: Harper Collins, 2007.

Shogan, Robert. *Backlash: The Killing of the New Deal*. Chicago: Ivan R. Dee, 2006.

Sirevag, Torbjorn. *The Eclipse of the New Deal and the Fall of Vice-President Wallace, 1944*. New York: Garland Publishing, Inc, 1985.

Skorupski, John. ed. *The Cambridge Companion*. Cambridge: Cambridge University Press, 1998.

Sky, Theodore. *To Provide For the General Welfare*. Newark: University of Delaware Press, 2003.

Smith, Jean Edward. *FDR*. New York: Random House, 2007.

Smith, Rogers. *Civic Ideals*. New Haven: Yale University Press. 1997.

Sternsher, Bernard. *Rexford Tugwell and the New Deal*. New Brunswick: Rutgers University Press, 1964.

Stipelman, Brian. "The New Deal's Theory of Practice." *New Political Science* 32, no. 3, (June 2010): 237-260

Stucky, Mary. *Defining Americans: The Presidency and National Identity*. Lawrence: University Press of Kansas, 2004.

Sullivan, Patrice. *Days of Hope*. Chapel Hill: The University of North Carolina Press, 1996.

Sunstein, Cass. *The Second Bill of Rights: FDR's Unfinished Revolution and Why We Need It Now More Than Ever*. New York: Basic Books, 2004.

Suskind, Ron. "Faith, Certainty, and the Presidency of George W. Bush." *The New York Times Magazine*, 17 Oct. 2004.

Thompson, Michael. *Politics of Inequality: A Political History of the Idea of Economic Inequality in America*. New York: Columbia University Press, 2007

Tocqueville, Alexis de. *Democracy in America*. Trans. Gerald E. Bevan. London: Penguin Books, 2003.

Trachtenberg, Alan. *The Incorporation of America: Culture and Society in the Gilded Age*. New York: Hill and Wang, 2007.

Vincent, M.D. and Beulah Amidon. "NRA: A Trial Balance." Freidel.

Wallace, Henry. *New Frontiers*. New York: Reynal & Hitchcock, 1934.

———. *Statesmanship and Religion*. New York: Round Table Press, Inc., 1934.

———. *Whose Constitution?: An Inquiry into the General Welfare*. New York: Reynal & Hitchcock, 1936.

———. *Democracy Reborn*, ed. Russell Lord. New York: Da Capo Press, 1973.

Waller, Spencer Weber. *Thurman Arnold: A Biography*. New York: New York University Press, 2005.

Wandersee, Winifred. "ER and American Youth: Politics and Personality in a Bureaucratic Age." Hoff-Wilson.

Wettergreen, John. "The Regulatory Policy of the New Deal." Eden.

White, G. Edward. *The Constitution and the New Deal*. Cambridge: Harvard University Press, 2000.

White, Graham and John Maze. *Henry A. Wallace: His Search for a New World Order*. Chapel Hill: The University of North Carolina Press, 1995.

Wiebe, Robert. *The Search for Order: 1877-1920*. New York: Hill and Wang, 1967.

Wilson, Fred. "Mill on Psychology and the Moral Sciences." Skorupski.

Wolin, Sheldon. *Politics and Vision: Continuity and Innovation in Western Political Thought*. Expanded edition. Princeton: Princeton University Press, 2004.

———. *Democracy Inc.: Managed Democracy and the Specter of Inverted Totalitarianism*. Princeton: Princeton University Press, 2008.

Young, James. *Reconsidering American Liberalism: The Troubled Odyssey of the Liberal Idea*. Boulder: Westview Press, 1996.

Zangrando, Joanna and Robert L. Zangrando. "ER and Black Civil Rights." Hoff-Wilson.

Zinn, Howard, ed. *New Deal Thought*. Indianapolis: Hackett, 2003.

———. *A People's History of the United States*. New York: The New Press, 1997.

Index

Abbot, Philip, 9, 13, 68, 109, 111, 174, 187
abundance, 80–85, 103; and consumption, 107, 110; distribution of, 141; folklore and, 189–90; FR on, 62; liberty and, 131; and self-development, 114; Wallace on, 207
accountability, 283–84, 286
Addams, Jane, 108
Adkins decision, 231
administration: critique of, 284, 286; FR on, 56, 67; New Deal and, 11; symbolism and, 205
aftermath of New Deal: FR and, 12, 230; Wallace on, 207
agency: and change, 249–50; mastery and, 78–80; New Deal and, 165–225; populism and, 41; progressivism and, 42–43; and symbols, 173
agrarian myth, 205
agriculture, 34, 63, 86, 209, 234
Alger, Horatio, 90n6, 198, 204
Anderson, Marian, 145
Arnold, Thurman: and Anti-Trust division, 110–11, 183, 219n97; and change, 246, 249–52; on Constitution, 208; on consumption, 108; on folklore, 16; on government, 281; importance of, 19, 21–23, 31n78; on power, 10; and

pragmatism, 3, 168–69, 171–208; on property, 71–75, 93n81; on reform, 33, 61
Arthurdale, 159n210, 186–87
assistance. *See* relief
autonomy. *See* liberty

Badger, Anthony, 9, 136, 21n22, 233, 245, 258n93
Barber, Benjamin, 108, 266, 272
baseball, 154n89, 157n168
Batten, Samuel, 46
Beard, Charles, 43
Berle, Adolph, 20, 22, 68, 89n4
Berlin, Isaiah, 79
Bernstein, Irving, 129, 246
Bill of Rights, 125; Second, 132–39
Black, Hugo, 91n32
Black, Ruby, 138
blacks: and Democratic Party, 239; New Deal and, 144–47, 151n29; and organization, 245–46; Social Security and, 259n109
Blum, John, 34
Brandeis, Louis, 44–45, 231
Brands, H. W., 219n96
Brinkley, Alan, 22, 110, 137, 273, 294–96
Bronner, Stephen, 274, 287, 290, 298–99
Brownlow, Louis, 256n53
Brownlow Report, 236, 256n53
Brownson, Orestes, 92n55
Bryan, William Jennings, 39

About the Author

Brian Stipelman is an assistant professor of political science at Dowling College in Oakdale, NY, where he teaches courses in American politics and political theory. He received his PhD from Rutgers University in 2008. He has authored several articles on the political thought of the New Deal. This is his first book. He looks forward to being able to get to his long backlog of projects, including research on Walter Lippmann, the political thought of Terry Pratchett, Internet communities and political socialization, and the institutional roadblocks that undermine democratic politics in the United States.